Curso Completo de Inglés
Teach Yourself

Habla Inglés desde la primera lección.
Niveles Uno - Cuatro
Aprenda Inglés sin profesor hoy.

Dr. Yeral E. Ogando

Curso Completo de Inglés Niveles Uno-Cuatro
© 2016 por Dr. Yeral E. Ogando
Publicado: Christian Translation LLC
Impreso en los EE.UU
Diseño de Portada por SAL media

ISBN 13: 978-1-946249-02-9
ISBN 10: 1-946249-02-5

1. Language Learning - Aprender un Idioma.
2. English Language – Idioma Inglés

DEDICACIÓN:

Éste libro está dedicado a la Única y duradera persona que siempre ha estado ahí para mí, sin importar cuán terco soy: DIOS

Sin Ti mi Dios, nada soy. Gracias por tu misericordia e inmerecedora Gracia.

AGRADECIMIENTOS:

Gracias a Dios por permitir que mi sueño se hiciera realidad y por darme fuerzas cuando sentí ganas de renunciar.

De no haber sido por el apoyo que he recibido a lo largo del camino de parte de éstas increíbles y sorprendentes personas, no estaría donde estoy hoy. Gracias a mi editora, Sharon A. Lavy y a los "Diseñadores de la Portada", SAL media por haber hecho un gran trabajo ayudándome con esta obra.

Elizabeth McAchren por su excelente colaboración e ideas durante la creación de este primer libro de la serie. Coleman Clarke y Kathryn Ganime-Leech por su increíble trabajo en el audio.

Ésta ha sido una muy larga jornada para mi familia, pero la recompensa es digna. Gracias a mi padre, Héctor y a mis hijas, Yeiris y Tiffany por permanecer a mi lado a través de éste viaje. Saben que les amo.

God bless you all
Dios les bendiga

Dr. Yeral E. Ogando
www.aprendeis.com

Tabla De Contenido

Curso Completo de Inglés
Teach Yourself English

Habla Inglés desde la primera lección.
Nivel inicial y avanzado.
Aprenda Inglés sin profesor hoy.

Dr. Yeral E. Ogando

Introducción

He publicado este método para que puedan aprender inglés en forma rápida y eficaz. Les pido que dediquen 20 minutos diarios al estudio del inglés sin interrupción, para que puedan concentrarse y digerir el contenido de esta obra. Uno de los desafíos más grande del aprendizaje es ser una persona Autodidacta, en otras palabras, que aprende por cuenta propia. Se requiere mucha disciplina y dedicación en el estudio para poder lograr un buen aprendizaje. Estudiar una hora completa cada día puede hacerlos sentirse aburridos o cansados rápidamente, esta es la razón por la que les recomiendo un mínimo de 20 minutos y un máximo de 40 minutos al día para mejor aprendizaje. De este modo podrán lograr mejores resultados.

Les deseo Buena suerte en este increíble viaje al mundo del aprendizaje del idioma inglés, y recuerden, "*Hablen sin vergüenza*"

Dr. Yeral E. Ogando
www.aprendeis.com

SÍMBOLOS Y ABREVIACIONES

Audio: Indica que se necesita el Audio MP3 para esta sección. No olviden que cada oración o palabra en inglés está disponible en audio MP3.

Dialogo: Indica dialogo o texto de lectura.

Gramática: Indica la gramática o explicación de la estructura del idioma

Ejercicios: Indica las secciones para ejercicios y prácticas.

Prólogo

Muchas personas creen que "*Aprender Inglés*" es una tarea muy difícil, de modo que se pasan la vida con el deseo de Aprender Inglés, pero nunca se deciden por el miedo o tabú que se les han inculcado, que el Inglés es muy difícil de aprender.

Estoy completamente de acuerdo con las personas que dicen que es difícil Aprender Inglés, puesto que nunca han tenido el método adecuado o la enseñanza correcta para aprenderlo. En otras palabras, siempre será difícil Aprender Inglés sino se tiene la herramienta adecuada.

No olviden que no todo el que enseña, sabe enseñar. Existen muchos profesores y muchos métodos para aprender, sin embargo, la mayoria de ellos no abordan la forma correcta para el aprendizaje del estudiante. Este método les demostrará lo sencillo que es poder "hablar Inglés" en poco tiempo. Después de mas de 10 años de experiencia y vivenciando la forma rápida del aprendizaje de mis estudiantes, pongo en sus manos este tesoro.

Les demostraré que desde la primera lección con este método, podrán comenzar a hablar Inglés. No tienen que esperar meses y años, pueden hablar al momento de haber terminado la primera lección. ¿Y si eso es con la primera lección? Imaginense después de haber terminado el curso completo.

Este curso es para enseñarles la forma correcta de Aprender Inglés, reconociendo los patrones y formas de hablar; aun podrán aprender un poco más de español en este increíble viaje.

Siempre recomiendo a mis alumnos que estudien un mínimo de 20 minutos y un máximo de 40 minutos al día. Esto les permitirá aprovechar al máximo su aprendizaje y a la vez a mantener la mente activa en el idioma. No traten de estudiar varias horas un día a la semana, porque se fatigarán y aburrirán, no llegando a sacarle provecho al aprendizaje. Es mejor un poco con calidad que mucho sin efectividad.

La mayoría de los métodos y cursos para aprender Inglés inician con el alfabeto; este no es uno de ellos. Permítanme decirles que el alfabeto en inglés, solo les sirve para deletrear las palabras. No es como en español que al saber el alfabeto, podemos conocer los sonidos y pronunciaciones. El inglés es distinto, los sonidos y pronunciaciones deberán ser escuchados y aprendidos en el transcurso del curso.

PASOS PARA USAR ESTE LIBRO Y SACARLE EL MEJOR PROVECHO

Asegúrense de **DESCARGAR** el Audio del libro con las instrucciones encontradas en la página "**BONO GRATIS**" este método no tiene la pronunciación marcada o habla de la pronunciación, es **IMPERATIVO** descargar el audio para poder aprender la pronunciación correcta del inglés.

Ve a la página de "**BONO GRATIS**" y descarga el audio del libro.

Lee la conversación del libro, escuchando la pronunciación directamente del audio. Asegúrate de captar la pronunciación y practicarla.

Lee y aprende las nuevas palabras, frases y expresiones encontradas en la sección "*New Words*" y "*Phrases and Expressions*".

Ahora debes concentrarte en la gramática de la lección. Esta es la parte más importante y lo que te permitirá hablar correctamente. Presta mucha atención a cada explicación y en especial a la estructura de las palabras. Recuerda que necesitas el audio para las oraciones o ejemplos encontrado en todo el libro. Nunca pases a otra sección o lección sin antes dominar completamente la gramática.

Ahora necesitas regresar al inicio de la lección y escuchar una vez más las conversaciones hasta que

puedas comprenderlas bien y asimilar la estructura.
Repasa las nuevas palabras, frases y expresiones hasta que las aprendas bien y asegúrate de lograr la pronunciación como la del audio. El desafío más grande que tienes es dominar la pronunciación y pronunciar como la voz nativa del audio MP3.

Es tiempo de realizar los ejercicios. Asegúrate de llenar y practicar cada ejercicio. Los mismos medirán tu comprensión de la gramática de la lección. Una vez llenes tus ejercicios, revísalos una y otra vez, y cuando ya estés seguro. Entonces, podrás ver las respuestas al final del libro, solo para comparar y asegurarte de que lo hiciste bien. No hagas trampa.

Ya terminaste la lección. Felicidades. Ahora debes regresar al inicio de la lección una vez más y repasarla por completo, como si fuera la primera vez. Si viste que los conceptos expresados los entendiste bien y los manejaste a la perfección, es porque estás listo para pasar a la siguiente lección. De lo contrario, entonces, deberás seguir el repaso de la lección hasta que la domines a la perfección.

Lesson 1
I speak English – Yo hablo Inglés

Conversation 1

Teacher: Good morning.

Students: Hi.

Teacher: What is your name?

Student A: My name is Allan.

Teacher: Allen, it's nice to meet you.

Student A: No, I am Allan.

Teacher: Oh, okay. Nice to meet you, Allan.

Conversation 2

Teacher: Hello. What is your name?

Spy: Mr. Knife.

Teacher: Tell me about yourself.

Spy: I speak English and Spanish. I live in Europe. I work in New York. And I like to eat three foods: meat, cheese, and cake.

Teacher: You live in Europe, and you work in New York, good.

Spy: Yes, I like to travel.

Teacher: I assume you travel on an airplane…

Spy: I travel in buses, cars, and airplanes.

Teacher: You need to rest!

New words – Nuevas palabras
Three foods – tres comidas
Airplane – avión

A car – un carro
A song – una canción
An email – un email
Baby – bebé
Beer – cerveza
Book – libro
Box – caja
Boy – chico / muchacho
Bus – bus / autobús
Cake – bizcocho
Cheese – queso
Chicken – pollo
Church – iglesia
City – ciudad
Dish – plato
English – inglés
Fast – rápido
Fish – pescado
French – francés
Fruit – fruta
German – alemán
Hard – duro
Ice cream – helado
Kiss – beso
Knife – cuchillo
Leaf – hoja *(de un árbol)*
Life – vida
My dog – mi perro
My father – mi padre
Potato – papa
Rice – arroz
Soup – sopa

Spanish – español
Spy – espía
The teacher – el profesor
To Europe – a Europa
Tomato – tomate
Wife – esposa

Phrases and Expressions - Frases y expresiones

Hello – hola *(usualmente al responder el teléfono)*
Hi - hola
Good morning - buenos días
Good afternoon - buenas tardes
Good evening - buenas noches *(al caer la noche)*
Good night – buenas noches *(al despedirse y después de las 10 pm)*
Please - por favor
Thank you - gracias
Excuse me – perdón / con permiso
What is your name? - ¿Cuál es tu nombre? / ¿Cómo te llamas?
My name is… - me llamo / mi nombre es…
Pleased to meet you – encantado de conocerte
Nice to meet you - mucho gusto
Thank you very much - muchas gracias
You're welcome - de nada
See you later - hasta luego
Have a nice day - qué pase un buen día
See you tomorrow – hasta mañana
Goodbye - adiós
Tell me about yourself – háblame acerca de ti

I assume – yo supongo

After work – después del trabajo

In New York – en Nueva York

In the pool – en la piscina

Like a baby – como un bebé (like *en este caso se traduce como, parecido a)*

With my wife – con mi esposa

In the park – en el parque

Grammar – Gramática

Vamos a iniciar nuestro aprendizaje y nuestra primera tarea es aprender a poner las palabras en plural, entiéndase, de una a varias cosas.

En español decimos:

Libro

Entendemos que está en singular, porque se refiere a una sola cosa.

Libros

Entendemos que está en plural, porque se refiere a varias cosas.

En español tenemos muchas maneras de formar el plural de las palabras; en inglés, en cambio, tenemos muy pocas y es bastante sencillo. Veamos.

The plural - El plural

Casi todas las palabras formarán el plural agregándole "*S*" o "*ES*". De entrada asumimos que todas las palabras forman el plural agregándole "*S*". Esta diferencia es el concepto general a aprender.

Book – libro

Book*s* – libros

*Bike – bicicleta
Bike**s** – bicicletas

Meat - carne
Meat**s** – tipos de carne

Soup – sopa
Soup**s** – tipos de sopa

Como ustedes pueden ver en "*bike*", las palabras que terminan en "*E*", solo se le agrega "*S*" al plural.

Practiquemos unos ejemplos más.
Beer – cerveza
Beer**s** – vasos de cerveza

Cake – bizcocho
Cake**s** – bizcochos

Fruit – fruta
Fruit**s** – tipos de fruta

Las palabras que terminan en "*CH, SH, O, S, X, Z*" forman su plural agregándoles "*ES*".

Church – iglesia
Church**es** – Iglesias

Dish – plato
Dish**es** – platos

Potato – papa
Potato**es** – papas

Tomato – tomate
Tomato**es** – tomates

Bus – bus / autobús
Buses – bus*es* – autobuses

Kiss – beso
Kiss*es* - besos

Box – caja
Box*es* – cajas

Las palabras que terminan en "*Y*" precedida de una consonante, entiéndase, cuando antes de la "*Y*" hay una consonante, forman su plural cambiando la "*Y*" por una "*i*", después agregándole "*ES*".

Baby – bebé
Bab*ies* – bebés

City – ciudad
Cit*ies* – ciudades

Spy – espía
Sp*ies* – espías

Veamos si aprendimos bien el concepto. *¿Cómo formaríamos el plural de la palabra "boy"?*
El plural es normal, como todas las palabras, agregándole "*S*".

Boy – chico / muchacho
Boy*s* – chicos / muchachos

Aunque termina en "*Y*", como pueden ver, está precedida por una vocal, y la regla dice que solo cuando esté precedida de una consonante. No lo olviden.

Las palabras que terminan en *"F"* o *"FE"* cambian la *"F"* por una *"V"* y entonces se le agrega *"ES"* o *"S"*.

Kni*fe* – cuchillo
Kni*ves* – cuchillos

Wi*fe* – esposa
Wi*ves* – esposas

Li*fe* – vida
Li*ves* – vidas
Lea*f* – hoja (de un árbol)
Lea*ves* – hojas

Este es el concepto general que es necesario que aprendan muy bien antes de continuar. Como siempre, existen palabras irregulares al plural, las cuales veremos mientras vamos desarrollando nuestro aprendizaje. Si aún no dominan este concepto básico del plural, es necesario que lo repasen y lo dominen completamente; de esto depende el éxito de este curso.

Personal pronouns - Los pronombres personales

Aprenderemos los pronombres personales, en inglés. Los dividiré en 2 grupos para mejor entendimiento.

Singular. Estos son los pronombres que se refieren a una sola persona.

I	- yo
You	- tú o usted
He	- él
She	- ella
It	- él o ella para animal o cosa.

Plural. Estos son los pronombres que se refieren a dos o varias personas.

We	- nosotros
You	- ustedes
They	- ellos / ellas

Como ustedes pueden notar *"tú"* *"usted"* y *"ustedes"* es lo mismo en inglés. Presten mucha atención y no se confundan.

Deben prestar mucha atención a las terceras personas del singular *"He / She / it".* Por lo general éstas van juntas. Esta es la razón por la cual hemos aprendido el plural de las palabras primero. En inglés, estos pronombres personales *"He / She / It"* son los que hacen la diferencia y los que pueden complicar las cosas si no se dominan bien. *Entremos en materia importante ahora.*

Conjugation of verbs in present tense - Conjugación de los verbos en el presente simple.

Nivel Uno

En español sabemos que un verbo está en infinitivo, esto es, en su forma del diccionario sin conjugar, cuando tiene la terminación "*Ar / Er / Ir*".

Hablar
Comer
Vivir
Como sabemos, no es lógico ni posible decir "*Yo hablar*". Estaríamos hablando como cavernícolas. ¿No es verdad?

En español, le quitamos la terminación "*Ar / Er / Ir*" y entonces agregamos la terminación correspondiente al pronombre personal.

Hablar	- *habl*
Yo hablo	
Tú hablas	
Comer	- *com*
Yo como	
Tú comes	
Vivir	- *viv*
Yo vivo	
Tú vives	

En inglés, no tenemos que preocuparnos por nada de eso; de hecho, en inglés es bastante sencillo, como verán a continuación.

Sabemos que un verbo está en infinitivo, esto es, en su forma sin conjugar en inglés cuando lleva la partícula "*To*" al inicio.

To speak – hablar
To eat – comer
To live – vivir

Al igual que en español, en inglés no podemos decir "*I to speak*". Estaríamos diciendo "*Yo hablar*", y como la época de cavernícolas ya pasó, debemos hablar correctamente.

Para conjugar el verbo en inglés, solo tenemos que quitarle la partícula "*To*" y agregar los pronombres personales.

To speak – hablar

I	speak	– Yo hablo
You	speak	– Tú hablas / Usted habla
He	*speaks*	*– Él habla*
She	*speaks*	*– Ella habla*
We	speak	– Nosotros hablamos
You	speak	– Ustedes hablan
They	speak	– Ellos / Ellas hablan

To eat – comer

I	eat	- Yo como
You	eat	- Tú comes / Usted come
He	*eats*	*- Él come*
She	*eats*	*- Ella come*
We	eat	- Nosotros comemos
You	eat	- Ustedes comen
They	eat	- Ellos / Ellas comen

To live – vivir

I	live	- Yo vivo
You	live	- Tú vives / Usted vive
He	*lives*	*- Él vive*
She	*lives*	*- Ella vive*
We	live	- Nosotros vivimos

| You | live | - Ustedes viven |
| They | live | - Ellos / Ellas viven |

No veo nada difícil, ¿Acaso ustedes ven alguna dificultad? Exacto. Todo es sencillo y fácil de aprender con el método correcto.

Recuerden que "*You*" significa tanto "*tú o usted*" y en su forma plural "*ustedes*".

También ya habrán visto que la conjugación es la misma para todos estos pronombres (*I, You, We, You, They*). Solo tenemos que quitar el "*To*" y ya podemos hablar.

Para conjugar un verbo con "*He / She / It*" en inglés, solo tenemos que aplicar la regla que ya aprendimos para formar el plural de las palabras con los verbos. Por ahora concéntrense en la conjugación de "*I / You / We / You / They*". Más adelante trataremos a fondo la conjugación para "*He / She / It*".

Yo les dije que podrían hablar inglés desde su primera lección, ¿*no es así?*, bueno, les mentí. No tienen que terminar la primera lección; de hecho, ya pueden comenzar a hablar inglés. ¿*Acaso no me creen?* Vamos a ver.

¿*Cómo se dice frutas?* Recordemos que ya aprendimos esta palabra, la cual es "*fruits*".

¿*Cómo se dice* "*yo como*"? También acabamos de aprenderlo, lo cual es, "*I eat*".

I eat fruit. – yo como fruta.
We eat fruit. – nosotros comemos fruta.

¿Estamos o no hablando inglés? Aprendamos 3 palabras más.

English – inglés
Spanish – español
In New York – en Nueva York

I live in New York – yo vivo en Nueva York.
I speak English – yo hablo inglés.
You speak Spanish – tú hablas español / usted habla español / ustedes hablan español.

Con este poco que hemos aprendido, ya podemos hablar cosas básicas. Solo tenemos que aprender algunas palabras o vocabularios de complemento. Y listo, ya estamos hablando inglés.

Por ejemplo, en vez de *New York,* pueden decir cualquier otro estado o lugar donde vivan. En vez de *English* o *Spanish*, pueden decir cualquier otro idioma que sepan. En vez de *fruit* pueden decir cualquier otra cosa que coman.

Vamos a ver si es verdad lo que les estoy diciendo.

A few words – Unas pocas palabras

At night - por la noche / en la noche

Cheese – queso	Chicken – pollo
Correct – correcto	Fish – pescado
French – Francés	German – Alemán
Ice cream – helado	Now - ahora
People – personas	Rice – arroz

Slowly - despacio / lentamente

Some - algunos	Spy - espia

Students - estudiantes
True - verdad /verdadero
Two - dos

¿Cómo diríamos las siguientes frases?
Tú comes arroz
Nosotros comemos pescado
Ellos comen carne
Usted come helado
Ellas comen queso
Nosotros hablamos alemán
Ustedes hablan francés
Ya aprendimos la estructura y forma de crear todas estas frases. Como sé que lo han hecho bien, solo para que estén seguros les colocaré las respuestas más abajo.

You eat rice
We eat fish
They eat meat
You eat ice cream
They eat cheese
We speak German
You speak French

Como pueden ver, es mucho más fácil de lo que les había dicho. Ya sé que están hambrientos por aprender más y hablar inglés fluido. Es por esto que les voy a presentar una lista de verbos que les ayudarán en su pronto hablar.

List of verbs in present tense - Listado de verbos en el presente simple.

- *To argue* with my wife – discutir con mi esposa
- *To circle* the correct word – encerrar la palabra correcta
- *To cook* rice – cocinar arroz
- *To dance* merengue – bailar merengue
- *To drink* a beer – beber una cerveza
- *To drive* a car – conducir un carro
- *To eat* fruit – comer fruta
- *To fish* a fish – pescar un pez
- *To hug* my father – abrazar a mi padre
- *To kiss* my dog – besar a mi perro
- *To put down* the knife - bajar el cuchillo
- *To read* a book – leer un libro
- *To rest* after work – descansar después del trabajo
- *To run* fast – correr rápido
- *To sing* a song – cantar una canción
- *To sleep* like a baby – dormir como un bebé
- *To study* English – estudiar inglés
- *To swim* in the pool – nadar en la piscina
- *To talk* to the teacher – hablar con el profesor
- *To travel* to Europe – viajar a Europa
- *To walk* in the park – caminar en el parque
- *To wash up the* dishes - lavar los platos
- *To work* hard – trabajar duro
- *To write* an email – escribir un email

Three model verbs - Tres verbos modales.

To want – querer
I want - yo quiero
You want- tú quieres / usted quiere
He wants - él quiere
She wants - ella quiere
We want- nosotros queremos
You want- ustedes quieren
They want - ellos / ellas quieren

To need – necesitar
I need - yo necesito
You need - tú necesitas / usted necesita
He needs - él necesita
She needs - ella necesita
We need - nosotros necesitamos
You need - ustedes necesitan
They need - ellos / ellas necesitan

To like – gustar
I like - me gusta
You like - te gusta / le gusta (a usted)
He likes - le gusta (a él)
She likes - le gusta (a ella)
We like - nos gusta
You like - les gusta (a ustedes)
They like - les gusta (a ellos / ellas)

Con estos tres verbos modales además de la lista de verbos anterior, ustedes pueden hablar inglés sin problema, un inglés básico, pero pueden hablar muchísimo. Vamos a ver algunos ejemplos usando los verbos ya aprendidos y los verbos modales.

I drink a beer – yo bebo una cerveza

I want to drink a beer – yo quiero beber una cerveza

I need to drink a beer – yo necesito beber una cerveza

I like to drink beer – me gusta beber cervezas

Veamos rápidamente la estructura con los verbos modales.

En español decimos "*yo quiero beber una cerveza*". El verbo después de *quiero* está en infinitivo "*beber*", porque ya hemos conjugado el primero "*quiero*". Es el mismo concepto en inglés.

I want **to drink** a beer – Yo quiero beber una cerveza.

Como ya conjugamos "*I want – yo quiero*" el verbo que le sigue debe estar en infinitivo "*to drink – beber*".

We want **to dance** merengue – queremos bailar merengue

They need **to run** fast – ellos necesitan correr rápido

You like **to cook** fish– te gusta cocinar pescado

I need **to work** hard – necesito trabajar duro

I want **to kiss** my dog – quiero besar mi perro

We need **to talk** to the teacher – necesitamos hablar con el profesor

¿Pueden entender la estructura o patrón? Espero que sí, porque les he explicado de una forma clara y fácil. Esto quiere decir que ustedes saben mucho más de lo que se imaginan. Con el contenido de esta primera lección, pueden hablar lo que han estado tratando de hablar durante varios años. Hoy pueden decirlo con confianza con solo aprender esta primera lección. *Lo prometido es deuda. Ya pueden hablar inglés.* Por supuesto, ya se habrán dado cuenta que no hemos hablado de *"He / She / It".* No se preocupen, en las próximas lecciones estaremos hablando de estos pronombres. Por ahora, necesito que conjuguen cada uno de los verbos que les he dado. Vamos a necesitarlos en la segunda lección. Recuerden, al conjugar los verbos, presten mucha atención cuando hablen de *"He / She / It".* Deberán usar las reglas que aprendieron al inicio formando las palabras en plural; el concepto que les enseñé para formar el plural, es el mismo que se aplica cuando conjugamos un verbo con *"He / She / It".* Presten mucha atención a cada verbo cuando estén conjugando con estos pronombres. No olviden que solo tienen que quitar el *"to"* y colocar los pronombres personales delante del verbo.

Exercises – Ejercicios

Exercise 1.1: Write the plural form – Escribe el plural.

book_____   bike_____

church_____   kiss_____

beer_____   cake_____

dish_____bus_____

boy _____   box_____

potato_____   wife _____

city _____   spy_____

leaf_____knife_____

Exercise 1.2: Complete the phrase using the plural form. – Complete la frase usando el plural.

The _____ (wife) of two _____

(boy) want some _____ (kiss).

The _____ (boy) eat the _____

(cake) and the _____ (cheese).

They put down the _____ (knife).

No _____ (hug) for the _____ (wife).

Now the _____ (boy) need to wash up the

_____ (dish).

Exercise 1.3: Write sentences using pronouns (I, you, we, they) conjugating the verbs. – Escribe oraciones usando los pronombres (I, you, we, they) conjugando los verbos.

Example:

Dogs + to dance merengue   <u>They   dance merengue.</u>

People on bikes + to work hard

_____.

People in Europe + to drive fast

_____.

Spies and teachers + to work hard

_____.

Spies and teachers + to study people

_____.

Dogs + to sing at night

_____.

Students + to sleep like a baby

_____.

Boys + to eat fast _____.

Fish + to swim fast   _____.

People + to swim slowly _____.

People + to eat fish _____.

Exercise 1.4: Write sentences conjugating the verbs – Escribe oraciones conjugando los verbos.

1- Wives + to talk_____.

2- They + to write emails_____.

3- Teachers + to need sleep_____.

4- Babies + to sleep in church_____.

5- They + to need kisses_____.
6- You and I + to need English

_____ _____.

7- We + to like English books_____.
8- I + to cook meat with potatoes and tomatoes

_____.

9- We + to eat fast_____.

10- You + to wash the dishes_____.

Exercise 1.5: Write the correct word. – Escribe la palabra correcta.

Example: They want _to drive_ the car.
to sing / to cook / to drive

I like _____ in the pool.
to work / to swim / to travel

I want _____ in the park.
to argue / to cook / to fish

I need _____ an English book.
to hug / to read / to drive

Boys like _____ cake.
to eat / to live / to drink

We need _____ English.
to sleep / to speak / to kiss

They want _____ a fish.
to walk / to sing / to cook

Exercise 1.6: Circle the true answers. – Encierra la respuesta correcta.

I like to eat chicken / fish / rice / cheese / cake.

I want to study English / German / Spanish / French.

I kiss babies / dogs / books / my wife.

I sleep like a baby / after work / in the park / in the pool.

I travel in the car / in the bus / in Europe / in a book.

Lesson 2
Do you study English? - ¿Estudias Inglés?

Conversation 1

Salesman: Here you are, Mrs.— What's your name?

Customer: It's Miss—Miss Mason.

Salesman: Pleased to meet you, Miss Mason. Here's the music you want. Do you like music?

Customer: Yes, I do—I listen in the car, at my house.

Salesman: What else do you like to do in your free time?

Customer: Well, I watch television and read.

Salesman: Do you play chess?

Customer: Yes, actually! Do you?

Salesman: No, I don't, but we have a chess book here.

Customer: Oh, uh, no. No, thank you.

Salesman: Do you study English?

Customer: Yes, I do.

Salesman: Do you want a book about English?

Customer: No, thank you. I just want the music.

Salesman: Okay. Have a nice day!

Conversation 2

Waiter: Good evening, Sir, what can I do for

you?

Customer: Do you have coffee?

Waiter: Yes, we do. We have coffee, tea, wine . . .

.

Customer: Excellent. Coffee, please.

[15 minutes later.]

Customer: Waiter?

Waiter: Yes?

Customer: The coffee spilled.

Waiter: That's a shame. Don't worry about it. Here you are, another coffee. Anything else?

Customer: Uh, yes, actually. I forgot my money.

Waiter: That is a shame!

Conversation 3

Child: Mommy?

Mother: Yes?

Child: I want coffee.

Mother: No, Honey.

Child: Mommy?

Mother: Yes?

Child: I want tea.

Mother: No, Honey.

Child: Mommy? Mommy? Mommy!

Mother: What do you want?

Child: Coffee? "No." Tea? "No." Orange juice?

Mother: Okay.

From here the waiter takes the customer into the back of the alley, mugs him and leaves him by the garbage.

Conversation 4:

Boy: Do you like me?
Girl: Yes, I do.
Boy: Do you want to have lunch with me?
Girl: No, I don't.
Boy: Do you really like me?
Girl: Yes, I do, but I like Billy, too. And I want to have lunch with him.

Conversation 5:

Car Salesman: Do you like this car?
Man: Yes, I do.
Car Salesman: Do you want to buy it?
Man: No, I don't.
Car Salesman: Do you really like the car?
Man: Yes, I like the car, but I don't have any money.

New words – Nuevas palabras

Well – bien   Something – algo
Here you are – aquí tiene
Wine - vino
That's a shame – es una pena / lastima.
Don't worry – no se preocupe
An orange juice – un jugo de naranja
Excellent - Excelente
Mr. – Señor   Mrs. – Señora
Miss – Señorita (*también se abrevia como Ms. Recuerden, que Ms. Se usa tanto para mujer como para señorita, protegiendo su estatus marital*)
Chess – ajedrez   Money – dinero
Coffee – café   The beach – la playa

Tea – té   Music – música

Television – televisión (También *se abrevia como TV*).

The movies – cine / películas

Parties – fiestas

What – qué (*se usa para preguntar*)

Then – entonces   Sir – Señor

An apple – una manzana

Actually - de hecho   Just - solo

Okay – ok   Can – poder

To have lunch - almorzar

Really - de veras   This - esto / esta

Phrases and Expressions - Frases y expresiones

I listen - yo escucho

At my house - en mi casa

What else - ¿qué más?

Your free time - tu tiempo libre

To watch television - ver televisión

To play chess - jugar ajedrez

15 minutes later - 15 minutos después

Spilled - se derramó

About it - acerca de eso

Another coffee - otro café

Anything else? - ¿algo más?

I forgot my money - olvidé mi dinero

To buy it - comprarlo

Any money - nada de dinero

Do you like me? - ¿te agrado?

Every day - cada dia

To walk together - caminar juntos
Every morning - cada mañana
Many cities - muchas ciudades
After dinner - despues de cena
Specific source of money - fuente especifica de dinero
Any dog is okay - cualquier perro está bien
One specific type of wine - un tipo de vino especifico
Specific piece or collection - pieza o colección especifica
From here – desde aqui
Back of the alley – parte de atras del callejón
Mugs him – le da con la taza
And leaves him by the garbage – y lo deja en la basura

Grammar – Gramática

Ya somos expertos conjugando una serie de verbos y hablando en inglés. Estoy completamente seguro que han demostrado sus habilidades y ejercido sus nuevos conocimientos hablando inglés con sus familiares, amigos y personas allegadas.

Aún no sabemos cómo hacer preguntas o responder en forma afirmativa o negativa. Les tengo buenas noticias: es tiempo de aprender esas pequeñas cosas que necesitan para seguir creciendo en su aprendizaje del idioma inglés.

Recuerden que decíamos en la primera lección, que solo necesitamos quitar el "To" y entonces agregar los pronombres personales al verbo. Eso lo aprendimos muy bien y sabemos cómo usarlo. Vamos a recapitular.

¿Cómo decimos "Yo quiero estudiar inglés"?

Sabemos que "***To want***" es querer. Sabemos que "***To study***" es estudiar y también sabemos que "***English***" es inglés.

I want   to study English - Yo quiero estudiar inglés.

Recordemos como conjugar el verbo.
To want – querer.

I want - yo quiero
You want – tú quieres / usted quiere
He wants – él quiere
She wants - ella quiere
We want – nosotros queremos
You want – ustedes quieren
They want – ellos / ellas quieren

The auxiliary verb "To do" - El verbo auxiliar "To do".

Vamos a aprender nuestro primer verbo auxiliar, esto es, el verbo que nos permitirá realizar otras acciones o dará sentido a nuestra conversación. *Recuerden que si conjugáramos el verbo "to do" tendríamos (I do, you, do, we, do, they do) y (he does, she does).* Vamos a usar "***To do***" como verbo auxiliar, esto es, auxiliando otros verbos para formar una oración.

Si recordamos la conjugación, tenemos los pronombres "***I, You, We, You, They***" para "***Do***". ¿No es verdad? Excelente.

General rules on how to use "do" as an auxiliary - Reglas generales para usar el "Do" como auxiliar.

Do: Se usa con los pronombres personales "*I, You, We, You, They*" en el presente simple para *preguntas y respuestas cortas afirmativas.* Parafraseando, *preguntar y responder en formas cortas afirmativas.* Veamos.

Do you like to eat? – ¿Te gusta comer?

Para hacer preguntas. Como pueden ver se coloca al inicio de la oración, seguido del pronombre personal.

Yes, I do. – Si, me gusta.

En respuesta corta afirmativa se coloca el "do" después del pronombre personal.

Yes, I like to eat. – Si, me gusta comer.

Como ven en la respuesta larga afirmativa, no se usa el "do". Esto es porque tenemos el pronombre personal *"I"* y el verbo conjugado "*like*", entonces, no necesitamos ningún complemento, porque ya tenemos el verbo conjugado. No lo olviden.

Continuemos viendo otros ejemplos y practicando el uso del auxiliar "Do".

Do you want to eat? ¿Quieres comer?

Yes, I do. – Sí.

Yes, I want to eat. – Sí, yo quiero comer.

Do they need to work? – ¿Necesitan ellos trabajar?

Yes, they do. – Sí.

Yes, they need to work. – Sí, ellos necesitan trabajar.

Do you like to study? – ¿Les gusta a ustedes estudiar?

Yes, we do. – Sí.

Yes, we like to study. – Sí, a nosotros nos gusta estudiar.

Con esta estructura ustedes pueden hacer combinaciones infinitas y hablar de cualquier cosa, haciendo preguntas y respuestas. Veamos un poquito más de esta estructura o patrón.

Do you study English? – ¿Estudias inglés?

Yes, I do. – Sí.

Yes, I study English. – Sí, yo studio inglés.

Do they drink beer? ¿Beben ellas cerveza?

Yes, they do. – Sí.

Yes, they drink beer. – Sí, ellas beben cerveza.

Do you speak English? – ¿Habla usted inglés?

Yes, I do. – Sí.

Yes, I speak English. – Sí, yo hablo inglés.

Don't (Do not): Se usa en respuestas cortas y largas negativas. Como pueden ver la forma normal es "**Do not**", pero en el inglés hablado se usa más la contracción "**Don't**". Se quita la "**o**" del "**not**" y se coloca un apóstrofe.

Do you want to study English with me? – ¿Quieres

estudiar inglés conmigo?

Yes, I do. – Sí.

Yes, I want to study English with you. – Sí, quiero estudiar inglés contigo.

No, I don't. – No.

No, I don't want to study English with you. – No, no quiero estudiar inglés contigo.

Esta es la estructura completa—bastante simple y fácil de usar. Repasemos.

Para preguntar y responder oraciones afirmativas cortas usamos "*Do*".

Para respuestas cortas y largas negativas usamos "*Don't*".

Hemos aprendido dos palabras nuevas "*with me* – conmigo" y "*with you* – contigo".

Ahora vamos a aprender dos adverbios y dos conjunciones que nos ayudarán mucho en nuestro aprendizaje.

Conjunctions - Conjunciones

And – y: se usa para unir dos oraciones positivas o negativas.

But – pero: se usa para unir una oración positiva y una negativa o viceversa. O siempre que haya contraste en la oración.

Adverbs – Adverbios.

Too – también: se usa al final de dos oraciones

afirmativas.

Either – Tampoco: se usa al final de dos oraciones negativas.

I like to cook **and** I like to eat **too.** – Me gusta cocinar **y** me gusta comer **también.**

Sería ilógico decir en español "*me gusta cocinar y me gusta comer tampoco*". No tiene sentido, *¿verdad?* Es imperativo usar **también.** Es lo mismo en inglés.

I don't like to work **and** I don't like to study **either.** – No me gusta trabajar **y** no me gusta estudiar **tampoco.** *(either tiene dos formas de pronunciarse, presten atención al audio)*

Sería ilógico decir en español "*no me gusta trabajar y no me gusta estudiar también*". No tiene ningún sentido, ¿verdad? Es imperativo usar **tampoco.** Es lo mismo en inglés.

I like to walk, **but** I don't like to run. – Me gusta caminar, **pero** no me gusta correr.

I like meat, **but** I prefer vegetables – me gusta la carne, pero prefiero vegetales.

Sería ilógico decir en español "*me gusta caminar, pero me gusta correr*". No tiene ningún sentido, ¿verdad? Es imperativo al usar "pero", que la segunda oración sea de contraste. Es lo mismo en inglés. Recuerden que siempre que hay un "pero", algo de contraste viene.

Definite and Indefinite articles - Articulo definido e indefinido.

En español tenemos muchas formas y variantes para los artículos, definidos e indefinidos. Veamos lo fácil que es en inglés.

Definite article - Articulo definido.

En inglés usamos *"The"*, que es el único articulo definido, equivalente a todas las versiones en español "el, lo, la, los, las".

Cuando hablamos del articulo definido, nos referimos a algo en específico o que sabemos de qué estamos hablando.

I want the car - quiero el carro. El es el artículo definido, y sabemos que al usarlo nos estamos refiriendo a un carro en específico, no uno cualquiera, más bien uno en particular. Es lo mismo en inglés.

The car – el carro.

The house – la casa.

The cake – el bizcocho.

Como pueden ver no importa si es femenino o masculino, en inglés solo se usa *"The"*, aun para el plural. No tienen que romperse la cabeza pensando o analizando qué usar, siempre usarán *"the"*.

Indefinite article - Artículo indefinido.

Cuando hablamos del artículo indefinido, nos referimos a cualquier cosa, no hablamos de nada en específico. Decimos *"quiero un carro"*, no importa cuál sea; el fin es que queremos un carro, nada en específico. En inglés es lo mismo.

En inglés usamos "A" cuando las palabras

comienzan con consonante y "An" cuando las palabras comienzan con vocal. Veamos.

I want a car – quiero un carro.

I want an ice cream – quiero un helado.

Como "*ice cream*" inicia con vocal, usamos "*an*". Recuerden, "*A / An*" solo se usan en el singular. Y no hace diferencia si es femenino o masculino, solo si la palabra inicia en vocal.

An apple – una manzana
An ice cream – un helado
A car – un carro
A boy – un chico

Si queremos usar el plural, usamos "*Some-algún-alguno*".

Some cars – algunos carros o unos carros
Some boys – algunos chicos o unos chicos.

Vamos a repasar un poco a ver cómo va nuestro aprendizaje.

¿*Cómo se dice "qué" en inglés?* Acabamos de ver que se dice "*what*", ¿correcto?

Decíamos:

Do you like to eat? – ¿Te gusta comer?
Yes, I do. – Sí.
No, I don't. – No.

Yes, I like to eat – Sí, me gusta comer.
No, I don't like to eat – No, no me gusta comer.

¿Cómo decimos, entonces, "Qué te gusta comer?"
Sencillo, solo tenemos que colocar el "what" al inicio de la oración.

What do you like to eat? - ¿Qué te gusta comer?

I like to eat rice and meat. – Me gusta comer arroz y carne.

I like to eat potatoes, but I don't like to eat fruit. – Me gusta comer papas, pero no me gusta comer fruta.

Todas las palabras y construcciones en esta conversación, ya las hemos aprendido. Esto quiere decir que hemos comprendido bien esta conversación. Felicidades.

Cardinal numbers – Números cardinales

1	one	2	two
3	three	4	four
5	five	6	six
7	seven	8	eight
9	nine	10	ten
11	eleven	12	twelve
13	thirteen	14	fourteen
15	fifteen	16	sixteen
17	seventeen	18	eighteen
19	nineteen	20	twenty
21	twenty-one	22	twenty-two
23	twenty-three	24	twenty-four
25	twenty-five	26	twenty-six
27	twenty-seven	28	twenty-eight
29	twenty-nine	30	thirty
31	thirty-one	40	forty

50	fifty	60	sixty
70	seventy	80	eighty
90	ninety		

100	a/one hundred
200	two hundred
300	three hundred
400 f	our hundred
1,000	a/one thousand
2,000	two thousand
3,000	three thousand
100,000	a/one hundred thousand
200,000	two hundred thousand
1,000,000	a/one million

Asegúrense de aprender bien los números del 1 al 19; después de ahí, siempre usarán los números del 1 al 9. Presten atención a la pronunciación nativa en el Audio.

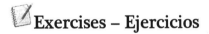 ## Exercises – Ejercicios

Exercise 2.1: Write *either, some,* **or** *too – Escribe "either, some, o too".*
Example: "I rest after church." "I do, __too__.

"I don't like TV." "I don't like it (1)_____."

"I need (2)_____ coffee." "I need some (3)_____."
"It's nice to meet you." "It's nice to meet you,

(4)_____ "

"I don't swim." "I don't (5)_____."

"Do you want (6)_____ wine?" "No, thank you."

"And you?" "I don't want wine (7)_____."

"I don't want to go to the party." "I don't want to go

(8)_____."

"I like to drink (9)_____ orange juice in the

morning."

"Do you study English?" "Yes, I do." "And you?"

Yes, I do, (10)_____."

Exercise 2.2: Write *and* or *but* – Escribe "and o but"
Example: I like coffee, _and_ I like tea.

I like coffee, (1)_____ I don't want coffee now.

I sleep during the day, (2)_____ I work at night.

They swim every day, (3)_____ they walk

together at night.

Every morning, she hugs her cat, (4)_____

she kisses her dog.

I don't speak English, (5)_____ I want to.

They drive to many cities, (6)_____ they don't travel by plane.

He drinks, (7)_____ he drives, (8)_____ he doesn't drink and drive.

-We like to talk, (9)_____ we don't like to argue.

We cook together, (10)_____ we drink some wine after dinner.

Exercise 2.3: Match the sentence with the explanation – Combina la oración con su explicación.
Example:
I need the money. ⤬ Any money is okay.

I need some money.   You have a specific source of money.

I want to buy a dog.   It's a specific dog.
I want to buy the dog. Any dog is okay.

I like to read a book at night.   Any book is okay.
I like to read the book at night. I read a specific book.

I need to talk to a teacher.   I need my teacher.

I need to talk to the teacher.   Any   teacher   is okay.

I like to drink the wine at night.   I   drink   one specific type of wine.
I like to drink some wine at night.   Any   wine   is okay.

I like music.   It's a specific piece or collection.
I like the music.   Any music is okay.

I want to rest at the beach.   It's a specific beach.
I want to rest at a beach. Any beach is okay.

Lesson 3
Does she speak English? – ¿Habla ella inglés?

Conversation 1

Taxi driver: Where to, sir?

Customer: Well, I want to find Gus.

Taxi driver: Where do you want to go?

Customer: I don't know. He has his guitar with him.

Taxi driver: Does he have a girlfriend?

Customer: No, he doesn't.

Taxi driver: Does he like parties?

Customer: No, he doesn't.

Taxi driver: Does he play the guitar in the park?

Customer: I don't know. He needs money.

Taxi driver: Well, do you want to go to the park?

Customer: Okay.

Conversation 2

Host: Ladies and gentlemen, welcome to the Culture Game! To answer a question, just push the button! Okay. Let's start the game. What do Americans eat for Thanksgiving dinner?

Janeth: Um, turkey?

Host: That's right! They eat turkey. Next

question: What is a *rondalla*?

Julie: Men play their guitars and sing together.

Host: Excellent! And when do people in the US eat sandwiches?

Janeth: They eat sandwiches for lunch.

Host: That's right! Janeth goes to Hawaii!

Janeth: Yay!

Mini – conversation 1

Salem: We need to buy a car.

Paola: Really? My mom sells cars.

Salem: Oh. Good idea. Um, does she speak English? I have a lot of questions.

Paola: Yes, she does. She has the answers for your questions!

Salem: Great! Well, I have to go home now. I need to find something to eat. Thanks!

Paola: You're welcome!

Mini – conversation 2

Student A: I need something to eat.

Student B: I have some chicken.

Student A: Yummy! Good idea!

Student B: Uh, do you want some?

Student A: Yes, I do! Mmm. It's delicious!

Student B: I am glad you like it.

New words – Nuevas palabras

Newspaper – periódico

Letter – carta

Guitar – guitarra
Cards – cartas (juego de cartas)
Soccer – fútbol americano (de pie)
Gentleman – caballero
Gentlemen – caballeros
Lady - dama
Ladies – damas
Man – hombre
Men – hombres
Woman – mujer
Women – mujeres
Ma'am – señora
Sugar – azúcar
Milk – leche
Turkey – pavo
Butter – mantequilla
Beef – carne de res
Lamb – cordero
Cookies – galletas / galleticas
Soup – sopa, caldo
Dessert – postre
Salad – ensalada
Hot dogs – perro caliente / salchicha
Hamburgers – hamburguesa
Sandwich – sándwich
*How much – cuanto (para cosas incontables)
*How many – cuantos (para cosas contables)
*What for? - ¿Para qué? (se usa para hacer preguntas)
    *For – por / para
Delicious – delicioso
Dad – papi

Mom – mami

Taxi driver – taxista

*Where? - ¿Dónde?

*Who? - ¿Quién?

*To – a / hacia

Presten atención especial al plural irregular de las palabras mencionadas.

Recuerden, siempre que cualquier palabra termina con "*man - hombre*" el plural será "*men - hombres*". Lo mismo sucede con "*woman - mujer*": el plural será "*women - mujeres*". Es súper importante aprender la pronunciación del plural de "*woman*": cambia mucho. Deben aprenderlo de memoria y nunca olvidarlo.

Phrases and expressions – Frases y expresiones

Something to drink – algo para beber / algo de beber.

Something to eat – algo para comer / algo de comer.

I am glad you like it – estoy contento que le guste.

Pardon? – ¿perdón?

Good idea – buena idea.

To find Gus - encontrar a Gus.

Welcome to the Culture Game - Bienvenidos a los Juegos Culturales.

Just push the button! - solo presiona el botón.

Let's start the game - comencemos el juego.

Thanksgiving dinner - cena de acción de gracias.

That's right! - eso es correcto.

Next question - próxima pregunta.

Janeth goes to Hawaii! - Janeth va a Hawaii.

My mom sells cars - Mi madre venda autos.

I have a lot of questions - tengo muchas preguntas.

Yummy! – delicioso.

Fill in – llenar.

A pound and a half - una libra y media.

Two slices - dos rodajas / dos pedazos.

One bag - una bolsa / una funda / un saco.

A gallon - un galón.

One stick - una barra.

Grammar – Gramática

Como ya sabemos el uso del "*Do*" como auxiliar y con los pronombres que se usa, ahora vamos a practicar el "*Does*", el cual se usa con "*He / She / It*". Esto es obvio, porque si recordamos la conjugación, sería "*He does, she does, it does*". ¿Correcto? De modo que es lógico suponer que es imperativo usar "does" con "*He / She / It*".

Se usa de la misma forma que el "do", lo único es que con "He / She / It" tenemos que seguir la reglas del plural que aprendimos al inicio, cuando usamos estos pronombres, debido a que la terminación del verbo les dirá si tienen que agregarle "S" o "ES" a la conjugación.

Does: Se usa para preguntar y responder oraciones cortas afirmativas en el presente simple con los pronombres personales "*He / She / It*".

Does he like to eat? – ¿Le gusta a él comer?

Yes, he does. – Sí.

Yes, he likes to eat. – Sí, a él le gusta comer.

Repasemos lo que hemos visto en estas tres frases. *Pregunta: Does al inicio de la oración.* ***Does*** he like to eat? *Respuesta corta afirmativa: Does al final de la oración.* Yes, he ***does.*** *Respuesta larga afirmativa: aquí es donde está la parte engañosa. Deben colocar la terminación "S" o "ES", dependiendo como termine el verbo.* Yes, he likes to eat.

Como pueden ver, "***Does***" está en la pregunta y la respuesta corta afirmativa. *Presten mucha atención a la respuesta larga afirmativa.* Como vemos, aquí es donde tenemos que aplicar las reglas del plural para poder conjugar correctamente. Siempre que después del pronombre personal haya un verbo, el mismo deberá estar conjugado. Por esta razón, en la respuesta larga afirmativa, colócale "*S*" o "*ES*" al verbo conjugado. Vamos a practicar este tan importante concepto. Recuerden, esta es la única diferencia en inglés, y es imperativo que dominemos el concepto a la perfección; de lo contrario sería como si dijéramos en español "*ella comes manzana*". Qué horrible se escucha esa oración, ¿verdad? Si queremos hablar correctamente, tenemos que prestar atención a este concepto.

Does she speak English? – ¿Habla ella inglés?

Yes, she *does*. – Sí.

Yes, she *speaks* English. – Sí, ella habla inglés.

Does he want to work? – *¿quiere él trabajar?*

Yes, he *does*. – Sí.

Yes, he *wants* to work. – Sí, él quiere trabajar.

Does Tiffany need to study? - *¿necesita Tiffany estudiar?*

Yes, she *does*. – Sí.

Yes, she *needs* to study. – Sí, ella necesita estudiar.

What *does* Ruth want to eat? - *¿qué quiere Ruth comer?*

She *wants* to eat pizza. – Ella quiere comer pizza.

Doesn't (Does not): Se usa en respuestas negativas cortas y largas con los pronombres personales "*He / She / It*".

Does he like to sleep? - *¿le gusta a ella dormir?*

No, he *doesn't*. – No.

No, he *doesn't* like to sleep. – No, a ella no le gusta dormir.

Como podemos ver, es el mismo uso que el "*don't*", lo único que el "*doesn't*" se usa los pronombres correspondientes a la conjugación.

Grammar summary – Resumen gramatical.

I want to sing a song – yo quiero cantar una canción.

You want to sing a song – tú quieres cantar una canción o usted quiere cantar una canción.

He *wants* to sing a song – él quiere cantar una canción.

She *wants* to sing a song – ella quiere cantar una canción.

We want to sing a song – nosotros queremos cantar una canción.

You want to sing a song – ustedes quieren cantar una canción.

They want to sing a song – ellos(as) quieren cantar una canción.

Ask and answer – Preguntar y responder.

Do you want to sing a song? - *¿quieres cantar una canción?*

Yes, I do. – Sí.

Yes, I want to sing a song. – Sí, quiero cantar una canción.

No, I don't. – No.

No, I don't want to sing a song. – No, no quiero cantar una canción.

What do you want to study then? - ¿qué quieres estudiar entonces?

I want to study German and French. – quiero estudiar alemán y francés.

Does she want to sing a song? - *¿quiere ella cantar una canción?*

Yes, she does. – Sí.

Yes, she **wants** to sing a song. – Sí, ella quiere cantar una canción.

No, she doesn't. – No.

No, she doesn't want to sing a song. – No, ella no quiere cantar una canción.

What does she want to cook then? - ¿qué quiere ella cocinar entonces?

She **wants** to cook rice and meat. – ella quiere cocinar arroz y carne.

Affirmative and negative statements – Declaraciones afirmativas y negativas.

I want to drive **and** I want to travel **too**. – quiero conducir y quiero viajar también.

I don't want to write **and** I don't want to read **either**. – No quiero escribir y no quiero leer tampoco.

I want to walk, **but** I don't want to run. – quiero caminar, pero no quiero correr.

She **likes** to cook **and** she **likes** to eat **too**. – A ella le gusta cocinar y le gusta comer también.

She doesn't like to hug *and* she doesn't like to kiss *either.* – A ella no le gusta abrazar y no le gusta besar tampoco.

She *likes* to talk, *but* she doesn't like to argue. – a ella le gusta hablar, pero no le gusta discutir.

We need the money – Necesitamos el dinero.
They need a car – ellos necesitan un carro.

List of new verbs – Listado de nuevos verbos

To answer a question – responder una pregunta.
To ask a question – hacer una pregunta. *(To ask significa pedir o preguntar).*
To buy a car – comprar un carro.
To do the homework – hacer la tarea.
To go home – ir a casa *(hogar).*
To hate injustice – odiar la injusticia.
To listen to the radio – escuchar la radio.
To play golf – jugar golf.
To play the piano – tocar el piano.
To prefer something – preferir algo.
To start the game – comenzar el juego.
To watch the game – mirar el juego.

Asegurense de estudiar bien esta corta lista de verbos. Recuerden que siempre se dice *"To listen to".*
I listen to music – yo escucho música.
You listen to the radio – usted escucha la radio.
To play significa tanto jugar como tocar cualquier

tipo de instrumento musical.

I want to play the piano – quiero tocar el piano.

We want to play tennis – queremos jugar tenis.

Remarks - Notas

How much / How many – Cuántos

Es importante que aprendamos a usar estas dos palabras, las cuales significan lo mismo en español, pero en inglés tienen diferente uso.

How much: Se usa para cosas infinitas o incontables. Siempre se usa con el dinero.

How much money do you need? ¿Cuánto dinero necesitas?

I need one hundred dollars – necesito cien dólares.

Aunque puedes contar el dinero, pero el mismo es infinito.

How much sugar do you need? ¿Cuánta azúcar necesitas?

I need two teaspoons – necesito dos cucharaditas.

Puedes contar las cucharaditas de azúcar, pero no el azúcar.

How many: Se usa para cosas que se pueden contar.

How many apples do you want? - ¿cuántas manzanas quieres?

I want two apples – quiero dos manzanas.

Importante, cuando nos referimos a la moneda,

usamos **how many.** *Solo cuando nos referimos a la moneda.*

How many pesos do you need? - ¿cuántos pesos necesitas?

How many dollars do you want? - ¿cuántos dólares quieres?

Noten la diferencia y no se confundan. Para dinero y cosas infinitas usamos **how much;** en cambio para referirnos a la moneda de un país y para cosas contables usamos **how many.**

Where? - ¿Dónde?
Where do you want to eat tonight? ¿Dónde quieres comer esta noche?

I want to eat in a restaurant – quiero comer en un restaurante.

Who? - ¿Quién?
Who want*s* to eat? - ¿quién quiere comer?
Who like*s* cake? - ¿A quién le gusta el bizcocho?
I do. – A mí.

Siempre recuerden que cuando usan "who", el verbo siguiente debe estar conjugado como si fuera para "He / She", esto es, con "*S*" o "*ES*". Esto es porque estamos preguntando en un grupo, a nadie en específico, esto es, a una tercera persona y alguien va a contestar la pregunta.

For – Por / para
Necesitamos prestar mucha atención a esta

preposición.

We need money – necesitamos dinero.

What for? - ¿para qué?

For a car – para un carro.

We want a guitar – queremos una guitarra.

What for? - ¿para qué?

To play the guitar– para tocar la guitarra.

Esto es muy importante, aunque en español usamos un verbo en infinitivo después de "*para*", en inglés es diferente. *NUNCA* se usa "*for*", simplemente se usa el verbo en infinitivo y esto expresa la idea del español "para". Veamos.

I need a bike – necesito una bicicleta.

What for? - ¿para qué?

To ride it – para montarla.

I need food to eat it – necesita comida para comerla.

We want a beer to drink it – queremos una cerveza para beberla.

To go – Ir

Vamos a dedicar una sección al verbo "to go". Prestemos mucha atención en cómo se usa. Vamos a conjugarlo primero.

I go – yo voy

You go – tú vas / usted va

He goes – él va

She goes – *ella va*
We go – nosotros vamos
You go – ustedes van
They go – ellos / ellas van

Aprendimos hace poco que "*to* – *a / hacia*" significa en dirección a, el cual se usa en combinación con el verbo "*to go*". Les daré una lista de lugares que deben aprender de memoria. El uso no tiene mucha explicación: simplemente con unos se usa el "*to*" con otros se usa "*to the*" y con otros no se usa.

We go downtown – vamos al centro de la ciudad. *(No se usa nada delante de downtown).*

She goes home – ella va a casa (hogar). *(No se usa nada delante de home).*

They go to school – ellos van a la escuela. *(Siempre se dice to school).*

You go to the post office – usted va al correo postal. *(Siempre se dice to the post office).*

We want to go to the park – queremos ir al parque. *(Siempre se dice to the park).*

He goes to the hospital – él va al hospital. *(Siempre se dice to the hospital).*

I need to go to the bank – necesito ir al banco. *(Siempre se dice to the bank).*

We prefer to go to the restaurant – preferimos ir al restaurante. *(Siempre se dice to the restaurant).*

I don't want to go to the police station – no quiero ir a la estación de policía. *(Siempre se dice to the police station)*.

Pedro and Maria want to go to the nightclub – Ellos quieren ir al club nocturno. *(Siempre se dice to the nightclub)*.

I need to go to the hotel – necesito ir al hotel. *(Siempre se dice to the hotel)*.

You go to the train station – ustedes van a la estación de tren. *(Siempre se dice to the train station)*.

We go to the airport – vamos al aeropuerto. *(Siempre se dice to the airport)*.

He doesn't want to go to the office – él no quiere ir a la oficina. *(Siempre se dice to the office)*.

They need to go to the bus station – ellas necesitan ir la estación de autobús. *(Siempre se dice to the bus station)*.

Where do you want to go to? - ¿A dónde quieres ir?

I want to go home – quiero ir a casa.

También puede ver *"Where to?"* ¿A dónde? en su forma contracción.

Where to Sir? - ¿A dónde señor?

To the airport – al aeropuerto.

To have – tener

Vamos a ver nuestro primer verbo irregular en inglés.

I have   - yo tengo
You have   - tú tienes / usted tiene
He has   - *él tiene*
She has   - *ella tiene*
It has   - *él o ella tiene (animal o cosa)*
We have   - nosotros tenemos
You have   - ustedes tienen
They have - ellos / ellas tienen

Como podrán ver solo es irregular en las voces para "*He / She / It*".

I have a car – tengo un carro.

She has a guitar – ella tiene una guitarra.

We have money – tenemos dinero.

He *doesn't have* money – él no tiene dinero.

Recuerden, que cuando estamos hablando en negativo, no usamos la conjugación "*has*", solamente en oraciones afirmativas. No lo olviden.

She has a dog – ella tiene un perro

She *doesn't have* a dog – ella no tiene un perro

He has a cat – él tiene un gato

He *doesn't have* a cat – él no tiene un gato.

Practiquemos lo que hemos aprendido en estas tres lecciones antes de continuar con la próxima lección.

Exercises – Ejercicios

Exercise 3.1:   Fill in with "How much?" or

"How many?" – Llena con "How much" o "How many".

Example: "I need some hamburgers." "How many?" Five.

"I need some <u>chicken</u>." "_____?" "A pound and a half."

"I need some <u>cake</u>." "_____?" "Two slices."

"I need some <u>cookies</u>." "_____?" "Two."

"I need some <u>coffee</u>." "_____?" One bag.

"I need some <u>hot dogs</u>." "_____?" "Three."

"I need some <u>sugar</u>." "_____?" "Two bags."

"I need some <u>milk</u>." "_____?" "A gallon."

"I need some <u>beef</u>." "_____?" "Half a pound."

"I need some <u>butter</u>." "_____?" "One stick."

"I need some <u>potatoes</u>." "_____?" "Just one."

Exercise 3.2: Write *who, what,* or *where*. – Escribe "who, what o where"

Example: "Where do you want to go after work?" "To the pool."

"_____ do you want to go?" "To the park."

"_____ do you want to eat?" "Lamb and potatoes!"

"_____ do you play golf with?" "My dad."

"_____ do you study English?" "In New York."

"_____ do you study English with?" "My wife."

"_____ do you like to watch the game?" "At home."

"_____ do you want for dessert?" "Cookies."

"_____ do you like to drink with cookies?" "Coffee."

"_____ do you go to church with?" "My mom."

"_____ do you do your homework?" "In the park."

Exercise 3.3: Conjugate the verbs – Conjugar el verbo.

Mom _____ (kiss) Dad every night.

I _____ (eat) ice cream after work.

You _____ (hate) injustice, don't you?

My father _____ (drive) fast.

The game _____ (start) in five minutes.

Women _____ (like) to talk.

I _____ (like) sugar with my coffee.

The sandwich _____ (need) some cheese.

The teachers _____ (prefer) to go home.

_____ (do) you like to play the piano?

* Lesson 4
Review Lesson – Lección de repaso

Con la lección tres concluimos el tiempo gramatical del presente simple. Vamos a dedicar esta lección cuatro a repasar lo ya aprendido y a trabajar en algunos ejercicios para ejercitar nuestras habilidades. Recuerden, no pasen a la próxima lección si no están 100% seguros de dominar las primeras tres lecciones, las cuales son la base y esencia de todo el aprendizaje.

Haga 5 preguntas usando el modelo presentado más abajo, con la lista de verbos. En sus respuestas, favor de usar afirmativo y negativo en su forma corta y larga.
Do you like to work?
Yes, I do.
Yes, I like to work.
No, I don't.
No, I don't like to work.

Verbos: To study, to swim, to travel, to sleep, to write.

Haga 5 preguntas usando el modelo presentado más abajo, con la lista de verbos. En sus respuestas, favor de usar afirmativo y negativo en su forma corta

y larga.
Does he want to cook?
Yes, he does.
Yes, he wants to cook.
No, he doesn't.
No, he doesn't like to cook.

Verbos: To read, to argue, to kiss, to hug, to walk.

Haga tres oraciones usando "and" y "too".
I like to cook, and I like to eat too.
Haga tres oraciones usando "and" y "either".
I don't like to cook, and I don't like to eat either.
Haga 5 oraciones usando "but".
I like to eat, but I don't like to cook.
Escriba un corto dialogo expresando qué le gusta comer y qué no le gusta comer.
Escriba un corto dialogo expresando lo que necesita y lo que prefiere.
Traduzca el siguiente párrafo al español.
Good morning, Dad. I want to talk to you today. I need money. What for? For a car and I want to go to college, but right now I prefer to go downtown.
Excuse me, Sir. Do you want something to drink? Yes, please. I want an orange juice. And do you want something to eat? No, thanks.
Traduzca al inglés el siguiente texto.
Buenos días, mamá. ¿Qué quieres cocinar hoy? Hoy quiero cocinar arroz con carne, pero no tengo frutas. ¿Quieres tú comer frutas? No, mamá. No me gustan las frutas, pero me gusta el vino. Quiero beber vino con la comida. Buena idea.

Traducir las siguientes frases al inglés.
Hola Papá, necesito 2500 dólares para comprar un carro.
María quiere comprar una bicicleta, pero no tiene dinero.
¿Cuántos dólares tienes?
Necesito una bicicleta, pero prefiero un carro.
Answer the questions about your preferences. – Responde las preguntas con tu preferencia.
Example: Do you prefer to listen to music or play the piano? _Play the piano._
Do you prefer to cook or wash the dishes?
Do you prefer to listen to music or read?
Do you prefer to fish or swim?
Do you prefer to talk or dance?
Do you prefer to run or walk?
Do you prefer to work or study?
Do you prefer to watch golf or play golf?
Do you prefer to do your homework or listen to the radio?
Do you prefer to ask a question or answer a question?
Do you prefer to sleep like a baby or like a mom?

12. Complete the conversation using the correct phrase. – Completa la conversación usando la frase correcta.

Here you are.   That's a shame.   Don't worry.
It's nice to meet you.   I'm glad you like it. Good idea.

"Dad, I want to buy a car, but I don't have any money."

"_____"

"This chicken is delicious!"

" _____ "

"Hi. My name is Emily." "_____ "
"Oh, no. I want to cook for you, but I don't have any fruit or meat."

" _____ "
"I want some coffee, please."

" _____ "
"I need some money. I want to work.

" _____ "

13: Write the pronoun – Escribe el pronombre (I, you, he, she, it, we, they).

My mom likes wine. _____ drinks it at night.

My name is Ronnie. _____ teach piano.

What is your name? Where do _____ work?

My mom and dad don't like to rest.

_____ prefer to work.

Dad and I play a lot of games, but _____ don't

play chess.

Lesson 5
Who are you? - ¿Quién eres?

Conversation 1

Mac: My car doesn't work.

Joe: well...

Mac: It is here at the garage. Do you want to see it?

Joe: No, I don't.

Mac: But I need it.

Joe: Really?

Mac: Who are you?

Joe: I'm Joe.

Mac: Are you the mechanic?

Joe: No, I'm a bus driver. My bus doesn't work.

Conversation 2

Anthony: What does your brother do?

Bart: Hmmm, uh—he visits people.

Anthony: Is he a pastor?

Bart: No, he drives a car.

Anthony: Is he a doctor?

Bart: No, he works in an office.

Anthony: Oh, is he a salesman?

Bart: No, he works for the government.

Anthony: Is he a police officer?

Bart: No, he—

Anthony: He drives a car, and works in an office. But he also visits people and works for the government. Hmmm, is he a mailman?

Bart: Yes!

Conversation 3

Jessica: I want to buy some furniture, but I have money for just one thing.

Shaun: What do you need?

Jessica: Well, a need a couch, a dresser, a bed, and a lamp.

Shaun: Wow, Jessica, don't you have a bed?

Jessica: Yes, I do. I need it for the guest room.

Shaun: What do you need the dresser for?

Jessica: Well, my things are in boxes.

Shaun: Oh. And the couch?

Jessica: I have a couch upstairs, but I want one downstairs, too.

Shaun: Okay. And do you really need a lamp?

Jessica: Mmm, I want it for my bedroom. I don't need it, I guess.

Shaun: You need the dresser for your things.

Jessica: Yeah. You're right. It's just what I need.

New words – Nuevas palabras

Actor - actor
Actress - actriz
Bus driver - chofer de autobús
Businessman - hombre de negocios
Businesswoman - mujer de negocios
Cook - cocinero

Dentist - dentista
Department store - tienda por departamentos
Doctor - doctor
Flight attendant - azafata
Garage - garaje / taller
Hotel - hotel
Housewife - ama de casa
Mailman - cartero
Mechanic - mecánico
Nightclub - club nocturno
Office - oficina
Pastor - pastor
Pharmacist - farmacéutico
Pilot - piloto
Plane - avión
Police officer - oficial de policía
Police station - estación de policía
Porter - portero
Post office - oficina postal / correo
Salesman - vendedor
Saleswoman - vendedora
School - escuela / colegio
Secretary - secretaria
Singer - cantante
Soccer player - futbolista
Theater - teatro
Waiter - camarero
Waitress - camarera
Broom – escoba
Butterfly – mariposa
Job – trabajo
Drugstore – farmacia

Nivel Uno

Stadium – estadio
Apartment – apartamento / departamento
Bathroom – sala de baño
Bed – cama
Bedroom – cuarto / dormitorio
Closet – closet
Couch – sofá
Curtain – cortina
Dining room – comedor
Door – puerta
Dresser – gavetero / cómoda
Fence – cerca / valla
Gate – portón
Lamp – lámpara
Living room – sala de estar
Mirror – espejo
Picture – cuadro / foto
Refrigerator / fridge – refrigerador / nevera
Rent – renta
Room - habitación
Rug – alfombra
Shelf – estante
Sink – lavamanos
Stairs – escaleras
Stove – estufa
Street – calle
Toilet – inodoro
Tree – árbol
Wall – pared
Window – ventana
Upstairs – Planta de arriba / último piso
Downstairs – planta baja / primer piso

Phrases and expressions – Frases y expresiones

What do you do? - ¿Qué haces? / ¿A qué te dedicas? *(en cuanto a trabajo se refiere).*

What do you want to be? - ¿Qué quieres ser?

How nice – que agradable / que bien.

What do they do? – ¿Qué hacen ellos? *(en cuanto a trabajo).*

I'm afraid (not) – Me temo *(que no).*

It's just what I need – Es justo lo que necesito.

Of course – por supuesto.

He visits people - él visita personas.

He works for the government - él trabaja para el gobierno.

He also visits people - él también visita personas.

The guest room - el cuarto de huésped.

My things are in boxes - mis cosas están en cajas.

You're right - tienes razón.

I guess – supongo.

Estudien muy bien cada una de las nuevas palabras, el nuevo vocabulario de esta lección antes de continuar. El éxito depende de esto.

Grammar – Gramática

Vamos a trabajar con el verbo "*to be*". Como ya dominamos bien el contenido de las pasadas tres lecciones, ahora nos concentraremos en el avance de nuestros estudios. En español tenemos los verbos "*ser y estar*", ambos con usos diferentes. Decimos, "yo estoy aquí" o "yo soy Pedro". Les sorprenderá saber que en inglés se usa un solo verbo para ambos.

To be – Ser o Estar.

I'm (I + am) – yo soy o estoy

You're (You + are) – tu eres o estás / usted es o está

He's (He + is) – él es o está

She's (She + is) – ella es o está

It's (It + is) – él o ella (animal o casa) es o está

We're (We + are) – nosotros somos o estamos

You're (You + are) – ustedes son o están

They're (They + are) – ellos / ellas son o están

Para la forma de contracción, solo quitamos la "*a*" en *Are* o la "*i*" en *is* y le agregamos un apóstrofe. Ambas formas son usadas; ya dependerá del estilo de la persona hablando. Es imperativo aprender ambas formas. Vamos a practicar un poco antes de ver las versiones para preguntar y responder del verbo "*to be*".

I am an *actor,* and I work in a *theater.* –Yo soy un actor y trabajo en un teatro.

You are a *doctor,* and you work at a hospital. – Usted es un doctor y trabaja en un hospital.

He is a *pilot,* and he flies a *plane.* – Él es un piloto y vuela un avión.

She is a *singer,* and she works in a nightclub. – Ella es una cantante y trabaja en un club nocturno.

We are teachers, and we work at a school. – Somos profesores y trabajamos en una escuela.

You are secretaries, and you work in an office. – Ustedes son secretarias y trabajan en una oficina.

They are porters, and they work at a hotel. – Ellos son porteros y trabajan en un hotel.

Sandra is an *actress,* and she works in a theater, too. – Sandra es una actriz y trabaja en un teatro también.

Peter is a *police officer,* and he works at the *police station.* – Peter es un oficial de policia y trabaja en la estación de policia.

Lenin and Melvin are mechanics, and they work in a *garage.* – Lenin y Melvin son mecanicos y trabajan en un taller.

Ruth is a *housewife,* and she works at home. – Ruth es una ama de casa y trabaja en la casa.

Hector is a *salesman,* and Silvia is a *saleswoman;* they work in a *department store.* – Héctor es un vendedor y Silvia es una vendedora; ellos trabajan en una tienda por departamentos.

Larry is a *mailman,* and he works at the *post office.* – Larry es un cartero y trabaja en la oficina postal.

Leris is a *flight attendant,* and she works on a *plane.* – Leris es una azafata y trabaja en un avión.

Nelson is a *taxi driver,* and he drives a taxi. – Nelson es un taxista y conduce un taxi.

Sarah is a *bus driver;* she drives a bus. – Sara es un conductor de autobús; ella conduce un autobús.

Rudy is a *businessman,* and *Alba is* a *businesswoman;* *they are* business *people,* and they are at the office. – Rudy es un hombre de negocios y Alba es una mujer de negocios, ellos son personas de negocios y están en la oficina.

Theo is a *dentist,* and he works at the office. – Theo es dentista y trabaja en la oficina.

Louis is a *waiter,* and *Nelly is* a *waitress;* they work at a restaurant. – Louis es camarero y Nelly es camarera, ellos trabajan en un restaurante.

Tenemos mucha información nueva que estudiar y aprender. Asegúrense de repasar y aprender cada palabra nueva y las profesiones.

Ya dominamos la forma de contracción y la forma normal del verbo "to be" en afirmativo. Veamos la forma negativa y la forma para preguntas.

Ask and answer – Preguntar y responder.

En español decimos ¿*Eres tú doctor?* Colocamos el

verbo "*ser*" y después el pronombre personal. Ésta es la forma correcta. Bueno, se sorprenderán en saber qué es lo mismo en inglés; no tienen que pensar mucho. La estructura es la misma. Veamos.

Am I a doctor? – *¿Soy yo doctor?*
Are you a doctor? - ¿Eres tú *doctor?*
Is he a doctor? - ¿Es él *doctor?*
Is she a doctor? - ¿Es ella *doctor?*
Is it a donkey? - ¿Es él (ella) un burro*?*
Are we doctors? – ¿Somos nosotros *doctores?*
Are you doctors? - ¿Son ustedes *doctores?*
Are they doctors? - ¿Son ellos (ellas) *doctores?*

Are you a dentist? - ¿Eres dentista?
Yes, I am. – Sí, lo soy.
Yes, I am a dentist. – Sí, soy dentista.

Is he a doctor? – ¿Es él doctor?
Yes, he is. – Sí, lo es.
Yes, he is a doctor. – Sí, él es doctor.

Is she a cook? - ¿Es ella cocinera?
Yes, she is. – Sí, lo es.
Yes, she is a cook. – Sí, ella es cocinera.

Who are you? - ¿Quién eres?
I am the teacher – Soy el profesor.
I am not the pastor; I am the teacher – No soy el pastor, soy el profesor.

Prestar atención que con la forma interrogativa, nunca se usa la forma de contracción. Siempre se usará la forma completa.

Negative answers – Respuestas negativas

I'm not (am + not) – yo no soy o no estoy

You aren't (are + not) – tú no eres o no estás / usted no es o no está

He isn't (is + not) – él no es o no está

She isn't (is + not) – ella no es o no está

It isn't (is + not) – él (ella) no es o no está

We aren't (are + not) – nosotros no somos o no estamos

You aren't (are + not) – ustedes no son o no están

They aren't (are + not) – ellos / ellas no son o no están

Como pueden ver, existe la forma de contracción y la forma normal; solo recuerden que en la forma negativa la contracción se efectúa en la negación, esto es, con el "not". Se substituye la "o" del "not" por un apóstrofe y tenemos la forma de contracción. Presten mucha atención a la pronunciación. Es de suma importancia que usen el audio para asegurar una pronunciación perfecta. Veamos la estructura completa.

Are you a soccer player? - ¿es usted futbolista?

Yes, *I am*. – Sí, lo soy.

Yes, *I am* a soccer player. – Sí, yo soy futbolista.

No, *I am not*. – No, no lo soy.

No, *I am not* a soccer player. – No, yo no soy futbolista.

Are you a pharmacist? - ¿Son ustedes farmacéuticos?

Yes, *we are*. – Sí, lo somos.

Yes, *we are* pharmacists. – Sí, somos farmacéuticos.

No, *we are not* (no, *we aren't*). – No, no lo somos.

No, *we are not* pharmacists (no, *we aren't* pharmacists). – No, no somos farmacéuticos.

La forma de contracción en oraciones afirmativas, solo se usará en respuestas largas. Cuando usamos el negativo, se puede usar la forma de contracción tanto en la respuesta corta como larga.

Is it good? - ¿Es esto bueno?

Yes, *it is*. – Sí, lo es.

Yes, *it is* good. – Sí, esto es bueno.

No, *it is not* (*it isn't*). – No, no lo es.

No, *it is not* good (*it isn't*). – No, esto no es bueno.

Exercises – Ejercicios

Exercise 5.1: Write the profession using the verb to be. – *Escribe las profesiones usando el verbo "to be"*

Example: Jerry works in a hospital. He <u>is a</u>

doctor._

Marge answers the telephone in an office. She

_____.

Max works with cars at a garage. He

_____.

Sally works at home. She cooks and washes the

dishes. She _____.

Ralph works at a department store. He

_____.

Paul works at a church. He _____.

Jill sells medicine at a pharmacy. She

_____.

Mark works on an airplane. He isn't a flight

attendant. He _____.

Roseanne works at a theater. She

_____.

Ken drives a car. He _____.

Walter works at a police station. He's not a secretary. He _____.

Exercise 5.2: Answer with short answers – Contesta en respuesta corta.

Example: Are we English students? _Yes, we are._

Is the couch in the living room?

_____.

Are the pictures in the sink? _____.

Is the toilet in the street? _____.

Is the orange juice in the refrigerator?

_____.

Is the tree in the bathroom? _____.

Is the car upstairs? _____.

Are the books in the refrigerator?

_____.

Are the pictures in the closet?

_____.

Is the dresser in the bedroom?

_____.

Are the shelves on the wall? _____.

Lesson 6
Can I come in? - ¿Puedo entrar?

Conversation 1

Mary: [knock, knock] Hello?

John: Hi.

Mary: Are you there?

John: Yes. Who is it?

Mary: It's Mary.

John: [no answer]

Mary: I'm Mary . . . your sister.

John: Oh.

Mary: Can I come in?

John: Oh, uh, okay.

Mary: Where are you?

John: I'm behind the couch.

Mary: I don't see you.

John: I'm on the floor.

Mary: You're on the floor?

John: With the dog.

Mary: Did you buy a dog? Awwww. What's his name?

John: Her name is . . . Mary.

Mary: Mary!

Conversation 2

Mary: So, what does your dog do?

John: She can ask for food.

Mary: All dogs ask for food.
John: She sits in the window.
Mary: Okay.
John: You can see her outside. People don't walk near the house.
Mary: Really? Nice.
John: And she sings.
Mary: She sings?
John: Yes. She listens to the radio and sings.
Mary: What music does she sing?
John: Any music.
Mary: Excellent. We can sell—
John: We? She's my dog.
Mary: Uh, yes. But I can make videos.

New words – Nuevas palabras

Beautiful - lindo / hermoso
Brother -   hermano
Chair - silla
Glass - vaso
Intelligent -inteligente
Kitchen - cocina
Miles - millas
Nice - lindo
Sister - hermana
Son - hijo
Table - mesa
Yard - patio / yarda
Black - negro
Blue - azul
Brown - marrón

Gold - dorado / oro
Green - verde
Grey - gris
Orange - anaranjado / naranja
Pink - rosa
Purple - morado
Red - rojo
Silver - plateado
White - blanco
Yellow – amarillo

Phrases and Expressions - Frases y expresiones

Knock, knock - cuando se toca la puerta.
To ask for food - pedir comida.
All dogs - todos los perros.
She sits in the window - ella se sienta en la ventana.
But I can make videos - pero puedo hacer videos.

Grammar – Gramática
There is / There are – Hay

En español usamos *"hay"* tanto en el singular como en el plural. En inglés en cambio, tenemos el uso del singular, plural, preguntas y respuestas. Vamos a ver cómo funciona en inglés.

There is – Hay

Se usa para una sola cosa, esto es, en el singular. También se usa con las palabras que no se cuentan.

There is a chair in the kitchen – Hay una silla en la

cocina.

There is a dog in the yard – Hay un perro en el patio.

Ask and answer – preguntar y responder

Is there a dog in the yard? - ¿Hay un perro en el patio?

Yes, *there is.* – Sí, lo hay.

Yes, *there is* a dog in the yard. – Sí, hay un perro en el patio.

No, *there is not.* – No, no lo hay.

No, *there is not* a dog in the yard. – No, no hay un perro en el patio.

There's a glass on the table – Hay un vaso en la mesa.

There isn't a glass on the table – No hay un vaso en la mesa.

Como pueden ver, hay una forma de contracción para el positivo y negativo.

There are – Hay

Se usa para dos o más cosas, entiéndase, para el plural. La estructura es la misma que con "*there is*" a excepción que "*there are*" no tiene forma de contracción en el afirmativo.

There are two dogs in the yard – hay dos perros en el patio.

There are four chairs in the kitchen – hay cuatro

sillas en la cocina.

Ask and answer – preguntar y responder.

Are there any chairs in the house? – ¿hay algunas sillas en la casa?

Yes, *there are* some. – Sí, hay algunas.

Yes, *there are* some chairs in the house – Sí, hay algunas sillas en la casa.

No, *there are not* (*there aren't*). – No, no las hay.

No, *there are not* (*there aren't*) any chairs in the house. – No, no hay ninguna silla en la casa.

Es importante aprender a usar "*some-algún, algunos*"; siempre se usa en la forma afirmativa del plural "*there are*".

There are some dogs in the house – Hay algunos perros en la casa.

"*Any-ninguno*" siempre se usa en preguntas y respuestas negativas del singular y plural. Veamos.

Is there any fruit in the house? - ¿Hay alguna fruta en la casa?

There isn't any fruit in the house – No hay nada de fruta en la casa.

Are there any dogs in the house? - ¿Hay algún o algunos perros en la casa?

There aren't any dogs in the house – No hay ningún o ningunos perros en la casa.

Prepositions "In / At / On" – Preposiciones "In / At / On".

Hemos estado viendo estas preposiciones en el transcurso de las lecciones pasadas. Vamos a ver cómo funcionan. Estas tres preposiciones pueden ser traducidas como "*En*" en español.

In – *en* (dentro de algo)
At – *en* (localidad y dirección)
On – *en* (sobre o encima de algo).

There is money *in* the wallet – Hay dinero en la cartera (*entiéndase, el dinero está **dentro** de la cartera.Wallet es usado para la cartera de hombre solamente*).

The keys are *in* the purse – las llaves estan en la cartera *(dentro de la cartera. Purse es usado para la cartera de mujer solamente)*

There are apples *in* the refrigerator – hay manzanas en la nevera.

I am *at* school – Estoy en la escuela (entiéndase, como dirección o localidad)

Dad is *at* the hospital – papa está en el hospital.

We are *at* the restaurant – estamos en el restaurante.

There is a book *on* the table – -hay un libro en la mesa (*entiéndase, el libro está **sobre** la mesa).*

The papers are *on* the floor – los papeles están en el piso.

I am *on* the bike – estoy en la bicicleta.

Possessive adjectives – Adjetivos posesivos.

Ahora es tiempo de aprender a decir cuando algo nos pertenece o a alguien más. Los adjetivos posesivos funcionan igual que en español. Veamos.

My - mi
Your – tu / su (de usted)
His – su (de él)
Her – su (de ella)
Our - nuestro
Your – su (de ustedes)
Their – su (de ellos / ellas)

My car is beautiful – mi carro es hermoso.

Your house is nice - tu casa es linda / su casa es linda (de usted).

His dog is black – su perro es negro o el perro de él es negro.

Her cat is white – su gato es blanco o el gato de ella es blanco.

Our brother is intelligent – nuestro hermano es inteligente.

Your sister is sad – su hermana está triste o la hermana de ustedes está triste.

Their son is ugly – su hijo es feo o el hijo de ellos es feo.

Como pueden ver es verdaderamente fácil usarlos.

The preposition "Of - De" – La preposición "of - de".

Se usa por lo general al igual que en español. Prestemos atención a los ejemplos citados.

A house *of* stone - Una casa de piedra.

The city *of* New York – La ciudad de Nueva York.

The leg *of* the table – La pata de la mesa.

Como pueden ver, no hay nada difícil en usar y aprender esta preposición.

Possessive Case "'S" – El caso posesivo "'s"

En inglés existe lo que llamamos el caso posesivo; ahí es cuando los hispano-hablantes dicen que los de habla inglesa dicen las cosas al revés, pero no es así. Veamos y aprendamos el por qué.

El caso posesivo es representado por "'s", entiéndase, un apostrofe antes de la "s". Y significa "de" en español.

The house *of* Pedro – La casa de Pedro.

Pedro *'s* house – La casa de Pedro.

Solo tienen que colocar la 'S después de quien posee el artículo o palabra en cuestión; esto indicará que esta persona posee el objeto o cosa.

The car *of* Maria – El carro de María. ¿Quién posee el carro? María, ¿verdad? Entonces, solo tenemos que adherir la 's al nombre de María.

Maria *'s* car – El carro de María.

Carlo*s'* Apple – La manzana de Carlos.

Si quien posee termina en "S", solo colocamos el apostrofe después de la "S" del nombre de la persona. Recuerden que esta regla se aplica cuando la palabra está en plural.

The boys' projects – Los proyectos de los chicos
The Smiths' car – El carro de los Smiths.

Can – Poder

En español tenemos que conjugar el verbo "*poder*" para decir cuando somos capaces o no de hacer algo. En cambio, en inglés es bastante fácil, solo tenemos que usar "*can*", el cual se usa con todos los pronombres personales por igual, sin distinción alguna. Veamos.

I can – yo puedo
You can – tú puedes / usted puede
He can – él puede
She can – ella puede
We can – nosotros podemos
You can – ustedes pueden
They can – ellos / ellas pueden
I can talk to you – puedo hablar contigo.
She can walk ten miles – ella puede caminar 10 millas.
We can learn English – nosotros podemos aprender inglés.

Presten atención, después del "can" el verbo siempre va sin el "to". NUNCA usen un verbo en infinitivo, es decir, con el "to" después de "can". Eso es un error garrafal. También pueden notar que no se usa "s" o "es" cuando usamos "Can".

Ask and answer – Preguntar y responder

Can I work with you? - ¿puedo trabajar contigo?

Yes, you can. – Sí, puedes.

Yes, you can work with me. – Sí, puedes trabajar conmigo.

No, you cannot. – No, no puedes.

No, you cannot work with me. – No, no puedes trabajar conmigo.

I can't work today – no puedo trabajar hoy.

Fíjense muy bien la forma de contracción negativa "*can't*". No tiene dos "n".

Can you arrive early tonight? - ¿puedes llegar temprano esta noche?

No, I can't. – No, no puedo.

Can she sing? - ¿puede ella cantar?

Yes, she can sing very well – Sí, ella puede cantar muy bien.

Can I come in? - ¿puedo entrar?

Yes, you can come in – Sí, puedes entrar.

Can you help me, please? - ¿puedes ayudarme, por favor?

No, I can't help you – No, no puedo ayudarte.

Can I help you? - ¿puedo ayudarte?

Yes, you can help me – Si tú puedes ayudarme.

No, you can't help me – No, no puedes ayudarme.

Can we rent a car? ¿Podemos rentar un auto?

Yes, we can. – Sí, podemos.
No, we can't. – No, no podemos.

Prepositions – Preposiciones
Behind – detrás
There is a dog **behind** the car – hay un perro detrás del carro.
Between – entre
There is a dog **between** the car and the house – hay un perro entre el carro y la casa.

In front of – en frente de
There is a dog **in front of** the house – hay un perro en frente de la casa.

Next to – al lado de
There is a dog **next to** the window – hay un perro al lado de la ventana.

Over – sobre
There is a man **over** the table – hay un hombre sobre la mesa *(entiéndase, over es cuando no se está tocando la superficie)*
Under – debajo
There is a child **under** the table – hay un niño debajo de la mesa.
Near – cerca
There is a clinic **near** the house – hay una clínica cerca de la casa.

Hemos aprendido muchas cosas nuevas. El nivel de inglés actual es muy alto y están listos para hablar sobre casi cualquier cosa, pero aun nos faltan muchas cosas por aprender. Repasen las lecciones pasadas y asegúrense de aprender bien cualquier palabra, término o concepto que aún no dominen bien.

Reading - Lectura

Do you know how many people speak English? There are 400 million native speakers of English, but there are 1.5 million people who speak English as a second language! Who says what is correct in English? There is no Royal Academy of English. And many non-native speakers do not need to understand British or American English. They need to understand their neighbors—Russians, Chinese, or Mexicans—who combine English with their native language. Now, native speakers can go on the Internet and learn to speak non-native English!

Exercises - Ejercicios

Exercise 6.1: Write the correct preposition.

Example: The curtains are _in_ (under / on / in) the window.

The tree is _____ (next to / on / over) the street.

The lamp is _____ (between / at / over) the table.

The guitar is _____ (in / on / at) the chair.

The dogs are _____ (on / behind /over) the house.

The dishes are _____ (in / on / at) the table.

The teachers are _____ (under / on / at) the school.

The fruit is _____ (behind / over / between) the fridge and the stove.

Exercise 6.2: Make questions with *can*. Ask for help.

Verbs: arrive, buy come, cook, go, teach

Example: I need to learn Spanish. _Can you teach Spanish?_

My brother wants to go to church. Can he

_____ with you?

Mom needs something to eat. Can

_____ something for her?

I want to have a party. Can _____ to my party?

There is **a lot of** work. Can _____ early?

I need to buy a table for the party. Can I

_____ your table?

Exercise 6.3: Make questions with *can* to ask for permission. Write the verb.

Example: We need to buy a couch. Can we _buy_ a

couch today?

I want to cook. Can I _____?

George wants to play with your dog. Can he

_____ with your dog?

Natalie wants to run in the street. Can she _____ in the street?

They want to sing in church. Can they _____ in church?

You speak English! Can I _____ English with you?

Exercise 6.4: Write the correct possessive pronoun: *my, your, his, her, its,* or *their.*

I want _____ mom.

Mom wants _____ cat.

The cat wants _____ food.

The brother likes _____ house.

Do you want _____ car?

The teachers need _____ money.

Exercise 6.5: Answer the questions with a short answer.

Curso Completo de Inglés

Example: Can you speak English? _Yes, I can._ / Can you speak Russian? _No, I can't._

Can you drive a taxi? _____

Can you speak German? _____

Can you play the guitar? _____

Can you play chess? _____

Can you cook fish? _____

Lesson 7
What are you doing? - ¿Qué estás haciendo?

Conversation 1

Tamika:	Hey, Leila, what are you doing?
Leila:	I'm taking a shower.
Tamika:	Where are you going?
Leila:	To work.
Tamika:	You're getting an early start.
Leila:	Yes, well, I have a lot of work to do.
Tamika:	What do you have to do?
Leila:	I have to plan a trip for my boss. He's going to Korea.
Tamika:	Wow!
Leila:	I know. I'm going to buy his ticket today.
Tamika:	Okay. What do you feel like eating for dinner?
Leila:	Shrimp!
Tamika:	Mmm. With wine and some vegetables?
Leila:	Good idea. Well, have a nice day!
Tamika:	Thanks. Enjoy sleeping!
Leila:	Of course!

New words – Nuevas palabras
Bath – baño   Bed - cama

Check – cheque

Clothes – ropa

Door – puerta

Early – temprano

Exam – examen

Great – estupendo

Late – tarde

Now – ahora

Picture - foto / cuadro

President - presidente

Reality – realidad

Shrimp – camarones

Ticket - ticket / boleto

Church - iglesia

Day - día

Drink - bebida / trago

Email - email

Floor - piso

Job - trabajo

Letter - carta

Party - fiesta

Show - espectáculo

Something - algo

Ticket counter - mostrador de ticket / boletería

Tonight -- esta noche

Phrases and Expressions - Frases y expresiones

Very well - muy bien.

And so on - y así por el estilo, etcétera.

This weekend - este fin de semana.

My daughter – mi hija.

Choose the correct sentence - escoge la respuesta correcta.

An early start - un temprano comienzo / un inicio temprano.

What do you have to do? - ¿qué tienes que hacer?

And some vegetables - y algunos vegetales.

Healthy routine - rutina saludable.

Is essential - es esencial.

Drinking water - agua potable.

Before or during meals - antes o durante comidas.

When do you exercise? - ¿cuándo te ejercitas?

They eat healthful foods - ellos comen comida saludable.

And weather - y el clima.

I'm looking at prices of airline tickets - estoy mirando los precios de los tickets de las aerolíneas.

Lightweight clothes - ropas ligeras.

My friends - mis amigos.

I can't wait! - no puedo esperar - ansío el momento - estoy ansiosa.

To set the table - poner la mesa.

Grammar – Gramática

Como ya dominamos el verbo "to be", vamos entonces a dar un paso más en nuestro aprendizaje del idioma inglés.

Present progressive "Going to" – Presente progresivo "Going to".

El presente progresivo en español se forma con el verbo "*ir + a*". Decimos "*Voy a México*". En inglés se usa "*going to*". Cuando usamos el "going to" indica una acción futura o por realizar próximamente. Veamos cómo se usa.

Going to – Ir a

I am going to – yo voy a - iré

You are going to – tú vas a / usted va a – irá(s) a

He is going to – él va a – irá a

She is going to – ella va a – irá a

It is going to – él o ella va a – irá a

We are going to – nosotros vamos a – iremos a
You are going to – ustedes van a – irán a
They are going to – ellos / ellas van a – irán a
Como habrán notado, para formar este tiempo en inglés siempre tendrán que usar la conjugación correspondiente del verbo "*to be*". No olviden que también indica una acción futura o cercana a su realización.

I'*m going to* London – voy a Londres. / Iré a Londres.
You *are going to* study French – tú vas a estudiar francés. / Tú aprenderás francés.

She'*s going to* cook tonight – ella va a cocinar esta noche. / Ella cocinará esta noche.
He'*s going to* learn English – él va a aprender inglés. / Él aprenderá inglés.
It *is going to* rain today – va a llover hoy. / Lloverá hoy.
We'*re going to* eat – vamos a comer / comeremos.
You *are going to* Italy – ustedes van a Italia. / Ustedes irán a Italia.
They *are going to* sing tonight – Ellas van a cantar esta noche. / Ellas cantarán esta noche.

Ask and answer – Preguntar y responder

Am I going to? - ¿voy yo a?
Are you going to? - ¿vas tú a? ¿va usted a?
Is he going to? - ¿va él a?
Is she going to? - ¿va ella a?
Is it going to? - ¿va a?

Are we going to? - ¿vamos nosotros a?
Are you going to? - ¿van ustedes a?
Are they going to? - ¿van ellos / ellas a?

Como pueden ver, si dominan el verbo "*to be*" no tendrán ningún inconveniente, puesto que es el verbo "*to be*" que hace la forma interrogativa, negativa y afirmativa. Veamos.

Are you going to study English? - ¿vas a estudiar inglés?
Yes, I am. – Sí, voy.
Yes, I am going to study English – Sí, voy a estudiar inglés.

No, I am not. – No, no voy.
No, I am not going to study English – No, no voy a estudiar inglés.

Is he going to learn English? - ¿va él a aprender inglés?
Yes, he is. – Sí, él va.
Yes, he is going to learn English – Sí, él va a aprender inglés.

No, he isn't. – No, él no va.
No, he isn't going to learn English – No, él no va a aprender inglés.

Is she going to France? ¿va ella a Francia?
Yes, she is. – Sí, ella va.
Yes, she is going to france – Sí, ella va a Francia.

No, she is not. – No, ella no va.

No, she is not going to france – No, ella no va a Francia.

Where are you going (to)? – ¿Adónde vas?

I am going to Germany – voy a Alemania.

Como ustedes pueden ver la estructura es la misma, solo deben cambiar el "*verbo*" o la "*palabra*" para indicar lo que ustedes quieren decir. Este es un tiempo que se usa tanto como en español. Lo mejor parte es, que no es difícil, como ustedes creían. A practicar.

Vamos a aprender algunos nombres de países y sus idiomas para completar nuestro ciclo de aprendizaje del futuro próximo.

Countries – Países

Australia - Australia

Belgium - Bélgica

Cambodia - Cambodia

Canada - Canadá

China - China

Cuba - Cuba

Dominican Republic – República Dominicana

France - Francia

Germany - Alemania

Greece - Grecia

Haiti - Haití

India - India

Indonesia - Indonesia
Israel - Israel
Italy - Italia
Japan - Japón
Korea - Corea
Mexico - México
Norway - Noruega
Philippines - Filipina
Portugal - Portugal
Russia - Rusia
Spain - España
Thailand - Tailandia
Turkey - Turquía
UK – Reino Unido
USA – Estados Unidos de América

Nationalities – Nacionalidades
Australian - Australiano
Belgian - Belga
Cambodian - Camboyano
Canadian - Canadiense
Chinese - Chino
Cuban - Cubano
Dominican - Dominicano
French - Francés
German - Alemán
Greek - Griego
Haitian - Haitiano
Indian - Indio
Indonesian - Indonesio
Israeli - Israelí

Italian - Italiano
Japanese - Japonés
Korean - Coreano
Mexican - Mejicano
Norwegian - Noruego
Filipino - Filipino
Portuguese - Portugués
Russian - Ruso
Spanish - Español
Thai - Tailandés
Turk - Turco
Englishman - Inglés
American - Americano

Languages – Idiomas
Arabic - Árabe
Chinese - Chino
Creole - Creol
Dutch - Holandés
English - Inglés
French - Francés
German - Alemán
Greek - Griego
Hebrew - Hebreo
Hindi - Hindi
Indonesian - Indonesio
Italian - Italiano
Japanese - Japonés
Korean - Coreano
Polish - Polaco
Portuguese - Portugués

Russian - Ruso
Turkish - Turco

The gerund "ing" – El gerundio "ing".

El gerundio es también llamado presente progresivo, pero para que no se confundan lo seguiremos llamando, gerundio. Como saben, en español siempre se usa el verbo "*estar*" y después al verbo que le sigue se le agrega "*ando – iendo*". El gerundio en inglés es muy simple; de hecho ustedes ya han usado el gerundio, pero con otro significado. El gerundio es representado por "*ing*". Primero aprendemos a colocar el "*ing*" a los verbos. Debemos suponer que a todos los verbos le agregamos "*ing*", quitamos el "*to*" del infinitivo y le agregamos el "*ing*".

To cook – *cooking*   - cocinando
To eat – *eating*   - comiendo
To work – *working*   - trabajando
To drink – *drinking*   - bebiendo

A los verbos que terminan en "*e*", quitamos la "*e*" y le agregamos el "*ing*".
To write – *writing*   - escribiendo
To argue – *arguing*   - discutiendo
To arrive – *arriving*   - llegando
To drive – *driving*   - conduciendo
To dance – *dancing*   - bailando
To leave – *leaving*   - partiendo
To come – *coming*   - viniendo

To smoke – *smoking* - fumando
To take – *taking* - tomando / llevando

Si el verbo termina en una consonante, precedida de un vocal y una consonante a la vez, duplicamos le consonante final y agregamos "*ing*". Veamos.
To hug – *hugging* - abrazando
To swim – *swimming* - nadando
To run – *running* - corriendo

Recuerden, no se dobla la consonante cuando el verbo termina en "*W, X, Y*". Veamos.
To fix – *fixing* - reparando
To enjoy – *enjoying* - disfrutando
To snow – *snowing* - nevando

Si el verbo termina en "*ie*" lo cambiamos to "*ying*".
To lie – *lying* - mintiendo
To tie – *tying* - amarrando
To die – *dying* - muriendo

Si el verbo termina en una vocal acentuada más "*r*", duplicamos la consonante final. Veamos. Recuerden que el acento no se marca, es en la pronunciación, escuchen el audio y podrán notar la vocal acentuada.
To refer – *referring* - refiriendo
To defer – *deferring* - difiriendo

Recuerden, si el verbo termina en una vocal no acentuada más "*r*" no se duplica la "*r*". Una vez más, el acento es en la pronunciación y no se marca.

Nivel Uno

Escuchen bien el audio. Veamos.

To offer – *offering*	- ofreciendo
To suffer – *suffering*	- sufriendo
To whisper – *whispering*	- susurrando

Ya aprendimos como agregar el "*ing*" a los verbos. Es hora de aprender cómo usar el gerundio. Veamos.

I am cooking – yo estoy cocinando

You are cooking – tú estás cocinando / usted está cocinando

He is cooking – él está cocinando

She is cooking – ella está cocinando

We are cooking – nosotros estamos cocinando

You are cooking – ustedes están cocinando

They are cooking – ellos / ellas están cocinando

No olvidemos que el gerundio se refiere a una acción que está pasando en ese mismo momento. No hay porque pensar mucho, debido a que es similar que en español.

The plane is arriving at the airport – el avión está llegando al aeropuerto.

We are speaking to the president – estamos hablando con el presidente.

115

Curso Completo de Inglés

They are writing an email – ellos están escribiendo un email.

I am cashing a check – estoy cambiando un cheque.

He is taking a picture – él está tomando una foto.

You are coming from church – usted está viniendo de la iglesia.

I am dreaming now – estoy soñando ahora.

We are standing in front of the school – estamos parados en frente de la escuela.

She is waiting for her brother – ella está esperando por su hermano.

I am waiting for you – estoy esperando por ti / te estoy esperando.

You are reporting from the police station – ustedes están reportando desde la estación de policía.

Ask and answer – preguntar y responder
What *is she cooking* tonight? - ¿Qué está ella cocinando esta noche?

She is cooking shrimp – Ella está cocinando

116

camarones.

What *are you doing*? ¿Qué estás haciendo?
I am studying for my exam – estoy estudiando para mi examen.

Is he enjoying the party? - ¿está él disfrutando la fiesta?
Yes, *he is.* – Sí, él está.
Yes, *he is enjoying* the party. – Sí, él está disfrutando de la fiesta.

No, *he isn't.* – No, él no está.
No, *he is not enjoying* the party. – No, él no está disfrutando de la fiesta.

How are you doing? - ¿Cómo te va?
I am doing great – Me está yendo súper bien.
I am not doing very well – No, me está yendo muy bien.

Si nos detenemos un momento a evaluar lo que ya hemos aprendido, estaríamos sorprendidos con el nivel de inglés obtenido. Recuerden, la clave es practicar y practicar.

New verbs – Nuevos verbos
- *To board* the plane – abordar el avión
- *To buy* the ticket – comprar el ticket
- *To check in* at the ticket counter – registrarse en el mostrador de boletería

- *To come* from Europe – venir de Europa
- *To declare* something – declarar algo
- *To finish* the job – terminar el trabajo
- *To get up* early – levantarse temprano
- *To go out* for a drink – salir por un trago
- *To go to* bed late – acostarse tarde
- *To mail* the letter – enviar la carta *(es decir, por correo postal)*
- *To make* something – hacer algo *(expresa la idea de fabricar algo)*
- *To open* the door – abrir la puerta
- *To see* the reality – ver la realidad
- *To sell* cars – vender autos
- *To sit* on the floor – sentarse en el piso
- *To start* the day – comenzar el día
- *To stay* at home – quedarse en casa
- *To take a bath* – tomar un baño
- *To take a shower* – tomar una ducha
- *To think about* you – pensar en ti
- *To wear* nice clothes – usar ropas lindas *(llevar puesto)*

Repasemos y aprendamos bien cada uno de estos verbos. Los necesitamos para las siguientes lecciones. Buena suerte y continúen hablando. Les recomiendo hacer una pequeña pausa para revisar todo lo aprendido hasta ahora y después continuamos nuestros estudios.

Reading 1

What is a healthy routine? Do healthy people

exercise all day? Do they eat just fruit and vegetables? Do they sleep a lot? Work a lot? Today, many people are talking about healthy routines. Getting to bed early is essential. Drinking water is important, too. But when do you drink water? In the morning? Before or during meals? Before going to bed? When do you exercise? In the morning? At night? Some people get up early, start the work day, take a break for exercise, and then go back to work. They eat snacks in the morning and afternoon. They eat healthful foods: almonds, apples, and fish.

Reading 2

I'm planning a trip to the Dominican Republic. I'm reading about the culture and weather. I'm looking at prices of airline tickets. I need to buy one soon! I'm making a list of things I need: lightweight clothes, sandals, toothbrush, and so on. I'm talking to my friends about places to visit. And I'm taking swimming lessons. I can't wait!

Exercises – Ejercicios

Exercies 7.1: Write sentences using Going to – Escribe oraciones usando Going to.

Example: What are you going to eat for lunch?
_I'm going to buy pizza._____ (buy pizza)

What are you going to cook for dinner?

_____ (make shrimp cocktail)

What are you going to do after dinner?

_____ (practice speaking English)

What are you going to do this weekend?

_____ (play with my daughter)

What are you going to do this summer?

_____ (work a lot)

What are you going to do next year?

_____ (travel to Greece)

Exercise 7.2: Complete the telephone conversation using the verb in present progressive – Completa la conversación Telefónica usando el verbo en presente progresivo.

"Yes, Aunt Jill, we're all here. Hmmm? What _are_

we _doing_? (1) Well, I _____ (talk) to you, of

course. (2) Dad _____ (cook) some chicken for

dinner. (3) Mom _____ (make) juice. (4) Janet

_____ (set) the table. (5) Mark _____

(finish) his homework. (6) The baby _____ (eat),

as usual. (7) Frank and Fufu—our dogs, you know—

_____ (enjoy) their bone. (8) And the cat

_____ (play) with a mouse."

Exercise 7.3: Read the sentence in Spanish. Choose the correct sentence: simple present tense or present progressive.

Mamá está cocinando ahora.

Mom cooks. / Mom is cooking.

Mi hermana siempre lava los trastes.

My sister washes the dishes. / My sister is washing the dishes.

Papá arregla el techo cada año.

Dad fixes the roof every year. / Dad is fixing the roof every year.

Mi hermano está bañándose ahorita.

My brother takes a shower. / My brother is taking a shower.

Mamá siempre se duerme tarde.

Mom goes to bed late. / Mom is going to bed late.

Lesson 8
What time is it? ¿Qué hora es?

Reading 1

Early in the morning, a car stops in front of the airport. A man runs inside. He waits in line. "What time is it?" he asks the clerk, "you see my plane leaves early." The clerk asks him for his documents. "Do you have a passport, Sir? This is an international flight." He has only one carry-on bag, so he finishes quickly. "Where is my gate?" he asks. He follows the clerk's directions and quickly arrives at the departure gate. "What time is it?" he asks the clerk. "Your plane is delayed, Sir. There is bad weather in Chicago." He answers, "There is always bad weather in Chicago." The man sits, eats, sits, reads a book, and sits some more. "What time is it?" he asks again. "The time is on the screen, Sir," the clerk tells him. "Oh, okay. Thank you." The man sits again, saying to himself, "This is going to be a long day."

Reading 2

"Zzzzzzzz. Snort." The man wakes up to the sound of many people talking. "What time is it?" he asks in a panic. "Boarding time," a passenger answers. "Thank you," the man yells, running to get in line. But when it is his turn, the airline attendant tells him the plane is full. "But I have a ticket!" he insists. "I'm sorry. We're full." The man gets very angry and starts to complain. "My flight was supposed to leave at half past 6. What time is it now? It's noon, isn't it? I'm going to an important meeting!" The attendant asks to see his ticket. "This is not your plane. Your departure gate has changed." "Which one is my gate?" he asks. "Go to Gate E27." Embarrassed, the man looks for his new departure gate.

New words – Nuevas palabras
Bad - malo
Big - grande
Bike - bicicleta
Boat - bote / barco
Cheap - barato
Color - color
Cookies - galletas
Corner - esquina
Counter - mostrador
Delicious - delicioso
Expensive - caro
Flowers - flores
Good - bueno
Here - aquí
Inexpensive - barato
Lady - dama
Money - dinero
Motorbike - motocicleta (es un tipo de moto muy

ligera)
Nervous - nervioso
On foot - a pie
Pretty - lindo
Red - rojo
Salad - ensalada
Small - pequeño
There - allá
Train - tren
Airline Clerk – empleado de aerolínea
Boarding gate – puerta de abordaje
Departure lounge – sala de espera (en aeropuerto)
Flight – vuelo
Luggage – equipaje
Passport – pasaporte
Seat – asiento
Ticket – boleto
Trip – viaje
Vacation – vacaciones
Capital – capital
Radio station – estación de radio
Breakfast – desayuno
Lunch – almuerzo
Meeting – reunión
News – noticias
Person (people) – persona (s)
Snack – picadera
Customer – cliente
Pair – par
Size – medida
Style – estilo
Animal – animal

Birds – pájaros
Horse – caballo
Bottle – botella
Box – caja
Calculator – calculadora
Camera – cámara
Cigarette – cigarrillo
Clock – reloj (de pared)
Computer – computadora
Customs officer – oficial de aduanas
Matches – fósforos
Package – paquete
Perfume – perfume
Product – producto
Suitcase – maleta / maletín
Watch – reloj (de mano)

Phrases and expressions – Frases y expresiones.

Have a good trip – tenga un buen viaje.
Is this seat taken? ¿Está ocupado este asiento?
On foot – a pie.
On vacation – de vacación.
Smoking or nonsmoking? ¿Fumadores o no fumadores? (*refiriéndose al área).*
Or – o (conjunción).
What's your nationality? ¿Cuál es tu nacionalidad?
A cup of coffee – una taza de café.
A glass of wine – un vaso de vino.
At night – en la noche / por la noche.
I see – ya veo.

You see – ya ves.

In the afternoon – en la tarde.

In the evening – en la noche (temprano).

In the morning – en la mañana.

Not at all – no del todo (también se usa para decir de nada).

You're welcome – de nada.

I'd like – me gustaría.

A pair of shoes – un par de zapatos.

In style – a la moda

What a shame – que lástima / que vergüenza.

Good-bye – adiós.

See you – nos vemos.

*Else – más.

What else do you want? ¿Qué más quieres?

What else? ¿Qué más?

Nothing else – nada más.

Grammar – Gramática

Ya hemos descansado bastante después de nuestra corta pausa. Continuemos con nuestro viaje al mundo de habla inglesa.

Prepositions – Preposiciones

By – por: se usa para medios de transporte

I travel to Europe *by car* – Viajo en carro

We go to church *by boat* – vamos a la iglesia en bote

She is going to france *by plane* – ella va a Francia en avión

I am going to school *by bus* – voy a la escuela en

autobús

They go to the supermarket *by bike* – ellas van al supermercado en bicicleta

We go downtown *by motorbike* – vamos al centro de la ciudad en motocicleta

We are going to Italy *by train* – vamos a Italia en tren.

Recuerden, siempre usamos *por* para expresar medios de transporte. Sin embargo, cuando decimos "a pie", se usa *"on foot".*

I go to school *on foot* – voy a la escuela a pie.

From – **desde / de**: se usa para indicar procedencia y origen.

I am *from* Italy – soy de Italia.

Where are you *from*? - ¿de dónde eres?

I am *from* Paris – soy de Paris.

Where are you coming *from*? ¿De dónde vienes? – I am coming *from* church – vengo de la iglesia.

Around – **alrededor** – **derredor**: se usa para indicar algo próximo o de cercanía.

Is she from *around* here? ¿Es ella de por aquí?

Yes, she is from *around* here – sí, ella es de por aquí.

There is a restaurant *around* the corner – hay un restaurante a la vuelta de la esquina *(al doblar la esquina)*.

I feel very nervous when I am *around* you – me siento muy nervioso cuando estoy cerca de ti (contigo).

Demonstrative pronouns – Pronombres demostrativos

Ahora vamos a aprender a usar los pronombres demostrativos, los cuales también funcionan como adjetivos.

This – este / esto / esta: Se usa en el singular. Recuerden que cuando usamos "this" es porque el objeto o cosa de la que hablamos está a nuestro alcance, es decir, próximo a nosotros, que podemos tocarlo con nuestras manos.

This car is small – este carro es pequeño
This table is big – esta mesa es grande
This is good – esto es bueno.

These – estos / estas: Es el plural de "this"; tiene el mismo uso, pero en el plural.

These cars are small – estos carros son pequeños
These tables are big – estas mesas son grandes
Es bastante sencillo el uso, puesto que es igual que en español. Practiquen bien y aprendan el uso correcto.

That – ese / eso / esa: Se usa en el singular y cuando estamos refiriéndonos a un objeto o cosa que está lejos de nuestro alcance, lejos de nosotros.

That car is expensive – ese carro es caro
That dress is inexpensive – ese vestido es barato
That woman is pretty – esa mujer es linda.
That is not good – eso no es bueno

Those – esos / esas: Es el plural de "that"; tiene el mismo uso, pero el plural.

Those women are very pretty – esas mujeres son muy lindas.

Those cars are very cheap – esos carros son muy baratos.

Those tables are too expensive – esas mesas son demasiadas caras.

Por lo general cuando usamos los adjetivos demostrativos, tendemos a usar los adverbios de grado:

Very – muy
That car is very expensive – Ese carro es muy caro.
That dress is very cheap – Ese vestido es muy barato.

Too – demasiado / muy
This car is too expensive – este carro es demasiado caro.
This dress is too short – este vestido es muy corto.

Over here – aquí / por aquí
This car is very nice – esta carro es muy lindo.
This one here is very nice – este de aquí es muy lindo.
This one over here is very nice – este de por aquí es muy lindo.

Over there – aquel (aquella) – aquel de allá
That car over there is very nice – ese carro de allá es muy lindo / aquel carro de allá es muy lindo.

Recuerden que pueden usarlo tanto en el singular como en plural. También pueden usar "*here* – *aquí, acá*" y "*there* – *allí / allá*" solos.

También tendemos a usar el pronombre "*one* – *ones / uno* – *unos*"

That one is good – ese es bueno.

Those ones are delicious – esos son deliciosos.

This one is bad – este es malo.

These ones are not good – estos no son buenos.

Adjectives – Adjetivos

Vamos a continuar aprendiendo el uso de otros adjetivos para incrementar nuestro conocimiento y mejorar nuestras habilidades en inglés.

* *Any* – *algún / ningún*

Solo se usa en preguntas y oraciones negativas.

Do you have any salad? - ¿Tienes algo de ensalada?

No, I don't have any. – No, no tengo nada (ninguna).

Bedside – al lado de la cama

Brand new – Nuevo (de paquete)

Furnished - amueblado

* *Some* – *algún*

Solo se usa en preguntas y oraciones afirmativas y cuando se ofrece algo. Denota un grupo de palabras que describen cosas irreales cuando no estamos seguros de que existan.

Do you want some cookies? ¿Quieres algunas galleticas?

Yes, I want some cookies– Sí, quiero algunas galleticas.

Overweight – pasado de peso / con sobrepeso
Important - importante
Many – muchos
Se usa en todo caso, preguntas, afirmación, negación, siempre que hablemos de cosas contables.
Does she have many cookies? ¿Tiene ella muchas galletas?
Yes, she has many cookies – Sí, ella tiene muchas galletas.
No, she doesn't have many cookies – No, ella no tiene muchas galletas.

Big - grande
Busy - ocupado
Every – cada / todo
Interesting - interesante
Light – liviano / ligero
Heavy - pesado
Favorite - favorito
Beautiful - hermoso
Clean - limpio
Dirty - sucio
Empty - vacío
Full - lleno
Long – largo
New - nuevo
Old - viejo
Short - corto
Thick - grueso

Thin - delgado

Unattractive – feo (no atractivo)

Ugly - feo

Modern - moderno

Much –mucho

Se usa en preguntas y respuestas negativas. No usamos "much" en oraciones afirmativas. Recuerden, se usa con cosas que no se pueden contar.

How much salad do you need? - ¿cuánta ensalada necesitas?

I need a little – necesito un poco.

I don't need much – no necesito mucha.

A lot (of) - mucho

Se usa en todo caso: preguntas, respuestas afirmativas y negativas.

I have a lot of money – tengo mucha dinero.

I don't have a lot of money – no tengo mucho dinero.

Do you have a lot of money? - ¿tienes mucho dinero?

Yes, I have a lot of money – Sí, tengo mucho dinero.

No, I don't have a lot of money – No, no tengo mucho dinero.

Possessive pronouns – Pronombres posesivos

Hemos aprendido los adjetivos posesivos, que como ya sabemos, siempre van al inicio o en medio de la oración. Recordemos.

My car is nice – mi carro es lindo

This is *my* car – este es mi carro.

Ahora vamos a aprender los pronombres posesivos, los cuales se usan igual que en español. Nosotros decimos en español "este carro es mío". No podemos decir "este es mio carro"... no tendría ningún sentido. Esa es la diferencia entre en adjetivo y el pronombre posesivo. Aprendamos.

Mine - mío

Yours – tuyo / suyo

His - de él

Hers – de ella

Ours - nuestro

Yours – de ustedes

Theirs – de ellos / de ellas

Como pueden ver, casi todos terminan en "s" y no olviden que solo se usan al final de una oración. Muy importante, cuando ya sabemos de qué estamos hablando, entonces podemos usarlo en cualquier lugar de la oración. Veámoslo en acción.

This car is *mine* – este carro es mío.

This one over here is *yours* – este de aquí es tuyo.

That apple is *his* – esa manzana es de él.

That book is *hers* – ese libro es de ella.

That dog over there is *ours* – ese perro de allá es nuestro.

Those books on the counter are *yours* – esos libros en el mostrador son de ustedes.

These nice flowers over here are *theirs* – esas hermosas flores de aquí son de ellas.

Como pueden ver, es fácil de usarlos; se usan como en español. Presten mucha atención a la pronunciación del audio y asegúrense de dominarla a la perfección.

Cuando sabemos a qué nos referimos.
Where's your computer? – ¿Dónde está la computadora?

Mine is broken – la mía está rota (es decir, mi computadora está rota, en respuesta a la pregunta).

Dad took *mine* to work with him – papi se llevó la mía para trabajar (se llevó mi computadora, esto es en respuesta a la pregunta)

Con estos pronombres casi siempre se usan las palabras de preguntas:
Which – *¿cuál / cuáles?*
Which car is yours? ¿Cuál es tu carro?
The red one – el de color rojo
Which one? ¿Cuál?
The red one, next to the beautiful lady over there – el de color rojo, próximo a la hermosa dama de allá.

Whose - *¿de quién / de quiénes?*
Whose car is this? ¿De quién es este carro?
It is mine – es mío.
This is mine – es el mío.

Telling the time – Dando la hora

Vamos a aprender ahora como hablar del tiempo, como saber la hora y referirnos a una hora en específico. En español tenemos dos formas para preguntar la hora: ¿Qué hora es? Y ¿Qué horas son? Bueno, les sorprenderá saber que en inglés solo existe una forma de decirlo; es mucho más fácil que en español. Veamos.

What time is it? ¿Qué hora es? / ¿Qué horas son?

Sabemos que "what" significa "que" y time "tiempo"; también sabemos que "is" es del verbo "to be" y conocemos el pronombre "it", lo cual usamos porque nos referimos al tiempo. Y como pueden ver, no importa la hora, siempre será la misma pregunta. La hora siempre es en singular al igual que la respuesta.

What time is it? ¿Qué hora es?
It is three fifteen (3:15) – Son las 3:15
It is three o'clock – Son las tres en punto.

Cuando queremos preguntar la hora en que hacemos algo, entonces usamos "at" al inicio de la pregunta.

At what time do you get up everyday? - ¿a qué hora te levantas cada día?
I get up at 6:00 a.m. – Me levanto a las 6:00 a.m.

At what time do you start your day? ¿A qué hora inicias tu día?

I start my day at 5:00 o'clock – Inicio mi día a las 5:00 en punto.

Es bastante fácil como pueden ver. Vamos a aprender algunas variaciones y frases que nos ayudarán al momento de hablar de la hora.

It's 5:00 a.m. / p.m. – Son las 5:00 a.m. / p.m.
It's two-thirty – son las 2:30
It's half past two – son las 2:30 (pasa media hora de las 2 o son las 2 y media).

It's thirty minutes *past* two – son las 2:30 (pasan 30 minutos de las 2)

It's thirty minutes to three – son las 2:30 (30 minutos para las 3)

En inglés usamos "half – mitad (media)" para decir 30 minutos.

Usamos el *"past* – pasado (pasan)" para indicar cuando pasa cierto tiempo después de la hora.

Usamos *"to – para"* para indicar que va a dar una hora. Veamos más ejemplos.

It is two fifteen – son las dos y quince
It is a quarter *past* two – pasa un cuarto de las dos.
It is three forty five – son las 3:45
It is a quarter *to* four – falta un cuarto para las cuatro.

Es muy importante entender este concepto. Cuando pasan de una hora usamos "past-pasado" y cuando va a ser una hora usamos "to-para".

It is noon – es mediodía
It is midday – es mediodía
It is midnight – es medianoche

When are you coming home? ¿Cuándo vas a regresar a casa?
I'm coming home (at) about 7:00 o'clock – Voy a regresar a casa como a las 7 en punto.
I'm coming home after 7 – Vengo a casa después de las 7.
I'm coming home before 7 – vengo a casa antes de las 7.
I am coming home late tonight – vengo a casa tarde esta noche.
I am coming home early today – vengo a casa temprano hoy.

Adverbs – Adverbios

Vamos a continuar aprendiendo algunos adverbios que ya conocemos y otros nuevos.

About – acerca / más o menos
After – después
Before – antes
Early – temprano
Half past – pasan treinta minutos de
Late – tarde
O'clock – en punto
Quarter past – pasa un cuarto de
Quarter to / falta un cuarto para
Only – solamente

Today – hoy
Tomorrow – mañana
Tonight – esta noche
After tomorrow – pasado mañana
*Still – *todavía (siempre se usa en medio de palabras y algunas veces al inicio, pero nunca al final. Pueden indicar "aún" en muchos casos.*
I still don't want to eat – Todavía no quiero comer o aún no quiero comer.
*Yet – todavía *(siempre se usa al final de la oración, y puede indicar "aún" en muchos casos).*
She doesn't want to eat yet – ella no quiere comer todavía o ella no quiere comer aún.
Nearby – próximo / en los alrededores

Frequency Adverbs – Adverbios de frecuencia

Always – siempre
Every day – cada día
Every morning – cada mañana
Every week – cada semana
Every month – cada mes
Every year – cada año
Often – a menudo / con frecuencia
Sometimes – algunas veces
Usually – usualmente
Never – nunca

Exercises – Ejercicios

Exercise 8.1: Rewrite the sentence using the example.

Example: Which one is your car? _Which car is yours?_

Which one is their boat? _____

Which one is his seat? _____
Which one is her bicycle?

_____

Which one is my salad?_____
Which ones are their flowers?

_____

Which one is our flight?

_____

Which one is my passport?

_____

Which ones are her suitcases?

_____

Which one is your calculator?

_____

Which one is their box? _____

Exercise 8.2: Write the correct demonstrative pronoun using *this, that, these,* or *those.*
Example:

_____ (1) dress here is not in style, but

_____ (2) dress over there is expensive. _____

(3) section here is nonsmoking. _____ (4) section

over there is smoking.

_____ (5) snack here is cheap, but _____ (6)

cookies over there are delicious.

_____ (7) lady here is my mom, and _____

(8) man over there is my dad.

_____ (9) shoes here are nice, but _____ (10)

shoes over there are attractive.

Exercise 8.3: Write the means of transportation you use.

Example: How do you go to Australia? _by plane_

How do you go to Spain?   _____

How do you go to church?   _____

How do you go to the park?   _____

How do you go to work?   _____

How do you go to New York? _____

Exercise 8.4: Write how often you do these things.

Example: How often do you go to the park? _every morning_

How often do you go to church? _____

How often do you go shopping? _____

How often do you fly? _____

How often do you ride a horse? _____

Lesson 9
What would you like to know? – ¿Qué te gustaría saber?

Conversation 1

Patron: I need some information.

Librarian: What would you like to know?

Patron: Do you have any books on Spain?

Librarian: Yes, let me show you. They are right here—oh, no. They're checked out. Sorry.

Patron: I'd like to study European culture.

Librarian: Books on culture . . . . Here we are.

Patron: No, these are mainly picture books. I want facts.

Librarian: Okay. What would you like to know?

Patron: When did Napoleon conquer Spain?

Librarian: Oh, I can tell you that. On February 16th, 1808. That date marks the beginning of the Peninsular Wars.

Patron: Oh. Thank you.

Librarian: That's all?

Patron: Yes. Have a nice night.

Conversation 2

Karen: Yummy! Steak!

Aunt Fae: Oh, no. Karen. Don't eat that food.

Karen: Why not? Is it poisonous?

Aunt Fae: No. Why don't you have a turkey sandwich?

Karen: What's wrong with the steak? Is it too old?

Aunt Fae: No. Try the cheese-filled hot dogs.

Karen: Is the steak spicy?

Aunt Fae: No.

Karen: Is it fattening?

Aunt Fae: No, but—

Karen: Well, what's wrong with it?

Aunt Fae: Well, it's just that my husband wants it.

Karen: Oh, I see.

Aunt Fae: Would you like some lasagna? It's better than steak.

Karen: No, thanks.

Conversation 3

Bryan: Aunt Conchis, we're so happy you're visiting us. Would you like to watch TV?

Aunt Conchis : I don't watch TV on vacation.

Bryan: Oh. Would you like to see a movie?

Aunt Conchis : I never go to the movies.

Bryan: Would you like to see some caves or a waterfall?

Aunt Conchis : I don't like walking a lot.

Bryan: Would you like to go shopping?

Aunt Conchis : I don't have much money.

Bryan: Okay. Would you like some water?

Aunt Conchis : Is that all you can offer your poor aunt?

New words – Nuevas palabras

Angry - enojado
Better - mejor
Difficult - difícil
Food - comida
Husband - esposo
Months - meses
More - más
Phone - teléfono
Weeks - semanas
Wine - vino
Worthy - valioso
Year - año
Aunt - tía
Brother - hermano
Brother-in-law - cuñado
Cousin - primo
Daughter - hija
Father - padre
Father-in-law - suegro
Grandson - nieto
Grandchild - nieto
Granddaughter - nieta
Grandfather - abuelo
Grandmother - abuela
Husband -- marido / esposo
Mother - madre
Mother-in-law - suegra
Nephew - sobrino
Niece - sobrina
Parents - padres

Sister - hermana
Sister-in-law - cuñada
Son - hijo
Son-in-law - yerno
Stepchild - hijastro
Stepfather - padrastro
Stepmother - madrastra
Uncle - tío
Widow - viuda
Widower - viudo
Wife - mujer / esposa

Phrases and Expressions – Frases y Expresiones

Let me show you – déjame mostrarte / permíteme mostrarte.

They're checked out. – No están *(es decir los libros los han tomado prestado, por eso no están en el sistema, check-out).*

Mainly picture books – mayormente libros de imagines.

I want facts – quiero hechos (no imágenes, más bien hechos reales, datos históricos).

When did Napoleon conquer Spain? ¿Cuándo conquisto Napoleón España?

That date marks – Esa fecha marca.

The beginning of - el inicio de / el comienzo de.

The Peninsular Wars. – las guerras peninsulares.

That's all? - ¿eso es todo?

Yummy! – delicioso.

Is it poisonous? - ¿es venenoso?

What's wrong – ¿Qué pasa...? ¿Cuál es el problema...?

Is it too old? - ¿está demasiado viejo?

Is the steak spicy? - ¿está el filete picante?

Is it fattening? - ¿tiene demasiada grasa?

It's just that – es solo que.

Some caves or a waterfall? - ¿algunas cuevas o cascada?

Offer your poor aunt – ofrecerle a tu pobre tía.

Grammar – Gramática

Hemos estado aprendiendo cosas pequeñas para incrementar nuestro conocimiento. Como ven, ya están hablando inglés. Vamos a aprender ahora como ser educados y formular deseos. Escuchen bien la pronunciación del audio para aprender el sonido correcto.

Polite form "Would like" – Forma educada "Would like"

I would like – me gustaría

You would like – te gustaría

He would like – le gustaría

She would like – le gustaría

We would like – nos gustaría

You would like – les gustaría

They would like –les gustaría

I would like some juice – me gustaría algo de jugo

I'd like to speak with you – me gustaría hablar contigo.

La forma de contracción ('d) se usa mucho,

escuchen bien la pronunciación.

I'd like

You'd like

He'd like

She'd like

We'd like

You'd like

They'd like

Veamos como expresamos deseos con "would like".
I would like to be a teacher – me gustaría ser profesor.

She'd like to have a better husband – a ella le gustaría tener un mejor esposo.

He'd like to know you more – a él le gustaría conocerte mejor.

Veamos cuando ofrecemos algo con "would like".
Cuando queremos ofrecer algo, usamos la forma interrogativa siempre.

Would you like to eat? – ¿te gustaría comer?

Yes, I would – Si.

Yes, I would like to eat – si, me gustaría comer.

No, I would not – No.

No, I would not like to eat – No, no me gustaría comer.

La forma contracción negativa es más usada.

Would you like to come with me? - ¿te gustaría venir conmigo?

Yes, I would – Si.

Yes, I'd like to. – Si, me gustaría.

Yes, I'd like to go with you – Si, me gustaría ir contigo.

No, I wouldn't – No.

No, I wouldn't like to. – No, no me gustaría.

No, I wouldn't like to go with you – No, no me gustaría ir contigo.

Espero que hayan podido notar que pueden contestar con las respuestas afirmativas y negativas en la forma de contracción.

Would you like a glass of wine? ¿Te gustaría un vaso de vino?

Yes, please. – Si, por favor.

Yes, I would. – Si.

Yes, I would like one. – Si, me gustaría.

Yes, I would like a glass of wine – Si, me gustaría un vaso de vino.

No, thanks. – No, gracias.

No, I wouldn't. No.

No, I wouldn't like one. – No, no me gustaría.

No, I wouldn't like a glass of wine – No, no me gustaría un vaso de vino.

I'd like some more wine, please – Me gustaría más vino, por favor o ¿me das más vino, por favor?

I'd like to ask you something – me gustaría preguntarte algo.

Yes, please. What would you like to ask? – Si, por favor. ¿Qué te gustaría preguntar?

I'd like to know something – me gustaría saber algo.

Yes, please. What would you like to know? – Sí, por favor. ¿Qué te gustaría saber?

Recuerden, estamos aprendiendo como usar el "*would like*", más adelante estaremos viendo el condicional. Por ahora, nos conformamos con aprender el "would like".

Commands – ordenes o mandatos

Ordenes o mandatos en inglés son muy simples y sencillos de usar a diferencia del español.

Solo se comienza con el verbo conjugado para "*you*". Decimos "*you eat – tú comes*", entonces, solo necesitamos "*eat*" para formar el imperativo.

Eat the food – cómete la comida / cómase la comida / cómanse la comida.

Answer the phone – contesta el teléfono / conteste el teléfono / contesten el teléfono.

Walk the dog – camina al perro / camine el perro / caminen el perro.

Para el mandato negativo, usamos primero "don't", el cual ya sabemos que es la negación, y agregamos el verbo.

Don't walk the dog – no camines al perro / no camine al perro / no caminen al perro.

Don't eat that food – no te comas esa comida / no

se coma esa comida / no se coman esa comida.

¡Vieron que fácil es! Podemos usar "please" para no sonar tan rudos en el mandato y convertirlo en un mandato cortés o con educación. Siempre usaremos una coma antes de "please" al usarlo en imperativo. Walk the dog, please – camina al perro, por favor. Don't walk the dog, please – no camines al perro, por favor. Answer the phone, please – contesta el teléfono, por favor. Don't answer the phone, please – no contestes el teléfono, por favor.

Let us (let's) – vamos.

Para usar el imperativo con "nosotros" en inglés se usa la forma "let's - vamos". Este mandado puede sonar como una sugerencia o como un mandato dependiendo el tono de voz y la conversación. Veamos.
Let's eat – vamos a comer / comamos / a comer.
Let's talk – vamos a hablar / hablemos / a hablar.

Let's not eat – no comamos.
Let us not speak – no hablemos.
Usualmente se usa más la forma larga con la forma negativa en la versión de la Biblia, debido a que en el inglés hablado esta forma está en desuso.
Let us not sing – no cantemos.

Presten mucha atención a la posición del "not" de

la negación.

Cuando queremos ser más educados y formales en nuestro mandado, usamos "please", siempre colocando una coma antes de "please".

Let's study, please – vamos a estudiar, por favor / estudiemos, por favor / a estudiar, por favor.

Let us not study, please – no estudiemos, por favor.

Recuerden, el *let's* lo podemos usar con cualquier verbo y es muy usado en inglés, así que **"let's practice - a practicar"**.

Prepositions of time – Preposiciones de tiempo

Como ya hemos aprendido casi todo sobre la hora en la lección anterior, vamos a aprender algunas preposiciones del tiempo para complementar.

At / about – **en / acerca** *(cuando hablamos de hora)*

See you at 7:00 – nos vemos a las 7:00

See you at about 7:00 – nos vemos alrededor de las 7:00.

On – **en** (*cuando queremos referirnos a los días de la semana y cuando hablamos de una fecha específica, dando el mes y el día*)

See you *on* Tuesday – nos vemos el martes

We are coming *on* Wednesday – llegamos el miércoles / Vamos para allá el miércoles.

See you *on* November 3rd – nos vemos el tres de noviembre.

I am coming home *on* december 25th – regreso a

casa el 25 de diciembre.

For – por / para *(cuando nos referimos a tiempo de duración)*

For how long are you traveling ¿Por cuánto tiempo estás viajando? / ¿vas a viajar?

I am traveling *for* three weeks – estoy viajando por tres semanas.

For how long is she leaving? ¿Por cuánto tiempo se marcha ella?

She is leaving *for* two months – ella se va por dos meses.

In – en *(cuando solo mencionamos un lapso de tiempo— días, semanas, un mes o un año, sin dar ninguna fecha)*

See you *in* November – nos vemos en noviembre

They are coming *in* December – ellos vienen en diciembre.

See you **in** two weeks – nos vemos en dos semanas.

See you *in* two months – nos vemos en dos meses.

See you **in** a year – nos vemos en un año.

On – en

See you *on* November 3rd – nos vemos el tres de noviembre.

I am coming home *on* December 25th – regreso a casa el 25 de diciembre.

Days of the week – Días de la semana.

Monday - lunes

Tuesday - martes
Wednesday - miércoles
Thursday - jueves
Friday - viernes
Saturday - sábado
Sunday – domingo
Los días de la semana siempre inician con letra mayúscula.

Months of the year – Meses del año

January - enero
February - febrero
March - marzo
April - abril
May - mayo
June - junio
July - julio
August - agosto
September - septiembre
October - octubre
November - noviembre
December - diciembre
Los meses del año siempre inician con letra mayúscula.

Seasons of the Year – Estaciones del año

spring - primavera
summer – verano
autumn / fall – otoño
winter - invierno

Usamos "fall" en Estados Unidos y "autumn" en otras partes del mundo. Recuerden que las estaciones del año no van en mayúsculas, a menos que sea al inicio de la oración.

Ordinal numbers – Números ordinales.

En inglés es muy fácil formar los números ordinales; solo tenemos que agregar "th" a los números cardinales y eso los convierte en ordinales. Prestamos atención a los que son irregulares, y su forma abreviada en paréntesis.

First (1st) - primero
Second (2nd) - segundo
Third (3rd) - tercero
Fourth (4th) - *cuarto*
Fifth (5th) - quinto
Sixth (6th) - sexto
Seventh (7th) - séptimo
Eighth (8th) - octavo
Ninth (9th) - noveno
Tenth (10th) - décimo
Eleventh (11th)
Twelfth (12th)
Thirteenth (13th)
Fourteenth (14th)
Fifteenth (15th).

Así sigue agregando solo "th"a los números cardinales formando los números ordinales. Recuerden las formas irregulares o las que tienen cambios. Es muy sencillo.

The pronoun "It" – El pronombre "It".

Ya hemos visto el pronombre "it" que significa "él o ella" para animal o cosa. Vamos a dedicarle unas cortas líneas para asegurarnos que saben cómo usarlo apropiadamente. Recuerden, se usa para animal o cosa.

The apple is good – la manzana está buena. Como sabemos que nos referimos a la manzana, entonces podemos decir

It is good – Está buena. *(It es sustituyendo la manzana)*.

I like the apple – me gusta la manzana
I like it – me gusta (es decir, la manzana).

Veamos un ejemplo más avanzado.

I don't like to speak about *it* – No me gusta hablar sobre eso (de eso).

Vieron como usamos el "it", porque se supone que sabemos a lo que nos estamos refiriendo. Practiquemos con otros ejemplos.

I want the book – quiero el libro.
I want *it* – lo quiero.
I don't want the book – no quiero el libro.
I don't want *it* – no lo quiero.
I need the money – necesito el dinero.
I don't need *it* – no lo necesito.
The food is delicious – la comida está deliciosa.

155

How is it? ¿Cómo está?

It is delicious – está deliciosa.

It isn't delicious, it is ok – no está deliciosa, está aceptable.

Como pueden ver es muy sencillo, solo tienen que usar la lógica o el sentido común, puesto que es igual que en español.

Negative questions – Preguntas negativas.

Al igual que en español que usamos preguntas negativas como ¿Por qué no comes?, en inglés tenemos la misma construcción también como podemos ver debajo.

Why don't I learn English? - ¿Por qué no aprendo inglés?

Because *they say* it is very difficult. – porque dicen que es muy difícil.

Why don't you learn English? ¿Por qué no aprendes inglés?

Because I don't have a book – porque no tengo un libro.

Why doesn't he learn English? - ¿Por qué no aprende él inglés?

Because he doesn't like English – porque a él no le gusta el inglés.

Why doesn't she learn English? - ¿Por qué no aprende ella inglés?

Nivel Uno

Because she doesn't like it – porque a ella no le gusta.

Why don't we learn English? - ¿Por qué no aprendemos inglés?
Because they say it isn't worth it – porque dicen que no vale la pena.

Why don't you learn English? - ¿Por qué no aprenden ustedes inglés?
Because we don't need it – porque no lo necesitamos.

Why don't they learn English? - ¿Por qué no aprenden ellas inglés?
Because they hate it – porque ellas lo odian.

Vimos la estructura de cómo funciona y nos hemos dado cuenta que no es tan complicado como dicen. Recuerden:
Why? – ¿por qué?
Se usa para preguntar.

Because – porque
Se usa para responder.

*They say – dicen, o se dice
Equivale a un pensamiento general, es decir muchas personas dicen.

Veamos ahora con el verbo "to be". Solo presten atención cuando usamos las preguntas negativas con el verbo "to be" y "I".

*Why **aren't I** studying English? - ¿Por qué no estoy estudiando inglés?

Because I am very tired – porque estoy muy cansado.

Why aren't you studying English? - ¿Por qué no estás estudiando inglés?

Because I am very sad – porque estoy muy triste.

Why isn't he studying English? - ¿Por qué no está él estudiando inglés?

Because he is very angry – porque él está muy enojado.

Why isn't she studying English? - ¿Por qué no está ella estudiando inglés?

Because she is very sick – porque ella está muy enferma.

Why aren't we studying English? - ¿Por qué no estamos nosotros estudiando inglés?

Because we are very worried – porque estamos muy preocupados.

Why aren't you studying English? - ¿Por qué no están ustedes estudiando inglés?

Because we are very sleepy – porque tenemos mucho sueño.

Why aren't they studying English? - ¿Por qué no están ellas estudiando inglés?

Because they are very cold – porque tenemos

mucho frio.

Recuerden la diferencia. Cuando es una pregunta normal, usamos "*Am I*" cuando es una pregunta negativa, entonces, usamos "*Aren't I*". No lo olviden.

Why **am I** studying? ¿Por qué estoy estudiando?

Why **aren't I** studying? ¿Por qué no estoy estudiando?

Object pronouns – pronombres objetivos

Presten mucha atención a los pronombres objetivos; normalmente en español se colocan antes del verbo "te conozco", a diferencia del inglés en el cual se usa después del verbo o una preposición. Recuerden que los "object pronouns" se usan cuando sabemos cuál es el objeto de la oración para evitar repetición y para que la oración se entienda mejor. Veamos.

Me	- me
You	- te
Him	- le
Her	- le
It	- lo /la
Us	- nos
You	- los / les
Them	- los / las / les

Are you talking to **me**? - ¿estás hablando conmigo?

I love **her** – la amo *(sabemos de quien estamos hablando)*

I hate **him** – lo odio *(sabemos de quien estamos*

hablando)

She needs you – ella te necesita

They are speaking to *us* – ellos están hablando con nosotros.

Do you want *them*? – ¿las quieres? *(sabemos de quien estamos hablando).*

Practiquen mucho esta sección, porque necesitan dominar este concepto muy bien para poder hablar correctamente. Vamos a ver algunos ejemplos más complejos, siguiendo el mismo patrón.

She wants to speak to *me*, but I feel nervous around *her* – Ella quiere hablar conmigo, pero me siento nervioso a su lado.

I don't understand why he needs *us*, but we don't need *him* – no entiendo porque él nos necesita, pero nosotros no lo necesitamos.

Do you love *me*? – ¿me amas?

You don't need *her*, you need *me* – no la necesitas; me necesitas a mí.

Aseguremos de practicar y practicar. La clave para un buen aprendizaje es practicar cada palabra o concepto que aprendan.

Reading –

Dear Grandma Lois,

How are you? Are you feeling well? Do you still play cards with your friends?

Mom says you are coming to Greenville! Are you coming in December? You can come for Christmas! I want to see you so much. Would you like to stay with us? You don't have to stay at a hotel. We have a beautiful guest room with a couch, a bathroom, and everything!

Please let me know! We'd love to have you!

Love,

Lauren

✍️ Exercises – Ejercicios

Exercise 9.1: Write the word for the family relationship.

Example: My brother's daughter is my _niece_.

My dad's dad is my _____.

My mom's brother is my _____.

My uncle's daughter is my _____.

My brother's wife is my _____.

My daughter's son is my _____.

Exercise 9.2: Make an appropriate offer. Use "to" with verbs.

Example: "My sister is angry." _Would she like to listen to music?_

go to bed   some pizza   some soup   take them to the doctor   talk

"I'm hungry."_____

"Mom is worried."_____

"Dad is tired." _____

"The babies are sick." _____

"Grandma is cold." _____

Exercise 9.3: Make an appropriate plural ("Let's") command.

Example: The concert is on Thursday. _Let's_ _buy_
tickets._

    buy some warm clothes clean the house   eat
        go to sleep   study

We have a test tomorrow. _____

It's quarter after twelve. _____

Fall starts in two weeks. _____

Our flight leaves early. _____

Grandma is coming to visit tomorrow._____

Exercise 9.4: Write the correct preposition.

_____ March 21st

_____-_ 1611

_____ Saturday

_____ three days

_____ noon

🔒Lesson 10

Did you study English in school? - ¿Estudiaste inglés en la escuela?

🗨Reading 1

English Teacher: So, how do you know English? Did you study English in school?

College student: Well, sort of. I mean, I didn't learn a lot.

English Teacher: Really? So did you study on your own or what?

College student: Well, I watched English movies with subtitles.

English Teacher: You put the subtitles in Spanish?

College student: No, in English.

English Teacher: Oh, that's smart.

College student: That's all you did to learn English?

English Teacher: No, I listened to music too.

College student: Yeah? Did you have any friends you talked to in English?

English Teacher: Yeah. My neighbors were Canadian.

College student: Wow! That's great!

🗨Reading 2

Teacher: So, class, what did you do last summer?

Student 1: I went to Florida.

Teacher: Nice.

Student 2: I washed cars.

Teacher: Okay.

Student 3: I helped my dad with his business.

Teacher: Really? What does your dad do?

Student 3: He fixes cars.

Teacher: Great? Anyone else? Jason?

Jason: Nothing.

Teacher: You didn't do anything?

Jason: No.

Teacher: Where were you last summer?

Jason: Um, England.

Teacher: You went to England, but you say you didn't do anything?

Jason: Well, it was boring.

Teacher: Boring? What did you do?

Jason: We just saw a bunch of old buildings.

Teacher: Sounds fun to me!

Reading 3

Sam: What were you doing last night?

Judy: Well, you know, I had a lot of paperwork.

Sam: I called you three times.

Judy: Really? I guess I was listening to music.

Sam: I came by the house around 9 p.m.

Judy: Oh, at 9 p.m.? I was taking a bath.

Sam: I saw a light in the kitchen.

Judy: Oh, maybe I was cooking.

Sam: At 9 p.m.?

Judy: Well, you know, I didn't want to take a sandwich to work.

Sam: Okay. Well, maybe we can talk tonight.

Judy: Yeah, maybe.

New words – Nuevas palabras

Results - resultados
Pants - pantalones
Basic English – inglés básico
Comedy - comedia
Detective - detective
Disaster – desastre
Horror – horror - terror
Key - llave
Plan - plan
Science fiction – ciencia ficción
*Story – historia
War - guerra
Weekend – fin de semana
Western – del oeste (películas de vaqueros)
Double - doble
Food - comida
Test - examen
Trouble - problema / dificultad
Building - edificio
Farm - granja
Hometown – pueblo natal
Market - mercado
Population – población
Post card – tarjeta postal
River – río
Town – pueblo, ciudad, villa
Vegetable – vegetal / verdura
Weather – temperatura

*Boyfriend - novio
*Girlfriend - novia
Eye - ojo
Glasses – lentes / gafas
Hair - cabello
Place - lugar
Thing - cosa
Fault - culpa
Help - ayuda
Rain - lluvia
Good-looking – buen parecido / lindo
Young - joven
Elementary school – escuela primaria
*Kind (s) of – clase(s) de
*Story – historia

What kind of wine do you like to drink? - ¿Qué tipo de vino te gusta beber?

Don't tell me stories – no me hagas historias.

Hay una gran diferencia entre "***history – historia***" y "***story – historia***". En español se usa la misma palabra pero en inglés cuando hablamos de "history – historia" nos referimos a la historia en general, de hechos ya acontecidos. Y cuando hablamos de "story" es de un cuento o relato.

The history of Canada is very interesting – la historia de Canadá es muy interesante.

Don't come with old stories – no vengas con cuentos viejos.

*Boyfriend – novio

En inglés esta palabra también puede significar un amigo. Prestar atención al contexto para no confundir.

*Girlfriend – novia

En inglés también esta palabra puede significar una amiga. Prestar atención al contexto para no confundir.

Phrases and expressions – Frases y expresiones

Follow me – sígueme / sígame.

Terrific – estupendo.

Right – correcto / bien.

*In trouble – en problemas.

*To have trouble with – tener problemas con.

What's the matter (with)? - ¿Cuál es el problema (con)? / ¿Qué pasa (con)?

I'd love to – me encantaría.

I guess – supongo.

To have a good time – pasar un buen tiempo.

*In trouble – en problemas

*To have trouble with – tener problemas con

En inglés se tienen "problems – problemas", pero se está en "trouble – problemas".

I *have problems* with my boss – tengo problemas con mi jefe.

I *have a problem* – tengo un problema.

You are *in* deep *trouble* – estás es serios problemas.

*What's the matter? - ¿Cuál es el problema? / ¿Qué pasa?

What's the matter with you? - ¿Qué pasa contigo? / ¿Cuál es el problema contigo?

Well, sort of. – más o menos.

On your own or what? ¿Solo o qué?

To come by - pasar a recoger (buscar) a alguien.

To pay back - devolver dinero (cuando se debe y hay que pagar)

Movies with subtitles – películas con subtítulos.

A bunch of old buildings – un montón de edificios viejos.

Sounds fun to me! – me parece divertido / suena divertido.

Paperwork – papeleo.

I called you three times – te llamé tres veces.

I saw a light – vi una luz.

Maybe I was cooking – talvez estaba cocinando.

Hemos recorrido un gran camino; nuestra jornada ha sido muy fácil hasta ahora. Hemos visto que el inglés no está tan difícil ni complicado como siempre nos decían. Ya tenemos conocimiento para hablar de cualquier tema. ¿Qué les parece si hablamos del pasado? Excelente, vamos a tratar con el pasado ahora.

Grammar – Gramática

Ya estamos listos para iniciar está lección porque ya dominamos las lecciones anteriores y estamos hablando inglés casi fluido. Nos faltan muchas cosas por aprender, pero lo importante es que estamos ya comunicándonos en inglés. Continuemos nuestro viaje al mundo de habla inglesa.

Compound nouns – Nombres compuestos

En inglés a menudo se usan dos nombres o sustantivos para formar un solo.
Bus driver – chofer de autobús
Taxi driver – taxista
Plane ticket – ticket de avión
Chicken sandwich – sándwich de pollo
Chocolate ice cream – helado de chocolate
Orange juice – jugo de naranja
Lemon juice – jugo de limón
Action movie – película de acción

Algunas veces los dos nombres se escriben como una sola palabra como ya hemos visto.
Mailman - cartero
Businessman – hombre de negocios
Businesswoman – mujer de negocios
Motorbike – motocicleta

Adjectives – Adjetivos

Muchos de estos adjetivos ya lo hemos visto en los ejemplos y oraciones anteriores. Prestemos mucha atención.

All right – está bien / de acuerdo

Angry – enojado	Bald - calvo
Cold – frío	Cool – frío / fresco
Delicious – delicioso	Fat - gordo
Fine – bien	Fresh - fresco
Happy – feliz / contento	
Hot – caliente	Hungry - hambriento
Large – grande	Last – último
Lovely – encantador	Married - casado

Poor - pobre
Pretty – lindo / hermoso *(no se usa con hombres)*
Rich – rico   Sad - triste
Sick – enfermo
Sleepy – soñoliento / con sueño
Single - soltero   Sorry – lo siento
Strong - fuerte   Tall - alto
Terrible – terrible
Thirsty – sediento / con sed
Tired – cansado   Warm – caliente / tibio
Weak – débil   Worried - eocupado
Young – joven   Wonderful - maravilloso

New verbs – Nuevos verbos

To show – mostrar
Show me the results – muéstrame los resultados.

To project - proyectar
What are you trying to project? ¿Qué estas tratando de mostrar?
I am trying to project the presentation – estoy tratando de mostrar las presentación.

To put on – ponerse (refiriéndose a ropa)
Put on your pants – ponte los pantalones

To rain – llover (se usa con la tercera persona "it". Se llama verbo impersonal)
It is raining – está lloviendo.

To snow – nevar (se usa con la tercera persona "it". Se llama verbo impersonal)
It is going to snow – va a nevar

To think about – *pensar en*
I am thinking about you – estoy pensando en ti.

Simple Past – Pasado simple

Como el nombre lo dice, el pasado simple se refiere a eventos del pasado.

Tenemos la forma para los verbos regulares, los verbos irregulares y la forma del verbo "**to be**". Vamos a iniciar con los verbos regulares.
Regular verbs in simple past – Verbos regulares en el pasado simple.

La regla general es que formamos el pasado simple agregando "*d*" o "*ed*" a los verbos regulares. Veamos.

To love – *loved* - amar
To snow – *snowed* - nevar
To stay – *stayed* - permanecer
To travel – *traveled* - viajar
To walk – *walked* - caminar
To watch – *watched* - mirar
To argue – *argued* - discutir
To arrive – *arrived* - llegar
To declare – *declared* - declarar
To finish – *finished* - terminar
*To hate – *hated* - odiar
*To live – *lived* - vivir
To need – *needed* - necesitar
To play – *played* - jugar
To show – *showed* - mostrar

To wait for – *waited for* – esperar por
To help – *helped* - ayudar
To enjoy – *enjoyed* - disfrutar
To obey – *obeyed* - obedecer
To fix – *fixed* - arreglar
To mix – *mixed* - mezclar

Es bastante fácil con los verbos regulares, recuerden, solo tienen que agregar "d" o "ed". Veamos algunos pequeños cambios de vocal en el pasado simple regular. Los verbos que ya terminan en "e" solo tienen que agregarles la "d".

Si el verbo termina en "y" precedido de consonante, se cambia la "*y*" por "*i*" y se le agrega "ed".

To study – *studied* - estudiar
To cry – *cried* - llorar
To try – *tried* - tratar
To spy – *spied* - espiar
To apply – *applied* - solicitar
To bury – *buried* - enterrar
To fry – *fried* - freír
To marry – *married* – casarse

Si el verbo termina en una sola consonante que no sea "x", precedido por una sola vocal, duplicamos le consonante antes de agregar "ed".

To beg – *begged* - rogar
To hug – *hugged* - abrazar
To plan – *planned* - planear
To rob – *robbed* - robar

Si el verbo regular tiene dos o más silabas y si

termina en "l" o "r", y si la última silaba está acentuada, duplicamos la "l" o "r" y agregamos "ed".

To prefer – *preferred* - preferir
To fulfil – *fulfilled* - cumplir
To control – *controlled* - controlar

Si el verbo regular tiene dos o más silabas y si termina en "l" o "r", y si la última silaba NO está acentuada, NO duplicamos la "l" o "r"; SOLO agregamos "ed".

To cancel – *canceled* - cancelar
To travel – *traveled* - viajar
To suffer – *suffered* - sufrir
To honor – *honored* – honrar
To spell – *spelled* - deletrear

Recuerden, está regla solo funciona en USA; en el Inglés Británico verán las consonantes duplicadas. Esto es para que no se sorprendan si lo ven en alguna parte.

Irregular verbs in the simple past – Verbos irregulares en el presente simple.

Antes de comenzar a ver como se usa y dar ejemplos, vamos a ver algunos verbos irregulares. Como son irregulares, solo hay una forma de aprenderlos y es memorizándolos.

To begin – *began* – iniciar / comenzar
To break - *broke* - romper
To bring - *brought* - traer
To buy - *bought* - comprar
To build - *built* - construir

To choose - *chose*	- escoger
To come - *came*	- venir
To cost - *cost*	- costar
To cut - *cut*	- cortar
To do - *did*	- hacer
To draw - *drew*	- dibujar
To drink - *drank* -	beber
To drive - *drove*	- conducir
To eat - *ate*	- comer
To feel - *felt*	- sentir
To find - *found*	- encontrar
To get - *got*	- obtener
To give - *gave*	- dar
To go - *went*	- ir
To have - *had*	- tener
To hear - *heard*	- escuchar
To hold - *held*	- sostener
To keep - *kept*	– guardar o mantener
To know - *knew*	– saber o conocer
To leave - *left*	– dejar o marcharse
To lead - *led*	- dirigir
To let - *let*	- permitir
To lose - *lost*	- perder
To make - *made*	- hacer
To mean - *meant*	- significar
To meet - *met*	- conocer
To pay - *paid*	- pagar
To put - *put*	- poner
To read - **read*	- leer
To run - *ran*	- correr
To say - *said*	- decir
To see - *saw*	- ver

To sell - *sold*	- vender
To send - *sent*	- enviar
To set - *set*	- colocar
To sit - *sat*	- sentarse
To sing - *sang*	- cantar
To sleep - *slept*	- dormir
To speak - *spoke* -	hablar
To spend - *spent*	- gastar
To stand - *stood* –	pararse o ponerse de pie
To take - *took*	– tomar o coger
To teach - *taught* -	enseñar
To tell - *told*	- decir / contar
To think - *thought*	- pensar
To understand - *understood*	- entender
To wear - *wore*	– llevar puesto / usar
To win - *won*	– ganar
To write - *wrote*	- escribir

Prestar mucha atención a la pronunciación del verbo "read" en pasado.

Veamos ahora como usamos el pasado simple en inglés. Recordemos que para hacer preguntas en el presente simple usamos "do – does" dependiendo de los pronombres. Hemos aprendido el pasado del verbo "to do" el cual es "did". Como ya sabemos la procedencia de "did" podemos comenzar.

Did: se usa para hacer preguntas en el pasado simple con todos los pronombres personales y en respuestas cortas afirmativas.

Did you come home yesterday? ¿Viniste a casa

175

ayer?

Podemos ver que el *"did"* está al inicio de la oración seguido del pronombre; también vemos que el verbo que le sigue *"to come - venir"* está en presente. *Como ya "did" está en pasado, el verbo principal siempre estará en presente.* No lo olviden.

Yes, I did. – Sí.
Si recordamos como usar "do" no tendremos problemas, porque el uso es igual, lo único que ahora es en el pasado.
Did you go to church last Sunday? - ¿fuiste a la iglesia el pasado domingo?

Yes, I did. – Sí.
Yes, I *went* to church last Sunday. – Si, fui a la iglesia el pasado domingo.

Prestemos mucha atención a la respuesta larga afirmativa, puesto que esta es la parte engañosa, si no prestamos atención. Como no podemos usar "did" en la respuesta larga afirmativa, entonces, el verbo tiene que estar en pasado *"went"*.
What *did* you cook yesterday? - ¿Qué cocinaste ayer?
I *cooked* rice and beans – cociné arroz y habichuelas.
Did you study English at school? - ¿estudiaste inglés en la escuela?
Yes, I *did*.
Yes, I *studied* English at school.

No, I *did not.* – No.

No, I *did not* study English at school. – No, no estudié inglés en la escuela.

Como pueden ver, en las respuestas negativas usamos "*did not*"; por lo tanto el verbo tiene que permanecer en presente, porque ya tenemos a "*did not*" en pasado.

Did you work last week? - ¿trabajaste la semana pasada?

Yes, I *did.* – Si.

Yes, I *worked* last week. – Si, trabajé la semana pasada.

No, *I didn't.* – No.

No, *I didn't* work last week. – No, no trabajé la semana pasada.

¿Vieron la contracción de "did not"? Presten mucha atención a la pronunciación de "*didn't*".

What *did* you do last summer? - ¿qué hiciste el pasado verano?

I *went* to a summer school and *studied* basic English – fui a una escuela de verano y estudié inglés básico.

Did you read my book? - ¿leíste mi libro?

Yes, I *did.* – Si.

Yes, I **read* your book – sí, leí tu libro.

No, I *didn't.* – No.

No, I *didn't* read your book – No, no leí tu libro.

Prestar atención a la pronunciación de "*read*" en pasado, porque cambia completamente.

Did she talk to you about the problem? - ¿habló

ella contigo acerca del problema?

Yes, she *did.* – Si.

Yes, she *talked* to me about the problem – Si, ella habló conmigo acerca del problema.

No, she *didn't.* – No.

No, she *didn't* talk to me about the problem – No, ella no habló conmigo acerca del problema.

Did she spell my name wrong? - ¿deletreó ella mi nombre mal?

Yes, she *did.* – Si.

Yes, she *spelled* your name wrong – Si, ella deletreó tu nombre mal.

No, she *didn't.* – No.

No, she *didn't* spell your name wrong – No, ella no deletreó tu nombre mal.

Como les expliqué, se usan con todos los pronombres por igual; no hay ninguna diferencia.

Practiquen muy bien cada uno de los conceptos ya explicados y asegúrense de dominarlos bien antes de pasar a la siguiente lección.

Espero que hayan estudiado bien las lecciones pasadas y que estén listos para continuar.

Como vimos el verbo *"to spell – deletrear"*, estamos listos para aprendernos el abecedario en inglés

.

The alphabet – El alfabeto

A B C D E F G H I J K L M N O P Q R S T U V W X Y Z

Escuchen bien la pronunciación de cada letra para que puedan aprender a deletrar bien. Recuerden que ese es el único uso del alfabeto en inglés.

Verb to be in simple past – El verbo "to be" en pasado simple.

"To be" – Ser o estar

I was –   yo fui o estuve
You were –   tú fuiste o estuviste
He was –   él fue o estuvo
She was –   ella fue o estuvo
It was –   él o ella (animal o cosa) fue o estuvo
We were –   nosotros fuimos o estuvimos
You were –   ustedes fueron o estuvieron
They were –   ellos / ellas fueron o estuvieron.

Questions – preguntas

Was I?   - ¿fui o estuve yo?
Were you?   - ¿fuiste o estuviste tú?
Was he?   - ¿fue o estuvo él?
Was she?   - ¿fue o estuvo ella?
Was it?   - ¿fue o estuvo él / ella?
Were we?   - ¿fuimos o estuvimos nosotros?
Where you?   - ¿fueron o estuvieron ustedes?
Where they?   - ¿fueron o estuvieron ellos / ellas?

Es muy importante recordar que el "simple past" puede referirse no solo al "pasado simple" en español, pero también al "pasado imperfecto". Veamos.

Where were you yesterday? - ¿Dónde estuviste ayer? / *¿Dónde estabas ayer?*

I was at home – Estuve en casa. / *Estaba en casa.*

Were you at the church last week? - ¿estabas en la

iglesia la semana pasada?

Yes, I was. – Si.

Yes, I was at the church last week. – Si, estaba en la iglesia la semana pasada.

No, I was not. – No.

No, I was not at the church last week. – No, no estaba en la iglesia la semana pasada.

Was she here two days ago? - ¿estuvo ella aquí hace dos días?

Yes, she was. – Si.

Yes, she was here two days go – Si, ella estuvo aquí hace dos días.

No, she wasn't. No.

No, she wasn't here two days ago – No, ella no estuvo aquí dos días atrás.

Presten atención a la forma de contracción de la negación, especialmente en la pronunciación.

She was a beautiful singer when she was young. – Ella era una hermosa cantante cuando era joven.

I heard she was very pretty – escuché que ella era muy hermosa.

He was my teacher in elementary school – él era mi profesor en la escuela primaria.

En inglés se usa mucho "last – pasado / ultimo" y "ago – hace" cuando se habla del pasado.

Last night - anoche

Last week – la semana pasada

Last month – el mes pasado

Last year – el año pasado

Yesterday – ayer

The day before yesterday – anteayer
One hour ago – hace una hora
Two days ago – hace dos días
A week ago – hace una semana

The gerund in the past – El gerundio en el pasado.

Si recordamos como formar el gerundio "ing" en el presente, no tendremos ningún inconveniente, porque es lo mismo, lo único que es en pasado. Usamos el verbo "to be" en el pasado. Veamos.

Were you studying last night? - ¿estabas estudiando anoche?

Yes, I was. – Si.

Yes, I was studying last night – Si, yo estaba estudiando anoche.

No, I wasn't studying last night; I was resting – No, no estaba estudiando anoche; estaba descansando.

What were you doing? - ¿Qué estaba usted haciendo?

I was just waiting for you – solo estaba esperando por ti.

When my father arrived, I was getting ready to look for him – cuando mi padre llegó, me estaba preparando para buscarlo.

What were you doing when I called? - ¿Qué estabas haciendo cuando llamé?

I was sleeping when you called. You woke me up. – estaba durmiendo cuando llamaste. Me despertaste.

Como pueden ver, es bastante sencillo. El conocimiento adquirido les es suficiente para hablar de cualquier cosa en cualquier lugar. Recuerden que si no practican no podrán adquirir fluidez, concéntrense en usar lo que han aprendido.

Con esta lección llegamos al final de la primera parte de este increíble método de enseñanza y aprendizaje del idioma inglés. Estudien muy bien y dominen los conceptos ya dados a plenitud ya que la segunda parte viene con más inglés y conocimientos más profundos, pero fáciles de usar. Good luck – buena suerte.

Pero antes, les tengo una sorpresita preparada para después de los ejercicios. Espero la disfruten.

 Exercises – Ejercicios

Exercise 10.1: Read the sentence. Write the best **word.**

bald   fresh   rich   single thirsty

Ken wants some water. He is _____.

George doesn't have any hair. He is _____.

Mary isn't married. She is_____.
Lily has a lot of money. She is

_____.

I bought these vegetables yesterday. They're

_____.

Exercise 10.2: Write the letter of the grammatical answer.

_____ What was Mom doing when you gave her the flowers?

_____ What were you doing when I called?

_____ What was he doing when she sang to him?

_____ What were they doing when you paid them back?

_____ What was I doing when you left?

_____ What was the dog doing when you took him his water?

They were talking.

You were reading the newspaper.

She was washing the dishes.

It was burying a bone.

He was watching TV.

I was sleeping.

Exercise 10.3: Write sentences in the simple past.

Example: You / follow me / last night You followed me last night.

It / snow / last week_____

They / argue / last night _____

We / cry / yesterday_____

He / finish / last year_____
I / watch the movie / two weeks ago

_____

Exercise 10.4: Write sentences in the past progressive. (Some sentences have the simple past, too.)

Example: I / study publishing / in 2000.   _I was studying publishing in 2000._

She / walk / when it rained_____
They / rob the store / when the police officer drove

by _____

He / write her a letter / she arrived_____
We / do homework and drink coffee / when Mom

went to sleep_____
I / teach my class / when my daughter came to the

door_____

Conversational Level One – Nivel de Conversación Uno

At the stadium

Pam loves football. She has invited her niece to a football game so that her niece, Lisa, can find out how wonderfully and exciting football really is. "Nice move!" she shouts. Her team is in a good position to win the game.

"It's such a beautiful day," Lisa comments.

Pam does not hear her. "Go, go," she shouts. "Oh, he was so close to another touchdown."

"What happened?" Lisa asks.

"Aren't you paying attention, Lisa?"

Lisa is lost. She does not understand football and doesn't know why all the men tackle each other. "I want another hotdog."

"Shhh! Pay attention." Lisa watches as the men hunch over and pass the ball back: "Hut-hut," says the quarterback.

Lisa looks around. She's the only person not wearing orange. It's not her color. Besides, she's from out of state. Everyone is yelling "Get 'em" and "Tackle 'em."

Soon the orange team has the ball again. "Go, go . . . 3rd touchdown!!!"

Pam looks over at her niece. She is not enjoying

the touchdown. "Listen, this is how it works. They have four tries to make 10 yards."

Lisa still doesn't look excited. Her aunt continues, "It's the anticipation of what play the coach is going to call. People agree or disagree with the play. And you see the guys working so hard. It's very exciting."

Lisa listens to the shouts around her. She watches the game. She watches the players running down the field. She sees the receiver running, and "Touchdown!" Everyone is shouting, and Lisa's shouting too. She's hooked.

Phrases and Expressions

Nice move! – Buena jugado, Buena movida, bien *pensado (se usa cuando tenemos una idea o acción inesperada que traerá los resultados deseados).*

Lisa comments – Lisa comenta.

Tackle each other – se taquean mutuamente.

Hunch over and pass the ball back – se doblan (encorvan) y pasan el balon *(se refiere a la posicion que adoptan los futbolistas para cada jugada).*

Says the quarterback – dice el quarterback *(posición en footbol de atacar).*

She's from out of state – ella es de otro estado.

Get 'em and Tackle 'em – atrapalos y taquealos *(en el idioma hablado se usa mucho este tipo de forma, get them and tackle them seria lo formal).*

She is not enjoying the down – ella no esta disfrutando la entrada *(un down es un tiempo en cada partido, parecibo a "inning" en béisbol).*

They have four tries to make 10 yards – tiene cuatro intentos para correr 10 yardas.

The anticipation of - la anticipacion de.

What play the coach – que jugada el entrenador…

People agree or disagree with the play – las personas aceptan o no la jugada *(están en acuerdo o en desacuerdo)*.

Running down the field – corriendo en el campo.

She sees the receiver running – ella ve al receptor corriendo

And "Touchdown!" - y "Gol"

She's hooked – ella está emocionada *(esta expresión quiere decir que ella ya está en el juego, ya estaáatrapada y emocionada con el juego)*.

⌨ College enrolling

⌨ *Dana:* So what major did you choose?

Mattie: Well, I don't know for sure what I want to do, so I put undecided.

Dana: So did I. Then at the end of my first year, I chose my major.

Mattie: How did you decide on a major?

Dana: Well, you know, in the first year or two, you take the general courses—English, history, computer applications, math, speech, and so on. So you find out which courses you enjoy the most. And you talk to people in different majors and ask what they plan to do after graduation. Then you choose the area you like.

Mattie: So, what do you plan to do after graduation?

Dana: Actually, for my internship, I'm doing some design—logos and such. And I started doing it as a freelancer online. I'm getting really good at it.

Mattie: That's great!

Dana: Do you like design?

Mattie: I can't even draw a fish.

Dana: Oh. Well, do you like math, science, humanities?

Mattie: Uh, no.

Dana: What do you like?

Mattie: I like sewing, crafts.

Dana: How about interior design?

Mattie: Ah, that sounds nice.

Dana: But it's a science major. Do you like science?

Mattie: It's okay.

Dana: In that major, they take a lot of science courses. I'm going to have lunch with an interior design friend. Do you want to come along? You can ask her questions and decide if you want to study it.

Mattie: That sounds great. Thanks so much! I don't like the sound of the label "undecided."

Phrases and Expressions

College enrolling - inscribiendose en la Universidad.

So what major did you choose? – que Carrera escogiste *(major en este caso se refiere a estudios universitarios dos o 4 años).*

I don't know for sure - no lo se aun (no estoy segura aun).

I put undecided – puse "indecisa"

You enjoy the most – que disfrutes más.

Then you choose the area you like – entonces seleccionas el area que te gusta.

For my internship – para mi pasantía.

As a freelancer online – como trabajador independiente en linea.

I'm getting really good at it – me estoy volviendo Buena en eso.

Do you like design? – ¿te gusta el diseño?

I can't even draw a fish – no puedo ni dibujar un pescado.

I like sewing, crafts – me gusta la costura, manualidades.

How about interior design? – ¿qué tal desiños de interiores?

Do you want to come along? – ¿Quieres acompañarme? *(come along es acompañar al aguien).*

Graduation's day

Mom:　It's a beautiful day for a graduation.

Dad:　Yeah, I love gray, cloudy depressing days.

Mom:　Well, you don't have to worry about sunburn.

Dad:　Yeah. There isn't any more money for medical bills.

Mom:　Stop complaining and look for Greg. . . . Tell me when you see him.

Dad:　I'm not telling you anything. I can just see you waving and screaming and making a fuss.

Mom:　Oh, what's the fun if you don't get excited?

Dad: You have to promise you won't make a scene.

Mom: Ok.

Dad: There he is.

Mom: Already? Where?

Dad: Right in front of you.

Mom: There he is. He's talking to the president! What do you think they're talking about.

Dad: Probably his tie is crooked.

Mom: You can be so difficult.

Dad: Haha. He dropped his diploma. That's my boy.

Mom: When does this service end?

Dad: Another hour. You know, they all have to walk across the stage, not just Greg.

Mom: Oh, okay. Wake me when it's over.

Dad: Well, they're almost done. . . . . Ah, here comes Greg.

Mom: Greg, the president talked to you. I saw him. What did he say?

Greg: Keep moving.

Mom: Oh, okay. Well, stand over there with your dad. I want a nice picture of the two of you.

Greg: Like this? (He sticks out his tongue.)

Mom: No. I want a natural pose.

Greg: *[Makes bunny ears with his fingers behind his dad's head.]*

Mom: Put your hand around his waist.

Dad: If you want it natural, he can put his hand in my pocket!

Phrases and Expressions

Cloudy depressing days – dias nublados y depresivos.

To worry about sunburn – preocuparse por quemaduras del sol.

For medical bills – para facturas medicas.

Stop complaining – deja de quejarte / para de quejarte.

I can just see you waving – solo puede verte moviendo los brazos *(wave – es mover los brazon o haciendo señales con los brazos)*.

And making a fuss – y haciendo un escandalo (una bulla).

You won't make a scene – no haras una escena.

Probably his tie is crooked – probablemente su corbata está doblada.

You can be so difficult – puedes ser tan difícil.

That is my boy – ese es mi chico.

To walk across the stage – caminar por el escenario.

Wake me when it's over – despiertame cuando se acabe.

Keep moving – muevanse *(no se detengan, muevanse)*.

He sticks out his tongue – saca la lengua.

I want a natural pose – quiero una pose natural.

Makes bunny ears with his fingers behind his dad's head – pone orejas de conejo con sus dedos en la cabeza de su papa.

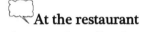

At the restaurant

A couple (husband and wife) walk into a restaurant. "How many are there in your party?"

"Just us two," they answer.

The waitress shows them to their table and gives them their menus. "Good evening. Here are your menus. Can I bring you something to drink?"

"Not right now," replies the husband. "We need to look at the menu first." The waitress tells them to let her know when they are ready.

They both look at their menus for a couple minutes. Then the wife asks her husband, "Do you see anything you like?"

"Well, I really want shrimp cocktail, but I can't find it on the menu. How about you?"

"Oh," she replies, "I thought I would get some chicken fried chicken, although it's a little expensive."

He agrees: "It's really expensive."

"Are you ready to order?" asks the waitress.

"Well, . . . " the wife begins, but her husband interrupts.

"Do you have shrimp cocktail?"

"No, I'm sorry," replies the waitress. "We do not. We have fried fish." But the husband does not want fish. He wants shrimp.

The wife asks, "Is the chicken fried chicken good?"

"Everyone says it's delicious."

"Mmm, then I think—"

"Do you have grilled shrimp?" asks the husband.

"No, we do not."

"I think I—" begins the wife.

"Fried shrimp?"

"No."

"I—"

"Hot and spicy shrimp?"

"Sir," replies the waitress, "we do not have shrimp. How about I give you a few more minutes to decide?"

"That would be nice," answers the wife. She then says to her husband, "Honey, if you like, we can go somewhere else."

"Let's do that," he answers. So they go to their favorite all-you-can-eat restaurant.

"That comes to $25 for two adults with refills," says the cashier.

"Great," says the husband, "where's the shrimp cocktail?"

"Oh, I'm sorry," replies the cashier, "We don't have shrimp cocktail."

Phrases and Expressions

A couple – un par / una pareja

How many are there in your party?" – ¿cuántos hay en el grupo? *(party significa partido, pero en términos legales y en restaurantes se usa como grupo)*

For a couple minutes – por un par de minutos.

Chicken fried chicken - Milanesa de pollo empanizada y frita.

How about I give you – ¿qué tal si les doy?

A few more minutes – un par de minutos más.

All-you-can-eat restaurant – un restaurant en donde comes todo lo que puedas comer

With refills – con repetición *(puedes repetir las veces que quieras)*

⌖ **At the drugstore:**
A customer at a popular drugstore looked around for a long time. An employee asked him, "Can I help you?"

He answered, "I'm looking for men's shampoo."

"This bottle is for men," she said.

"No, it's purple."

"But it says here, see? Men's Shampoo."

"Can't you see? It's purple. It's not for men."

"Ok, sorry, sir. Anything else I can do for you?"

But the customer wanted to keep looking, so the employee went back to the other aisle and continued stocking shelves.

Soon, the man went to the pharmacy counter. "Do you have montelukast?"

"Yes, do you have your prescription?" the pharmacist asked.

"No, but I always get it here," the man answered.

"I'll check your record." The pharmacist told him, "Actually, we have your prescription on record, and it is still valid."

"So are you going to give me my pills?"

"Just a minute, Sir. I'll get them for you."

A few minutes later, the man brought a few items to the cash register, and the cashier asked him, "How are you, Sir?"

"You tell me!" he answered.

The employee looked at the items the man was

buying: a box of tissues, cough drops, ibuprofen, and ginger tea for a sick stomach. "Oh, sorry you're not feeling well, Sir. Did you find everything you were looking for?" The man told her he didn't need anything else.

Before giving him his total, the cashier said, "Did you notice our BOGO sale on the tissues?" When the man just stared at her, she explained, "They're buy one get one free."

The man looked irritated. "You people are always trying to get me to spend more money."

The cashier realized the man did not understand, so she just said, "Okay, Sir, that's $7.99."

The man started looking in his wallet. "Mmm? Do you accept credit?" he asked and then handed the cashier an expired credit card. The clerk told him that the card was expired and asked him if he had cash.

"Well, yeah, but I don't have an eight-dollar bill," he said, laughing. He handed her a ten-dollar bill and walked off with his things.

"Don't you want your change, Sir?" asked the cashier. "Nope!" he yelled back.

Phrases and Expressions
Looked around for a long time - Pasarlo viendo qué hay *(look around – mirar alrededor, o cuando se camina por los pasillos de la tienda mirando productos o artículo)*

Other aisle – otro pasillo

Continued stocking shelves – continuó poniendo los productos en los estantes.

montelukast?" – medicina para las alergias

A few items – algunos artículos
You tell me - Tú, dime
Cough drops – gotas para la toz
Ginger tea – te de jengibre
BOGO sale - dos por uno
Stared at her – se quedó mirándola fijamente *(stare es mirar fijamente)*

Handed the cashier an expired credit card –le entrego una tarjeta vencida a la cajera *(to hand es entregar o pasar con la mano algo a alguien)*

Walked off with his things – se marchó con sus cosas *(walk off es marcharse o irse caminando)*

Nope!" he yelled back. – no, él le respondió

 At the ER

A young man and his mother walked into a hospital. The boy didn't really notice what was happening, but his mother was already upset because she had to drive to two different hospitals. "I didn't know the hospitals took turns taking emergency cases on weekends," she complained.

"Mmm," said the boy.

The mother walked up to the receptionist and explained her son's problem, and the receptionist told her to take a seat. So she and her son sat down in the waiting room. They sat, and sat, and sat. The mother started talking to a friendly woman who spoke Spanish. They talked for three hours. But when the nurse called the boy's name, the mother was in the restroom, and the Hispanic woman walked with the boy to explain his problem. "He's intoxicated," she said.

The nurse said he would not help the boy. At that point, the mother returned. "My son needs help."

"I'm sorry, but we don't help in these cases," the nurse said.

"Why not?" the mother asked.

"Just take him home to sleep it off," said the nurse.

"Sleep it off? He's very sick!"

"What are the symptoms?" asked the nurse.

"Well, he ate some fish that had been sitting out for a couple hours in the hot weather, and he started throwing up. Now he's a little better, but he's in a lot of pain."

The nurse said he probably had food poisoning, but he also asked, "How much did he drink?"

"Drink?" the mother asked. "He had some water."

"I'm sorry. You're friend told me he was intoxicated. But don't worry. I understand the problem. In Spanish, food poisoning is called *intoxicación*. We can help you. Come right back with me.

Phrases and Expression

At the ER – En la sala de emergencia *(ER es la abreviación de Emergency Room)*

To drive to two different hospitals – conducir a dos hospitales diferentes

Took turns - se turnaron *(take turn es turnarse)*

In the waiting room – en la sala de espera

A friendly woman – una mujer amistosa

The nurse called the boy's name – le enfermera

llamó el nombre del chico

In the restroom – en el lavabo / en el baño

He's intoxicated – él está borracho *(intoxicated en inglés es cuando alguien esta borracho)*

To sleep it off - que se le pase durmiendo

That had been sitting out – que se habían quedado fuera del refrigerador

Come right back with me. - indicando que le acompañe por la puerta hasta el área más restringido de las camas de emergencias

* Level One Tests – Examenes del Nivel Uno

Estos son los exámenes para pasar el nivel uno. Asegúrense de tomar su tiempo y completarlos correctamente. Una vez los hayan completado y estén completamente seguros que han terminado. Pueden presentarlos a un amigo de habla inglesa para que los revise y les diga si lo hicieron bien, o pueden enviarme un email con sus exámenes. Sin en algún punto, aun están dudosos, deberán repasarlo y asegurarse de dominarlo muy bien. El primer nivel es la base para todo el aprendizaje, sin dominarlo bien, no podremos aprender bien. Es imperativo dominar a la perfeccion cada uno de los conceptos presentados en este nivel. *Good luck once again!*

Test 1.1: Choose the correct plural form.

bike	bikes	bikies
books	bookes	bookies
boxs	boxes	boxies
boys	boyes	boies
potato	potatoes	potaties
spys	spyes	spies
wifes	wives	wivies

Test 1.2: Choose the correct answer. Write the letter.

_____ Where to?

_____ Who with?

_____ What for?

My mom

The park

To buy a car

After work

Test 1.3: Replace the noun with the correct personal pronoun: *I, you, he, she, it, we,* or *they.*

Example. People like fruit. _They_ like meat, too.

Mom cooks vegetables. _____ eats fruit, too.

The car doesn't have a radio. _____ doesn't have **comfortable seats** either.

Dad drives to work. _____ walks, too.

My husband and I don't go to work. _____ don't have money either.

Matt and Jerry don't like to read. _____ don't like to read either.

Test 1.4: Write the correct form of the verb.

Example: She / go / to work _She goes to work._

students / need / fruit _____

my   dog   /   swim   /   in   the   pool

_____

I   /   want   /   something   to   drink

_____

You   /   do   /   your   homework   /   fast

_____

We / prefer / to buy a car

_____

Test 2.1 Write the correct possessive pronoun: my, your, his, her, its, our, their.

Example: They need _their_ car.

Julie cooks for _____ husband.

Dad drives _____ car to work.

The fish swims in _____ **aquarium**.

We like _____ little park.

Test 2.2: Write the sentence in *going to* future.

Example: I _am going to go to bed_ (go to bed). I'm tired.

Dad _____ (fix) the roof. He is putting on his work clothes.

It _____ (rain). The **sky** is black.

Jenny_____ (cook). She is taking the meat out of the refrigerator.

Grandpa _____ (come) to our house! He has his ticket.

Moses and Josh _____ (learn) the lesson. They are studying.

You _____ (like) this movie. It's great!

Test 2.3: Write the verb in present progressive.

He _____ (work). He has some cars to sell.

She _____ (not wear) nice clothes. She's in bed.

I _____ (not study). I'm sick.

We _____ (not board) the plane. Our plane is late.

They aren't enjoying their day. They _____ (argue).

Test 2.4: What's in the fridge? Use *there is* or *there are.*

_____ some cake.

_____ five apples.

_____ some rice.

_____ a package of hot dogs.

_____ some cookies.

Test 2.5: Write the possessive form.

Example: The dog has a bone. _the dog's bone_

Mom has a car. _____

Dad has a job. _____

John and Susie have some letters. _____

Margaret has a party. _____
Mae, Rae, and Jay have tickets.

_____ _____

Test 3.1: Write *this, that, these,* or *those*.

(1) _____ flowers over here are really

expensive, but (2) _____ flowers over there are pretty, too.

(3) _____ fish that I'm eating is really good,

but (4) _____ turkey over there looks good, too.

(5) _____ customer I'm helping is really

angry, but (6) _____ customer waiting over there looks nice.

(7) _____ couch over there is too heavy,

but (8) _____ chair over here is too light.

Test 3.2: Underline the correct word.
We don't need **(many / much)** cake. My husband doesn't like cake.
They want **(a / some)** suitcases for their trip. They don't have any.

The dress is (**too** / **very**) pretty. I want to buy it.

There are (**many** /**much**) animals at the zoo.

I'd like (**a lot of** / **much**) chocolate ice cream. It's really hot outside!

Test 3.3: Underline the best sentence.

Drink some wine! / Would you like to drink some wine?

You were bad! **Stand in the corner. / Let's stand in the corner.**

Let's eat the cake now! / Eat the cake now!

Test 3.4: Write the verb in the correct form: simple past or past progressive.

I _____ (watched / was watching) a show

when the woman _____ (arrived / was arriving).

I _____ (waited / was waiting) for my friend

when the movie _____ (started / was starting).

I _____ (begged / was begging) for the job

when this terrific person _____ (applied / was applying) for it.

When he _____ (asked / was asking) to marry

me, I _____ (planned / was planning) to leave him.

Test 4.1: Under the correct verb form.

We (**go** / **are going** / **went**) to a party later tonight.

We always (**eat / are eating / ate / are going to eat**) chicken on Sundays.

I (**wash / am washing / washed / am going to wash**) the car now.

She (**buys / is buying / bought / is going to buy**) her car last year.

Test 4.2: Read the answer choices. Write the correct word.

I would like _____ help with this. (any/some)

He told us lots of _____ about his trip. (history/stories)

_____ a butterfly on the flower! (There is/There are)

I like this car over _____. (here/there)

I like fish _____ it is healthy. (because/why)

_____ people don't eat meat. (many/much)

_____ three types of people: those who can **count** and those who can't. (There is/There are)

Test 4.3: Underline the correct word.

This is (**me / my / mine**) car.

Those keys are (**they / their / theirs**).

(**He / His**) is my husband.

Are these (**you / your / yours**) cookies?

Test 4.4: Underline the correct preposition.

We're neighbors! Our house is (**between / for / next to**) yours.

"Where are my keys?" / "They're (**at /over/ under**) you, on the couch."

She is coming (**about / at / on**) Wednesday.

The bike is (**about / behind / on**) the school.

Verb list – Lista de verbos

To stick – pegarse - adherirse

To tell - decir

Hunch over – encorvarse – doblarse

To agree – estar de acuerdo - acordar

To answer – contestar - responder

To apply – solicitar

To argue – discutir

To arrive – llegar

To ask – pedir o preguntar

To be – Ser o Estar.

To beg – rogar

To begin - iniciar - comenzar

To board – abordar

To break - romper

To bring - traer

To build - construir

To bury – enterrar

To buy - comprar

To cancel – cancelar

To cash – cambiar dinero

To check in – registrarse

To choose - escoger

To circle - encerrar

To come – venir

To come along – acompañar

To come in - entrar
To comment - comentar
To complain - quejarse
To complete - completa
To conjugate - conjugar
To continue - continuar
To control – controlar
To cook – cocinar
To cost - costar - valer
To cough - toser
To cry – llorar
To cut - cortar
To dance – bailar
To declare – declarar
To defer – diferir
To die – morir
To disagree – estar en desacuerdo
To do - hacer
To draw - dibujar
To dream - soñar
To drink – beber
To drive – conducir
To eat – comer
To enjoy – disfrutar
To feel - sentir
To fill in – llenar
To find - encontrar
To finish– terminar
To fish – pescar
To fix – reparar - arreglar
To fry – freír
To fulfil – cumplir

To get – obtener - conseguir
To get up – levantarse
To give - dar
To go – Ir
To go out – salir
To hand - entregar
To hate – odiar
To have – tener
To have lunch - almorzar
To hear - escuchar - oir
To help – ayudar
To hold - sostener - sujetar
To honor – honrar
To hook – enganchar
To hug – abrazar
To keep - mantener - guardar
To kiss – besar
To knock - tocar
To know – saber - conocer
To lead - dirigir
To learn - aprender
To leave - dejar - irse
To leave – - partir
To let - permitir
To lie – - mentir
To like - gustar
To listen to – escuchar
To live – vivir
To look around – mirar alrededor
To lose - perder
To love – amar
To mail – enviar

To make – hacer
To marry – casarse
To match - combinar
To mean - significar - querer decir
To meet - conocer - econtrarse - reunirse
To mix – mezclar
To need – necesitar
To obey – obedecer
To offer – ofrecer
To open – abrir
To pay - pagar
To plan – planear
To play – jugar
To prefer – preferir
To project - proyectar
To put - poner
To put down - bajar
To put on – ponerse
To rain – llover
To read – leer
To refer – referir
To refill - rellenar
To report - reportar
To rest – descansar
To rewrite - reescribir
To rob – robar
To run – correr
To say - decir
To see – ver
To sell – vender
To send - enviar
To set – establecer, montar, fijar

To show – mostrar
To sing – cantar
To sit - sentarse
To sleep – dormir
To smoke – fumar
To snow – nevar
To speak – hablar
To spell – deletrear
To spend - gastar
To spy – espiar
To stand – pararse - levantarse
To start – comenzar
To stay – quedarse - permanecer
To stock - almacenar
To stop – detener - parar
To study – estudiar
To suffer – sufrir
To swim – nadar
To tackle - taquear
To take – tomar - coger - llevar
To talk – hablar
To teach
To tell - decir - contar
To think – pensar
To tie – amarrar
To travel – viajar
To try – tratar
To understand - entender
To wait - esperar
To wait for – esperar por
To walk – caminar
To walk off - irse

To want – querer
To wash - lavar
To watch - ver - mirar - observar
To wave - agitar
To wear – usar - llevar puesto
To whisper – susurrar
To win - ganar
To work – trabajar
To worry - preocuparse
To write – escribir
To write – escribir
To yell – gritar – vociferar

Grammar Summary

Lesson 1

The plural
Personal pronouns
Conjugation of verbs in present tense
List of verbs in present tense
Three model verbs

Lesson 2

The auxiliary verb "To do"
Conjunctions
Adverbs
Definite article
Indefinite article
Cardinal numbers

Lesson 3

Does
Grammar summary
List of new verbs

Lesson 5

To be
Lesson 6
There is / There are
Prepositions "In / At / On"
Possessive adjectives
The preposition "Of
Possessive Case
Can
Prepositions
Lesson 7
Present progressive "Going to"
Countries
Nationalities
Languages
The gerund
New verbs
Lesson 8
Prepositions
Demonstrative pronouns
Adjectives
Possessive pronouns
Telling the time
Adverbs
Frequency Adverbs
Lesson 9
Polite form "Would like"
Commands
Prepositions of time
Days of the week
Months of the year
Seasons of the Year
Ordinal numbers

The pronoun "It"
Negative questions
Object pronouns
Lesson 10
Compound nouns
Adjectives
New verbs
Simple Past
Regular verbs in simple past
Irregular verbs in the simple past
Did
Alphabet
Verb to be in simple past
The gerund in the past

Answers to exercises – Respuestas de los ejercicios

Como terminaron sus exámenes y se aseguraron de dominar cada concepto, pueden verificar las respuestas al final del libro. Me he tomado la libertad de ofrecerles las respuestas de todos los ejercicios de cada lección asi también como los del examen de nivel. Pero no hagan trampa, solo ustedes pierden si hacen trampa. *See you on the second volume.*

Lesson 1

Answers to Exercise 1.1:

books	bikes	churches	kisses
beers	cakes	dishes buses	
boys	boxes	potatoes	wives
cities	spies	leaves knives	

Answers to Exercise 1.2:

The wives of two boys want some kisses.

The boys eat the cakes and the cheeses.

They put down the knives.

No hugs for the wives.

Now the boys need to wash up the dishes.

Answers to Exercise 1.3:

They work hard.

They drive fast.

They work hard.

They study people.

They sing at night.

They / I sleep like a baby.
They eat fast.
They swim fast.
They swim slowly.
They eat fish.
Answers to Exercise 1.4:
Wives talk.
They write emails.
Teachers need sleep.
Babies sleep in church.
They need kisses.
You and I need English.
We like English books.
I cook meat with potatoes and tomatoes.
We eat fast.
You wash the dishes.
Answers to Exercise 1.5:
I like to swim in the pool.
I want to fish in the park.
I need to read an English book.
Boys like to eat cake.
We need to speak English.
They want to cook a fish.
Answers to Exercise 1.6 will vary. They should be true for each student.

Lesson 2
Answers to Exercise 2.1:
some
too
either
too

either
some
either
either
some
too
Answers to Exercise 2.2:
but
and
and
and
but
but
and
but
but
and

Answers to Exercise 2.3:
I want to **buy** a dog.   **Any** dog is okay.
I want to **buy** the dog.   It's a specific dog.

I like to read a book at night.   Any book is okay.
I like to read the book at night. I read a specific book.

I need to talk to a teacher.   Any teacher is okay.
I need to talk to the teacher.   I need a specific teacher.

I like to drink the wine at night.   I drink one

specific **type or bottle** of wine.

I like to drink some wine at night.   Any wine is okay.

I like music.   Any music is okay.
I like the music. It's a specific **piece** or **collection**.

I want to rest at the beach.   It's a specific beach.
I want to rest at a beach. Any beach is okay.

Lesson 3
Answers to Exercise 3.1:
How much?
How much?
How many?
How much?
How many?
How much?
How much?
How much?
How much?
How many? / How much?
Answers to Exercise 3.2:
Where
What
Who
Where
Who
Where
What
What
Who

Where

Answers to Exercise 3.3:

Kisses

Eat

Hate

Drives

Starts

Like

Like

Needs

Prefer

Do

Lesson 4

Answers to Exercise 11: Answers will vary.

Answers to Exercise 12:

That's a shame.

I'm glad you like it.

It's nice to meet you.

Don't worry.

Here you are.

Good idea.

Answers to Exercise 13:

She

I

you

They

we

Lesson 5

Answers to Exercise 5.1:

She is a secretary.

He is a mechanic.

She is a housewife.

He is a salesman.
He is a pastor.
She is a pharmacist.
He is a pilot.
She is an actress.
He is a taxi driver.
He is a police officer.
Answers to Exercise 5.2:
Yes, it is.
No, they aren't.
No, it isn't.
Yes, it is.
No, it isn't.
No, it isn't.
No, they aren't.
No, they aren't.
Yes, it is.
Yes, they are.
Lesson 6
Exercise 6.6: Write "There is" or "There are."

_____ a bike in the house.

_____ a dog on the bike.

_____ some dishes on the dog.

_____ some sandwiches on the dishes.

_____ some meat in the sandwiches.
Answers to Exercise 6.1:
next to

over
on
behind
on
at
between
Answers to Exercise 6.2:
go
you cook
you come
you arrive
buy
Answers to Exercise 6.3:
cook
play
run
sing
speak
Answers to Exercise 6.4:
my
her
its
his
your
their
Answers to Exercise 6.5 will vary.
Answers to Exercise 6.6:
There is
There is
There are
There are
There is

Lesson 7
Answers to Exercise 7.1:
I'm going to make shrimp cocktail.
I'm going to practice speaking English.
I'm going to play with my **daughter.**
I'm going to work a lot.
I'm going to travel to Greece.
Answers to Exercise 7.2:
am talking
is cooking
is making
is setting
is finishing
is eating
are enjoying
is playing
Answers to Exercise 7.3:
Mom is cooking.
My sister washes the dishes.
Dad fixes the roof every year.
My brother is taking a shower.
Mom goes to bed late.
Lesson 8
Answers to Exercise 8.1:
Which boat is theirs?
Which seat is his?
Which bicycle is hers?
Which salad is mine?
Which flowers are theirs?
Which flight is ours?
Which passport is mine?
Which suitcases are hers?

Which calculator is yours?
Which box is theirs?

Answers to Exercise 8.2:
This
That
This
That
This
Those
This
That
These
Those
Answers to Exercise 8.3 will vary.
Answers to Exercise 8.4 will vary.
Lesson 9
Answers to Exercise 9.1:
grandfather
uncle
cousin
sister-in-law
grandson
Answers to Exercise 9.2:
Would you like some pizza?
Would she like to talk?
Would he like to go to bed?
Would you like to take them to the doctor?
Would she like some soup?
Answers to Exercise 9.3:
Let's study.
Let's eat.

Let's buy some warm clothes.

Let's go to sleep.

Let's clean the house.

Answers to Exercise 9.4:

on

in

on

in

at

Lesson 10

Answers to Exercise 10.1:

thirsty

bald

single

rich

fresh

Answers to Exercise 10.2:

C

F

E

A

B

D

Answers to Exercise 10.3:

It snowed last week.

They argued last night.

We cried yesterday.

He finished last year.

I watched the movie two weeks ago.

Answers to Exercise 10.4:

She was walking when it rained.

They were robbing the store when the police officer drove by.

He was writing her a letter when she arrived.

We were doing homework and drinking coffee when Mom went to sleep.

I was teaching my class when my daughter came to the door.

Answers to Level One Tests – Respuesta de los Examenes del Nivel Uno

Answers to Test 1.1:

bikes

books

boxes

boys

potatoes

spies

wives

Answers to Test 1.2:

b

a

c

Answers to Test 1.3:

She

It

He

We

They

Answers to Test 1.4:

Students need fruit.

My dog swims in the pool.

I want something to drink.

You do your homework fast.

We prefer to buy a car.

Answers to Test 2.1:

her

his
its
our
Answers to Test 2.2:
is going to fix
is going to rain
is going to cook
is going to come
are going to learn
are going to like
Answers to Test 2.3:
is working
isn't wearing
am not studying
are not boarding
are arguing
Answers to Test 2.4:
There is
There are
There is
There is
There are

Answers to Test 2.5:
Mom's car
Dad's job
John and Susie's letters
Margaret's party
Mae, Rae, and Jay's tickets
Answers to Test 3.1:
These
those

This
that
This
that
That
this
Answers to Test 3.2:
much
some
very
many
a lot of
Answers to Test 3.3:
Would you like to drink some wine?
Stand in the corner.
Let's eat the cake now!
Answers to Test 3.4:
was watching; arrived
was waiting; started
was begging; applied
asked; was planning
Answers to Test 4.1:
are going
eat
am washing
bought
Answers to Test 4.2:
some
stories
There is
there
because

Many
There are

Answers to Test 4.3:
my
theirs
he
your

Answers to Test 4.4:
next to
under
on
behind

Nivel Uno Conclusión

Muchas gracias por seleccionar el *Curso Completo de Inglés – Nivel Uno* por Yeral E. Ogando para su aprendizaje. Por fin, han llegado al final del primer nivel, por lo tanto, ya pueden hablar inglés fluido y están listos para el nivel dos.

Les exhorto que continúen practicando y hablando inglés en todo momento, ya les he dicho que la Practica hace al Maestro. Visiten mi pagina de internet para más información.

God bless you and see you in volumen two.

Dr. Yeral E. Ogando
www.aprendeis.com

Nivel Uno BONO GRATIS

Estimado Estudiante,

Necesitas descargar el audio MP3 para usar este increible método para aprender inglés. Visita este link:

http://aprendeis.com/ingles-audio-nivel1/

Usuario "ennivel1"

Contraseña "enl2016"

Solo tienes que descargar el archivo comprimido, descomprimirlo y estas listo para iniciar tu experiencia al mundo del inglés.

Si quieres compartir tu experiencia, comentario o possible sugerencia, siempre podrás contactarme a info@aprendeis.com

Muchas gracias por estudiar el *Curso Completo de Inglés – Nivel Uno* y por escuchar mis instrucciones.

Caros afectos,

Dr. Yeral E. Ogando

Curso Completo de Inglés
Teach Yourself English

Habla Inglés desde la segundo lección.
Nivel Dos avanzado.
Aprenda Inglés sin profesor hoy.

Dr. Yeral E. Ogando

🔒Lesson 1

Looking after the house and the children – Cuidando la casa y nos niños

🗨Conversation 1

Doorbell: *[Ding dong]*

Karen: Hello?

Cindy: Hi. My name is Cindy.

Karen: It's nice to meet you.

Cindy: Nice to meet you, too. I'm looking for volunteers for the Neighborhood Watch program.

Karen: Yes?

Cindy: Well, we need someone to keep an eye on activity on this street between the hours of 9 a.m. and 12 p.m.

Karen: I'm sorry. I'm very busy during those hours.

Cindy: Oh, really? Since you don't work, I thought—

Karen: What?

Cindy: Well, you're just a housewife, right?

Karen: *Just* a housewife?

Cindy: Yes, I mean, you don't have a job, do you?

Karen: I don't have a job, but I work. I pick up, dust, sweep, and mop. I do the laundry, fix lunch, and I have to finish any extra projects—shopping, sewing, etc.—before my kids come home from school.

Cindy: Right, but I'm sure you can listen to what's happening in the street and check to see if everything's okay.

Karen: If I hear anything, I will check on it. But most of the time I listen to music to help me keep moving.

Cindy: Do you have to listen to music all the time?

Karen: Look, I think you'd better find someone else to help you, okay?

Conversation 2

Waiter: Good afternoon. Can I take your order?

Customer: Well, I'm waiting for a friend, but I don't have much time, so . . . do you have a seniors menu?

Waiter: Yes, one moment, please. . . . Here you are.

Customer: Thank you. . . . I'd like the stuffed mushrooms to start with.

Waiter: Would you like anything to drink?

Customer: Yes. Is the cider pretty good?

Waiter: Delicious. All of our customers rave about it.

Customer: Sounds great.

[15 minutes later]

Waiter: How was your appetizer?

Customer: Delicious, thank you.

Waiter: Would you like to order the main dish?

Customer: Well, I'd like to wait for my friend,

but—tell you what—why don't you bring my dessert first?

Waiter: That's fine. What would you like? Our apple tart is quite popular.

Customer: Well, today, I think I'd like the bread pudding.

Waiter: Great. Would you like some coffee with that?

Customer: Sure.

[15 minutes later]

Waiter: How was your dessert?

Customer: Wonderful. You know what, I don't think my friend is coming, so why don't you bring me the bill.

Waiter: Sure. If you would like, I can prepare a box of food to go. The special today is veal parmigiana, and the roast beef is also excellent.

Customer: No, I've had enough, thank you.

Conversation 3

Diana: You wouldn't believe what your children did today! Jason wrote on the walls. At least he used chalk, and it's not permanent. Then Carrie got into the shortening and got it all over the house. Look! You can see her footprints on the floor. They are always making more work for me. And you too! How many times do I have to tell you to leave your shoes by the door?

Shawn: But I'm on my way out, darling. I'm going to see your mother—to see how she's doing.

Diana: Can't you find the snake out back and

kill it first?

Shawn: I'll do it later.

Diana: Well, don't take too long. Give my regards to mother.

Shawn: Okay, dear.

Opal: Hi, Shawn. What's the matter? Is Diana in one of her moods?

Shawn: You can say that again. She's really stressed out with her new job. She sends her regards, by the way.

Opal: Thanks. New job?

Shawn: You know, she's selling bags and purses.

Opal: Bags and purses? Is that a lot of work?

Shawn: I guess it's hard to get started, and she already has her hands full with the kids.

Opal: Hmmm. Well, I've already got a visitor, but that's okay. Come on in to the living room. I'd like you to meet my friend, Darice. This is my son-in-law, Shawn.

Shawn: Hi, Darice, it's nice to meet you.

Darice: Nice to meet you, too, Shawn. You're a handsome young man.

Shawn: Thank you [chuckling].

Opal: If you're hungry, you can check the fridge.

Shawn: Okay, thanks! . . . Yum, is this shrimp cocktail?

Opal: Oh, that's no good. I made that on Sunday. There's some steak on the bottom shelf.

Darice: So what do you do, Shawn?

Shawn: I'm a writer.

Darice: Where do you work?

Shawn: At the Herald.

Darice: Really? Do you wear khakis to work?

Shawn: Yes. We dress pretty casual.

Darice: Oh, that's too bad. Young men never dress up anymore. You would look so nice in a suit.

Shawn: Thank you. I do wear a suit when I have an important interview.

Darice: Really? Who do you interview?

Shawn: Oh, sometimes the mayor or some of the wealthier women who are involved in a lot of social activities. That's when I really dress up.

Darice: Yes, we appreciate formality.

Shawn: Do you like to participate in society, Darice?

Darice: Well, yes, I host some fundraising events, and I volunteer at the local school.

Shawn: Really?

Darice: Yes, I read to the children.

Shawn: That's nice. Actually, I guess I'd better be going. I should help Diana get the kids to bed. They like at least three stories at bedtime.

Opal: Okay. She still watches soap operas, doesn't she? Tell her I said no more soap operas. If she wants to have time for extra jobs, she has to get the housework done before the kids get home from school.

Shawn: Why don't you call her? I think she'd take it better from you.

Opal: All right. First thing tomorrow. Make sure she gets to bed early, too. No TV.

New words – Nuevas palabras
Address – dirección
Phone number – número telefónico
Darling - querido (a)
Regards – saludos / recuerdos
Announcer – locutor / anunciador
Channel - canal
Cruise - crucero
The Caribbean – El caribe
Island – isla
Through – a través
*If – si
*All of - todo
Passport control – control de pasaporte / verificación de pasaporte
Port - puerto
Soap – jabón
Sun - sol
Swimming pool - piscina
Travel agency – agencia de viajes
Travel agent – agente de viajes
Bill – factura / cuenta
Birthday - cumpleaños
Bread - pan
Carrot - zanahoria
Cheesecake – bizcocho de queso
Chopstick – palitos chinos
Century - siglo
Main course – plato principal
First course – plato de entrada
Dessert - postre
Duck - pato

Fork - tenedor
French fries – papas fritas
Hand - mano
Lettuce - lechuga
Melon - melón
Menu - menú
Mushrooms – hongos / champiñones
Onion - cebolla
Peas - guisantes
Poison - veneno
Pudding - pudin
Sauce - salsa
Shrimp – camarones (es singular y plural a la vez, no se le agrega s)
Shrimp cocktail – coctel de camarones
Snail - caracol
Snake - serpiente
Spoon - cuchara
Steak – filete / bistec
Veal – ternera
Volunteers - voluntarios

Remarks:

If – si condicional:

If you want to eat, you have to work. – Si quieres comer, tienes que trabajar.

All of – todo: da la idea del todo sobre una cantidad.

All of you – todos ustedes (de un grupo).

All of the boys – todos los chicos (de un grupo)

Phrases and Expressions - Frases y expresiones
A Friend of mine – un amigo mío
Cheers – salud *(cuando se brinda)*
How do you do? - ¿Cómo te va?
I'd like you to meet my friend – me gustaría que conocieras a mi amiga.
We'd like you to meet our friends- nos gustaría que conocieras a nuestros amigos.
Nice to meet you – encantado de conocerte
Pleased to meet you – es un placer conocerte
Look – mira *(usada como comodín al hablar)*
To send your regards – enviar recuerdos / saludos
You know – tú sabes
All the time – todo el tiempo
Congratulations - felicidades
Can I take your order? - ¿Puedo tomar su orden?
House specialty – especialidad de la casa
Could you help me, please? - ¿Podrías ayudarme, por favor?
Happy birthday – feliz cumpleaños
How old are you? - ¿Qué edad tienes?
To have your hands full – tener las manos llenas
Nowadays – hoy en día
Neighborhood Watch program – programa de vigilancia del vecindario.
To keep an eye on activity - vigilar la actividades
To rave about it – alardear a cerca de algo

Grammar – Gramática

Como les había comentado, en este segundo nivel tendremos menos explicaciones y más acción, debido a que la base para todo son las lecciones pasadas. Vamos a incrementar nuestros conocimientos y a iniciar este segundo nivel.

Tag questions – Coletilla interrogativa

Se usa cuando el hablante espera que quien escucha confirme o niegue lo que está diciendo, o espera que el oyente este de acuerdo con lo dicho. Cuando tenemos una declaración negativa, el "*tag question*" estará en afirmativo y cuando tenemos una declaración afirmativa, el "*tag question*" estará en negativo. Recuerden, siempre será lo inverso al igual que en español.

Decimos ¿te comiste la comida? *¿No es verdad?* O ¿no te comiste la comida? *¿Verdad?* A esto nos referimos con "tag question", veamos en inglés ahora.

I am clever, *aren't* I? – soy inteligente. ¿No es así?
Yes, you are. – Si, lo eres.
Yes, you are clever – Si, tú eres inteligente.

You aren't crazy, *are you*? – tú no estás loco. ¿O sí?
No, I am not. – No, no lo estoy.
No, I am not crazy – No, no estoy loco.

He is smart, *isn't he*? – él es inteligente. ¿No es así?
Yes, he is – Si, lo es.
Yes, he is clever – Si, él es inteligente.

She isn't young, *is she*? – ella no es joven. ¿O sí?
No, she isn't – No, no lo es.
No, she isn't young – No, ella no es joven.

It is good, *isn't it?* – Es bueno. ¿No es así?
Yes, it is – Si lo es.
Yes, it is good. – Si, es bueno.

We are rich, **aren't we?** – Somos ricos. ¿No es verdad?
Yes, we are. – Si, lo somos.
Yes, we are rich – Si, somos ricos.

You are foolish, **aren't you?** – Eres tonto. ¿No es así?
Yes, I am – Si, lo soy.
Yes, I am foolish – Si, soy tonto.

They aren't fat, **are they?** – Ellas no son gordas. ¿O sí?
No, they aren't – No, no lo son.
No, they aren't fat – No, ellas no son gordas.

Presten atención al "tag question" I am, siempre será "aren't I? cuando la declaración sea afirmativa. Pero cuando la declaración sea negativa, se usa la conjugación normal.
I am not crazy. *Am I?* – No estoy loco, ¿O sí?
No, you're not – No, no lo eres.
No, you're not crazy – No, no estás loco.

Would (wouldn't) like – Gustaría (no)
En lecciones anteriores ya vimos el uso del "would like"; repasemos un poco el "would like".
Questions – preguntas
Whom would I like to see? – ¿A quién me gustaría

ver?

What would you like to see? - ¿Qué te gustaría ver?

Why would you like to see it? - ¿Por qué te gustaría verlo?

Where would you like to see it? - ¿Dónde te gustaría verlo?

When would you like to see it? - ¿Cuándo le gustaría verlo?

Which would he like to see? - ¿Cuál le gustaría ver?

How would she like to see it? - ¿Cómo le gustaría verlo?

How long would we like to see it? - ¿Por cuánto tiempo nos gustaría verlo?

How much would you like to pay? - ¿Cuánto les gustaría pagar?

How many would they like to buy? - ¿Cuántos les gustaría comprar?

Affirmative answers – Respuestas afirmativas

I'd like (I + would) … – me gustaría…

You'd like (you + would) … – te gustaría / le gustaría…

He'd like (he + would)… – le gustaría…

She'd like (she + would) … – le gustaría…

It'd like (it + would) … – le gustaría…

We'd like (we + would) … – nos gustaría…

You'd like (you + would) … – les gustaría…

They'd like (they + would) … – les gustaría…

Negative answers – Respuestas negativas

I wouldn't like… - no me gustaría…

You wouldn't like… - no te gustaría…

He wouldn't like... - no le gustaría...
She wouldn't like... - no le gustaría...
It wouldn't like... - no le gustaría...
We wouldn't like... - no nos gustaría...
You wouldn't like... - no les gustaría...
They wouldn't like... - no les gustaría...

Would you like to eat with me today? - ¿te gustaría almorzar conmigo hoy?
Yes, I would – Sí.
Yes, I'd like to eat with you today – Sí, me gustaría comer contigo hoy.
No, I wouldn't – No.
No, I wouldn't like to eat with you today – No, no me gustaría comer contigo hoy.

Recuerden,
Respondemos "wouldn't" para cosas que no queremos hacer. Pero cuando alguien nos ofrece algo, entonces, decimos "No, thank you".
Would you like some cake? – ¿te gustaría algo de bizcocho?
No, thank you – No, gracias.
No, I wouldn't, thanks. I'd prefer some juice – No, gracias. Preferiría algo de jugo.

Adjectives – Adjetivos
*Alone - solo
Same – igual / mismo
Duty-free – libre de impuestos
Excited - emocionado
Main – principal / primordial

Pleasant -agradable
Boiled - hervido
Broiled – asado a la parrilla
Different - diferente
Enough - suficiente
Fried - frito
Medium – medio cocido
Rare – casi crudo
Roasted - asado
Special - especial
Well-done – bien cocido (referente a comida)
*Alone: lo usamos solo cuando nos referimos a la persona "I am alone – estoy solo".
Pero decimos:
I just want to talk to you - solo quiero hablar contigo.
I only want to talk to you – solamente quiero hablar contigo.
Presten mucha atención y no se confundan.

Adverbs – Adverbios
Ago – hace (solo se usa en el pasado)
The day before yesterday – Antes de ayer
Hard – duro, difícil
Last – último / pasado
Never - nunca
Normally - normalmente
Rarely - raramente
Really – realmente
Immediately - inmediatamente
Also - también
Anywhere – en cualquier lugar

Certainly - ciertamente
Instead (of) – en vez de
Somewhere – en algún lugar
Always - siempre
Usually - usualmente
Often – a menudo
Sometimes – algunas veces

New regular verbs – Nuevos verbos regulares
To call – called - llamar
To look after – looked after - cuidar
To pick up – picked up - recoger
To cash – cashed – cambiar *(dinero)*
To cook – cooked - cocinar
To dance – danced - bailar
To fish – fished - pescar
To listen to – listened to – escuchar a
To report – reported - reportar
To smoke – smoked - fumar
To start – started – iniciar / comenzar
To talk – talked - hablar
To want – wanted - querer
To work – worked - trabajar
To land – landed - aterrizar
To use – used - usar
To board – boarded - abordar
To check in – checked in - registrarse
To kiss – kissed - besar
To like – liked - gustar
To mail – mailed – enviar por correo
To open – opened - abrir
To rain – rained - llover

To rent – rented - rentar
To rest – rested - descansar

New irregular verbs – Nuevos verbos irregulares
To forget – forgot - olvidar
To get – got – conseguir / obtener
To go dancing – went dancing – salir a bailar
To send – sent - enviar
To get up – got up - levantarse
To make – made – hacer - fabricar
To put on – put on – ponerse *(ropas)*
To get to – got to – llegar a *(un lugar o destino)*
To give – gave - dar
To go in – went in – entrar *(cuando la persona está afuera y va a entrar)*
To come in – came in – entrar *(cuando la persona está dentro y quiere que entres)*
To take off – took off – despegar (un avión)
To fly – flew - volar
To run – ran - correr
To swim – swam - nadar
To wear – wore – usar / llevar puesto
To bring – brought - traer
To eat out – ate out – comer fuera *(un restaurante, etc)*

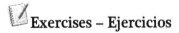**Exercises – Ejercicios**

Exercise 1.1: Write the tag question. Use the correct pronoun to rename the subject of the first sentence. If the sentence uses the verb *to be*, use the

verb *to be*. If it contains a helping verb, use the same helping verb. If it uses some other verb, use the verb *do*. Keep the verb tense the same, but remember to change from negative to affirmative or from affirmative to negative.

He's smart, _isn't he?_
My parents didn't call me, _did they?_
You love her, _don't you?_

1. She's a happy baby, _____

2. It didn't rain, _____

3. You like chocolate, _____

4. Mom is really busy, _____

5. Dad wasn't sleeping, _____
6. You can't rest with all that noise,

_____

7. Mom doesn't know you're sick,

_____

8. You can walk, _____

9. Mr. Walker isn't here, _____

10. You go running every day, _____

Exercise 1.2: Underline the logical sentence. Remember, the condition should begin with *if.*

Example: If you want to get a job, you need to dress formally. / If you need to dress formally, you want to get a job.

1. If she wants to get her work done, she shouldn't watch soap operas. / If she shouldn't watch soap operas, she wants to get her work done.

2. If they can deliver newspapers, they want to make extra money. / If they want to make extra money, they can deliver newspapers.

3. If you call me first, Mom lets you go to the movies. / If Mom lets you go to the movies, call me first!

4. If you finish your work early, we can go out to eat! / If we can go out to eat, you finish your work early.

5. If I can't do the laundry, it rains. / If it rains, I can't do the laundry.

Exercise 1.3: Write the correct question word.
Example: When are visiting hours? Right now. _Whom_ would you like to see?

1. "I'd like some pens. _____

2. ____ would you like to buy?" "Five, please."

3. "Let's go to the movies. _____ would you like to see?"
"An action movie, of course!"

4. "I want to go see my mom. _____ would you like to see her?"
"On Sunday."

5. "I need to see the schedule. _____ do

you need to see it?"

"I want to see who is talking first—my boss or me."

6. "Let's go out. _____ do you want to go?"

"Let's go to the park downtown!"

Lesson 2

Getting ready for the wedding – Preparandose para la boda

Conversation 1

Haidresser:　　Come right in, honey. So you're getting married in a couple hours? How do you feel?

Bride:　　Oh, nervous, excited, you know, like everyone.

Haidresser:　　Yeah. I remember my wedding day. I thought life would be so perfect. But it's just work, work, work.

Bride:　　Really?

Haidresser:　　Well, you know, before you're married, he comes to see you, takes you out to eat, and gives you presents. After you're married, he comes home to eat, takes you to the grocery store, and gives you dirty laundry.

Bride:　　Ah, right. What do you do to keep the love alive?

Haidresser:　　Well, I guess I don't do much. I just try to keep him alive. Haha. Okay, we're almost done with the hair. Do you want to see it? Now, for your makeup: do you want a dramatic look or something more subtle?

Bride:　　I'd like it natural, please.

Haidresser:　　Okay. And for your lipstick? I

251

recommend red for those pictures.

Bride: Um, I guess red would be nice.

Haidresser: Good. Would you like your nails red, too?

Bride: Sure.

Haidresser: So, where are you going for your honeymoon?

Bride: I don't know. It's a surprise!

Haidresser: Oh, that could be nice. The groom doesn't like camping, does he?

The wedding

There was the bridge, two left turns, the eternal traffic light, and a right turn into the parking lot. Frank could hardly believe the day was finally here. As he walked into the church, there was a quick flash of white and a door closed. Christie would cry if he saw her before the wedding. She was very traditional. He knocked on the closed door. "How are things going in there?" he asked. There was no answer. He slipped a note under the door and continued down the hall to the men's restroom.

Behind the door, Christie read the note and cried. After years of dreaming of her wedding day, there were so many unexpected emotions. It wasn't all flowers and romance. She was making a big commitment! From now on, she would plan meals, wash dishes, pick up socks, dust, sweep, and mop— and she would do this after getting out of work. It wouldn't be easy. Could she do it? Could she work all day and still be nice to Frank at the end of the day?

She read the note again. She was promising loyalty to the man she loved, to the man who bought her flowers and chocolates, to the man who taught her Scrabble and golf. Frank was an expert at basketball and poetry. She couldn't imagine life without him. She dried her tears, reapplied her makeup, and arranged the train of her dress behind her.

As she walked up to the door, she could just see Frank by the altar. He was so handsome—and kind. The usher opened the door. Her father took her arm, wiping tears from his own eyes. Everyone was crying, apparently, even the flower girl, who became nervous and ran to her mother. Christie laughed and walked down the aisle toward Frank. Her father gave her to her husband. The pianist played terribly. He had two jobs and no time to practice. But the bride and groom didn't notice. They said their vows, exchanged rings, and kissed, all the time promising eternal love with their eyes.

When they turned around, the saw their parents crying and smiling. It would be difficult, but they would make each other happy. And even if they weren't always happy—because Christie knew that sometimes they wouldn't feel happy—they would still love each other. She could learn a new type of love: one that didn't depend on chocolates and flowers. Her love would create sunshine on rainy days. She chose to face the future with hope instead of fear.

Frank looked at his wife. He was completely happy. She was so beautiful, so radiant. They practically flew out of the auditorium. Everyone congratulated them and promised to help them through the future months and years. It was a perfect day, a day to remember in hard times. Now they just had to find a job.

Conversation 2

Clerk: Welcome to Legend Lodge. We're so glad you chose to stay with us! Let's see. Do you have a reservation?

Frank: Yes, for five nights.

Clerk: Hmmm. Well, it looks like your reservation is for tomorrow night.

Frank: No, there must be some mistake. I made it from Saturday to Wednesday.

Clerk: I'm sorry. You are currently booked from Sunday to Thursday, but we'll see if we can change it. . . . You're in luck! We have a free room tonight, but it's not the bridal suite. How about we put you in the forest room tonight and tomorrow you can change to the bridal suite?

Frank: Is there an extra charge?

Clerk: No, if you are only staying five nights, the cost remains the same.

Frank: Great!

Clerk: Would you like some supper? There's a buffet in the dining room to your right. It's complementary—included in the price of the room. Go right in and see what's there while I process your card.

Frank: Looks delicious!

Clerk: Fantastic. Here's your key. Your room is straight down the hall. Would you like some help

with your bags?
Frank: No, we're fine, thanks.
Clerk: Call me if you need anything!

New words – Nuevas palabras
Barber shop – barbería / peluquería
Bridge - puente
Bus stop – estación de autobús
Chemistry - química
Class - clase
Corner – esquina
Hall – corredor / pasillo
Driver – conductor / chofer
Hairdresser - estilista
Jail – cárcel
Jeweler - joyero
Left - izquierda
Right - derecha
Library – bliblioteca
Math / Mathematics – matemáticas
Mistake - error
Museum - museo
Parking lot – parqueo / estacionamiento
Professor – profesor
Real estate agency – agencia de bienes raíces
Receptionist – recepcionista
Road – carretera / calle
Subway – subterráneo / metro
Supermarket – supermercado
Traffic light – semáforo
University - universidad
Area – área

Band – banda / grupo
Best man – padrino (de una boda)
Bride – novia (de la boda)
Bridesmaid – damas de honor
Future - futuro
Groom – novio (de la boda)
Guest - invitado
Honeymoon – luna de miel
Meter - metro
Reception – recepción
Studio – estudio
Surprise - sorpresa
Truck – camión
Usher – ujier
Wedding - boda
Answer – respuesta
Application – solicitud
Appointment – cita
Business – negocio
Company - compañía
Form – forma
Manager – gerente
Personnel – personal
Question - pregunta
Salary – salario
Word - palabra
Worker - trabajador
Aunt – tía
High school – escuela secundaria / bachillerato
Life - vida
Tourist – turista
Uncle - tío

Writer - escritor**Phrases and Expressions - Frases y expresiones**

To be right – estar en lo cierto (correcto) / tener la razón

To be wrong – estar equivocado

Could you tell me ...? - ¿Podrías decirme...?

Could you tell us...? - ¿podrías decirnos?

Do you mind if...? - ¿te importaría si...?

To make a mistake – cometer un error / meter la pata

Sure - seguro

To take the bus – tomar el autobús *(abordarlo)*

To take the plane – tomar al avión *(abordarlo)*

I hope so – eso espero

I think so – eso pienso / creo

I guess so – eso supongo

I hope not – espero que no

I guess not – supongo que no

I don't think so – no lo creo

To take a vacation – tomar vacaciones

To come right in – entrar de inmediato *(cuando la persona está dentro y te invita a entrar)*

To go right in – entrar de inmediato *(cuando la persona está afuera y te indica que entres)*

Good to see you – es bueno verte / encantado de verte

What can I do for you? - ¿Qué puedo hacer por ti? ¿En qué te puedo servir?

What can we do for you? - ¿Qué podemos hacer por ti?

To get a job – conseguir un trabajo / empleo.

257

📖 Grammar – Gramática

Aprendemos un poco más sobre la forma cortés de pedir o preguntar las cosas. Veamos las preguntas y oraciones normales y como las convertimos en formal o cortes.

"Could you tell... May I ask...".

How old *are you*? - ¿Qué edad tienes?

Could you tell me how old *you are*? - ¿podrías decirme que edad tienes?

May I ask how old *you are*? - ¿puedo preguntar qué edad tienes?

Ustedes pueden ver como la simple pregunta "how old are you?" se convierte en una pregunta cortes con tan solo usar **"could you tell... May I ask...".**

Presten mucha atención a la estructura, porque cuando usamos esta forma de cortesía, ya la pregunta original no está como pregunta. Veamos lo que les estoy explicando.

Decimos "How old *are you*?" Recuerdan que "*Are you*" es la forma para preguntas del verbo "to be".

Pero cuando usamos "May I ask how old *you are*?", estamos diciendo "*You are*" no en forma de pregunta, sino como afirmación, porque ya el "May I ask" o "Could you tell..." hace la forma de pregunta. ¿Comprenden la idea? Vamos a seguir practicando el modelo.

Excuse me; could you tell us what time it is? -

¿excuseme, podrías decirnos que hora es?

May I ask what time it is, please? - ¿podrías decirnos que hora es, por favor?

May I ask if I made any mistakes? - ¿puedo preguntar si cometí algún error?

Could you tell me if I made any mistakes? - ¿podrías decirme si cometí algún error?

Ustedes pueden convertir cualquier pregunta en forma cortes. Recuerden, cuando usamos el "may", la pregunta es más suave y cortes. En cambio, cuando usamos "could" la pregunta tiene un tono un poco más fuerte en comparación con el "may".

Modal verb *Can* / *Could* – Verbo modal *Can* / *Could*.

Recuerden que ya vimos el uso del "Can" en lecciones pasadas, de modo que solo daremos un repaso y nos concentraremos en "could".

I can talk now – puedo hablar ahora.

I can't talk now – no puedo hablar ahora.

Can I speak now? - ¿Puedo hablar ahora?

Yes, you can. – Si, puedes.

No, no you can't. – No, no puedes.

Ahora vamos a aprender el uso del "could". Tiene dos usos diferentes dependiendo de la conversación y el contexto.

Could – podría

I can speak now – puedo hablar ahora.

I could speak now – podría hablar ahora.

I can fly the plane – puedo volar el avión.
I could fly the plane – podría volar el avión.

I can't sing opera – no puedo cantar ópera.
I couldn't sing opera – no podría cantar ópera.
Could you sing opera? - ¿podrías cantar ópera?
Yes, I could. – sí, podría.
Yes, I could sing opera – si, podría cantar ópera.
No, I couldn't – no, no podría.
No, I couldn't sing opera – no, no podría cantar ópera.

Recuerden, el patrón es el mismo. Nunca se usa un verbo en infinitivo cuando usamos "could".
Could you sing then? - ¿podrías volar entonces?
No, I couldn't fly anymore – no, no podría volar más.

Could – pasado de "can"

Este es el segundo uso del "could", el cual es el pasado de can y tenemos que tomar muy en cuenta esto, dependiendo el contexto o la oración. Veamos.
Could you talk to the teacher yesterday? - ¿pudiste hablar con el profesor ayer?
Yes, I could. – Si, pude.
Yes, I could talk to the teacher yesterday – Si, pude hablar con el profesor ayer.
No, I couldn't. – No, no pude.
No, I couldn't tak to the teacher yesterday – No, no pude hablar con el profesor ayer.

Como pueden ver, siempre que usamos "could" para el pasado el verbo permanece en presente; es como cuando aprendimos el "did". No lo olviden.

What happened to you yesterday? - ¿Qué te pasó ayer?

I couldn't swim, I had cramps – No pude nadar, tenía calambres.

I couldn't come yesterday, because I was sick. – No, pude venir ayer porque estaba enfermo.

El concepto está claro, solo tienen que comenzar a usarlo con los otros conocimientos ya adquiridos. Si se ponen a analizar, ustedes tienen un nivel de inglés casi equivalente a un año de universidad. Ya pueden hablar en casi todos los tiempos. Sigamos nuestro aprendizaje.

Auxiliary verb "used to" – Verbo auxiliar"used to" – solía.

Usamos el "used to" para cosas que solían pasar regularmente en el pasado, pero ya no ocurren más.

I used to cook – solía cocinar *o* acostumbraba a cocinar *(pero ya no cocino más)*.

I used to go to church every Sunday – acostumbraba ir a la iglesia todos los domingos *(pero ya no más)*.

She used to play the piano – ella solía tocar el piano *(pero ya no más)*.

Para preguntas y respuestas negativas, como es el pasado, usamos el "*did / didn't*". Veamos.

Did you use to play the piano? - ¿acostumbrabas tocar el piano?

Yes, I used to. – Sí, solía.

Yes, I did. – Sí.

No, I didn't use to. – No, no solía.

No, I didn't. – No.

Tenemos la opción de contestar de dos formas, con el "did" o con el "*used to*".

Recuerden que cuando usamos el "*did*" el verbo debe ir en presente, es por esto que usamos "*use to*" en preguntas y respuestas negativas. Continuemos practicando.

Did you use to cook for your husband? - ¿acostumbrabas cocinar para tu esposo?

Yes, I used to. – Si, solía.

Yes, I did. – Si.

Yes, I used to cook for my husband. – Si, solía cocinar para mi esposo.

No, I didn't use to. – No, no solía.

No, I didn't. – No.

No, I didn't use to cook for my husband. –No, no solía cocinar para mi esposo.

Did you use to play cards? - ¿acostumbrabas jugar cartas?

Yes, I used to play cards – Si, acostumbraba jugar cartas.

No, I didn't use to play cards – No, no acostumbraba jugar cartas.

Algunas veces cuando usamos el negativo,

podemos reemplazar el "didn't" por el "never". Cuando usamos "never" el "used to" tiene que ir en pasado.

I didn't use to sing at home – No acostumbraba a cantar en casa.

I never used to sing at home – nunca acostumbraba a cantar en casa.

Did you use to smoke? - ¿acostumbrabas a fumar?

I never used to smoke – nunca acostumbraba a fumar.

I didn't use to smoke – no acostumbraba a fumar.

Siempre que no se use el "did", entonces el "used to" deberá estar en pasado. No lo olviden.

I always used to smoke – yo siempre acostumbraba a fumar.

I used to work from time to time – acostumbraba a trabajar de tiempo en tiempo.

I used to flirt a lot – solía coquetear mucho.

New regular verbs – Nuevos verbos regulares
To look for – looked for – buscar
To turn – turned – girar / doblar
To hope – hoped – esperar *(de esperanza)*
To intend – intended – tener la intención
To answer – answered - responder
To apply for – applied for - solicitar
To ask – asked – pedir o preguntar
To earn – earned - ganar
To expect – expected - esperar
To fill out – filled out – llenar *(formulario)*
To type – typed – digitar / escribir en la

computadora

To bore – bored - aburrirse

To die – died - morir

To learn – learned - aprender

New irregular verbs – Nuevos verbos irregulares

To be born – was / were born - nacer

To become – became - convertirse

To hit – hit - golpear

To say – said - decir

To pay – paid - pagar

To sit down – sat down - sentarse

To understand – understood - entender

To find – found – encontrar / buscar

To get married – got married - casarse

To get on – got on – montarse / subirse *(en un vehículo)*

To get off – got off – desmontarse / bajarse *(de un vehículo)*

To tell – told – decir / contar

Prepositions – Preposiciones

Across – a través de / de un lado a otro

Across the Street – al otro lado de la calle *(esto es, cruzando la calle)*

Along – a lo largo

Walk along the street – camine a lo largo de la calle

Down – abajo – hacia abajo

Turn down the Street – gire hacia abajo en la calle

Over – sobre / encima

We have to go over the bridge – tenemos que pasar por encima del puente

Up – arriba / hacia arriba
Let's go up – vamos a subir
On top of – en la cima de / en la parte superior
They are on top of the mountain – ellos están encima de la montaña. *(Es decir, en la parte superior, en el pico de la montaña)*
Straight ahead – al frente / todo derecho
Continue straight ahead and then turn right at the first traffic light – continúa todo derecho y entonces gira a la derecha en el semáforo.

Estas preposiciones las usamos usualmente cuando estamos dando dirección e indicaciones.

Adjectives – Adjetivos
Left – izquierda
Turn left at the next corner – gira a la izquierda en la siguiente esquina.
Right – derecha
Don't turn right – no gires a la derecha
Boring - aburrido
Closed - cerrado
Enormous - enorme
Fantastic - fantástico
High - alto
Lucky - suertudo
Old-fashioned – pasado de moda
Open - abierto
Square – plaza / manda
Sure - seguro
Total - total
Careful – cuidadoso / cuidado

Careless - descuidado
Fast - rápido
Immediate - inmediato
Loud – alto (de volumen)
Low – bajito / bajo
Hard – duro / rudo
Noisy - ruidoso
Present – presente / regalo
Quick – rápido / ágil
Slow – lento / despacio
Soft – suave / blando
Famous - famoso
Following – siguiente

Adverbs – Adverbios
A Little – un poco
Maybe – tal vez / quizás / puede ser
Yet - todavía
Anymore – nunca más / ya
Badly – gravemente / mal
Carelessly – descuidadamente
Carefully - cuidadosamente
Happily - felizmente
Loudly – altísimo
Noisily - ruidosamente
Quickly – rápidamente / ágilmente
Quietly - tranquilamente
Sadly – tristemente
Slowly – lentamente
Softly – suavemente
Terribly – terriblemente

Como pueden ver, para formar la terminación "mente" en inglés, solo tenemos que agregar "ly" al adjetivo y lo convertimos en adverbio. Veamos.

He is a bad pilot – él es un mal piloto

He flies the plane badly – el vuela el avión malamente.

You are careful – eres cuidadoso

You speak carefully – tú hablas cuidadosamente

You are a careless driver – eres un conductor descuidado

You drive carelessly – conduces descuidadamente

We need an inmediate answer – necesitamos una respuesta inmediata

Answer immediately – responde inmediatamente

He's a quick mechanic – él es un mecánico rápido

He works quicky – él trabaja rápidamente

The music is terrible because they sing terribly – la música es terrible porque ellos cantan terriblemente

Recuerden que con los adjetivos que terminan en "y", se cambia por una "i" y entonces se le agrega "ly". Los adjetivos que terminan en "le", quitamos l "e" y le agregamos la "ly".

Estos son irregulares y nunca cambian.

Fast – fast

She is a fast driver – ella es una conductora rápida

She drives fast – ella conduce rápido

*Good – well

I am a good teacher – soy un buen profesor

I teach well – yo enseño bien.

Hard –hard
You are a hard worker – eres un arduo trabajador
You work so hard - trabajas muy duro

Presten mucha atención, especialmente a "good – well". Nunca pueden decir "I speak good", eso sería como decir "Yo hablar bueno". Y ya establecimos que la era de los cavernículas pasó. Tenemos que decir
I speak well – yo hablo bien
They learn well – ellas aprenden bien
I am a good learner – soy un buen aprendiz

The word "so" – La palabra "so"
So puede variar su significado dependiendo del contexto; veamos.
So – muy / tan
It is *so* good, isn't it? – es tan bueno, ¿no es así?
They are *so* beautiful, aren't they? – ellas son muy hermosas, ¿no es así?
I am *so* happy – estoy tan feliz
So – por motivo de eso / así que / de modo que
I listened to the radio *because* I didn't like the TV shows – Escuchaba la radio porque no me gustaban los programas de TV.
I didn't like the TV shows, *so* I listened to the radio. – No me gustaban los programas de TV, así que escuché la radio.
I changed the channel *because* I didn't like the movie – cambié el canal porque no me gustaba la película.
I didn't like the movie, *so* I changed the channel. – No me gustaba la película, sí que cambié de canal.

So – Si, No

Are they saying something? I think *so*... ¿están ellos diciendo algo? Creo que si...

Sería lo mismo que contestar.

Yes, I think they are saying something - Sí, creo que ellos están diciendo algo.

Is she doing something? I don't think *so* - ¿está haciendo algo? Creo que no.

Sería lo mismo que contestar.

No, I don't think she's doing anything – No, no creo que ella esté haciendo algo.

Como siempre, deben repasar y aprender bien cada sección antes de continuar a la siguiente. A partir de esta lección, vamos a incluir una nueva sección en cada lección "***Word Definitions***". Esta nueva sección tendrá algunas palabras en inglés con sus definiciones en inglés.

Word Definitions

- ***Writer:*** *a person who writes in a particular way, books, stories, or articles as a job or occupation. Someone who has written something.*

- ***Famous:*** *known or recognized by many people. Having fame and widely known.*

- ***Usher:*** *a person who leads people to their seats in a theater, at a wedding, etc.*

- ***Groom:*** *a man who has just been married or is about to be married.*

- ***Bride:*** *a woman who has just been married or is about to be married.*

- ***To shoot:*** *kill or wound (a person or animal)*

with a bullet or arrow. Fire a bullet from a gun or discharge an arrow from a bow. Use a firearm with a specified degree of skill.

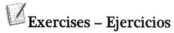 Exercises – Ejercicios

Exercise 2.1: Underline the word that does not belong (that is not in the same category as the others).

Example: told   expected   smoked   ask
1. tourist barber shop   museum   supermarket
2. turn   jail   expect learn
3. loud   noisy   noisily high
4. left   right   straight ahead   ground
5. band   professor   groom aunt

Exercise 2.2: Write the correct form of the verbs in parentheses. All of the sentences are in the simple past. Remember not to use the past after *did*.

Did you already _pay_ (pay) for your hotel room?

No, I didn't (1) _____ (say) I cannot make a

reservation. You (2) _____ (speak) too quickly.

You did not (3) _____ (understand) my question.

If you already (4) _____ (pay), you would lose

your money if you stayed somewhere else.

Margaret (5) _____ (look) everywhere for the

gold ring. But she (6) _____ (can) not find it. She

(7)_____ (get) down on her knees to look under

the couch. But it (8) _____ (be) not there. She

finally (9) _____ (sit) down on the floor,

discouraged. And then she (10) _____ (see) it on

top of the chair opposite her. She almost (11)

_____ (cry), she was so happy!

Exercise 2.3: Unscramble the sentence. Write the words in the correct order.
Example: at / turn / traffic light / the / don't / right
Don't turn right at the traffic light.
 1.   noisily / down / the hall / the guest / walked
 2.   the bridge / the groom / kissed / quickly
 3.   the class / quietly / boring / he / left
 4.   the rings / they / happily / for / paid / gold
 5.   the hall / artist's / the / across / is / studio

Exercise 2.4:
Make indirect questions. Add a phrase to make the sentence more polite.
Example: Why are you sad? _May I ask why you are sad?_
 1.   Where is the restroom?

_____

Curso Completo de Inglés

2. What is your name? _____

3. Where are you from?

_____

4. When does the movie start?

_____

5. Where is the museum?

_____

Lesson 3
The robbery – El robo

Conversation

Customer: Excuse me. Could you help me, please?

Clerk: Sure. What can I do for you?

Customer: Could I see the ring with all the little diamonds?

Clerk: The silver one?

Customer: No, the other one, the one with the diamonds in the shape of a flower.

Clerk: Ah. The gold one. Here it is.

Customer: Yes. Is it okay if I put it on?

Clerk: Well, um, okay, I guess so. The silver ring is also very popular.

Customer: It's kind of boring, though.

Clerk: It has less detail, but touch it. See how comfortable it is. All those details can hurt a lady's hand when the ring moves. The silver ring is very practical.

Customer: Yes, ... but she would like the gold one better.

Clerk: Okay. Would you like to set up payments or . . . . ?

Customer: I have a traveler's check.

Clerk: I'm sorry, Sir, but we don't accept traveler's checks.

Customer: Okay. Well, here, here's my credit card.

Clerk: Hmmm. It says payment is denied.
Customer: Do you mind if I use your phone?
Clerk: No problem.
Customer: I'd like to place a collect call. ... Hi. Yes, I know you have an 800 number. I'm sorry I didn't bring it with me. I'm on vacation. I think my card is blocked. I'm at the jewelry store, and I'm trying to buy a ring. ... Yes, that would be great. Thank you! Okay. Can you try it again?
Clerk: Sure. Oh, I'm sorry. Our system is down. Do you have cash?
Customer: No. I'm on vacation.
Clerk: How about I fill out a pen-and-paper charge slip?
Customer: Um, no. Let's just forget about it.
[Men with hankerchiefs over their mouths enter, waving guns around.] Put your hands up! Put everything in this bag. ... Give me your wallet—oh, great. He has a gun. [The men run out of the store with the sound of gunfire.]
Clerk: Where are the police? Were you shot?
Customer: No, they fired the gun by accident. I'm fine.
Clerk: Thank you so much, Sir. Do you want to try to run your credit card through the system again?
Customer: No, thanks. I just want to know where to go to report the attempted robbery.

New words – Nuevas palabras
Boxing – boxeo
Champion – campeón
Foot – feet – pie / pies

Millionaire - millonario
Movie star – estrella de cine
Politician - político
Politics - política
Prime minister – primer ministro
Accident - accidente
Arm - brazo
Diamond - diamante
Ear – oreja / oído
Earring – arete / pendiente
Finger – dedo (de la mano)
Gold - oro
Ground – suelo / tierra
Gun - arma
Handkerchief – pañuelo
Jewel - joya
Jewelry – joyería
Karate - karate
Meal - comida
Mouth - boca
Neck - cuello
Necklace - collar
Nose - nariz
Note - nota
Ring - anillo
Thief – ladrón
Robbery - robo
Tooth – teeth – diente / dientes
Wallet - cartera
Age - edad
Call - llamada
Change - cambio

Clothes - ropa
Coin - moneda
Cow - vaca
Apartment - departamento
Driver's license – licencia de conducir
Foreigner – extranjero
Identification – identificación
Line - linea
Operator - operador
Paper – papel
Pen – lapicero / bolígrafo
Pepper - pimienta
Receiver – receptor / auricular
Sales - ventas
Salt - sal
Sheep - oveja
Traveler's check – cheque de viajero
Besides – además
Into – hacia adentro

Word Definitions

Suddenly: *very quickly, usually as a surprise.*

Collect call: *when the person who gets the call (not the person who is calling) pays for the call.*

Coin: *a piece of metal issued by the government to use as money.*

To dial: *establish or try to establish a telephone connection by operating the dial on a telephone.*

To ring: *give a clear resonant sound, as a bell when struck.*

Phrases and Expressions - Frases y expresiones

To answer the phone – contestar el teléfono
Forget it - olvídalo
Hold the line – espera en la línea
On the phone – al teléfono
To be robbed – ser robado
Man – hombre (expresión al hablar)
To be shot – ser baleado / recibir un tiro.

Grammar – Gramática

Vamos a aprender el uso de nuevos pronombres. Presten mucha atención a la forma en cómo se usan. Verdaderamente no existe una diferencia entre ellos, con excepción que la forma "body", que es un poco menos formal que la forma "one".

Pronouns in affirmative sentences – Pronombres en oraciones afirmativas.

Everybody – todo el mundo *(personas)*
Everyone – cada uno *(personas)*
Everything – todo *(cosas)*
Everywhere – en todo lugar *(lugar)*
Somebody – alguien *(personas)*
Someone - alguien *(personas)*
Something - algo *(cosas)*
Somewhere – en algún lugar *(lugares)*

There is **somebody** at the door – there is someone at the door – hay alguien en la puerta.

I would love to go **somewhere** this week – me encantaría ir a algún lugar esta semana.

Someone gave me a present – alguien me dio un

regalo.

I am not goint to tell my secret to **anyone** – no le contaré mi secreto a nadie.

I gave you *everything* I had – te di todo lo que tenía.

Pronouns in interrogative sentences – pronombres en oraciones interrogativas
Anybody – alguien *(personas)*
Anyone – alguien *(personas)*
Anything – algo *(cosas)*
Anywhere – algún lugar *(lugares)*

Is (there) **anybody** home? – Is (there) anyone home? – ¿hay alguien en casa?
Did **anyone** come? - ¿vino alguien?
If you need **anything**, just tell me - si necesitas algo, solo dime

Pronouns in negative sentences – Pronombres en oraciones negativas
Nobody – *anybody – nadie (*personas*)
No one – anyone – nadie *(personas)*
Nothing – anything – nada *(cosa)*
Nowhere – anywhere – en ningún lugar *(lugares)*

I don't want to go **anywhere** with you – no quiero ir a ningún lado contigo.
I don't have **anything** to eat – no tengo nada de comer.
I can't find **anyone** – no puedo encontrar a nadie.
Es muy importante entender que cuando la

oración esta en negativo, solo se podrán usar los que comienzan con "any".

Cuando usamos *"nobody, no one, nothing, nowhere"*, la oración está en afirmativo, pero con un significado negativo. Veamos.

There is *nothing* I can do – no hay nada que yo pueda hacer.

There is *nowhere* you can go – no hay lugar donde puedas ir.

She has *nobody* to talk to – ella no tiene a nadie con quien hablar.

There was *no one* at the party – no había nadie en la fiesta.

Cuando una de estas palabras es usada como el sujeto de la oración, entonces es seguido por la conjugación del verbo para "he / she".

Everybody loves him – todo el mundo lo ama

Everything is ready – todo está listo

Everybody wants to go – todo el mundo quiere ir.

Everybody knows the truth – todo el mundo sabe la verdad.

Everything looks nice – todo luce bien.

Recuerden que *"somebody"* es para referirse a una sola persona. Si queremos referirnos a más de una persona, usamos *"some people"*.

Somebody wants to see you – alguien quiere verte.

Some people want to see you – algunas personas quieren verte.

Nobody came to the church yesterday – nadie vino a la iglesia ayer.

Somebody left a message for you – alguien dejó un mensaje para ti.

Podemos usar "*someone, something, somebody, somewhere*" en preguntas. Pero cuando lo usamos en preguntas, es porque estamos esperando que nos contesten con "Sí", es decir, que la respuesta sea positiva.

Are you going *somewhere*? - ¿vas a algún lado?
Yes, I am going home – Sí, voy a casa.
Are you looking for *something*? - ¿estás buscando algo?
Yes, I am looking for my watch – Si, estoy buscando mi reloj.
Can *somebody* help me, please? - ¿puede alguien ayudarme, por favor?
Yes, I can help you. – Si, puedo ayudarte.
Are you looking for *someone*? - ¿estás buscando a alguien?
Yes, I am looking for my sister – Si, estoy buscando a mi hermana.

Ahora, si hacen sus preguntas en formas negativas, es porque están 100% seguros de que la respuesta es "Sí", sin lugar a dudas. Veamos.
Aren't you going *somewhere*? - ¿no vas a algún lado?
Yes, I am going home – Si, voy a casa.
Aren't you looking for *someone*? - ¿no estás buscando a alguien?
Yes, I am looking for my sister – Si, estoy buscando

a mi hermana.

Aren't you looking for *something*? - ¿no estás buscando algo?

Yes, I am looking for my watch – Si, estoy buscando mi reloj.

Tambien hay que tener mucho cuidado con este estilo, puesto que en muchos casos las usamos para cuestionar a la persona "aren't you going somewhere? Ya vete, no?"

Relative pronouns as a subject "Who / That" – Pronombres relativos como sujeto "Who / That".

Recordemos el significado de "who – quien" y "that – eso, esta". Los pronombres relativos siempre son seguidos por la conjugación del verbo en la tercera persona singular o plural. Podemos usar "who – that" para personas, pero cuando nos referimos a cosas solo podemos usar "that". No olviden que en este contexto, "that" lo traducimos como "que".

I lost the money – perdí el dinero.

I am the one *who* lost the money – soy quien perdió el dinero.

I am the one *that* lost the money – soy quien perdió el dinero.

These flowers are very expensive – estas flores son muy caras.

These are the ones *that* are very expensive – Esas son las que son muy caras.

I am the one *who* knows everything – soy el que sabe todo.

You are the man *who* is learning English – tú eres el hombre que (quien) está aprendiendo inglés.

Noten que casi siempre usamos "the one – el que / la que" cuando nos referimos a personas.

The one *who* is looking at you – el que te está mirando.

The one *that* is looking at you – el que te está mirando.

I want the expensive ice cream. I want the one *that* is expensive – quiero el helado barato. Quiero el que es barato.

Recuerden,

Cuando "who / that" se refieren al objeto de la oración, no es obligatorio usarlos. Podemos omitirlos. Veamos.

I have the contract. Peter signed it. – Tengo el contrato. Peter lo firmó.

I have the contract *(that)* Peter signed – tengo el contrato que Peter firmó.

This is the man. I hit him – este es el hombre. Yo lo golpeé.

This the man *(who[m] / that)* I hit – este es el hombre (a quien – que) yo golpeé.

Question words plus infinitive / Present progressive – Palabras interrogativas más el infinitivo / Presente progresivo.

We know *who to call* – sabemos a quién llamar.

We know *who we are calling* – sabemos a quién estamos llamando.

We know *what to do* – sabemos qué hacer.

We know *what we are doing* – sabemos lo que estamos haciendo.

We know *when to leave* – sabemos cuándo partir.
We know *when we are leaving* – sabemos cuándo partiremos.

We know *where to go* – sabemos a dónde ir.
We know *where we are going* – sabemos a dónde vamos.

We know *how to get there* – sabemos cómo llegar.
We know *how we are getting there* – sabemos cómo llegaremos.

Como pueden ver, el uso es bastante sencillo, pueden usar tanto el infinito como el presente progresivo. Veamos algunos ejemplos en preguntas y respuestas.

Do you *know who(m) to call*? - ¿sabes a quien llamar?
Yes, I know *who(m) to call* – sí, sé a quién llamar.
No, I don't know *who(m) to call* – no, no sé a quién llamar.

Do you know *who you are calling*? - ¿sabes a quien estas llamando?
Yes, I know *who I am calling* – sí, sé a quién estoy llamando.
No, I don't know *who I am calling* – no, no sé a quién estoy llamando.

Do you know *what to do?* - ¿sabes qué hacer?
Yes, I know *what to do* – sí, sé qué hacer.
No, I don't know *what to do* – no, no sé qué hacer.

Do you know *what you are doing?* - ¿Sabes lo que estás haciendo?
Yes, I know *what I am doing* – sí, sé lo que estoy haciendo.
No, I don't know *what I am doing* – no, no sé lo que estoy haciendo.

Do you know *when to leave?* - ¿Sabes cuándo partir?
Yes, I know *when to leave* – si, se cuándo partir.
No, I don't know *when to leave* – no, no sé cuándo partir.

Do you know *when you are leaving?* - ¿sabes cuándo te marchas?
Yes, I know *when I am leaving* – sí, sé cuándo me marcho.
No, I don't know *when I am leaving* – No, no sé cuándo me marcho.

Do you know *where to go?* - ¿sabes a dónde ir?
Yes, I know *where to go* – si, sé a dónde ir.
No, I don't know *where to go* – no, no sé a dónde ir.

Do you know *where you are going?* - ¿sabes a dónde vas?
Yes, I know *where I am going* – sí, sé a dónde voy.
No, I don't know *where I am going* – no, no sé a

dónde voy.

Do you know *how to get there?* - ¿sabes cómo llegar?
Yes, I know *how to get there* – sí, sé cómo llegar.
No, I don't know *how to get there* – no, no sé cómo llegar.

Do you know *how you are getting there?* - ¿sabes cómo llegaras?
Yes, I know *how I am getting there* – Si, sé cómo llegare.
No, I don't know *how I am getting there* – no, no sé cómo llegare.

Como pueden ver, las preguntas y respuestas siempre van con el "do" aun cuando estamos usando el presente progresivo, porque la primera parte de la oración está en presente simple. Y si se fijan bien, solo la primera parte está en forma de pregunta, la segunda no. Si quieren hacerlo en forma negativa, solo tienen que usar el negativo.

Do you know *what to do?* - ¿sabes qué hacer?
I don't know *what to do* – no sé qué hacer.
Do you know *what you are doing?* - ¿sabes lo que estás haciendo?
I don't know *what I am doing* – no sé lo que estoy haciendo.

Conjunctions – Conjunciones
Vamos a aprender a usar "*when – cuando*" y "*while*

– *mientras*" como conjunciones.

Usamos "*while*" cuando dos cosas pasan al mismo tiempo.

My mother usually sings *while* she is cooking – mi mamá usualmente canta mientras está cocinando.

I sang *while* I played the piano – canté mientras tocaba el piano.

Si algo está sucediendo y entonces sucede algo más, usamos "*when*".

I talk. Everybody listens – hablo. Todos escuchan.

Everybody listens *when* I talk – todos escuchan cuando hablo.

The thief saw the police officer. She ran. – la ladrona vio al policía. Ella corrió.

The thief ran *when* she saw the police officer – la ladrona corrió cuando vio al policía.

When I talk, everybody listens – cuando hablo todos escuchan.

While I am cooking, I usually listen to the radio – mientras estoy cocinando, usualmente escucho la radio.

Pronouns and adjectives – Pronombres and adjetivos.

Continuemos aprendiendo otros pronombres y adjetivos.

Another – otro

Usamos **another** cuando hablamos del singular o queremos una cosa del montón. Es un adjetivo. Es "*an + other*" pero cuando los usamos juntos se convierten en una sola palabra. Expresa cantidad y significa "*uno más o adicional*".

I want **another** apple – quiero otra manzana.

Do you want **another** piece of fruit? - ¿quieres otra fruta?

Yes, I want **another** one. – sí, quiero otra.

No, I don't want any more – no, no quiero más.

También podemos usar **"another"** con **"one"** cuando en la frase o la oración está clara la alusión al texto anterior.

You ate a lot of apples. You can't eat **another one**. – comiste muchas manzanas. No puedes comer otra.

Do you want another apple? - ¿quieres otra manzana?

No, thanks – no gracias,

Yes, I want **another one** – sí, quiero otra.

También puede significar **"algo alterno o diferente"**.

I am not happy with this perfume. Next time I am going to buy **another** brand – no estoy contento con este perfume. La próxima vez compraré otra marca.

Other – otro

Es un adjetivo y significa "diferente o el segundo de dos cosas". Podemos usarlo cuando hablamos del singular o plural.

I can't find my **other** key – no puedo encontrar mi otra llave.

Do you have any **other** questions? - ¿tienes alguna otra pregunta?

Yes, there are other questions to answer. – sí, hay otras preguntas para contestar.

No, I don't have any more questions. – no, no tengo más preguntas.

I want the *other* basket of apples – quiero la otra canasta de manzanas.

También puede usarse con "*one – ones*" cuando el significado es claro por el contexto anterior.

I don't like this dog. I prefer *the other one* – no me gusta este perro. Prefiero el otro.

These shoes are nice, but *the other ones* look better – estos zapatos son lindos, pero los otros son mejores.

También podemos usar "*the other – the others*" como pronombres para referirnos a personas o cosas.

The others (the other people) are always ready – los demás siempre están listos.

Where are *the others*? - ¿Dónde están los demás?

The others are not here – los demás no están aquí.

I want juice, but *the others* prefer wine – quiero jugo, pero los otros (los demás) prefieren vino.

You have one, and I am going to have *the other* – tú tienes uno y yo voy a tomar el otro.

Each other – ambos
They love *each other* – se aman ambos / el uno al otro.

Regular verbs – Verbos regulares
To happen – *happened* – suceder / ocurrir / pasar
To remember – *remembered* - recordar
To weigh – *weighed* - pesar
To kill – *killed* - matar
To rob – *robbed* – robar / atracar
To sign – *signed* - firmar

To thank – *thanked* - agradecer
To try – *tried* – tratar / intentar
To borrow – *borrowed* – tomar prestado *(se toma prestado algo de alguien)*
To carry – *carried* – cargar / llevar
To dial – *dialed* - marcar
To exchange – *exchanged* – intercambiar

Irregular verbs – Verbos irregulares
To begin – *began* – empezar / comenzar
To hang up – *hung up* - colgar
To hear – *heard* - escuchar
To ring – *rang* – sonar
To lend – *lent* – prestar *(se presta algo a alguien)*
To break – *broke* - romper
To catch – *caught* – atrapar / agarrar
To choose – *chose* – elegir / escoger
To lie – *lay* – yacer / tenderse
To steal – *stole* - robar
To wake up – *woke up* - despertarse
To lose – *lost* - perder
To put – *put* - poner
To win – *won* - ganar

Adverbs - Adverbios
Even – aun / incluso
Someday – algún día
Ever – alguna vez / una vez
Inside - dentro
Outside - fuera
Suddenly – de repente
Again – de nuevo / otra vez

Adjectives – Adjetivos

A few – un poco

Representa una idea positiva y seguida del plural.

I have *a few* books – tengo pocos libros.

They still have *a few* good products – ellos aún tienen unos pocos productos buenos.

Si usamos *"few"* solo sin el artículo *"a"*, entonces denota una idea negativa, significando *"casi nada"*.

I have *few* good friends – tengo pocos amigos *(denotando que no tiene muchos amigos y que le gustaría tener más).*

Awful – terrible / horrible
Crazy – loco / descabellado
Exciting – emocionante / excitante
Funny – divertido / gracioso
Political - político
Asleep – dormido / adormecido
Collect – recolecta / colecta

The Champion

How can someone prepare to be a good politician—through sports, through fighting? Ask boxing champion Vitali Klitschko. His childhood dream was to be like Bruce Lee. And he did become a sports hero. He is very tall, he has long arms, and he has a strong chin. But he also has special training techniques that allow him to use a different strategy for each person he fights. He lost only two professional fights, and those losses were because of injuries—a cut above his eye and a shoulder injury; no one knocked him down. Vitali is the one who is famous for knockouts.

In real life, he is a champion in more than fighting. He was the first professional boxing world champion with a PhD. Vitali's brother followed in his footsteps, becoming world boxing champion and earning a doctorate in sports science. The two brothers work together in other areas as well.

So what prepares a boxing champion to be successful in politics? Is it strategy? Vitali also plays chess. He says that "chess is similar to boxing [because] you need to develop a strategy, and you need to think two or three steps ahead [of] . . . your opponent." The difference between chess and boxing, he says, is that in chess "nobody is an expert, but everybody plays. In boxing everybody is an expert, but nobody fights." And in politics? Who are the experts in politics?

Vitali Klitschko became involved in the Ukrainian democratic opposition movement. While he served in parliament, he protested against the president, Yanukovych. In that fight, around 100 protesters lost their lives before a peace deal promised new elections. The champion of human rights is now the mayor of Kiev, in Ukraine. When two political groups **merged** in 2015, Klitschko became the party leader. He says that what Ukraine needs is for everyone to have a decent job, to bring home enough money to live comfortably. Ukraine needs to honor those who gave their lives in the revolution of 2014 in order to make Ukraine a modern European democratic country.

Exercises – Ejercicios

Exercise 3.1: Write "another," "the other," or "each other."

Example: They're so funny! The girls are teaching _each other_ how to dance.

1. Would you like _____ piece of cake? We have a lot of cake!
2. Your parents are so nice. I can see they really love _____.
3. I don't want the blue pen. It doesn't work. I want _____ one.

4. I'm sorry to bother you again. Could you give me_____ coin? The machine didn't start.

5. I didn't buy the purple dress. I got _____ one.

Exercise 3.2: Max offends people with his direct questions. Rewrite the questions as indirect questions, to make them more polite.

Where is the restroom? _Do you know where the restroom is?_

1. Why is the bank closed?

_____

2. How can I rent a boat?

----

3.   When does the boat come back?

----

4.   Where are the other boats?

----

5.   Who is the manager?

Exercise 3.3: Norman is a know-it-all. Write sentences with "I know."

Example 1:   "Why did Marcus leave?"   _I know why he left._

Example 2:   "How do we get to the zoo?" _I know how to get there._

1.   "Where is the park?"

----

2.   "When does the movie start?"

----

3.   "What should I do?"

----

4. "Who is your dad calling?"

_____

5. "Where is your sister going?"

_____

Exercise 3.4: Write the best word.
anyone   anything   everyone   nobody
    nothing   something
Example: One the table? There's _nothing_ on the table.

1. I couldn't find _____ to eat.

2. _____ told me yesterday was your birthday.

3. I need _____ to open the box with.

4. I didn't see _____.

5. I thought you were sick. _____ said you were sick.

🔒 Lesson 4
Going for a walk – Dar un paseo

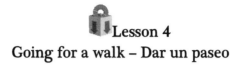Conversation 1

Mattie: Wow, you look terrible, Hannah!

Hannah: Thanks a lot!

Mattie: What's the matter?

Hannah: Oh, everything. Everything's the matter.

Mattie: Do you want to go for a walk? You might feel better.

Hannah: Okay. I've just had a terrible day.

Mattie: Tell me about it.

Hannah: Well, first, I don't like my haircut at all, so it took me forever to do my hair. So then I was late for work, and my boss gave me a speech about the importance of punctuality. My project was somehow erased from the computer system, and I lost two hours while the IT man worked to recover it. So then I had to stay late to finish. Then I missed the bus and had to walk home. The next bus didn't stop for me, but it splashed mud all over me. And now, I tried to wash my clothes, but the washing machine won't start. So now I have to handwash the laundry. I don't know how it could be worse.

Mattie: Um, I just felt something wet.

Hannah: Wet? Water? Great! Now, it's raining!

And my clothes are on the clothesline.

Conversation 2

Julie: [*Doorbell rings*]Hi, neighbor!

Luther: Hi, Julie. Are you ready to go?

Julie: Yep. Thanks. I see you washed your car. It looks great!

Luther: Thanks. So what have you done today?

Julie: Well, I just basically got ready to go out.

Luther: Really? That's all you did? *[laughs]*

Julie: Well, yeah. It's my day off, so I usually just work on my graduate class. But today was more relaxed. I ironed my clothes while the washing machine was running. I curled my hair while I washed the dishes. I thought of ideas for my homework while I mopped. And I did my makeup while the floor was drying.

Luther: So you did the laundry, did your hair, did the dishes, did your homework, did your makeup, and washed the floors, but you didn't really do anything. You work hard, don't you?

Julie: That's kind of you to say so. What did you do today?

Luther: Well, you know I have a difficult case right now, so I mainly spent my time researching similar cases to find some inspiration.

Julie: When do you get out of work?

Luther: At three.

Julie: Really? That's early.

Luther: Yeah, that gave me time to get a haircut and a shave.

Julie: That's nice. So hey, my mom asked me what I was doing, and I said I was going out with the neighbor. And she said, "Going out? On a date?" And I laughed.

Luther: Haha.

Julie: So . . .

Luther: [smiles]/So . . . . ?

Julie: Is this a date?

Conversation 3

Jake: Got everything?

Nate: Yep. Let's go.

Jake: All right. Now, you have the map, the compass, the water, and a first-aid kit, right?

Nate: First-aid kit? Where are we going?

Jake: Well, you never know. Better safe than sorry.

Nate: All right. I'll go get it. Just a second.

Jake: Let's go.

Nate: There aren't any snakes up there, are there?

Jake: No, I don't think so.

Nate: You don't think so? Have you ever seen any?

Jake: No, but I've never been on that trail before.

Nate: You've never gone there before?

Jake: No. But they say it's great.

Nate: I hope so. Did you bring any food?

Jake: No.

Nate: Neither did I.

Jake: If we're lucky, maybe we'll find some poison mushrooms.

Nate: Very funny.

Jake: So, how are you doing at work?

Nate: Great. My boss thinks I'm pretty good. He has me installing roofs.

Jake: You're quite the success, huh?

Nate: I'm doing okay. So are you sure this is the right way?

Jake: I think so.

Nate: That's comforting. There isn't a clear path. And I'm afraid one of these rocks might slip and I could faa-aa-aall *[falling].*

Jake: Now, aren't you glad we brought the first-aid kit?

Nate: Yeah, I guess so. Let's just wrap up my ankle and go back down.

Jake: Go back down? We're just getting started.

Nate: Well, I'm done. I have to—oh, no! Now, I won't be able to get up on the roof tomorrow.

Jake: I guess not. I'm sorry about that.

Nate: Oh, it's okay, I guess. I have to call my boss though. He's not going to be happy about this. I've already missed three days of work this month. . . . *[calling boss]* Hey, Fred, I have some bad news. I think I've sprained my ankle. Yeah, *[laughs]* I'm okay on the roof, but an absolute failure at mountain climbing. The thing is, I don't think I could get up on the roof tomorrow. . . . No, I mean, I can still finish the job. I just need to let my ankle heal first. . . . *Yeah.*

Thanks. See you tomorrow.

New words – Nuevas palabras

Ashtray - cenicero

Boss - jefe

Dish - plato

Failure - fracaso

Faucet – llave / grifo

Leg - pierna

Neighbor - vecino

Past - pasado

Present - presente

Success - éxito

Water - agua

Date – fecha / cita (cuando vamos a divertirnos con alguien con interes romantico)

Haircut – corte de pelo

Housework – tareas del hogar

Invitation – invitación

Laundry – lavandería

Mountain - montaña

Plate – plato (refiriéndose al recipiente)

Shave - afeitada

Swimming – natación

Umbrella – sombrilla / paraguas

Walk - caminata

Washing machine – lavadora

Appointment – cita (mayormente refiriéndose a negocios y no diversión)

Both – ambos

Quiche - Tarta de huevo (usualmente con carge o vegetales)

Word Definitions

Just: *now, a few minutes ago.*

To look: *to turn your eyes so you can see. To go and see.*

Neighbor: *a person who lives near you.*

To miss: *regret the absence or loss. Fail to be present at or for. Fail to hit or strike.*

Haircut: *an act or instance of cutting the hair. The style in which the hair is cut and worn, especially men's hair.*

To invite: *to ask someone to go somewhere.*

Phrases and Expressions - Frases y expresiones

To do (wash) the dishes – lavar los platos

To do your homework – hacer la tarea

To do the housework – hacer los deberes de la casa

To do the laundry – lavar la ropa

To get a haircut – recortarse el pelo

To get a shave - afeitarse

To go for a drive – dar un paseo en vehículo

To go for a meal – salir a comer

To go for a swim – salir a nadar

To go for a walk – salir a caminar

That's quite all right – está muy bien. Está bien, no hay inconvenientes.

That's very kind of you – es muy gentil (amable) de tu parte.

Grammar – Gramática

Hemos aprendido los tiempos gramaticales más

importantes y primordiales. Estamos listos para hablar del "*presente perfecto*".

Present perfect tense – Tiempo presente perfecto.
Ya somos expertos, de modo que no tienen que alarmarse. El presente perfecto funciona igual que en español. Se usa la conjugación de "*to have – haber*" en presente más el *pasado participio* del verbo.
En inglés a diferencia del español, el pasado simple de los verbos regulares es el mismo que el pasado participio; en otras palabras es mucho más fácil en inglés. Solo debemos aprender el pasado participio de los verbos irregulares. Veamos un ejemplo.

I *kissed* the princess – besé a la princesa.
I *have kissed* the princess – he besado a la princesa.

Structure of the Present perfect – Estructura del presente perfecto.
Affirmative - afirmativo
I *have (I've) walked* – he caminado
You *have (you've) walked* – has caminado
He *has (he's) walked* – ha caminado
She *has (she's) walked* – ha caminado
We *have (we've) walked* – hemos caminado
You *have (you've) walked* – han caminado
They *have (they've) walked* – han caminado

Negative – negativo
I *haven't walked* – no he caminado
You *haven't walked* – no has caminado
He *hasn't walked* – no ha caminado
She *hasn't walked* – no ha caminado

We *haven't walked* – no hemos caminado
You *haven't walked* – no han caminado
They *haven't walked* – no han caminado

Questions – preguntas

Have I *walked?* - ¿he caminado?
Have you *walked?* - ¿has caminado?
Has he *walked?* - ¿ha caminado?
Has she *walked?* - ¿ha caminado?
Have we *walked?* - ¿hemos caminado?
Have you *walked?* - ¿han caminado?
Have they *walked?* - ¿han caminado?

Como pueden ver, no es nada complicado; de hecho es más fácil que en español y la estructura funciona igual que en el idioma español. Practiquemos un poco este tiempo con verbos regulares e irregulares en el pasado participio.

I've already ***been*** there – ya he estado ahí.
I ***haven't been*** there yet – aún no he estado ahí.
I've just ***been*** there – acabo de estar ahí.
I've never ***been*** there – nunca he estado ahí.
Have you ever ***been*** there? - ¿alguna vez has estado allí?
No, never – no, nunca.
Yes, a few times – si, algunas veces.

Have you ever ***studied*** English? - ¿alguna vez has estudiado inglés?
Yes, *I've* already ***studied*** English – sí, ya he estudiado inglés.

No, *I have* never *studied* English – no, nunca he estudiado inglés.

I've just *studied* English – acabo de estudiar inglés.

Es bastante sencillo; solo necesitamos practicar.

Recuerden algunas notas importantes sobre estas palabras que hemos estado usando, dándole un mejor sentido a la oración.

Yet – todavía / aun
Solo se usa en preguntas y respuestas negativas. Y usualmente viene al final de la oración.

Just – solo / reciente
Siempre viene entre en verbo auxiliar "have / has" y el verbo principal.

Already – ya
Se usa en cualquier lugar.

Ever / never – alguna vez / nunca.
Solo se usa en preguntas y respuestas negativas y viene después del verbo auxiliar.

Past participle – Pasado participio
Existen cinco tipos de pasados participios en inglés.
El pasado participio de los verbos regulares, que es el mismo que el pasado simple.
To walk – *walked* – *walked* - caminar
To kiss – *kissed* – *kissed* - besar
To ask – *asked* – *asked* – pedir / preguntar
To have – *had* – *had* - tener
To clean – *cleaned* – *cleaned* - limpiar
To describe – *described* – *described* - describir
To fix – *fixed* – *fixed* – arreglar / reparar
To iron – *ironed* – *ironed* - planchar

To look – *looked* – *looked* – mirar / observar
To turn – *turned* – *turned* – girar / voltear
To wash – *washed* – *washed* - lavar
To worry – *worried* – *worried* - preocuparse
To invite – *invited* – *invited* - invitar
To miss – *missed* – *missed* – extrañar / faltar / errar
To refuse – *refused* – *refused* - rehúsar
To shave – *shaved* – *shaved* – afeitar

En el pasado participio algunos verbos usan la misma forma del pasado simple.

To feel – *felt* – *felt* - sentir
To tell – *told* – *told* - decir

El pasado participio de algunos verbos que es el mismo que el infinitivo.

To come – *came* – *come* - venir
To hit – *hit* – *hit* - golpear
To run – *ran* – *run* - correr
To become – *became* – *become* - convertirse

El pasado participio de algunos verbos que termina en "En, N".

To give – *gave* – *given* - dar
To fly – *flew* – *flown* - volar
To go – *went* – *gone* - ir
To break – *broke* – *broken* - romper
To choose – *chose* – *chosen* - escoger
To do – *did* – *done* - hacer
To drive – *drove* – *driven* - conducir
To eat – *ate* – *eaten* - comer
To forget – *forgot* – *forgotten* - olvidar
To get – *got* – *gotten* - obtener
To know – *knew* – *known* - saber

To lie – *lay* – *lain* - recostarse
To see – *saw* – *seen* – mirar / ver
To show – *showed* – *shown* - mostrar
To speak – *spoke* – *spoken* - hablar
To steal – *stole* – *stolen* – robar / hurtar
To take – *took* – *taken* – tomar / llevar
To wear – *wore* – *worn* - usar
To write – *wrote* – *written* - escribir
To be – *was / were* – *been* – ser o estar

El participio de algunos verbos que tienen "i" en el presente "a" en el pasado "u" en el participio.
To begin – *began* – *begun* – iniciar / comenzar
To sing – *sang* – *sung* - cantar
To swim – *swam* – *swum* - nadar
To drink – *drank* – *drunk* - beber
To ring – *rang* – *rung* - sonar

Aprendamos muy bien esta lista y el patrón mencionado, puesto que todos los verbos forman parte de una de estas cuatro divisiones. Continuemos practicando un poco más.

Has she *spoken* with you? - ¿ha ella hablado contigo?

Yes, she *has* already *spoken* with me – sí, ella ya ha hablado conmigo.

No, she *hasn't spoken* to me yet – no, ella aún no ha hablado conmigo.

What *have* you *told* them? - ¿qué les has dicho?

I *haven't told* them anything yet – aún no les digo nada.

I've told them the truth – les dije la verdad.

What *have* you *done?* - ¿Qué has hecho?
I *haven't done* anything – no he hecho nada.
I *have done* what you asked – he hecho lo que me pediste.

Have you *been* to Paris? - ¿has ido a Paris?
Yes, *I've* already *been* to Paris – sí, ya he estado en Paris.
Yes, *I've* just *come* from Paris – sí, acabo de llegar de Paris.
No, I *haven't been* to Paris yet – no, aún no he ido a Paris.
I *have* never *been* to Paris - nunca he estado en Paris.

Recuerden,
Usamos el pasado simple cuando algo ya no volverá a pasar, es decir, se quedó en el pasado.

Usamos el presente perfecto cuando pudiera volver o no a pasar, pero existe la posibilidad. Ya hemos aprendido el presente perfecto. Practiquemos y hablemos.

Have to – tener que
Ya vimos el verbo "*to have – tener*". Solo vamos a repasar un concepto muy sencillo cuando usamos "have + infinitive". Cuando usamos el "have" con el infinitivo del verbo, lo traducimos como "tener que". Veamos algunos ejemplos.

I *have to study* English – tengo que estudiar inglés.
She *doesn't have to study* hard – ella no tiene que

estudiar duro.

I *had to study* yesterday – tuve que estudiar ayer.

I *am going to have to study* tomorrow voy a tener que estudiar mañana.

I *used to have to study* hard – solia tener que estudiar duro.

I've had to study hard all my life – he tenido que estudiar duro toda mi vida.

Vean la estructura en todos los tiempos, y practiquen. Su nivel de inglés es asombroso. Si han asimilado el contenido correctamente hasta ahora, ustedes están hablando inglés casi fluido.

Adverbs – Adverbios
Actually – realmente / en realidad
Fortunately - afortunadamente
Perhaps – tal vez
Soon - pronto
Unfortunately - desafortunadamente

Adjectives – Adjetivos
Electric - eléctrico
Great - grandioso
Kind – amable - bondadoso
Serious - serio

Exercises – Ejercicios
Exercise 4.1: Write the verb in the present perfect (have/has + past participle).
Example: "I_'ve_ just _finished_ my homework (finish)." / "Great! Do you want to go see a movie?"

1. "_____ you _____ any lunch (have)?" / "No." / "Do you want to go out to eat?"

2. "Did you find your keys?" / "I _____n't _____ for them yet (look)."

3. "I_____ _____ my dress shoes (ruin)!" / "Oh, no. What are you going to wear for your speech?"

4. "My parents _____ _____ the house (sell)." / "Wonderful! Now they can move to Florida."

5. "Do you want to see the new science fiction movie?" / "No, I_____ already _____ it (see)."

6. "_____ you_____ _____ to Charleston (be)?" / "Yes, it's beautiful!"

7. "Do you want some quiche?" / "Yes, please. I_____ never _____ it before (try)."

8. "Do you like your new pants?" / "I _____n't _____ them yet (wear)."

9. "_____ you ever _____ on an international flight (fly)?" / "No, just national ones."

10.

11. "I _____ _____ the computer (fix). You can use it now." / "Thanks so

much!"

Exercise 4.2: Underline the correct vocabulary word.

1. My hair is really long. I need a (**haircut** / **meal** / **homework**).

2. Wow! This place is really dirty. We need to do some (**swim, homework, housework**).

3. Oh, no! The test is tomorrow, and I didn't do my (**haircut** / **homework** / **housework**).

4. I need some exercise. Let's go for a (**shave** / **swim** / **meal**).

5. I need a change of **scenery**. Let's go for a (**haircut** / **meal** / **drive**).

Exercise 4.3: Underline the correct word.

1. Have you (**ever/yet**) been to New York?

2. I have (**ever/already**) eaten lunch. I'm not hungry.

3. I've (**never/yet**) seen the ocean. I want to go next year.

4. What have you done lately? I've (**never/just**) finished writing a book.

5. Have you done your homework (**just/yet**)? There's a lot to do!

Lesson 5
Getting sick - Enfermandose

Conversation 1

Josh: Hi, Gene, how are you?

Gene: I'm okay. I have a little bit of a headache with all the work planning this dinner.

Josh: I'm sorry, but I'm afraid I feel worse than you.

Gene: Really? What's the matter?

Josh: I think I have the flu.

Gene: Are you throwing up?

Josh: Yeah, and I woke up in the middle of the night with nausea, so I took some pills. And now I have diarrhea.

Gene: Maybe you ate something that bothered your stomach.

Josh: Yeah, that must be it.

Gene: Well, I guess you'd better get some rest. Do you have ginger ale?

Josh: No, why? Is that good for the flu?

Gene: It really helps an upset stomach. Do you have a convenience store nearby?

Josh: Yeah. Just down the street.

Gene: Okay. Get yourself some ginger ale and salty crackers. Or you could eat some chicken noodle soup. When you're feeling a little better, you can eat rice, bananas, or toast, too.

Josh: I have some bean soup. How about that?

Gene: Bad idea, Josh. Stick to the crackers for now if you don't want to feel worse.

Conversation 2

Paul: All right, Shane, are you done studying? Let me give you a little quiz. Let's see. Let's say I have a sore throat.

Shane: No other symptoms?

Paul: No.

Shane: Take a little tea with honey and lemon.

Paul: Okay. And for a stomachache?

Shane: Well, it depends on the cause: you might have a virus or you could have eaten something that you need to get out of your system.

Paul: All right. And if I have a runny nose, sore throat, and a backache?

Shane: Sounds like a cold. Take some cough medicine and get a lot of rest.

Paul: Yep. And what if I feel dreamy and depressed?

Shane: Dreamy and depressed? Sounds like a sickness of the heart. Are you in love?

Paul: No, unfortunately. Well, you might pass your test. But you should probably keep studying all night. Do you have any symptoms?

Shane: Yeah. A pain-in-the-neck roommate!

Paul: Glad to help!

New words – Nuevas palabras
Ashtray - cenicero
Boss - jefe
Dish - plato
Failure - fracaso
Faucet – llave / grifo
Leg - pierna
Neighbor - vecino
Past - pasado
Present -presente
Success - éxito
Water - agua
Date – fecha / cita (cuando vamos a divertirnos con alguien con interes romantico)
Haircut – corte de pelo
Housework – tareas del hogar
Invitation – invitación
Laundry – lavandería
Mountain - montaña
Plate – plato (refiriéndose al recipiente)
Shave - afeitada
Swimming – natación
Umbrella – sombrilla / paraguas
Walk - caminata
Washing machine – lavadora
Appointment – cita (mayormente refiriéndose a negocios y no diversión)
Both – ambos
Quiche - Tarta de huevo (usualmente con carge o vegetales)

Word Definitions

Tasty: Having good flavor; yummy, delicious

Prescription: orders from the doctor for behavior or medicine to take

To examine to look over in order to evaluate

Patient: person being examined or treated by a doctor

Disease: serious illness

Flu: a virus causing vomiting and possibly diarrhea

Fever: consistently high temperature

Love at first sight: a romantic inclination that began from the first meeting

Phrases and Expressions - Frases y expresiones

Bless you – salud / bendición

Love at first sight – amor a primera vista

To be a pain in the neck – ser un fastidio

To be in love – estar enamorado

Different from – diferente de

To get sick - enfermarse

To get well - mejorarse

To get a disease – contraer una enfermedad

To have a look at – dar una mirada (ojeada)

To have an operation - operarse

To take someone's temperature – tomar la temperatura de alguien

What's wrong with…? - ¿Cuál es el problema con…? ¿Qué pasa con…?

The cost of living – el costo de la vida

To know why – saber el por qué

To understand why – entender el por qué

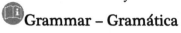Grammar – Gramática

Ya hemos visto el *"would like"*, que es una forma del condicional. Veamos el *"would"* como condicional en su forma completa. Como verán, ya saben usarlo, aun antes de explicárselo. Pero les daremos un repaso para mejor aprendizaje.

Would - condicional

Podemos usarlo con cualquier verbo; para la estructura usaremos el verbo "to go". Recuerden que el condicional demuestra una posibilidad, sugerencia o invitación y equivale a la terminación "ría" en español.

Affirmative – afirmativo

I would (I'd) go – yo iría
You would (you'd) go – tú irías
He would (he'd) go – él iría
She would (she'd) go – ella iría
We would (we'd) go – nosotros iríamos
You would (you'd) go – ustedes irían
They would (they'd) go – ellos / ellas irían

Negative – negativo

I wouldn't go – yo no iría
You wouldn't go – tú no irías
He wouldn't go – él no iría
She wouldn't go – ella no iría
We wouldn't go – nosotros no iríamos
You wouldn't go – ustedes no irían
They wouldn't go – ellos / ellas no irían

Questions – preguntas
Would I go? - ¿iría yo?
Would you go? - ¿irías tú?
Would he go? - ¿iría él?
Would she go? - ¿iría ella?
Would we go? - ¿iríamos nosotros?
Would you go? - ¿irían ustedes?
Would they go? - ¿irían ellos / ellas?

Would you go with me to the movies tonight? - ¿irías conmigo al cine esta noche?
Yes, I'd go with you. – Sí, iría contigo.
No, I wouldn't go with you – no, no iría contigo.

I would go with you, but I don't have time – iría contigo, pero no tengo tiempo.
I would study with you, but I don't have the book – estudiaría contigo, pero no tengo el libro.
I would buy the book, but I do not have money – compraría el libro, pero no tengo dinero.
Como pueden ver, ya sabían cómo usarlo; la estructura o patrón es el mismo que usamos anteriormente. Practiquen lo más que puedan y hablen en todo momento.

Comparing people and things with adjectives – Comparando personas y cosas con adjetivos.
Cuando queremos comparar personas o cosas, siempre tenemos que usar el comparativo. Existen tres grados del comparativo como veremos mas abajo.

Equity – Igualdad

En español usamos la combinación *"tan... como"* para el comparativo de igualdad; en inglés usaremos *"as... as"*. Veamos.

You are *as* intelligent *as* you look – eres tan inteligente como pareces.

She is *as* tall *as* her sister – ella es tan alta como su hermana.

He is *as* ugly *as* his brother – él es tan feo como su hermano.

Si queremos usar el comparativo de igualdad en negativo, tenemos que usar *"not as...as"*.

He is *not as* ugly *as* his brother – él no es tan feo como su hermano.

She *isn't as* tall *as* her sister – ella no es tan alta como su hermana.

You are *not as* intelligent *as* you look – no eres tan inteligente como pareces.

Como ven, es bastante sencillo; el concepto es prácticamente el mismo que en español.

Superiority – Superioridad

En español usamos la combinación *"más...que"*; en inglés vamos a usar la combinación *"more...than"* y *"er...than"*

Cuando el adjetivo tiene *más de una sílaba*, entonces usamos "*more...than*".

She is *more* important *than* you – ella es más importante que tú.

She is *more* beautiful *than* her sister – ella es más hermosa que su hermana.

You are *more* intelligent *than* me – tú eres más inteligente que yo.

Cuando el adjetivo tiene *una sílaba, o termina en "y" o "ly"*, entonces usamos "*er...than*".

She is tall*er than* her sister – ella es más alta que su hermana.

He is smart*er than* his brother – él es más inteligente que su hermano.

They are fast*er than* us – ellos son más rápido que nosotros.

Cuando termina en "*y*"o "*ly*", cambiamos la "*y*" por una "*i*" y le agregamos "*er*".

We are happ*ier than* them – somos más felices que ellos.

I am angr*ier than* you – estoy más enojado que tú.

She is ugl*ier than* you – ella es más fea que tú.

They are bus*ier than* you – ellas estan más ocupadas que ustedes.

I am funn*ier than* you – soy más divertido que usted.

Si el adjetivo de una sílaba termina en una consonante, tenemos que duplicar la consonante final antes de agregarle "*er*".

The water today is hot*ter than* yesterday – el agua hoy está más caliente que ayer.

She is wett*er than* you – ella está más mojada que tú.

No olviden la parte más importante: cuando la palabra tenga *más de una sílaba* siempre usamos "*more...than*" cuando es de *una sola sílaba o termina en "y" o "ly"*, entonces usamos "*er...than*".

También podemos usar "more...than" con verbos.

I study more than you – estudio más que tú.

I used to go out more than you – acostumbraba a salir más que tú.

Usando "*more...than*" o "*er...than*" con adverbios.

I run fast*er than* you – corro más rápido que tú.

You are *more* careful *than* me – eres más cuidadoso que yo.

Inferiority – Inferioridad

En español usamos la combinación "menos...que"; en inglés usaremos "*less...than*". Es muy importante que comprendan el concepto de "*less...than*" solo se usa cuando hablamos de cosas que no podemos contar, como "information".

I have *less* information *than* you – tengo menos información que tú.

The apple cost *less than* I thought – la manzana costó menos de lo que pensé.

Como pueden ver, pueden usar una palabra en

medio de "less...than" o no; depende de ustedes.
The apple cost *less (money) than* I thought – la manzana costó menos de lo que pensé.
Para cosas contables, entonces tenemos que usar "*fewer...than*".
I have *fewer* books *than* you – tengo menos libros que tú.
I have *fewer than* five products – tengo menos de cinco productos.

Usando "less...than" con verbos.
I run *less than* you – corro menos que tú
I eat *less* now *than* I used to eat – ahora como menos que lo que acostumbraba a comer.

Como siempre, tenemos algunos que son irregulares y que tenemos que aprender de memoria.
Good / well – better - bueno
Bad – worse - malo
Little – less - poco
I am *better than* you – soy mejor que usted
She is *worse than* me – ella es peor que yo

Superlative – Superlativo
Como el nombre lo dice, el superlativo es para indicar que alguien o algo es lo máximo. En español usamos "*el más, el menos*". En inglés usamos "the" seguido de la terminación "est" para los regulares. Veamos las reglas en inglés.
Palabra o sílaba que termina en "e": le agregamos "st" para el superlativo.
She is *the nicest* girl in town – ella es la chica más

linda del pueblo.

She is *the fastest* runner in the marathon – ella es la corredora más rápida del maratón.

Palabras o sílabas con una sola vocal y una consonante al final: se le duplica la consonante final y se le agrega "est".

Nicauris is *the hottest* girl in town – Nicauris es la chica más caliente del pueblo.

He is *the tallest* guy in the class – él es el hombre más alto de la clase.

You are *the biggest* clown in the world – eres el payaso más grande del mundo.

Palabras con una sílaba, con más de una vocal o más de una consonante al final: solo se le agrega "est".

This is *the highest* mountain in the world – ésta es la montaña más alta del mundo.

Palabras de dos sílabas terminando en "y": cambiamos la "y" por una "i" y agregamos "est".

I am *the happiest* man in the world – soy el hombre más feliz del mundo.

You are *the ugliest* girl in town – eres la chica más fea del pueblo.

You are *the prettiest* girl in the class – eres la chica más linda de la clase.

Palabras de dos o más sílabas que no terminan en "y": usamos "*the most*".

We are *the most popular* people in town – somos las personas más populares de la ciudad.

Nicauris is *the most beautiful* girl in my town – Nicauris es la chica más hermosa de mi pueblo.

You are *the most important* person in my life –

eres la persona más importante en mi vida.

Irregular superlatives – Superlativos irregulares
Good / well – better – the best
Bad – worse – the worst
Little – less – the least

You are *the best* student in the class – eres el mejor estudiante de la clase.

You are *the worst* driver – eres el peor conductor.

You are *the least* important person in my life – eres la persona menos importante en mi vida.

Con esto hemos concluido la parte del comparativo y superlativo. Asegúrense de practicar los conceptos presentados y hagan los ejercicios; de esto depende el éxito de su aprendizaje.

Auxiliary verb "must" – Verbo auxiliar "must".

Ya hemos aprendido los diferentes usos del "have to"; ahora vamos a aprender el uso del "must", que tiene el mismo significado en español: "tener que – deber"; pero en inglés tiene diferencia en su uso. *Recuerden, NUNCA se usa "TO" después de "must".*

Expresando una obligación o un deber.

You *must* take your medicine – tienes que tomarte tu medicina.

You *must* wear your seatbelt while you're driving – debes usar tu cinturón de seguridad mientras conduces.

You *mustn't* speak on the phone while driving – no debes hablar por teléfono mientras conduces.

Enfatizando la necesidad de algo.

You *must* drive carefully – debes conducir con

cuidado.

You *must not* smoke, it is not good for your health – no debes fumar, no es bueno para tu salud.

She *must* study her lessons to learn English well – ella debe estudiar sus lecciones para aprender bien inglés.

Cuando estás seguro de que algo es cierto, una deducción segura.

Lo usamos cuando no sabemos, pero estamos seguros basados en hechos o experiencias.

Tiffany *must* be home. I heard some voices – Tiffany debe estar en casa. Escuché unas voces.

They *must* be hungry, it is 3 p.m., and they haven't eaten yet – ellos deben estar hambrientos, son las 3 p.m. y aún no han comido.

Dando una fuerte recomendación.

You *must* taste the food here – debes probar la comida de aquí.

We *must* get together sometimes – debemos juntarnos alguna vez.

You *must* hear "Messin' Around" by Pitbull. It is fantastic. – debes escuchar "Messin' around" de Pitbull; es fantástica.

Expresando suposiciones lógicas positivas "must+have+past participle".

It *must have rained* yesterday – debió haber llovido ayer.

You *must have won* the lottery with the new car you just bought – debiste haberte ganado la loto con el nuevo carro que acabas de comprar.

Yeiris *must have eaten* all the food; there's nothing left – Yeiris debió haberse comido toda la comida, no queda nada.

Recuerden, en sentido general cuando usamos "**must**"; éste indica algún tipo de obligación impuesto por el hablante.

En caso de que tengan que hacer alguna pregunta, entonces deben usar "**have to**"; el "**must**" por lo general no se usa para preguntar.

Adjectives – Adjetivos
Dry - seco
Easy – fácil
Friendly – amigable / amistoso
Healthy - saludable
Narrow - estrecho
Relaxed - relajado
Safe - seguro
Smart – inteligente / astuto / listo
Sour – agrio / amargo
Strange – extraño
Sweet - dulce
Tasty - sabroso
Wide - ancho
Comfortable – cómodo / confortable
Dangerous – peligroso
Difficult – difícil
Cheap - barato
Better - mejor
Glad – contento / alegre
Uncomfortable - incómodo
Economical - económico
Whole – todo / entero / total
Prepositions – Preposiciones

Because of – por motivo de
I cannot eat *because of* you – no puedo comer por ti (por tu culpa).

In the middle of – en medio de
The glass is *in the middle of* the table – el vaso está en medio de la mesa.

Since - desde
Expresa cuando inició algo que aún no ha terminado.

I've had this car *since* 2002 – he tenido esta carro desde el 2002.

I have been here *since* 1998 – he estado aquí desde el 1998.

New regular verbs – Nuevos verbos regulares
To compare – compared - compared - comparar
To visit – visited – visited - visitar
To breathe – breathed – breathed - respirar
To examine – examined – examined - examinar
To jump – jumped – jumped – saltar / brincar
To last – lasted – lasted – durar / perdurar
To smell – smelled – smelled - oler
To sneeze – sneezed – sneezed - estornudar
To taste – tasted – tasted – probar / saborear

New irregular verbs – Nuevos verbos irregulares
To hurt – hurt – hurt – lastimar / doler
To lie down – lay down – lain down - recostarse
To take off – took off – taken off – despegar / quitarse

To cost – cost – cost - costar
To find out – found out – found out - descubrir

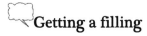**Getting a filling**

Gary called his friend's dental office in the middle of the afternoon. The secretary told him the dentist couldn't see him for two weeks. But Gary told her he had to see the dentist right away. He just couldn't take it anymore—his toothache was killing him. The secretary double-booked his appointment and told him they would try to fit him in that afternoon but she couldn't promise anything.

The dentist's waiting room was full when Gary got there. After a while, he was the only one left. And still, he waited. Finally, with only fifteen minutes left until closing, the dentist called him back.

"Gary, nice to see you. What's the matter?" asked the dentist. "Oh, it looks like you have a pretty bad cavity. You need a filling. Would you like me to schedule an appointment to fill your cavity?"

Gary asked, "Can't you do it now? It hurts so bad—more than any other toothaches I've ever had before."

"There really isn't time today. It's closing time."

"Please, Bill. I'd do anything to get rid of this pain."

"Tell you what. This is very unconventional, but I have a couple things I need to do tonight. If you can help me with one of them, I can fill your tooth.

"Sure. Bill, anything."

So the dentist filled his tooth. He first numbed Gary's gum. Then he used a syringe to insert an anesthetic so that the drilling wouldn't hurt. And it didn't hurt. Gary felt better than ever. Of course, his mouth was still numb.

"If you don't want to get a new filling every couple years, you must brush your teeth three times a day and floss," the dentist told Gary.

"So what's the favor you need?" Gary asked the dentist. He had to repeat himself a couple times. With his mouth numb, he was hard to understand.

"Ah," the dentist chuckled. "Mary wants a giant monster for her daughter's birthday party. I have the costume in the car."

"Are you serious?" Gary asked.

"Yes," the doctor answered. "That is one of two things I had to do tonight."

"What's the other thing," asked Gary, "if you don't mind telling me?"

"I have to write an article about time management. It's due tomorrow."

"I guess I'll enjoy being a monster more than writing an article!" Gary said, grateful at least to be feeling better.

Exercises – Ejercicios

Exercise 5.1: These sentences are missing something. Add *must (have)* or *have to* where appropriate.

1. It's 5:45. You leave now if you want to catch the bus.
2. I can't say no. My country needs me. I go.
3. Dan didn't come to work today. He be sick.
4. But, Mom, just look at all that snow! Do I

326

shovel the sidewalk?

5. Ingrid looks pretty happy. She finished her project.

Exercise 5.2: Say the same thing in other words.
Example: I love you more than I love chocolate. (as much as) I don't love chocolate as much as I love you.

1. John is taller than me. (short)
2. Chocolate bars cost less than chocolate chips. (more)
3. No one in the class is as smart as my boyfriend. (smart—superlative)
4. Our house is the least attractive house on the block. (ugly—superlative)
5. It's wetter inside than outside! (dry)

Exercise 5.3: Find the rest of the sentence. Write the letter.

1. _____ They would give you a discount,

2. _____ I would eat my vegetables,

3. _____ My dog would go to school,

4. _____ We would help you with your work,

5. _____ I would give you my ice cream,

6. _____ Mr. Smith would explain it to us,

a. but they won't let him in.

b.   but he was detained in traffic.
c.   but you have to take your ID card.
d.   but I need it for my sore throat.
e.   but they don't taste good.
f.   but we're really busy.

Lesson 6
Five star hotel – Hotel cinco estrella

Conversation 1

Customer: Good evening. I booked a room a couple weeks ago on the Internet.

Desk Clerk: Good evening. Can I have your name, please?

Customer: Here. It's on my card.

Desk Clerk: Did you use this card to book the room?

Customer: Yes.

Desk Clerk: Would you like me to charge the room on this card?

Customer: Yes.

Desk Clerk: Okay. You're all set. Room number 22C. Would you like me to show you to your room?

Customer: [30 minutes later] Hi. It's me again. I, well, it's the room. I asked for nonsmoking, but the room smells like smoke, and it's really bothering me. I just can't stand cigarette smoke.

Desk Clerk: Neither can I. We'll see if we can fix that for you. Which room were you in? . . . We'll have it ready in 10 minutes. I'll call your room when it's ready.

Customer: [Ring] Your new room is ready for you

now. Just come by the front desk for the key.

Desk Clerk: Here's your key. Sorry about the inconvenience. Will there be anything else?

Customer: Well, actually, is there anywhere I can buy a toothbrush? I can't believe I forgot my toothbrush.

Desk Clerk: It happens to everyone. Actually, I have a complimentary toothbrush I can give you. If you need any more towels or pillows or anything, just let me know. And you can call on the phone. You don't need to come to the desk.

Customer: No, five pillows is enough, thank you!

Conversation 2

Chad: Have you decided what to get Mom yet?

Sheryl: What to get Mom?

Chad: Yeah, you know, for Mother's Day.

Sheryl: Oh, no! I forgot. What are you getting her?

Chad: Well, you know, I've always sent her flowers. But I thought maybe the three of us could all go in together and buy Mom and Dad a night at the hotel by the lake.

Sheryl: Oh, that's a good idea. How much would it be?

Chad: Well, it'd cost us about $40 each.

Sheryl: That's not bad. Does it include a meal?

Chad: It includes continental breakfast, which is pretty nice there.

Sheryl: Yeah. What would it cost to include dinner, too?

Chad: I don't know. It'd depend on what she ordered.

Sheryl: Yeah, I guess so.

Chad: Actually, they have a snack room, and she can get a snack anytime.

Sheryl: Sounds good. Have you talked to Gina?

Chad: Yeah. She said she likes the idea.

Sheryl: Okay. Do you want me to reserve the room?

Chad: No, I'll do it. I'll use the points on my card to get the special price.

Sheryl: Oh, great. So I'll send you a check?

Chad: That works. Thanks, Sheryl. Oh, and Sheryl?

Sheryl: Yes?

Chad: Happy Mother's Day!

Sheryl: Thanks, Chad.

New words – Nuevas palabras
Blanket – frazada / cobija
Hair dryer – secador de pelo
Pillow - almohada
Pillowcase – funda (tapa) de almohada
Receipt – recibo
Service - servicio
Sheet – sábana
Star - estrella
Towel - toalla
Ball – pelota / bola
Doorbell – timbre de puerta
Envelope – sobre
Fool - tonto

Hole - hoyo
Race - carrera
Song – canción
Stamp – sello / estampilla
Telegram - telegrama
Brush - cepillo
Comb - peine
Father's day – día del padre
Mother's day – día de la madre
Electric razor – rasurador eléctrico
Pajamas - piyama
Pocket - bolsillo
Sea – mar
Stone – roca / piedra
Suggestion - sugerencia
Tennis racket – raqueta de tenis
Weight - peso
None - ninguno
During - durante
Except - excepto

Word Definitions
Tired of: when you don't like something or someone anymore.
Foot: one meter (3.28 feet)
Jump up and down: when you jump in the air and come down again.
Filthy: something very dirty.
Fool: a person who is not smart (not a good word)
To promise: to pledge that you will or will not do something. To give your word and commit to it.
Phrases and Expressions - Frases y expresiones

As soon as possible – lo antes posible
Not ... at all – no ... del todo
I am not happy at all – no estoy del todo contento /
no estoy para nada contento.

To do your best – hacer lo mejor, dar tu mejor
esfuerzo

To have something ready – tener algo listo

If you don't mind – si no te importa

What a fool! – que tonto

On business – de negocio

Full of – lleno de

To put on weight – subir de peso

To lose weight – perder peso

Up and down – arriba y abajo *(ir de una lugar a
otro, una y otra vez)*

To look like – parecerse / ser similar

How are things? - ¿Cómo están las cosas?

What's new? - ¿Qué hay de nuevo?

Grammar – Gramática

Como hemos visto en las lecciones anteriores
existen muchas formas de hablar sobre el futuro, al
igual que en español. Vamos a aprender el auxiliar
"will" y sus diferentes usos.

The future with "Will" – El futuro con "Will"
Affirmative - Afirmativo
I will – I'll
You will - you'll
He will - he'll
She will - she'll
We will - we'll

You will - you'll
They will - they'll
Negative – Negativo
I will not – I won't -
You will not - you won't -
He will not – he won't -
She will not – she won't -
We will not – we won't -
You will not - you won't -
They will not – they won't -

Questions - Preguntas
Will I? -
Will you? -
Will he? -
Will she? -
Will we? -
Will you? -
Will they? –

Como habrán podido ver, la forma contracta del afirmativo solo tiene que substituir la "wi" de *will* por un apostrofe en todos los pronombres. Para el negativo, la forma contracta es irregular: "*won't*". No lo olviden. "*will*" *siempre irá acompañado de otro verbo en su forma infinitiva sin el "to*". Vamos a ver los diferentes usos del "*will*" ahora.

Cuando hacemos predicciones sobre el futuro. Creemos o pensamos algo sobre el futuro.

You *will enjoy* her company, she is very funny. – disfrutarás de su compañía; ella es muy divertida.

I think it *will rain* tomorrow – creo que lloverá

mañana.

I think I *will win* the gold medal – creo que ganaré la medalla de oro.

Cuando decidimos hacer algo inmediato. Decisiones rápidas.

I'll pick you up now – te recogeré ahora

We'll call a taxi for you – llamaremos un taxi para ti.

I think *I will go* right now – creo que me iré ahora mismo *(acabo de tomar esa desición)*.

Cuando hacemos una promesa, amenaza, invitación, orden, solicitud u ofrecimiento.

If you say something, you *will regret* it – si dices algo, lo lamentarás.

I *will kill* you if you do something like that – te mataré si haces algo así

Don't worry. I *won't tell* anyone – no te preocupes. No se lo diré a nadie.

I *will do* my best to help you – haré todo lo posible para ayudarte.

I *will have* the documents ready for tonight – tendré los documentos listos para esta noche.

Will you help me? - ¿me ayudaras?

Will you have some cake? - ¿aceptarás un poco de bizcocho?

Cuando son acciones repetitivas o hábitos.

Yeiris *will fall asleep* as soon she starts reading – Yeiris se quedará dormida desde que comience a leer. *(ella siempre lo hace)*

My car *won't go* faster than this – mi carro no irá

más rápido de ahí *(siempre es así, es lo máximo que corre)*

Con algunas acciones y eventos pasando en el presente.
Will you have another glass of wine? - ¿quieres otro vaso de vino?
The car won't start – el carro no enciende.
The baby won't stop crying – el bebe no para de llorar.

Cuando alguien se rehúsa a hacer algo usamos "won't".
Your brother *won't listen* to anything I say – tu hermano no escuchará nada de lo que le diga.
I told her to clean the room, but I know she *won't do* it. – le dije que limpiara la habitación, pero sé que no lo hará.

Polite commands – Órdenes o mandatos de cortesía.
Si queremos que alguien haga o no haga algo, pero no conocemos a la persona bien, preguntamos.
Will you open the door, please? - ¿abrirás la puerta, por favor?
Would you open the door, please? - ¿abrirías la puerta, por favor?
Can you open the door, please? - ¿puedes abrir la puerta, por favor?
Could you open the door, please? - ¿podrías abrir la puerta, por favor?
También usamos esta forma para cuando conocemos la persona bien; esto demuestra cortesía

al hablar.

Cuando conocemos la persona bien, decimos también.

I want you to open the door – quiero que abras la puerta.

I don't want you to open the door – no quiero que abras la puerta.

I'd like you to open the door – me gustaría que abras la puerta.

I'd like you not to open the door – me gustaría que no abras la puerta.

Don't open the door – no abras la puerta.

Do not open the door – no abras la puerta.

Volunteering – Ofreciéndose como voluntario.

Cuando quieres saber si alguien quiere que hagas algo, pero no conoces bien a la persona, preguntas.

Do you want me to open the door? - ¿quiere usted que abra la puerta?

Do you want me not to open the door? - ¿quiere usted que no abra la puerta?

Would you like me to open the door? - ¿le gustaría que abra la puerta?

Would you like me not to open the door? - ¿le gustaría que no abra la puerta?

Si conoces bien a la persona, entonces puedes decir.

I'll open the door – abriré la puerta.

Let me open the door – déjame abrir la puerta.

Allow me to open the door – permíteme abrir la puerta.

Presten mucha atención a la estructura y forma tanto del afirmativo como del negativo.

The auxiliary verb "Should" – El verbo auxiliar "Should".

Usamos el verbo auxiliary "should" para hacer sugerencias. Es bastante fácil usarlo. Recuerden, después de "should" NUNCA usen "to" con los verbos. Siempre va acompañado de un verbo.

Affirmative – Afirmativo
I should
You should
He should
She should
We should
You should
They should

Questions – Preguntas
Should I?
Should you?
Should he?
Should she?
Should we?
Should you?
Should they?

Negative – Negativo
I should not – shouldn't
You should not – shouldn't
He should not – shouldn't

She should not – shouldn't
We should not – shouldn't
You should not – shouldn't
They should not – shouldn't

Dando consejos, recomendaciones o sugerencias.
You should go to the movies tonight – deberían ir al cine esta noche.
You should see a doctor about that problem – deberías ver un doctor acerca de ese problema.
You should comb your hair – deberías peinarte el cabello.

Expresando una situación que mayormente estaría pasando en el presente.
I am going to call Tiffany. She *should be* at home now – voy a llamar a Tiffany. Ella debería estar en casa ahora.
You *should have* the money. I sent it yesterday. – deberías tener el dinero. Lo envié ayer.

Expresando una situación que mayormente pasara en el futuro, una predicción.
She *should be* fine tomorrow – ella debería estar bien mañana.
France *should win* the cup, because their team is better. – Francia debería ganar la copa, porque su equipo es mejor.

Expresando una obligación más cortés y suave que con el "must".
You *should pay* more attention to my instructions – deberías prestar más atención a mis instrucciones.

You *should never lie* to your parents – nunca deberías mentirles a tus padres.

You *should be* here in 10 minutes – deberían estar aquí en 10 minutos.

Expresando cuando no se está cumpliendo con una obligación.
En este caso usamos "should+be+ing".

They *should be studying* for the exam – ellos deberían estar estudiando para el examen *(pero no lo están)*

You *should be taking* your pills – deberías estar tomándote tus pastillas *(pero no lo estás haciendo)*

She *should be looking after* the children – ella debería estar cuidando los niños *(pero no lo está haciendo)*

Expresando algo esperado en el pasado, pero que no pasó.
En esta caso usamos *"should+have+past participle".*

I *should have been* more understanding, but I wasn't. – debería haber sido más comprensible, pero no lo fui.

You *should have seen* her play the piano, but you didn't. – debiste haberla visto tocar el piano, pero no lo hiciste.

They *should have been* here, but they weren't. – ellos debieron haber estado aquí, pero no lo estuvieron.

Cuando estamos aconsejando a alguien que no haga algo, porque no es debido o es malo, usamos "shouldn't".

You *shouldn't talk* to your parents like that – no deberías hablarle a tus padres de ese modo.

You *shouldn't be* here now – no deberías estar aquí ahora *(es peligroso o indebido)*

He *shouldn't smoke* – él no debería fumar (es perjudicial para su salud).

The verb "to get" – El Verbo "to get".

Hemos visto en el transcurso de las lecciones pasadas como se usa el verbo "to get" para formar otros verbos y expresiones. Este es un verbo que tenemos que prestarle mucha atención, debido a que se usa mucho en inglés y puede ayudarnos a formar cualquier oración.

To look for and find – buscar y encontrar.

I am going *to get a job* – voy a conseguir un trabajo.

To look and buy – buscar y comprar.

I am going *to get a book* – voy a comprar un libro.

To receive something – recibir algo.

I *got an email* from Nicauris – recibí un email de Nicauris.

To catch someone – atrapar a alguien.

I am going to get you – voy a atraparte.

Existen muchísimas cosas que podemos hacer y construir con el verbo "to get"; ya iremos adquiriendo esos conocimientos con la práctica.

Adjectives "no / any" and Pronouns "None / Any" – Adjetivos "no / any" y Pronombres "none / any".

Vamos a ver como usamos estos dos adjetivos y pronombres. Es realmente sencillo. Presten mucha atención.

Estas cuatro oraciones significan lo mismo.
There is **no** cold water – no hay agua fría.
There is **none** – no hay nada.
There isn't **any** cold water – no hay nada de agua fría
There isn't **any** – no hay nada.

Estas cuatro oraciones significan lo mismo.
There are **no** napkins – no hay servilletas
There are **none** – No hay ninguna.
There aren't **any** napkins– no hay ninguna servilleta.
There aren't **any** – no hay ninguna.

Como pueden ver, el "no" siempre va a modificar una oración en afirmativo, dándole el sentido de la negación.
Siempre usaremos "any" en oraciones negativas.

Conjunctions – Conjunciones

Veamos como usamos las conjunciones "*So / too / neither / not … either*". Ya hemos visto el uso en lecciones pasadas. Vamos a dedicarles una corta sección con los diferentes tiempos y usos.

Affirmative – Afirmativo

I am sad – estoy triste
So am I – yo también
I am, too – yo también
I am working – estoy trabajando
So am I – yo también
I am, too – yo también
I *am going to sleep – voy a dormir*
So am I – yo también

I am, too – yo también
I was glad – estaba contento
So was I – yo también
I was, too – yo también
I like to cook – me gusta cocinar
So do I – a mí también
I do, too – a mí también
I went to law school – fui a la escuela de leyes.
So did I – yo también
I did, too – yo también
I have been to Paris – he ido a Paris.
So have I – yo también
I have, too – yo también
I can dance – puedo bailar
So can I – yo también
I can, too – yo también
I could speak when I was two – podía hablar
cuando tenía dos años
So could I – yo también
I could, too – yo también
I'll leave now – me iré ahora
So will I – yo también
I will, too – yo también
She would love to sing – a ella le encantaría cantar
So would he – a él también
He would, too – a él también
I should leave now – debería irme ahora
So should I – yo también
I should, too – yo también
I must work soon – debo trabajar pronto
So must I – yo también
I must, too – yo también

Recuerden que pueden usar cualquier pronombre personal con esta estructura. Es muy usada, de modo que les recomiendo que la estudien muy bien y la practiquen.

Negative – Negativo
I am not sad – no estoy triste
Neither am I – ni yo tampoco
I am not either – ni yo tampoco
I am not working – no estoy trabajando
Neither am I – ni yo tampoco
I am not either – ni yo tampoco
I *am not going to sleep – no voy a dormir*
Neither am I – ni yo tampoco
I am not either – ni yo tampoco
I wasn't glad – no estaba contento
Neither was I – ni yo tampoco
I wasn't either – ni yo tampoco
I don't like to cook – no me gusta cocinar
Neither do I – ni a mí tampoco
I don't either – ni a mí tampoco
I didn't go to law school – no fui a la escuela de leyes.
Neither did I – ni yo tampoco
I didn't either – ni yo tampoco
I haven't been to Paris – no he ido a Paris.
Neither have I – ni yo tampoco
I haven't either – ni yo tampoco
I can't dance – no puedo bailar
Neither can I – ni yo tampoco
I can't either – ni yo tampoco
I couldn't speak when I was two – no podía hablar

cuando tenía dos años
Neither could I – ni yo tampoco
I couldn't either – ni yo tampoco
I won't leave now – no me iré ahora
Neither will I – ni yo tampoco
I won't either – ni yo tampoco
*She wouldn't love to sing – a ella no le encantaría
cantar*
Neither would he – ni a él tampoco
He wouldn't either – ni a él tampoco
I shouldn't leave now – no debería irme ahora
Neither should I – ni yo tampoco
I shouldn't either – ni yo tampoco
I mustn't work soon – no debo trabajar pronto
Neither must I – ni yo tampoco
I mustn't either – ni yo tampoco
Recuerden que cuando usan "neither", la oración esta en afirmativo; con el uso del "neither", damos en sentido de la negación.

Adjectives – Adjetivos
Blanket – frazada / cobija
Hair dryer – secador de pelo
Pillow - almohada
Pillowcase – funda (tapa) de almohada
Receipt – recibo
Service - servicio
Sheet – sábana
Star - estrella
Towel - toalla
Ball – pelota / bola
Doorbell – timbre de puerta

Envelope – sobre
Fool - tonto
Hole - hoyo
Race - carrera
Song – canción
Stamp – sello / estampilla
Telegram - telegrama
Brush - cepillo
Comb - peine
Father's day – día del padre
Mother's day – día de la madre
Electric razor – rasurador eléctrico
Pajamas - piyama
Pocket - bolsillo
Sea – mar
Stone – roca / piedra
Suggestion - sugerencia
Tennis racket –   raqueta de tenis
Weight - peso
None - ninguno
During - durante
Except – excepto

Adverbs – Adverbios
In a minute – en un minute / muy pronto
Right now – ahora mismo /inmediatamente
Later – más tarde / luego

New regular verbs – Nuevos verbos regulares
To apologize – apologized – apologized – ofrecer disculpas, disculparse
To change – changed – changed - cambiar

To complain – complained – complained - quejarse
To close – closed – closed - cerrar
To cry – cried – cried - llorar
To promise – promised – promised - prometer
To turn up – turned up – turned up – subir el volumen
To turn down – turned down – turned down – bajar el volumen
To brush – brushed – brushed - cepillar
To comb – combed – combed - peinarse
To shout – shouted – shouted – gritar / vocear / vociferar

New irregular verbs – Nuevos verbos irregulares

To keep – kept – kept – mantener / guardar
To throw – threw – thrown – arrojar / lanzar
To ride – rode – ridden – montar (bicicleta, caballo, etc.)

Celebrating Mother's and Father's day

For the mother of young children, Mother's Day may be one of the most ironic celebrations of the year. The media help everyone in the US remember to prepare for the second Sunday of May. The most difficult part of Mother's Day, however, is that there is no correct way to celebrate the day. Every child and husband wants Mom to feel unique and special.

Children don't have much money or experience to help them with getting an exciting gift. So Mom has to pretend she doesn't know what her children are doing as she provides the materials and cleans up afterwards. Often Dad can help, buying a cake or taking the family out to dinner. Without Dad's help, some children make their own inventions to honor Mother. They might make their own cards with special drawings, stickers, or glitter. They might take her breakfast in bed: burnt toast, runny eggs, or cereal with orange juice. Older children will make her a cake, but then sometimes the mother has to clean up the kitchen afterward. If the family doesn't have the surprise ready in time, Mother may be isolated from the others while they finish.

Husbands often buy their wives and mothers cards, jewelry, clothes, or flowers. Actually, flowers have been a tradition on Mother's Day for over a hundred years, particularly carnations. Churches and stores sometimes give out carnations on Mother's Day: red or pink are for women whose mother is still living, and white for women whose mother has died.

Father's Day, celebrated in the US on the third Sunday of June, has not become as popular as Mother's Day. It's usually up to Mom to make Daddy's day special. She might decorate the house with paper ties or give him a decorated set of his favorite treats. But it's harder to make something that Dad will like. Some dads enjoy cards or ties on this day. But many would prefer more expensive gifts: tools, cars, or fishing poles. So most fathers probably only get a special meal. And some dads just get a friendly phone call or best wishes.

Exercises – Ejercicios
Exercise 6.1: You're out of everything! Write _there_

isn't any more or *there aren't any more.* If it's countable, use the plural (*aren't*).

Example: Can I have some bread?   _There isn't any more._

1. I'd like some orange juice.

    _____

2. These French fries are cold. You should give me another box.   _____

3. Will you bring some of your brownies?

    _____

4. Can I borrow some tape?

    _____

5. Could you pass me the rolls?

    _____

Exercise 6.2:   **You will not be outdone! Agree with everything they say. (You only need to use one method—*so* OR *too.*)**

Example 1:   It was terrible. I cried and cried.
So did I. / I did, too.

Example 2:   I didn't see anyone I knew.
Neither did I. / I didn't either.

349

1. I can play the glockenspiel.

_____

2. I should leave now.

_____

3. I was at the concert last night.

_____

4. I didn't like the spaghetti.

_____

5. I'll go the party after work.

_____

Exercise 6.3: Underline the best request for the situation.

1. Mother to little boy: I want you to do your homework. / Could you do your homework, please?

2. Man to boss: Can you send me that file again, please? / Send me the file again.

3. Child to aunt: I'd like you to give me some juice. / Can I have some juice?

4. Clerk to customer: Could you sign here, please? / I want you to sign here.

5. Woman to best friend: Would you not open the door, please? / Don't open the door.

Conversational Level Two – Nivel de Conversación Dos

Singing like a bird

Mary sings in the shower. It's one of those times when she feels uninhibited and completely happy. She feels like a fairy princess. The birds sing with her, providing harmony and orchestra.

"O mío babbino caro," she began one day. The birds sang along. Little butterflies hovered by the exhaust fan. One or two got too close.

Suddenly a load roar silenced everything else. Mary finished her shower. When she opened the door and saw her husband, she complained, "Ralph, you scared all the birds away."

"No, I didn't."

"Yes, you did. Listen. Do you hear birds singing?"

"Well, you're not in the shower anymore. They like the sound of the water." Ralph saw his wife was not convinced. "I suppose you're going to blame me for the butterfly wing in the exhaust fan, too, right?" he asked.

"Oh, poor little thing. He must have gotten too close."

"Really, Mary, you should make a CD—you and your birds and butterflies," Ralph said, laughing.

"Thanks." Mary ignored the sarcasm. "I've practiced for a long time."

"Well, so have I," argued Ralph. "In fact, that's where I learned to sing—in the shower. And I think the birds could appreciate my superior talent."

"Superior to what?"

"You won't hear a better shower singer in the neighborhood," Ralph boasted.

"Whatever you say!"

"I sing as well as you," Ralph insisted.

"You don't sing, Ralph. You shout."

"Oh, so you don't want me to take a shower?"

"No, no. Please do. Be my guest. If it's not your singing, it'll be your smell that will keep the birds away."

For a couple minutes, all Mary heard was the calming sound of the water. Then it started. He was singing in the rain. He sang the same line over and over again—not two times, but eight times! Then it was a sad romantic song. He sang about war, faithful dogs, and his favorite foods.

Now, the bathroom had no window, but the exhaust fan was installed on a wall of the house that was near the street. And since it was a hot day, the windows were open anyway. And the neighbors could hear him. Nobody said anything, but they all rolled their eyes when they heard him and turned on their radio or TV to drown out the noise.

But Mary was not as lucky as her neighbors. She could not drown out the noise, no matter how loud she turned up the radio. Ten minutes went by, twenty. He was still happily shouting in the shower. Finally,

Mary couldn't take it anymore, so she started to wash the dishes.

"Augh! . . . Hey, turn off the sink!"

"I'm sorry, Honey," she said, but you've been in there forever. If I wait any longer, there won't be any water left to wash the dishes. Besides, you don't want to damage your voice. Where would we be without our family's most valuable resource?"

"Very funny," he said. "Okay. I'll be out in a minute. I'll come and give you a private concert so you can hear me better."

Phrases and Expressions

Singing like a bird – cantando como una ave *(cuando canta muy bien)*

When she feels uninhibited - cuando ella se siente libre *(uninhibited se refiere a cuando puedes expresarte sin ningún inconveniente)*

Like a fairy princess – como una princesa de hada.

A load roar silenced – un fuerte rugido silenció

You scared all the birds away – asustaste todos los pájaros *(scare away es ahuyentar del susto)*

Be my guest – adelante *(es una expresión para que la otra persona haga lo que dice, aunque sabemos que fracasará)*

To drown out the noise – para mater el ruido *(ahora el ruido)*

Mary couldn't take it anymore – Mary ya no pudo soportarlo.

Hey, turn off the sink – Hey, Cierra la llave del fregadero.

Gossipy neighbor

Charlotte: I don't like to gossip, but I've heard that Joe has a new girlfriend.

Francine: Really?

Charlotte: Yes. Pauline has seen him with her several times now.

Francine: Do you think they'll get married?

Charlotte: I don't know. But you might not have a quiet bachelor for a neighbor anymore.

Francine: Do you believe everything Pauline says?

Charlotte: Why not?

Francine: She told me something about you the other day, but I don't believe her.

Charlotte: I don't either. . . . Um, so, what did she say?

Francine: About what?

Charlotte: What did she say about me?

Francine: Who?

Charlotte: Pauline!

Francine: Oh, you know Pauline. She always makes up interesting stories.

Charlotte: Interesting? What did she say about me?

Francine: Oh, nothing much. . . .Oh Look, who's this?

A car pulls up in front of the neighbor's house playing loud music. A young woman steps out and goes up to the door. She knocks. Joe walks out, and they both get in the car and drive off together.

Francine: Maybe Pauline's right.

Charlotte: You should tell me what Pauline said.

Francine: No, she wouldn't like it.

Charlotte: You know, she told me a couple things about you, too.

Francine: Really?

Charlotte: Yeah, but I probably shouldn't tell you.

Francine: Why not?

Charlotte: Well, you know, she told me in confidence.

Francine: But if it's a secret about me . . .

Charlotte: Tell you what, you tell me what she said about me, and I'll tell you what she said about you.

Francine: Ahhh, you just want to know what she said about you.

Charlotte: Don't you want to know?

Francine: Well, yes. Okay. You first.

Charlotte: No, you first.

Francine: No—Oh, okay. She told me—you won't be angry?

Charlotte: No. Well, I won't be angry at you.

Francine: She told me you have a son nobody knows about.

Charlotte: I don't have any children! I've told her I never even had an official boyfriend.

Francine: Well, I wouldn't worry about it. So, what did she say about me?

Charlotte: She said you talk about all the neighbors.

Francine: Me? You know I would never gossip.

Charlotte: Right.

Francine: I mean, I don't talk as much as Pauline.

Charlotte: Of course not. And since I'm busier

than both of you, I don't have time to stand around and talk.

Francine: What do you have to do now?

Charlotte: Well, I need to go see a friend.

Francine: A friend?

Charlotte: Yes. Um, she's not feeling well, and she asked me to ... to, uh ... to take her some cookies.

Francine: She needs cookies because she's not feeling well.

Charlotte: Uh, yeah.

Francine: If it's Pauline, tell her I have a great story about her.

Phrases and Expressions

Gossipy neighbor – Vecina chismosa

An official boyfriend – un novio oficial

you talk about all the neighbors – hablas de todos los vecinos.

To stand around and talk – estar por ahi y hablar.

A car breaks down on a road trip. The man tries to play the mechanic ...

It was a long weekend. On Friday night, Olivia and Jarold made lasagna and watched a movie. On Saturday, they cleaned the house and the garage. On Sunday afternoon, they were bored. They talked about doing exercise, writing a book, and putting a puzzle together. But they finally decided to go for a drive.

It was a beautiful day for a drive. It was fall. There

was a nice cool breeze and that natural fall smell in the air. The hills were covered with colorful leaves. They drove past the mall, past the outlets, past the baseball stadium, past the new high school. There were fewer buildings, more trees. They were so glad to be out in nature. Then they noticed a new smell: smoke.

They pulled over to the side of the road and stopped the car.

"It must have overheated," said Olivia.

"Let me check," said Jarold. He opened the hood of the car and stood back while steam blew everywhere. The engine was very hot. He took caps off and put them back on. Everything looked okay, except for the smoke and steam.

"Have you checked the antifreeze?" Olivia asked?

"No, I think it's fine. I'm going to add some more oil." Jarold got some oil out of the trunk and added a quart. He started up the car. The hot engine warning light was still on.

He started to remove pieces from the engine. Olivia asked him what he was doing. He was going to clean the jack valve. "Did you check the antifreeze?" she asked.

"Yes, but I can't see how high the antifreeze is."

"Have you ever cleaned the jack valve before?"

"Yes, I have—several times."

"Okay," Olivia said, and she got back in the car. She tried to work on a word puzzle, but she couldn't concentrate. She got out her cell phone and started killing little creatures that ran around in circles.

Finally, Jarold finished cleaning the jack valve. He

started the engine. It was cooler this time. They turned around and drove back for five minutes, and the hot engine light came on again. "It must be the antifreeze. Why don't you add some antifreeze, Honey?" Olivia asked.

"We'll see," he said. Jarold tried a couple more things he knew how to do. It took twenty minutes, but the car was cool again. They drove ten minutes, and the car heated up again. This time, they were near a plaza. Jared found a mechanic.

The mechanic looked the car over and added some water. "You were low on antifreeze."

Jared got back in the car. He wondered if Olivia heard what the mechanic said. He hoped she wouldn't say anything. And she didn't. He tried to start the car. He was pretty sure it would be okay this time. But it wouldn't go! He looked at the indicator. The hot engine light wasn't on, but another light was. The gas tank was empty!

"Aha!" he said. "I guess it was a simple problem after all. We're out of gas."

Olivia laughed. He looked at Olivia, but she didn't look up from her game.

Phrases and Expressions

Putting a puzzle together – Armando un rompecabeza

To be out in nature – estar fuera en la naturaleza

Steam blew everywhere – humo (vapor) salia por todos lados.

He looked at the indicator – miró el indicador

We're out of gas – nos quedamos sin combustible.

Booking a hotel room

A middle-aged man walks into a hotel out of the rain and stands in front of the front desk. The clerk is on the phone. "Yes, she did! I heard her. She said that her boyfriend is"— The clerk turns and sees the client and continues, "staying in room 42B. Yes, I'll be sure to tell him."

"How can I help you?" she asked the man.

"Hi. I'd like a room."

"Of course. Double bed?"

"Two."

"Two double beds?"

"Yes."

"Smoking or non?"

"Nonsmoking."

"Fine." She makes a quick call. "If you'll just wait a couple minutes."

"What am I waiting for?"

"The room."

"It's not ready?"

"Well, we're getting it ready for you right now."

The man goes out to the car and comes back with his wife and daughter and the suitcases. They sit down to wait. He asks for a magazine. The clerk hands him a celebrity magazine and a cooking magazine. Five minutes go by. He asks about the room.

"If you'd like one queen bed, I have a room ready right now," she tells him.

He says he can wait. After ten minutes, the clerk

gives him his keycard and tells him where his room is. But when they find the room, there are just a couples sheets on the beds, the bathroom has hair on the floor, and there is no refrigerator. He goes back to the front desk.

"I expected the room to be a little bit cleaner," he tells the clerk. "In fact, the room isn't at all what I was expecting."

She comes to see the room. She takes some toilet paper and uses it to pick up the hair. She offers to put their food in the staff refrigerator overnight and promises to bring some blankets. "Will that be all?" she asks when she returns.

"Do you have room service?" he asks.

"We do have room service until 10, but that's closed now. There's a vending machine down the hall with an ice machine and a washing machine."

"What about coffee? Can I get some coffee? I expected the room to have a coffee pot."

She promises to bring him a cup of coffee. While she is gone, he starts to take a shower, but he notices that water is dripping from the light bulb over the shower. He complains to the clerk.

"I'm sorry," she says. "Would you like another room?"

He agrees, but she tells him it will be another ten or fifteen minutes. When they finally get their new room, they notice it smells like smoke. The clerk apologizes but says it's the only room left.

The man says, "I'm really disappointed in this hotel. It's supposed to be a five-star hotel! Who gave this place its rating?"

"Oh, no, sir. This isn't rated a five-star hotel. That's the name of the hotel: Five Stars."

Phrases and Expressions
A middle-aged man – un hombre de mediana edad
Water is dripping from the light bulb – el agua esta goteando del bombillo
I'm really disappointed – estoy realmente decepcionado
Who gave this place its rating? – ¿quién dio la calificación a este lugar?
This isn't rated a five-star hotel – no esta calificado como un hotel cinco estrella.
That's the name of the hotel: Five Stars – ese es el nombre del hotel: Cinco Estrellas.

Reporting little Charlie

A man went up to a police officer and asked for help. "What can I do for you?" the officer asked.

"I've lost little Charlie," he replied with tears in his eyes.

"Missing person," said the police officer as he opened a notebook. "Can you describe Charlie?"

"Yes, he's short and muscular."

"Muscular?"

"Yes, he's very strong. You should see him run!"

"Okay. How old is he?" asked the policeman.

"He's almost three."

"Two. What color are his eyes and hair?"

"He has brown eyes, brown hair."

"What about his skin color—light or dark?"

"Um, I don't know," replied the man. "Dark, I guess."

The policeman stared at him. "Okay. What clothes is he wearing?"

"Clothes? He's not wearing any clothes."

"Just a diaper?"

"No. nothing. I know some people get them clothes and everything, but I think that's a waste of money."

The policeman looked surprised. He was beginning to think this man was probably very negligent with his little boy. "When did you last see him?" he asked.

"Well, you see, we were playing ball. And I threw it pretty far. He went running after the ball, and he didn't come back."

"How long ago was this?"

"Maybe ten minutes," answered the man. When he saw a look of disapprobation on the police officer's face, he explained, "I've looked everywhere for him."

"Are there any other unique identifiers you can think of—eyeglasses and such?"

The man seemed to think that was funny and said he couldn't think of anything unique except that he had pointed ears.

"Pointed ears?" repeated the policeman. "That's unusual."

The man said that it was actually quite common. The policeman was thinking that this man was really strange.

"And he's ugly," the man added. The policeman's

mouth feel open. He couldn't believe anyone would talk about their child that way. "Really," the man insisted. "He's very ugly. You know, he has spikey hair and all."

"Wow. Um, we'll get a couple officers on it as soon as we can. Meanwhile, you keep looking for him. Call to him, anything you can think of."

"Okay, thank you so much, Officer."

The policeman walked over into the shade and made a call to headquarters to report the missing child. When he finished, he joined the man to help him look. He found the man calling to Charlie.

"Here, Charlie, Charlie,"

"Is that how you normally call your son?" the officer asked.

"Oh, he's not my son. We adopted him."

"But still," argued the police officer, "that's not a very dignified way to refer to a little boy."

"Well, he's not a little boy."

"What is he?"

"He's a dog—a Peruvian Inca Orchid, actually, a very expensive breed."

The policeman sighed. "Uh, Sir. I'm sorry. But we can't help you look for a dog. We can only help in the case of missing persons. I'm going to have to cancel the report. But best of luck to you. I hope you find him soon, and if I see him, I'll be sure to let you know."

Phrases and Expressions
With tears in his eyes – con lagrimas en sus ojos
Missing person – persona desaparecida

he's short and muscular – él es bajito y musculoso
That's a waste of money – es una perdida de dinero
Very negligent with his little boy – muy negligente con su pequeño hijo.
He had pointed ears – tiene orejas puntiagudas
That's not a very dignified way – esa no es una forma digna

Surprise

A young man wearing a ski mask and and swimming trunks forced open a screen door on a nice home in the suburbs. He found himself surrounded by violets, doilies, and family portraits. Well, he knew this was an old lady's house and that he probably wouldn't find a lot of electronics, but there would be jewelry and maybe even money stashed somewhere.

When he walked into the kitchen, he was surprised to find a smartphone charging on the counter. "Nice!" he said under his breath. He was hungry, so he checked the fridge. Steak! He got some out and ate as he checked out the phone's features. The sink was empty. He washed his dishes. "Don't want to leave any evidence," he thought.

Then he headed into the living room. The TV console was ancient—vintage, actually. It even had a dial! He turned it on. The picture quality wasn't bad. There was a black-and-white program on. He felt as if he had gone back in time. He took a selfie with the new phone on the old sofa, with the doiles, watching vintage TV. He felt tired after eating the steak, and he soon fell asleep.

Suddenly, he woke up with the feeling that someone was watching him. A sweet little old lady with curlers in her hair was staring at him. She looked very entertained.

The burglar felt irritated at her for laughing at him.

"Now, listen, Ma'am. You're going to sit on the couch. I'll just take a few things and go away."

"You want to bet?" replied the old lady.

"Don't make a noise and don't even think of calling the police until I'm gone. I don't want to hurt you. Just sit down and calm down, and nothing will happen to you."

"No, nothing will happen to me. But you'll be surprised at what is going to happen to you!" She kicked him as he started to stand up. He tried to grab her, but she whirled around and kicked him again. He couldn't believe his eyes. She was a karate expert. What luck! Of all the houses on the block, he had to choose the one with a grandma karate champion.

He said, "Okay. I won't take anything else. I'll let you go easy. I'll just leave now."

"No, you won't," she said. "Where's my cell phone?"

He slowly took the cell phone out of his pocket and handed it to her. Then he started toward the door. She jumped in front of him. "What about the kitchen?" she demanded. "You got the floor all dirty. Get in there and clean it up."

Before he knew it, he was on his hands and knees scrubbing the floor with a rag. He'd never done this before, and he was disgusted by the hair on his hands.

When the floor looked pretty good, he asked, "Can I go now?" His tone of voice was much more respectful than when he saw the lady for the first time.

"You can go," she said. Then she showed him her cell phone. "I hope you've learned your lesson. But I've already uploaded this picture, and if you ever come back, I'll share it on my social network!"

Phrases and Expressions
Swimming trunks – traje de baño
Forced open a screen door – Abrió a la fuerza una puerta de tela metálica
An old lady's house – la casa de una anciana
Money stashed somewhere – dinero escondido en algún lugar
Don't want to leave any evidence – no quiero dejar evidencia
The burglar felt irritated – el ladrón se enojó
You want to bet? – ¿quieres apostarlo?
Grandma karate champion – Abuela campeona de karate
I'll let you go easy – te dejaré ir fácil (sin problemas)

Level Two Tests – Examenes del Nivel Dos

Estos son los exámenes para pasar el nivel dos. Asegúrense de tomar su tiempo y completarlos correctamente. Una vez los hayan completado y estén completamente seguros que han terminado. Pueden presentarlos a un amigo de habla inglesa para que los revise y les diga si lo hicieron bien, o pueden enviarme un email con sus exámenes. Sin en algún punto, aun están dudosos, deberán repasarlo y asegurarse de dominarlo muy bien. El segundo nivel es esencial para todo el aprendizaje, sin dominarlo bien, no podremos aprender bien. Es imperativo dominar a la perfección cada uno de los conceptos presentados en este nivel. ***Good luck once again!***

Test Level exams – Test 5 covers units 1 to 3.

Test 1.1: Adjectives and Adverbs—write the correct form of the word.

Example: She got up and _noisily_ walked to the bathroom. (noisy)

1. The _____ boy left the door open. (careless)
2. The baby's mom _____ closed the door. (quiet)
3. You have worked really _____. (hard)

4. That is a really _____ truck! (fast)
5. He was tired, and he worked very

_____. (slow)

6. I was so _____ when I found the cake! (happy)

7. I had a _____ day! (bad)

8. My pillow is so _____. (soft)

Test 1.2: Put the words in the correct spaces.

ahead   corner   turn

Go straight (1) _____. Then (2) _____

left at the (3) _____.

across   down   over

The store is on the other side of the street. It's (4)

_____ the street.

A bird flew (5) _____ the house.

Grandma walks (6) _____ the street to visit her friend.

Test 1.3: What comes next? Write the letter of a logical statement to come next.

1. _____ If you like the TV program,

2. _____ I used to play with blocks.

3. _____ Would you like a flower?

a.   I have lots of them, and they are so beautiful.

Nivel Dos

b. You can watch it tomorrow, too!

c. Now I work all the time.

Test 1.4: Make the questions more polite. Make indirect questions.

Example: What day is today?   Could you tell me _what day today is?_

1. Can I use the phone?   Do you mind if

_____

2. Why are you sad?   May   I   ask

_____

3. Where is the museum?   Do   you   know

_____

4. How is everyone getting to the party?   Could

you tell me _____

Test 6 covers units 4-6.

Test 6.1: Agree with everything (*so* or *too/neither* or *either*).

Example: I shouldn't stay up too late. _Neither should I. OR I shouldn't either._

1. I am always in a good mood.

_____

2. I can't stand milk.

_____

3. I should go home now.

_____

4. I won't go to the funeral.

_____

5. I haven't studied for the test!

_____

6. I've eaten a whole pizza!

_____

7. I'll give $200 to charity.

_____

8. I can swim faster than a goldfish.

_____

9. I'm not very happy

---

10. I shouldn't eat a lot of bread.

Test 6.2: You are always superior. Use the comparative to say you are better at everything.

Example: Jane can run very fast.   I can run faster than Jane.

1. Mark is really tall.

---

2. My dad is so funny.

---

3. Our teacher is really intelligent.

---

4. Yikes. That frog is really ugly.

---

5. My boyfriend studies all the time.

Test 6.3: Check [✓] if they mean the same thing. Do nothing if they mean something different.

1. ❑   This is terrible! You should be doing your homework. / You will be doing your homework.

2. ❑ I would go with you. / I will go with you.

3. ❑ Could you help me? / Would you help me?

4. ❑ They should eat first. / They will eat first.

5. ❑ She shouldn't pick up her toys. / She won't pick up her toys.

6. ❑ They should arrive tomorrow. / They will arrive tomorrow.

7. ❑ My mom? Hmm. Right now, she'll be at home right now. / Right now, she should be at home.

8. ❑ I will help you! / I should help you!

9. ❑ They should have asked permission. / They will have asked permission.

10. ❑ Let's see, it's 5 p.m. She must be on her way here. / She should be on her way here.

11. ❑ Do you want me to call your mom? / Would you like me to call your mom?

12. ❑ Should you open the door, please? / Will you open the door, please?

Test 7.1: Circle the letter of the best response.

1. Achoo! [sneeze]
a. Congratulations!
b. Bless you!
c. Thank you!

2. Why don't you work for Fran Friday night?
a. I can't. I have a dentist appointment.
b. I would do it, but I already have plans.
c. I could, but she hasn't asked me.
d. All are grammatical responses.

3. I'm going to be busy next week.
a. I can't either.

b. You're crazy.

c. Neither is Mom.

d. So am I.

4. Have you ever been to the Grand Canyon?

a. Yes. I've been there three times.

b. I went last year.

c. Never.

d. All are grammatical responses.

5. Could you help me with my homework?

a. Let's go next week.

b. Why don't you do it now?

c. I'd like to, but I'm really busy.

d. Yes, I'd like some.

6. Are you doing okay?

a. I think yes.

b. I guess so.

c. I hope not.

d. I yes, really.

7. What did you use to do before you met your wife?

a. I went hunting once.

b. I always clean the house.

c. I always played video games.

d. All are logical responses.

8. Would you like to go to the zoo?

a. Right now? Let's go!

b. We often go to the zoo.

c. Mom loves the zoo.

d. I haven't seen that one.

Test 7.2: Underline the correct word or phrase in parentheses.

1. The Amazon River is (**longer / the longest**)

373

river in the world!

2. If I finish my homework in time, I **(will / should)** help you.

3. Unfortunately, they are **(taller / the tallest)** than me.

4. I haven't **(ate / eaten)** dinner.

5. My brother is **(taller/ the tallest)** than my dad.

6. Don't give up! I **(am going to / will)** help you.

7. Have you **(saw / seen)** the new cartoon?

8. I've felt bad **(since / before)** I ate the shrimp cocktail.

9. I'm as slow **(as / to)** a sloth.

10. Mom, you just **(will / have to)** come. It's going to be great!

Test 7.3: Write the correct word: *in, off, on, out, up, to.*

Example: I didn't get _____ the store on time. It's closed.

1. Don't forget to check _____ to the hotel before you eat.

2. You have to get _____ early if you want to be successful.

3. Her flight takes _____ at 6 a.m.

4. We're going to eat _____ for her birthday.

5. Put _____ your sweater. It's cold outside.

Verb list – Lista de verbos

To answer the phone – contestar el teléfono

To apologize – ofrecer disculpas, disculparse

To ask – pedir / preguntar
To be a pain in the neck – ser un fastidio
To be in love – estar enamorado
To be right – estar en lo cierto (correcto) / tener la razón
To be robbed – ser robado
To be shot – ser baleado / recibir un tiro.
To be wrong – estar equivocado
To become - convertirse
To believe - creer
To borrow – tomar prestado (se toma prestado algo de alguien)
To breathe - respirar
To brush - cepillar
To call – llamar
To carry – cargar / llevar
To catch – atrapar / agarrar
To change - cambiar
To check in - registrarse
To choose – elegir / escoger
To chuckle - reír
To clean - limpiar
To close - cerrar
To comb – peinarse
To come right in – entrar de inmediato (cuando la persona está dentro y te invita a entrar)
To compare - comparar
To describe – describir
To dial – marcar
To do the housework – hacer los deberes de la casa
To do the laundry – lavar la ropa
To do your best – hacer lo mejor, dar tu mejor

esfuerzo

To do your homework – hacer la tarea

To dust - despolvar

To eat out – comer fuera (un restaurante, etc)

To examine - examinar

To exchange – intercambiar

To find out – descubrir

To fly – volar

To forget – olvidar

To get a disease – contraer una enfermedad

To get a haircut – recortarse el pelo

To get a job – conseguir un trabajo / empleo.

To get a shave - afeitarse

To get sick - enfermarse

To get to – llegar a (un lugar o destino)

To get well - mejorarse

To go dancing – salir a bailar

To go for a drive – dar un paseo en vehículo

To go for a meal – salir a comer

To go for a swim – salir a nadar

To go for a walk – salir a caminar

To go in – entrar (cuando la persona está afuera y va a entrar)

To go right in – entrar de inmediato (cuando la persona está afuera y te indica que entres)

To hang up - colgar

To happen – suceder / ocurrir / pasar

To have a look at – dar una mirada (ojeada)

To have an operation - operarse

To have something ready – tener algo listo

To have your hands full – tener las manos llenas

To hit – golpear

To hurt – lastimar / doler

To invite – invitar

To iron – planchar

To jump – saltar / brincar

To keep an eye on activity - vigilar la actividades

To kill – matar

To know why – saber el por qué

To land – aterrizar

To last – durar / perdurar

To lend – prestar (se presta algo a alguien)

To lie – yacer / tenderse

To lie down – recostarse

To look – mirar / observar

To look after – cuidar

To look like – parecerse / ser similar

To lose weight – perder peso

To make a mistake – cometer un error / meter la pata

To miss – extrañar / faltar / errar

To mop - trapear

To pick up – recoger

To promised – prometer

To put on weight – subir de peso

To rave about it – alardear a cerca de algo

To refuse – rehúsar

To remember – recordar

To rent – rentar

To ride – montar (bicicleta, caballo, etc.)

To ring – sonar

To shave – afeitar

To shout – gritar / vocear / vociferar

To sign – firmar

To smell – oler

To sneeze – estornudar

To steal – robar / hurtar

To sweep - barrer

To take a vacation – tomar vacaciones

To take off – despegar / quitarse

To take someone's temperature – tomar la temperatura de alguien

To take the bus – tomar el autobús (abordarlo)

To take the plane – tomar al avión (abordarlo)

To taste – probar / saborear

To thank – agradecer

To throw – arrojar / lanzar

To turn – girar / voltear

To turn down – bajar el volumen

To turn up – subir el volumen

To understand why – entender el por qué

To use – usar

To visit – visitar

To wake up –despertarse

To wear – usar

To weigh – pesar

Grammar Summary

Lesson One

Tag questions – Coletilla interrogativa
Would (wouldn't) like – Gustaría (no)
Adjectives – Adjetivos
Adverbs – Adverbios
New regular verbs – Nuevos verbos regulares
New irregular verbs – Nuevos verbos irregulares

Lesson Two

"could you tell… May I ask…"
Modal verb Can / Could – Verbo modal Can / Could.
Auxiliary verb "used to" – Verbo auxiliar"used to" – solía.
New regular verbs – Nuevos verbos regulares
New irregular verbs – Nuevos verbos irregulares
Prepositions – Preposiciones
Adjectives – Adjetivos
Adverbs – Adverbios
The word "so" – La palabra "so"

Lesson Three

Pronouns in affirmative sentences – Pronombres en oraciones afirmativas.

Pronouns in interrogative sentences – pronombres en oraciones interrogativas

Pronouns in negative sentences – Pronombres en

oraciones negativas

Relative pronouns as a subject "Who / That" – Pronombres relativos como sujeto "Who / That".

Question words plus infinitive / Present progressive – Palabras interrogativas más el infinitivo / Presente progresivo.

Conjunctions – Conjunciones

Pronouns and adjectives – Pronombres and adjetivos.

Regular verbs – Verbos regulares

Irregular verbs – Verbos irregulares

Adverbs - Adverbios

Adjectives – Adjetivos

Lesson Four

Present perfect tense – Tiempo presente perfecto.

Structure of the Present perfect – Estructura del presente perfecto.

Past participle – Pasado participio

Have to – tener que

Adverbs – Adverbios

Adjectives – Adjetivos

Lesson Five

Would - condicional

Comparing people and things with adjectives – Comparando personas y cosas con adjetivos.

Superlative – Superlativo

Irregular superlatives – Superlativos irregulares

Auxiliary verb "must" – Verbo auxiliar "must".

Adjectives – Adjetivos

Prepositions – Preposiciones

New regular verbos – Nuevos verbos regulares
New irregular verbs – Nuevos verbos irregulares

Lesson Six

The future with "Will" – El futuro con "Wll"

Polite commands – Órdenes o mandatos de cortesía.

The auxiliary verb "Should" – El verbo auxiliar "Should".

The verb "to get" – El Verbo "to get".

Adjectives "no / any" and Pronouns "None / Any" – Adjetivos "no / any" y Pronombres "none / any".

Conjunctions – Conjunciones

Adjectives – Adjetivos

Adverbs – Adverbios

New regular verbs – Nuevos verbos regulares

New irregular verbs – Nuevos verbos irregulares

Answers to exercises – Respuestas de los ejercicios

Como terminaron sus exámenes y se aseguraron de dominar cada concepto, pueden verificar las respuestas al final del libro. Me he tomado la libertad de ofrecerles las respuestas de todos los ejercicios de cada lección asi también como los del examen de nivel. Pero no hagan trampa, solo ustedes pierden si hacen trampa. *See you on the third volume.*

Lesson One

Answers to Exercise 1.1:

1. isn't she?
2. did it?
3. don't you?
4. isn't she?
5. was he?
6. can you?
7. does she?
8. can't you?
9. is he?
10. don't you?

Answers to Exercise 1.2:

1. If she wants to get her work done, she shouldn't watch soap operas.
2. If they want to make extra money, they can deliver newspapers.
3. If Mom lets you go to the movies, call me first!
4. If you finish your work early, we can go out to eat!
5. If it rains, I can't do the laundry.

Answers to Exercise 1.3:

1. How many
2. Which
3. When
4. Why
5. Where

Lesson Two
Answers to Exercise 2.1:
1. tourist (person, not place)
2. jail (place—noun, not verb)
3. noisily (adverb, not adjective)
4. ground (place, not direction)
5. band (group, not person)

Answers to Exercise 2.2:
1. say
2. spoke
3. understand
4. paid
5. looked
6. could
7. got
8. was
9. sat
10. saw
11. cried

Answers to Exercise 2.3:
1. The guest noisily walked down the hall.
2. The groom quickly kissed the bride.
3. He quietly left the boring class.
4. They happily paid for the gold rings.
5. The artist's studio is across the hall.

Answers to Exercise 2.4:
1. Can you tell me where the restroom is? / May I ask where the restroom is?
2. May I ask what your name is?
3. May I ask where you are from?
4. Can you tell me when the movie starts? / May I ask when the movie starts?
5. Can you tell me where the museum is? / May I ask where the museum is?

Lesson Three
Answers to Exercise 3.1:
1. Another
2. Each other
3. The other
4. Another
5. The other

Answers to Exercise 3.2:
1. Do you know why the bank is closed?
2. Do you know how I can rent a boat?
3. Do you know when the boat comes back?
4. Do you know where the other boats are?
5. Do you know who the manager is?

Answers to Exercise 3.3:
1. I know where it is.
2. I know when it starts.
3. I know what to do.
4. I know who he is calling.
5. I know where she is going.

Answers to Exercise 3.4:
1. anything
2. Nobody
3. something
4. anyone
5. Everyone

Lesson Four
Answers to Exercise 4.1:
1. Have, had
2. have, looked
3. 've ruined
4. have sold
5. 've seen
6. Have, been
7. 've, tried
8. have, worn
9. Have, flown
10. have fixed

Answers to Exercise 4.2
1. haircut
2. housework
3. homework
4. swim
5. drive

Answers to Exercise 4.3:
1. ever
2. already
3. never
4. just
5. yet

Lesson Five

Answers to Exercise 5.1:

1. It's 5:45. You must leave now if you want to catch the bus.

2. I can't say no. My country needs me. I must go.

3. Dan didn't come to work today. He must be sick.

4. But, Mom, just look at all that snow! Do I have to **shovel** the sidewalk?

5. Ingrid looks pretty happy. She must have finished her project.

Answers to Exercise 5.2:

1. I am shorter than John.

2. Chocolate chips cost more than chocolate bars.

3. My boyfriend is the smartest one in the class.

4. Our house is the ugliest house on the block.

5. It's dryer outside than inside.

Answers to Exercise 5.3:

1. c
2. e
3. a
4. f
5. d
6. b

Lesson Six

Answers to Exercise 6.1:

1. There isn't any more.
2. There aren't any more.
3. There aren't any more.

4. There isn't any more.
5. There aren't any more.

Answers to Exercise 6.2:
1. I can, too. / So can I.
2. I should, too. / So should I.
3. I was, too. / So was I.
4. I didn't either. / Neither did I.
5. I will, too. / So will I.

Answers to Exercise 6.3:
1. I want you to do your homework.
2. Can you send me the file again, please?
3. Can I have some juice?
4. Could you sign here, please?
5. Don't open the door.

Answers to Level Two Tests – Respuesta de los Examenes del Nivel Dos

Answers to Test 1.1:
1. careless (adj.)
2. quietly (adv.—¿cómo cerró la puerta?)
3. hard (adv. sin cambio de forma—¿cómo trabajó?)
4. fast (adj.)
5. slowly (adv.—¿cómo trabajó?)
6. happy (adj.)
7. bad (adj.)
8. soft (adj.)

Answers to Test 1.2:
1. ahead
2. turn
3. corner
4. across
5. over
6. down

Answers to Test 1.3:
1. B
2. C
3. A

Answers to Test 1.4:
1. I use the phone?
2. why you are sad?
3. where the museum is?
4. how everyone is getting to the party?

Answers to Test 6.1:
1. So am I. / I am, too.
2. I can't either. / Neither can I.
3. I should, too. / So should I.
4. I won't either. / Neither will I.
5. I haven't either. Neither have I.
6. I have, too. / So have I.
7. I will, too. / So will I.
8. I can, too. / So can I.
9. I'm not either. / Neither am I.
10. I shouldn't either. / Neither should I.

Answers to Test 6.2:
1. I am taller than Mark.
2. I'm funnier than your dad.
3. I'm more intelligent than your teacher.
4. I'm uglier than that frog.
5. I study more than your boyfriend.

Answers to Test 6.3:
1. ❑ *Should* shows advice or obligation; *will* shows a prediction or order for the future.
2. ❑ *Would* shows a desire or wish; *will* gives an offer or promise.
3. ☑ They both politely ask for help.
4. ❑ *Should* gives advice; *will* gives a prediction.
5. ❑ *Should* gives advice; *will* shows her refusal to do something.
6. ❑ *Should* gives a probability; *will* gives a more sure prediction.
7. ☑ Both are guesses/assumptions based on

habits.

8. ☐   *Will* gives an offer; *should* shows a feeling of responsibility.

9. ☐   *Should* shows a feeling of guilt; *will* gives a probability in the past.

10. ☑   Both make a prediction, although *must* is stronger than *should*.

11. ☑   Both politely offer to do something.

12. ☐   *Should* makes no sense *(no se puede)*; *will* asks for help.

Answers to Test 7.1:
1. B
2. D
3. D
4. D
5. C
6. B
7. C
8. A

Answers to Test 7.2:
1. the longest
2. will
3. taller
4. eaten
5. taller
6. will
7. seen
8. since
9. as
10. have to

Answers to Test 7.3:

1. in
2. up
3. off
4. out
5. on

Nivel Dos Conclusión

Muchas gracias por seleccionar el *Curso Completo de Inglés – Nivel Dos* por Yeral E. Ogando para su aprendizaje. Por fin, han llegado al final del segundo nivel, por lo tanto, ya pueden hablar inglés fluido y están listos para el nivel tres.

Les exhorto que continúen practicando y hablando inglés en todo momento, ya les he dicho que la Practica hace al Maestro. Visiten mi pagina de internet para más información.

God bless you and see you in volumen three.

Dr. Yeral E.Ogando
www.aprendeis.com

Nivel Dos BONO GRATIS

Estimado Estudiante,

Necesitas descargar el audio MP3 para usar este increíble método para aprender inglés. Visita este link:
http://aprendeis.com/ingles-audio-nivel2/
Usuario "ennivel2"
Contraseña "en22016"

Solo tienes que descargar el archivo comprimido, descomprimirlo y estas listo para iniciar tu experiencia al mundo del inglés.

Si quieres compartir tu experiencia, comentario o possible sugerencia, siempre podrás contactarme a info@aprendeis.com

Muchas gracias por estudiar el *Curso Completo de Inglés – Nivel Dos* y por escuchar mis instrucciones.

Caros afectos,
Dr. Yeral E. Ogando

Curso Completo de Inglés

Teach Yourself

Habla Inglés desde la primera lección.
Nivel Tres avanzado.
Aprenda Inglés sin profesor hoy.

Dr. Yeral E. Ogando

Lesson 1
I can't wait to graduate – No veo la hora de graduarme

Conversation

Mark: Hey, look at this. There are a bunch of high-paying jobs in the classified ads today. It says here they need a security guard, and they'll pay $24 an hour.

Steve: That's not bad.

Mark: No. Oh, but you have to have experience in public service.

Steve: Well, you know, my work as a fireman qualifies me for that. But I'd have to give two weeks' notice.

Mark: Yeah. And they need someone right now. Here's something different. They want someone to design video games.

Steve: Well, you can do that yourself.

Mark: No, I don't know anything about programming. I just know how to use design software. You're qualified for both of these jobs.

Steve: Are they full time?

Mark: Yeah. Oh, you're right. You wouldn't be able to finish your degree this year if you worked full time. Whatever you do, don't quit school.

Steve: Don't worry. I don't plan to. But I can't wait to graduate!

New words – Nuevas palabras
All over – por todos lados / en todas partes / por doquier
Altitude - altitud
Boot - bota
Camper - campista
Campground - campamento
Captain - capitán
Carpenter - carpintero
Cashier - cajero
Change - cambio
College - colegio / universidad
Computer programmer – programador de computadoras
Degree – grado *(refiriéndose a la temperatura, también en otro contexto significa título universitario)*
Electrician - electricista
Farmer – granjero / agricultor
Firefighter - bombero
Fisherman - pescador
Folks – gente / pueblo *(usado para personas que conoces o tu familia "mi gente")*
Fortune - fortuna
Heel – taco / tacón
Hit – éxito *(una canción se vuelve un hit)*
Indigestion - indigestión
Industry - industria
Joke – broma / chiste
Judge - juez
Kid – muchacho (a)

Lawyer - abogado
Liter - litro
Luck - suerte
Make-up - maquillaje
Oven - horno
Plumber - plomero
Razor (blade) – rasuradora
Recipe - receta
Repairman – reparador / técnico
Sailor – marino
Sale - venta
Sand - arena
Shoelace – cordón de zapato
Soldier - soldado
Souvenir - recuerdo
Speed - velocidad
Tent - tienda
Tour – gira / recorrido
Tour guide – guía turística
Tourism - turismo
Toys - juguetes
Tramp – vagabundo / pordiosero
Village - villa

Words Definitions

Keep in touch: when we want to tell someone to write us or call us because we want to keep communication open.

By the way: When we want to change the conversation because we remember something.

Likewise: when we think or feel the same as the

other person; a transition used to add another point.
Can't wait: *when we are happy because we want something to happen soon or we want to do it soon.*

Phrases and Expressions - Frases y expresiones
A bunch of – un montón de
Back home – pueblo natal / hogar *(se usa esta expresión para referirse al hogar o pueblo natal de uno, cuando no estamos ahí)*
By the way – a propósito
Classified ads – Anuncios clasificados
Don't quit school – no dejes (abandones) la escuela
High-paying jobs – trabajos bien pagos
To give two weeks' notice – dar dos semanas de pre-aviso (para dejar un trabajo)

Can't wait for (Can't wait to) – no veo el momento, no puedo esperar por, estoy deseando *(se usa esta expresión cuando estamos ansioso por que algo pase o acontezca. Usamos "can't wait to" cuando viene un verbo.* **Can't wait to see you** – *estoy loco por verte / anhelo verte)*

Come on – dime *(usamos esta expresión cuando queremos que nos digan lo que realmente paso. También Se usa para convencer a alguien que haga cualquier cosa. Vente conmigo. Trabaja el sábado. Dame tu postre. No le digas a mamá.)*

Darn – rayos *(usamos esta expresión cuando estamos enojados o cuando nos damos un golpe, los españoles dirían "joder", algunos latinos diríamos "coño")*

Dear – querido (a)

Howdy - ¿Cómo te va? *(es una expresión muy coloquial para decir, "que tal" usada en el norte de Texas)*

I thought she'd never leave – pensé que nunca se iría.

In the way – en medio / en el camino *(usamos esta expresión cuando alguien se mete en nuestro camino)*

It was nice talking to you – fue bueno hablar contigo

Keep in touch – mantente en contacto

Likewise – igualmente / de igual forma

On sale – en venta

Out of the way – fuera del camino *(usamos esta expresión cuando queremos que alguien se nos quite del medio, nos deje el camino libre, o para decir que no nos estorben)*

Take care - cuídate

To be called – ser llamado *(llamar a alguien, algo o algún lugar por su nombre)*

To go camping – irse de campamento

To go sailing – irse a navegar

To help yourself – ayudarse a uno mismo *(usualmente comiendo o bebiendo algo. También la usamos cuando le decimos a alguien "Help yourself" sírvete tú mismo o estás en tu casa)*

To look forward to – anhelar que algo suceda *(siempre va un verbo después de "to")*

To wish someone the best of luck – desearle a alguien buena suerte

Welcome - bienvenido
Welcome aboard – bienvenido a bordo
Who is it by? - ¿Quién canta? / ¿Quién lo escribió? *(usamos esta expresión cuando queremos saber quien compuso una obra o canción)*
You're kidding! – ¿estás bromeando? *(usamos esta expresión cuando estamos asombrados y no creemos lo que nos están diciendo o cuando es algo difícil de creer)*

Grammar – Gramática
Pronouns and adverbs – Pronombres y adverbios
Whatever – lo que sea / cualquier cosa
Whatever you say, it is fine with me – lo que sea que digas, está bien por mí.
Whoever – quien sea – cualquier persona
Whoever comes first will get the prize – cualquiera que llegue primero recibirá el premio.
Whenever – cuando sea / en cualquier momento
Whenever you come, I'll be here waiting for you – cuando sea que vengas, estará aquí esperando por ti.
Wherever – donde sea / en cualquier lugar
Wherever you are, I hope you are happy – en donde quiera que estés, espero que estés feliz.

También puedes usarlos al dar órdenes; cuando esto sucede, la orden o el mandato es más fuerte de lo normal.

Whatever you do, don't mess it up – no importa lo que hagas, pero no metas la pata.

Whoever you marry, marry her for love – con quien sea que te cases, hazlo por amor.

Reflexive – Emphatic pronouns – Pronombres reflexivos y enfáticos.

Myself – yo mismo
Yourself – tú mismo
Himself – él mismo
Herself – ella mismo
Itself – él o ella mismo
Ourselves – nosotros mismos
Yourselves – ustedes mismos
Themselves – ellos / ellas mismas

Como pueden ver, la palabra "*self* – *mismo*" convierte a los pronombres personales en pronombres reflexivos; y como aprendimos en la primera lección, el plural de "*self*" es "*selves*". No lo olviden.

Usamos estos pronombres para enfatizar e indicar que el sujeto efectuó la acción o que ha sido efectuada por uno mismo.

I learned English myself – aprendí inglés yo mismo *(nadie me ayudó).*

The secretary herself finished the project – la secretaria misma terminó el proyecto *(ella misma, nadie más)*

He considered himself handsome – Él se considere hermoso.

When he was discovered, he shot himself – cuando lo descubrieron, se dio un tiro.

They gave themselves a raise – ellos se aumentaron el sueldo.

A veces usamos "by" o "all by" para enfatizar que nadie más ayudó o tomó parte en la acción.

I fixed the computer by myself – arreglé la computadora yo mismo.

I fixed the computer all by myself – arreglé la computadora yo solito *(nadie me ayudó)*.

Pronoun + of – Pronombre más of

Sabemos por lecciones anteriores el significado y uso de "of", solo vamos a agregar algunos pronombres con el patrón para que continuemos incrementando nuestro conocimiento.

One of them is crying – una de ellas está llorando. *(Cuando hay más de dos personas en el grupo)*

Neither of us is crying – ninguno de nosotros está llorando. *(Cuando solo hablamos de dos personas)*

Both of them are crying – ambas están llorando. *(Cuando hay dos personas nada más)*

All of you are crying – todos ustedes están llorando. *(Cuando hay tres o más personas en el grupo)*.

Some of them are crying – algunos de ellos están llorando. *(Cuando hay un grupo de más de three personas)*.

None of them are crying – ninguno de ellos está llorando. *(Cuando hablamos de un grupo de tres o más personas)*.

Adjectives – Adjetivos

Old - viejo

Own – propio (esta palabra siempre se usa después de un adjetivo posesivo my own money – mi propio dinero)

Poor - pobre
Excellent - excelente
Loose – flojo (lo contrario de apretado)
Sharp – filoso
Sore – adolorido (cuando se tiene dolor)
Tight - apretado
Crowded – lleno de gente (lleno de personas o cosas).

Regular verbs – Verbos regulares

To marry - married - married - casarse
To solve - solved – solved - resolver
To cure – cured – cured - curar
To drop – dropped- dropped – caer / dejar caer
To laugh – laughed – laughed - reír
To serve – served – served - servir
To stop – stopped – stopped - detener
To try on – tried on – tried on – probarse *(ropa)*
To arrange – arranged – arranged – organizar / arreglar
To camp – camped – camped - acampar
To drown – drowned – drowned - ahogarse
To hire – hired – hired – contratar / emplear
To sail – sailed – sailed - navegar
To smile – smiled – smiled - sonreír
To surf – surfed – surfed – surfear
To trouble – troubled – troubled – molestar / preocupar
To welcome – welcomed – welcomed – dar la bienvenida

Irregular verbs – Verbos irregulares
To mean – meant – meant – significar / querer decir
To spend – spent – spent - gastar
To cut – cut – cut - cortar
To fall down – fell down – fallen down – caerse
To grow – grew – grown – crecer

Get out of the way

There was no stopping Zack. Traffic lights didn't intimidate him. Potholes just made the road more interesting. He needed to feel the wind blowing his hair. Whoever got in his way was sorry. If the other lane was empty, he'd just pull over into the other lane and fly by. Honk, honk, he'd honk his horn. "Come on, move!" Then he'd follow closely behind the car until the driver pulled over and allowed Derek to get around him.

Zack's last glorious ride was on Memorial Day. From the on-ramp, he saw a couple cars in the right lane. He laughed and laid his foot on the accelerator. Vroom! The car shot ahead, and he merged into the right lane, just ahead of the other cars. The drivers had to brake to avoid an accident and neither of them was happy about it. They held their hands on the horn for a long time. "Whatever," Zack said and ignored them.

He went faster and faster. The trees were a blur. Suddenly, he saw another blur, a spot of color on the road. He switched lanes just in time to miss the hitchhiker. "I almost gave him a ride to remember,"

Zack thought. He came up to the horse farm. He slowed down a little to look at the white-fenced fields. He wasn't looking at the road when he saw someone run off the road. Another near miss. "Wow, I've got to slow down," he thought. He went a little slower until he passed the commercial district. As he passed the mall, he started to accelerate again when he saw a boy in the road. "What on earth?" he said and swerved to miss him. After all of these mishaps, he asked himself if he should slow down. But he soon forgot and got back into his normal mode of driving. That's when he heard the siren. He looked in the rearview mirror and saw the flashing lights. "Darn," he said. He slowed down and pulled over onto the shoulder.

"In a hurry?" the policeman asked him. He tried to laugh, but he realized this was going to be a very expensive ticket. "Let's see, going 90 in a 60-mile zone. That's over $300." Zack said nothing, hoping the policeman would consider him respectful and lower the fine. No luck. The policeman handed him a citation and returned his papers.

Back home, Zack called his friend Martin, a lawyer. "What should I do?"

"Go to court. Say you were just going with the flow of traffic. Maybe he'll reduce your fine. And no jokes!"

Exercises – Ejercicios

Exercise 1.1: Add a reflexive/emphatic pronoun to each of the following sentences.

Example: My brother painted the portrait _himself_.

I _____ don't eat much fruit.

They had to build the house _____.

We're going to write the manual _____.

The dog _____ showed rescue workers where to find its owner.

You should talk to her _____ and explain the misunderstanding.

Exercise 1.2: Write *whatever, whoever, whenever, or wherever.*

Example: _Whenever_ she comes, I'll heat her food.

You can come _____ you want.

_____ you are, you can get in touch with our customer service.

_____ money she makes, she spends.

You can marry _____ you want.

I'll eat _____ you give me.

Exercise 1.3: Write the letter of the answer.

_____ Do you want chicken or beef?

_____ Did you like your teachers in college?

_____ Did the students pass the class?

_____ Will you take your books with you?

_____ Which of your boys plays soccer?

A. Yes, some of them did.
B. I want both of them.
C. Neither of them is involved in sports.
D. Well, one of them was really amazing. The rest were okay.
E. Yes, I'm going to need all of them.

Exercise 1.4: Complete the texts. Write the appropriate phrase from below.

by the way come on   help yourself   take care   you're kidding

Of course, I'll remind you. Ah, _____, don't forget to call Dad.

Oh, there's plenty of food in the fridge.

_____!

Do you have to leave? We'll miss you. Oh, all right.

_____.

He left your sister? _____.
He seemed so in love.

Oh, _____. Please! I really need your help!

Lesson 2
To run out of gas – Quedarse sin combustible

Conversation

"I'll be right back, Honey. I'm going to go get the rental car for our trip," John called to his wife.

"Okay," Trisha replied. "Don't forget anything. What did they say you need?"

"Let's see, my driver's license, insurance policy, credit card, of course, and, well, any cash in case I don't want them to charge the deposit to the card."

"You don't need any other ID?" she asked.

"They didn't mention any."

"Okay, I'll have the suitcases ready when you get back."

When John came back with the car, he checked it over to make sure it was ready for the trip. Then, he packed up the car, and they started their trip from Tennessee to Texas. The first day was uneventful. They stayed overnight at a hotel and drove for another ten hours when the car stopped in the middle of the road. John pushed it to the side of the road and checked everything—the oil and water, of course, the carburetor, the radiator. Everything seemed okay. He called his insurance company for roadside assistance. When the man checked the car over, he laughed and said, "I could tow you to the gas station over there by the off-ramp."

"Seriously?" John asked. "Sorry about that. I could've just walked there, I guess. I didn't realize it was just the gas! Can you just give me a ride there and back?"

"Sure," the driver replied. "Now that I'm here, I might as well be of some use to you." The tow truck driver made sure John had an approved gas can and gave him the promised ride.

New words – Nuevas palabras
Ambulance - ambulancia
Battery - batería
Carburetor - carburador
Deposit - deposito
Dirt - sucio
Engine – motor (de vehículo)
Gas - gas
Including – incluyendo
Insurance - seguro
Kilometer - kilómetro
Noise - ruido
Oil – aceite / petróleo
Plus - más
Radiator - radiador
Service station – estación de servicio
Spare – llanta de repuesto, neumático
Tank - tanque
Tire – llanta / neumático
Trunk – cajuela / baúl
Warranty - garantía

Wheel – volante / rueda / timón
Chance - oportunidad
Contract – contrato
Desk - escritorio
Drawer – gaveta / cajón
Experience - experiencia
Fair – feria / justo
Marketing – mercadotecnia
Matter - asunto
Message - mensaje
Order – orden
Until - hasta
Report - reporte
Bomb - bomba
Cameraman - camarógrafo
Explosion - explosión
Floor – piso / suelo
Guy – tipo (hombre)
Helicopter - helicóptero
Hijacker - secuestrador
Hijacking - secuestro
Passenger - pasajero
String – cuerda / hilo

Words Definitions
All over: *when you have finished something, we say "it is all over." "It is over" is the same as saying "it is finished." It also means "everywhere."*
Fair: *An event or place where companies gather to show their products to public view.*
Insurance: *when you buy a vehicle, you go the*

insurance company to buy the insurance, so if you have an accident, they will pay for the damages over/beyond the deductible.

Matter: when there is something important to discuss. However, in conversation you say, "What's the matter?" which is the same as "What's the problem?"

Pleased: when you are happy about something. You are satisfied.

To keep warm: when you help something or someone to keep warm or the same temperature; you can use "to keep" with many adjectives: to keep cold, to keep happy, etc.

Warranty: when you buy something, you might get a warranty, meaning that the manufacturer will fix certain types of problem you might have with the appliance in the next few months or years.

Phrases and Expressions - Frases y expresiones

Do as I say – haz como yo digo *(haz como te digo)*

To get hurt – lastimarse / salir lastimado

Listen – escucha *(cuando queremos que alguien nos mire o preste atención)*

Look here – mira aquí / Oye tú / usted *(cuando queremos que nos miren y presten atención)*

Or else – si no *(es una expresión de advertencia, hace lo que digo o si no, ya veras, te atienes a las consecuencias)*

To pay attention – prestar o poner atención

Shut up – cállate / no hables *(no es cortés)*

Smart aleck – sabelotodo – sabiendo *(cuando*

alguien no está haciendo lo que le dijimos que haga. No es una buena palabra, y frecuentemente indica que la persona has sido irrespetuosa con alguien de autoridad, mayor o un experto en el area)

Thank goodness – gracias a Dios *(cuando estamos contentos de que algo haya pasado)*

To be in – estar en *(cuando estamos en la casa, en la oficina, iglesia).*

To be out – no estar en *(cuando no estamos en la casa, oficina, iglesia)*

To give someone a chance – darle una oportunidad a alguien.

To have a seat – tomar asiento

Let me see – déjame ver *(estamos diciéndole a la otra persona que nos espere mientras verificamos)*

To let someone know – hacerle saber algo a alguien *(decirle algo a alguien)*

Tell him I am here – dile que estoy aquí

On time – a tiempo

See you later – nos vemos después / más tarde

Damn – diablo / *coño (esta expresión no es buena, a muchas personas no les gusta decirla ni escucharla. Solo cuando se está demasiado enfadado se podría decir está frase)*

Fill it up - llénalo

In 5 minutes – en 5 minutes

In fact – de hecho / en realidad

It depends – depende / eso depende

To run out of – quedarse sin / acabársele algo / agotarse algo

📖 Grammar – Gramática

Forms of "Can" and "To be able to" – Formas de "Can" y "To be able to".

Can: solo tiene dos formas "**can / can't**" y "**could / couldn't**". Como ya habíamos explicado, "**can**" es para el presente simple y "**could**" es para el pasado simple y el condicional. Siempre lo usamos con otro verbo.

I can work hard now – puedo trabajar duro ahora.

I could work hard when I was young – pude trabajar duro cuando era joven.

También usamos "can" para referirnos al futuro.

I can come tomorrow – puedo venir mañana.

I cannot go to church on Sunday – no puedo ir a la iglesia el domingo.

Usamos "could" también como ya hemos aprendido en la forma cortés de "can" para pedir permiso. En este caso significa lo mismo que "may".

Can I talk to you? - ¿puedo hablar contigo?

Yes, you can. – Sí, puedes.

No, you can't. – No, no puedes.

Could I talk to you? – ¿podría hablar contigo?

Yes, you could. – Sí, podrías.

No, you couldn't – No, no podrías.

May I talk to you? - ¿puedo hablar contigo?

Yes, you may. – Sí, puedes.

No, you may not – No, no puedes.

Usamos *"To be able to – ser capaz de / poder hacer algo / tener la capacidad de"* con otro verbo in infinitive (esto es con "to"). Podemos usarlo en cualquier tiempo o forma.

I am able to travel – puedo viajar / tengo la capacidad para viajar.

I wasn't able to travel – no podía viajar / no tenía la capacidad para viajar.

I didn't use to be able to travel – no solía poder viajar.

I've been able to travel – he sido capaz de viajar / he podido viajar.

I'll be able to travel – podre viajar

I am not going to be able to travel – no poder viajar / no tendrá la capacidad de viajar.

I wouldn't be able to travel – no sería capaz de viajar.

When to use "can / could / to be able to" – Cuando usar "can / could / to be able to".

Usamos "can / could / to be able to" para decir que tenemos la habilidad o posibilidad.

She can sing – ella puede cantar *(habilidad)*.

She is able to sing – ella puede cantar / ella tiene la capacidad para cantar *(habilidad)*

She couldn't sing – elle no pudo cantar *(habilidad)*

She wasn't able to sing – ella no pudo cantar *(habilidad)*

She can probably sing – probablemente ella puede

cantar *(posibilidad)*

She will probably be able to sing – ella probablemente podrá cantar *(posibilidad)*.

She probably couldn't sing – probablemente ella no pudo cantar *(posibilidad)*.

She probably wasn't able to sing – probablemente ella no pudo cantar *(probabilidad)*.

Recuerden que podemos o no usar la palabra "probably" en la oración y el significado vendría siendo el mismo; sin embargo, tiene mejor sentido cuando la usamos.

Para pedir permiso usamos "Can" o la forma cortés "could / may". Nunca usamos "to be able to" para permiso.

Forms of "must" and "have to" – Formas de "must" y "have to".

La palabra "must" solo tiene una forma y la usamos solo para referirnos al presente o futuro.

I must fix the car now – debo arreglar el carro ahora.

I must fix the car tomorrow – debo arreglar el carro mañana.

Podemos usar "to have to" en todos los tiempos y formas.

I have to fix the car now – tengo que arreglar el carro ahora.

I am going to have to fix the car tomorrow – tendré que arreglar el carro mañana.

I didn't have to fix the car – no tuve que arreglar el

carro.

Recuerden,

En la forma negative "*mustn't*" y "*don't have to*" tienen diferente significados.

You mustn't fix the car now – no debes arreglar el carro ahora *(you may not fix the car now)*

You don't have to fix the car now – no tienes que arreglar el carro ahora *(you don't need to fix the car now – no necesitas arreglar el carro ahora).*

No olviden que el "*must*" es un fuerte mandato, que hay que hacer la cosa si o si, mientras que "*have to*" tienes que hacerlo, pero también puede que no lo hagas.

The Adverb "Back" – El adverbio "back".

Podemos usar el adverbio "back – atrás, detrás" con muchos verbos. Veamos algunos.

To give back – devolver / dar de vuelta.

Give me my watch back – devuélveme mi reloj.

To want back – querer de vuelta.

I want my money back – quiero mi dinero de vuelta.

To need back – necesitar de vuelta.

I need you back – te necesito de vuelta – necesito que regreses.

To go back – retornar.

Go back the same way you came – retorna o regresa por el mismo camino que viniste. *(Cuando quien habla no está en el lugar de destino)*

To come back – regresar / retornar.

Come back, please. I cannot live without you – por favor, regresa. No puedo vivir sin ti. *(Cuando la persona que habla está en el lugar de destino).*

To take back – retornar / devolver.

Take the money back – regresa el dinero / devuelve el dinero.

To bring back – traer de vuelta – retornar.

Bring me my dog back, please – regrésame mi perro, por favor /tráeme mi perro de vuelta, por favor.

To walk back – regresar caminando.

I cannot walk back, it is too far – no puedo regresar caminando; es demasiado lejos.

To run back – regresar corriendo.

I ran back to the house when I heard the news – regrese corriendo a la casa cuando escuche la noticia.

To drive back – regresar conduciendo.

I must drive back to the service station for gas – debo regresar conduciendo a la estación de servicio por gas.

Indirect Commands – Órdenes indirectos.

"Don't use my perfume!" Tiffany's father said – Tiffany's father *told her not to use* his perfume. – "No uses mi perfume," dijo el padre de Tiffany. – El padre de Tiffany le dijo que no usara su perfume.

"Brush your hair, Yeiris!" her mother said – Yeiris mother *asked her to* brush her hair. – "Cepillate el cabello, Yeiris," dijo su madre – La madre de Yeiris le dijo que se cepillara el cabello.

"Please do it as quickly as possible," he said to me – He *asked me to do* it as quickly as possible. – "Por favor, hazlo lo más pronto posible," me dijo él – Él me pidió que lo hiciera lo más pronto posible.

Como pueden ver, estamos usando *"told- dijo"* y *"asked – pidió"* para expresar una mandato de una tercera persona. Es lo mismo que en español. Recuerden, cuando el mandato es negativo, el *"not"* vienes antes del *"to"*. "Don't worry," Hector's father said. Hector's father told him not to worry – No te preocupes, dijo le dijo el padre de Héctor. El papá de Héctor le dijo que no se preocupara.

Reported Speech – Discurso indirecto
Cuando queremos decir lo que otra persona dijo sin usar sus palabras exactas, usamos el "reported speech".

Doctor Peter *says* you'll be fine – el doctor Peter dice que estarás bien.

He *says* he doesn't want it – él dice que no lo quiere.

Algunas veces usamos "that" para unir la oración, más parecido al español. Veamos los mismos ejemplos.

Doctor Peter *says that* you'll be fine – el doctor Peter dice que estarás bien.

He *says that* he doesn't want it – él dice que no lo quiere.

Es muy sencillo y fácil usarlo. Solo tenemos que recordar "says – dice" y a opción nuestra agregamos el "that – que" o no. Como prefiramos.

The president *says that* he'll solve the electricity problem – el presidente dice que el resolverá el problema de la luz.

The girl *says* you are mean to her – la niña dice que eres malo con ella.

Conditional (type 1) – Condicional (tipo 1).

En inglés encontraremos diferentes tipos de condicionales con "if – si condicional", vamos a ver el primer tipo.

If – when – si condicional – cuando

Si o cuando algo pasa, algo más pasará.

You will be very happy *if* you come with me – serás muy feliz si vienes conmigo.

You will be very happy *when* you come with me – serás muy feliz cuando vengas conmigo.

She will be very sad *if* she goes with him – elle estará muy triste si ella se va con él.

She will be very sad *when* she goes with him – ella estará muy triste cuando se vaya con él.

Usamos el presente simple (no el futuro) después de "if" y "when".

If not - unless / either

Si algo no sucede o a menos que suceda, algo más sucederá. Recuerden que esta estructura es con el negativo. Son usadas para un condicional.

If you don't come, I won't talk to you – si no vienes, no hablaré contigo.

Unless you come, I won't talk to you – a menos que vengas, no hablaré contigo.

If she doesn't come, I won't give her the money – si ella no viene, no le daré el dinero.

Unless she comes, I won't give her the money – a menos que ella venga, no le daré el dinero.

También podemos usar "either... or" para describir la misma idea.

Either you come, *or* I won't talk to you – o vienes o no hablaré contigo.

Either she comes, *or* I won't give her the money – o ella viene o no le daré el dinero.

Either you come *or else...* - o vienes o te atienes a las consecuencias / o vienes o verás.

Conjunctions – Conjunciones.

Vamos a ver "*either... or*" y "*neither... nor*".

I'll finish the project. If I don't, John will – terminaré el proyecto. Si no lo hago, John lo hará.

Either Peter *or* I will finish the project. Lo termina Peter o lo termino yo.

En el negativo tenemos en español "*ni...ni*". Veamos.

You are not smoking. My father isn't either – No estás fumando. Mi padre tampoco.

Neither my father *nor* you are smoking – ni mi padre ni tú están fumando.

You not learning Spanish. My sister isn't either – No estás aprendiendo español. Mi hermana tampoco.

Neither my sister *nor* you are learning Spanish –

ni mi hermana ni tú están aprendiendo español. Normalmente usamos un verbo en plural después de *"either... or / neither... nor"*. Pero recuerden, cuando son usados como pronombres, entonces el verbo siempre estará en singular. *Either of them is* able to swim – cualquiera de ellos es capaz de nadar. *Neither of us wants* to start – ninguno de nosotros quiere iniciar.

Recuerden, al igual que en español, cuando eres parte de la conversación y eres el hablante, siempre deberás contarte de ultimo; no es correcto decir "yo y María"... ¿verdad? Lo correcto es decir "María y yo". Lo mismo acontece en inglés.

Either he or *I* – o él o yo.

They saw him and *me* – lo vieron a él y a mí.

Adjectives – Adjetivos
Available – disponible
Flat – desinflado / rueda pinchada
Medium sized – talla mediana
Plenty of – suficiente de
Spare – repuesta / extra
Convenient - conveniente
Pleased - satisfecho
Urgent - urgente
Deaf - sordo
Frightened – aterrado

Regular verbs – Verbos regulares
To check – checked – checked – chequear / verificar

To fill – filled – filled - llenar
To return – returned – returned - regresar
To suggest – suggested – suggested - sugerir
To discuss – discussed – discussed - discutir
To arrest – arrested – arrested - arrestar
To belong – belonged – belonged - pertenecer
To hijack – hijacked – hijacked - secuestrar
To pray – prayed – prayed - orar
To pull – pulled – pulled - halar
To push – pushed – pushed - empujar
To reduce – reduced – reduced - reducir

Irregular verbs – Verbos irregulares
To be able / was (were) able / been able – ser capaz
To break down / broke down / broken down - dañarse
To blow up – blew up – blown up – explotar
To hold – held – held – mantener / sostener
To run away – ran away – run away - huir

The hijacking

Randy knew he couldn't turn back. If he changed his mind now, he would go to jail for sure. He tied up his prisoner as tight as he could and threw him into the truck. The prisoner yelled and yelled, making ridiculous threats: "If you don't let me go, I'm going to call the police! You are definitely fired. Either you let me go, or you're going to lose your insurance. You're not going to see another pay check, you hear me? And I won't recommend you for other jobs either."

Randy just laughed. He'd wanted to kidnap his boss for a very long time. He enjoyed hearing the desperate pleas from the back of the truck. He took him out to a deserted cabin and locked him inside. The next day, he went to work as usual. He took his time on the **overdue** project. Around noon, he called his boss's home to ask about him. Then he reported the disappearance to the police: "I don't know what happened to my boss today. He didn't come in to work today. His wife said he didn't go home last night either. I'm a little worried about him."

After work, he wrote a ransom note and mailed it from the next town over. Then he waited. No money came. He had to go out and feed his boss the next day or he would be sick. While he was there, he heard a helicopter. "Great!" he thought. "They've seen my truck and will know it's me." But he had something else up his sleeve. He worked feverishly for a few minutes, and when the police arrived outside and demanded that he come out, he yelled, "I've got a bomb!" He set the timer and sneaked out the back window. As he ran, the trees and brush scratched his face and tore his clothes, but he was nearly a mile away when the bomb went off. He felt a little worried for his boss and his wife, but he comforted himself saying, "At least I won't have to finish my project today." Then he heard another explosion. He had only set one bomb. What was that noise? Again and again, he heard the explosions. He opened his eyes and saw the alarm clock. "No," he yelled as he jumped out of bed to get ready for work.

Exercises – Ejercicios

Exercise 2.1: Write the correct form of *can, could,* or *be able to.*

Cats _____ swim. (can)

Fish _____ fly. (can not)

The computer repairman _____ repair your computer. (be able to—past tense)

Your son _____ become a great singer. (could)

She has _____ finish the report. (not be able to)

Monkeys _____ climb. (can)

My mom _____ bake your wedding cake. (could)

I'm sorry, but I will _____ go to your wedding. (not be able to)

Exercise 2.2: Write "A" if the sentence shows ability, "P" for probability, and "A/P" for both ability and probability (if it's ambiguous).

_____ They couldn't help us escape.

_____ My boyfriend can lift an 85-pound bar 8 times!

_____ The company wasn't able to hide its criminal activity.

_____ She couldn't make soft chocolate chip cookies at high altitudes.

_____ They couldn't make it to the party.

_____ The girl wasn't able to give birth until she had a C-section.

_____ Can she type 70 words a minute?

_____ Nobody is able to live without sleep.

_____ Could this drink contain poison?

_____ I could never marry a pirate.

Exercise 2.3: Underline the correct verb.
I **need/run/come** my sewing machine **back**, please.
The boogieman **wanted/went/brought** the bad little boy **back** to his mother.
We had to **take back/give back/walk back** down the mountain.
She **needed/gave/went** the project **back** because she was too busy to do it.
They want you to **want/need/give** the car **back** since you didn't pay for it.
That terrible cat keeps **bringing back/coming**

back/giving back.

Can you **take/go/want** the movie **back** to the store for me?

Some friends **went/drove/gave** us **back** to our house.

I **want/walk/come** the crib **back**, please.

She **gave back/wanted back/ran back** for the key.

Exercise 2.4: Make the direct speech indirect.

Policeman: "If you collect four of these tickets, you win a bicycle."

Teacher: "Bring pictures to class tomorrow."

Uncle Jerry: "You catch more flies with honey."

Veterinarian: "The best thing is to wash him."

Mechanic: "Your car will be as good as new."

Exercise 2.5: Write the verb in the correct form.

Do as I say, and nobody _____ hurt. (get)

If she arrives in time, we _____ her with us. (take)

When you fail a class, they _____ you come to summer school. (make)

Unless you stop him, Boris _____ the moose. (kill)

Either we save water, or we _____ enough for the summer. (not have)

Lesson 3
My coach – my star

Conversation

Max: Wow. I really don't feel like working tonight. I'm so tired.

Bobbie: But maybe we'll get to see Spark. Come on. I want to get his autograph.

Max: Oh, okay. But he might be too busy; you understand that, right?

Bobbie: Yes, of course, but I think this is our lucky night.

Max: Our lucky night?

Bobbie: No, not yours. Spark's and mine. He's going to score more goals than when he won the cup. And I'm going to get his autograph. It'll be worth a lot of money.

Max: Maybe. There have been lots of people who have gotten his autograph. He loves signing his name.

Bobbie: Yeah, I know, but not all tonight—his lucky night. He said he has the feeling he's going to play like never before. Now that he's back to work after his injury, he's going to really stomp on the other team.

Max: We'll see. I hope it's at least an interesting game so I have something to write about.

New words – Nuevas palabras
Autograph - autógrafo
Coach - entrenador
Condition – condición *(situación de salud)*
Crowd - multitud
Cup - taza
Field - campo
Goal – gol *(cuando se mete un gol al jugar)*
Interview - entrevista
Kiss - beso
Opportunity - oportunidad
Pay - paga
Pollution – contaminación
Position – posición *(puesto en una compañía)*
Sleeve – manga *(de la camisa)*
Sport - deporte
Team - equipo
Trash - basura

Words Definitions
Never mind: *it is the same as saying "forget it," that's all right.*

Condition: *when something or someone is healthy or in good state of health.*

True: *when something is real. What really happened, is happening or will happen.*

Deep down: *in your heart. Expressing how you really feel about something. You can also say down deep.*

Sweet: *something that is not sour -* the opposite of

sour. *Also when someone is kind.*

Phrases and Expressions - Frases y expresiones
A bit – un poco
Day after day – día tras día
Deep down – en el fondo / en lo profundo
Down here (there) – aquí (allá) abajo
For the best – es lo mejor
For the worst – es lo peor
Good luck – buena suerte
Hour after hour – hora tras hora
Look who's talking – mira quien habla
Never mind – olvídalo / ya no importa
On the road – viajando / en la carretera / de camino
To feel that – sentir que / creer que
I feel that she is right – siento que ella está en lo correcto / creo que ella está en lo correcto.
To find that – encontrar que / pensar que
I find that hard to believe – creo que eso es difícil de creer – para mí es difícil creerlo.
To fix up – hacer que algo o alguien luzca bien o lindo. Reparar una relación.
To go back to work – regresar al trabajo
To make friends – hacer amigos
To make up your mind – decidirte *(cuando no estás seguro y tienes que tomar una decisión)*
Up here (there) – aquí (allá) arriba
What do you say? - ¿Qué dices? / ¿Cómo ves? / ¿Está bien? *(cuando buscamos la aprobación de alguien)*

Grammar – Gramática

The auxiliary "May" and "Maybe" – El auxiliar "May" y "Maybe".

En lecciones pasadas hemos aprendido como usar "may"; veamos un poquito más de lo que ya hemos aprendido y tomemos nota de este corto repaso.

Algunas veces cuando usamos "may", puede significar "*maybe – tal vez*" o "*perhaps – tal vez*". Recuerden, "*maybe*" y "*perhaps*" significan lo mismo. Veamos.

Are you going to travel? - ¿vas a viajar o viajarás?
I may – puede que sí
I may not – puede que no.
I may travel – puede que viaje
I may not travel – puede que no viaje
Maybe I will – tal vez lo haré
Maybe I won't – tal vez no lo haré

Do you know if she's coming tonight? - ¿sabes si ella vendrá esta noche?
She may – puede que sí
She may not – puede que no
Maybe she will – tal vez lo hará
Maybe she won't – tal vez no lo hará
O simplemente pueden contestar
Maybe – tal vez
Perhaps – a lo mejor, quien sabe
Recuerden, solo hacemos preguntas con "may" cuando estamos pidiendo permiso. May I come in? - ¿puedo entrar?

"There is / are" with auxiliary verbs – "There is / are" con verbos auxiliares.

Usamos "there is" y "there are" en todos los tiempos y con verbos auxiliaries.

There may be a party tomorrow – puede que haya una fiesta mañana.

There used to be parties every week, but *there haven't been* any in a long time – solían haber fiestas todas las semanas, pero no ha habido ninguna en mucho tiempo.

There weren't any last month, and I don't believe *there'll be* any this month – no hubo ninguna el mes pasado y no creo que habrá ninguna este mes.

There can't be a party tomorrow, and *there aren't going to be* any this weekend – no puede haber una fiesta mañana y no habrá ninguna este fin de semana.

Fíjense bien en cada uno de los ejemplos resaltados. Es bastante sencillo, usen casi todos los tiempos para que tengan una mejor idea.

Verbs plus "ing" form – Verbos más la forma "ing".

Ya sabemos que la forma "ing" equivale al gerundio "ando – iendo". Algunos verbos y expresiones en inglés usan el "ing" después del verbo principal. En español sería como usar el infinito después del verbo principal. Veamos.

To enjoy - disfrutar

I *enjoy playing* cards – disfruto jugar cartas.

Fíjense bien: el primer verbo esta conjugado y el segundo verbo está con el "ing", mientras que en español usan el segundo verbo en infinito. Continuemos viendo más ejemplos.

To finish – terminar
We haven't *finished discussing* the situation yet – aún no hemos terminado de platicar la situación. Tenemos "finished" en pasado y el próximo verbo con "ing".

I *finished talking* to you – terminé de hablar contigo.

To stop – detener / parar
Stop drinking, please – para de beber, por favor.

Please *stop running* away – por favor, deja de huir.

To be used to – estar acostumbrado
I *am used to waking up* early – estoy acostumbrado a levantarme temprano.

To get used to – acostumbrarse
I'll never *get used to getting* up so early – nunca me acostumbraré a levantarme tan temprano.

To feel like – sentir que
I *feel like eating* an apple – tengo ganas de o se me antoja comerme una manzana.

I *feel like taking* a shower – tengo ganas de tomar una ducha.

To have trouble – tener problemas
You'll always *have trouble trusting* people – siempre tendrás problemas para creer en las personas.

You'll never *have trouble finding* a job – nunca tendrás problemas para encontrar trabajo.

To think of – pensar en

I'm *thinking of opening* a new business – estoy pensando en abrir un nuevo negocio.

We're *thinking of traveling* to Italy – estamos pensando en viajar a Italia.

I'm *thinking of planning* a trip – pienso planear un viaje.

Algunos verbos especiales pueden llevar tanto el infinitivo como el "ing".

To begin – empezar

Suddenly she *began to cry* – de repente ella empezó a llorar.

Suddenly she *began crying* – de repente ella empezó a llorar.

They *began to play* cards – ellos empezaron a jugar cartas.

They *began playing* cards – ellos empezaron a jugar cartas.

To start – comenzar

When I told the story, they *started to laugh* – cuando les conté la historia comenzaron a reírse.

When I told the story, they *started laughing* – cuando les conté la historia comenzaron a reírse.

To like – gustar

I *like fishing* – me gusta pescar

I *like to fish* – me gusta pescar

She *likes cooking* – a ella le gusta cocinar
She *likes to cook* – a ella le gusta cocinar.

To prefer - preferir
I *prefer eating* fruit – prefiero comer frutas
I *prefer to eat* fruit – prefiero comer frutas
We *prefer running* – preferimos correr
We *prefer to run* – preferimos correr.
Como pueden ver, la estructura es fácil y sencilla; ustedes pueden usar cualquier de las dos formas.

Tenemos que prestar mucha atención al verbo "*to stop*", porque cuando le sigue un verbo en infinitivo significa una cosa y cuando es "*ing*" significo otra cosa. Veamos los ejemplos.

I stopped working – *paré de trabajar* (significa que estaba trabajando y me detuve)

I stopped to work – *me detuve para trabajar* (significa que estaba haciendo algo y lo dejé para trabajar).

She *stopped smoking* – ella dejó de fumar
She *stopped to smoke* – ella se detiene para fumar.

Reported Speech in Present and Past – Discurso indirecto en presente y pasado.

En la lección anterior, vimos el "reported speech"; vamos a ver un poco más sobre el tema.

Recuerden que algunas veces usamos "that" como ya aprendimos, pero es opcional; no es un deber.

My teacher says:, "*You train* very hard" – Mi profesor dice, "Tú entrenas muy duro".

My teacher says that I train very hard – mi

profesor dice que yo entreno muy duro.

Cuando el verbo principal "say / tell" está en pasado, el verbo del discurso indirecto a menudo está en pasado también.

She said, "*I want* a room" – ella dijo, "yo quiero una habitación".

She said (that) she wanted a room – ella dijo que quería una habitación.

Usamos el presente en el discurso directo, y el pasado en el discurso indirecto.

He used to say, "*You are* the best" – él solía decir, "Tú eres el mejor".

He used to say (that) I was the best – él solía decir que yo era el mejor.

Usamos el presente del verbo "to be" en el discurso directo, y el pasado del verbo "to be" en el discurso indirecto.

Peter said, "Mary has to study hard" – Peter dijo, "María tiene que estudiar duro".

Peter said that Mary had to study hard – Peter dijo que María tenía que estudiar duro.

Usamos "has" en el presente del discurso directo, y "had" en el pasado del discurso indirecto.

Hector said, "Tiffany is going to France" – Héctor dijo, "Tiffany va para Francia".

Hector said that Tiffany was going to France – Héctor dijo que Tiffany iba para Francia.

Usamos el gerundio en el discurso directo, y el pasado gerundio en el discurso indirecto.

They said, "We can sing" – ellos dijeron, "podemos cantar"

They said that they could sing – ellos dijeron que podían cantar.

Usamos "can" en el presente del discurso directo, y "could" en el pasado del discurso indirecto.

Ben said, "I'll go to Europe" – Ben dijo, "iré a Europa".

Ben said the he would go to Europe – Ben dijo que iría a Europa.

Usamos "will" en el presente del discurso directo y "would" en el pasado del discurso indirecto.

Recuerden que siempre que usen "tell" deberán usar un objeto indirecto.

Hector told me, "I used to train very hard" – Héctor me dijo, "Yo solía entrenar muy duro".

Hector told me that he used to train very hard – Héctor me dijo que él solía entrenar muy duro.

Reported questions "ask" – Preguntas discurso indirecto "ask".

Presten mucha atención en el órden de las palabras.

Hector always asks, "How many points did you get?" – Héctor siempre pregunta, "¿Cuántos puntos sacaste?"

Hector always *asks how many points I got* – Héctor siempre pregunta cuantos puntos saqué.

Tiffany *asked*, "Why *is* he happy?" – Tiffany preguntó, "¿Por qué está él feliz?"

Tiffany **asked** why he **was** happy – Tiffany preguntó por qué él estaba feliz.
Cuando no hay ningún pronombre interrogativo, entonces tenemos que usar "if- si condicional".
Tiffany asked, "Do you like apples?" – Tiffany preguntó, "Te gustan las manzanas"
Tiffany **asked me if I liked** apples – Tiffany me preguntó si me gustaban las manzanas.

Adverbs – Adverbios
At first – al principio /al inicio / al comienzo
Definitely - definitivamente
Nicely – agradablemente, con finura, bien
At least – al menos
Especially - especialmente
Together – juntos
Nearly – casi

Adjectives – Adjetivos
Deep - profundo
Sweet - dulce
True – verdadero / genuino
Embarrassed – avergonzado
I am embarrassed by her behavior – me siento avergonzado por su conducta
Embarrassing - vergonzoso
Nervous - nervioso
Shy - tímido
Messy – sucio / desastroso
Neat – limpio / pulcro / ordenado / puro

Regular verbos – Verbos regulares
To burn – burned – burned - quemar
To mess up – messed up – messed up – desordenar / estropear / arruinar / ensuciar
To paint – painted – painted - pintar
To roast – roasted – roasted - asar
To straighten up – straightened up – straightened up – enderezar / ordenar
To ask for – asked for – asked for – preguntar por / pedir
To cheer – cheered – cheered – animar / alentar
To interview – interviewed – interviewed - entrevistar
To save – saved – saved – salvar / guardar
To score – scored – scored - anotar
To train – trained – trained - entrenar
To believe – believed – believed - creer
To decide – decided – decided - decidir
To deserve – deserved – deserved - merecer
To manage – managed – managed – organizar / lograr / administrar
To move – moved – moved - mover
To settle down – settled down – settled down – establecerse / resolver / sentar cabeza

Irregular verbs – Verbos irregulares
To freeze – froze – frozen - congelar
To hide – hid – hidden - esconder
To put away – put away – put away – guardar / retirar
To tear – tore – torn - rasgar

To throw away – threw away – thrown away – botar / arrojar / desechar

To wear out – wore out – worn out – gastar / desgastar

To teach – taught – taught - enseñar

Pollution

News Anchor: We'll turn now to the local news. According to polls, Mr. Thompson is in the lead for the office of mayor. His campaign is based on cleaning up the city with the slogan "Cleaner politics, a cleaner city." In fliers and TV ads, you can see him at points all around town picking up trash—in a designer suit— and supervising cleanup efforts at rivers and along roadways. He's always criticizing current politicians and public works projects for corruption and lack of transparency. However, Thompson recently refused to release records of his campaign funding and expenses. Many people have begun to question the sincerity of Thompson's "clean" politics. But he doesn't have direct answers. Let's go now to this afternoon's interview:

Reporter 1: Mr. Thompson, many people are very excited about your campaign of cleaning up politics and cleaning up the city, but in spite of repeated requests for your funding records, nothing has been released. What explanation can you give us for this apparent contradiction in your message and practice?

Mr. Thompson: I'm glad to address this problem of cleaning up our city. Our society demands a general cleanup: a cleanup of politics and a cleanup of the parks, rivers, and streets. I am working to renew our city. You can depend on me.

Reporter 1: Mr. Thompson—

Mr. Thompson: Any other questions? I'm glad to answer your questions. Transparency is key for clean politics.

Reporter 2: Yes, Sir, some people have suggested that you may not really represent clean politics.

Mr. Thompson: There will always be people who criticize clean politics. They like talking about others so that no one will look at what they are doing. They are afraid that their corruption will be exposed. You can count on me to expose dirty politics and clean up our dirty streets.

Reporter 3: Mr. Thompson, you have not been transparent. You have not released funding reports. You have not answered our questions. How can you call that clean politics?

Mr. Thompson: I have based my campaign on clean funding. You can always count on me to fight corruption. I will be accountable to taxpayers, unlike those who are in office now, who have not explained their use of taxpayer funds. I will publish spending budgets and expenses. We will bring transparency to our great city.

Exercises – Ejercicios
Exercise 3.1: Make the direct speech indirect.
"I love her," said Mark.

"This town is beautiful," they said.

"Where are you?" he asked.

"We're not going to throw away your toys," her parents promised.

"Go to sleep," he told his daughter.

"I score more points than any other player," the player said.

"There may be mice down here," John said.

"I find that hard to believe," said the policeman.

"Are you sure your husband will come?" the principal asked.

"Tom stopped to help the lady cross the street," Mac reported.

Exercise 3.2: Write the correct form of the verb. If two forms are possible, write both forms.

There used to _____ a park here (be).

We finished _____after closing time (eat).

I feel like _____ three coffees (drink).

The president may _____ over Christmas vacation (travel).

They're thinking of _____ a new cashier (hire).

Suddenly, it began _____ (rain).

A lot of people like _____ the sunset (watch).

I don't want to buy a membership. I prefer

_____ for one visit (pay).

My boss asked me _____ the project tonight (finish).

We stopped _____ the new museum on our way to our parents' house (visit).

Exercise 3.3: Write the correct form of the adjective or adverb.

She _____ asked me to wash my dishes (sweet).

She's a _____ girl (nice).

My brother is very _____ (neat).

Tim _____ stood outside the store (nervous).

They _____ lost their dog (definite).

Lesson 4
Spaceship travel – Viaje en la nave espacial

Conversation

Lizzie: What are you doing, Grandpa?

Grandpa: I'm working.

Lizzie: You're working? It looks to me like you're playing.

Grandpa: Playing? Playing with a rocket? With meticulous flight and landing plans? If that's what you call playing, I'm doing a good job of it.

Lizzie: You don't need to get angry, Grandpa. Have you planned how it will fly?

Grandpa: Have I planned—Lizzie, you are incredible. I have planned the flight time and return trip. I have planned how to avoid damage on reentry. I have even found a pilot.

Lizzie: A pilot?

Grandpa: Yes. Look!

Lizzie: It's my stuffed elephant.

Grandpa: Yes. They're supposed to be very intelligent. But that's just for aesthetics. I am finally going to realize my dream of breaking the sound barrier, of reaching other realms, of going beyond the ordinary limits imposed on frail humanity.

Lizzie: So where's the fuel kept?

Grandpa: Fuel?

Lizzie: Yeah, fuel. I mean, it has to have fuel to

fly, right?

Grandpa: Yes, of course. It's not quite—that is—I'm going to do that next.

New words – Nuevas palabras

Air conditioner – aire acondicionado (también se puede decir AC).

Amount – monto / cantidad

Astronaut - astronauta

Blood - sangre

Bone - hueso

Bowl – recipiente / taza / tazón

Brain - cerebro

Button - botón

Corn - maíz

Cotton - algodón

Cover – tapa / cobertura

Detail - detalle

Divorce - divorcio

Downhill – cuesta abajo *(en una colina)*

Dream - sueño

Earth – tierra

Energy - energía

Equipment – equipo

Except (that) – excepto (que)

Face - cara

Flour - harina

Frog - sapo

Fuel - combustible

Fur – piel *(tipo de ropa)*

Furniture - muebles

Glass – vaso / vidrio
Grape - uva
Hill – colina
History - historia
Invention – invento / invención
Journey - jornada
Leather – cuero / piel
Light – luz
Mess – lío / confusión / enredo
Metal - metal
Nylon - Nilo
Piece - pieza
Planet - planeta
Plastic - plástico
Rainstorm – tormenta de lluvia
Rat - rata
Reason - razón
Research – investigación
Scientist - científico
Ship - barco
Skin – piel
Sky - cielo
Snowstorm – tormenta de nieve
Space – espacio
Spaceship – nave espacial
Storm - tormenta
Strawberry - fresa
Tail – cola *(de un animal)*
Tractor - tractor
Vehicle – vehículo
Uphill – cuesta arriba *(en una colina)*

Way – forma / modo
Wheat - trigo
Witch - bruja
Wood - madera
Wool - lana
World - mundo

Word Definitions

Brain: *what is inside our heads.*

Can't stand: *when you hate something or someone.*

Fed up: *when you are angry because something has happened more than once.*

Good for nothing: *when a person or thing never works.*

History: *events in the past.*

Lazy: *a person that doesn't like to work or do anything.*

Stunning: *when someone is very attractive.*

Your honor: *when we are speaking to a judge.*

Way: *how a person does something or goes somewhere.*

Phrases and Expressions - Frases y expresiones

Can't stand – no soportar algo / odiar algo

Ever since -- desde entonces

To fall asleep – caer dormido / dormirse

To get divorced (from) – divorciarse de alguien

To get to a point (where) – llegar a un punto en donde…

To get to the point (where) – llegar al punto donde…

Good for nothing – bueno para nada

I mean – quiero decir / esto es / es decir *(cuando queremos decir los mismo en diferente forma para explicar lo dicho o para justificar lo dicho)*

To lose a job – perder un trabajo

Off and on – de vez en cuando *(no muy a menudo)*

On purpose – a propósito / adrede

To put out a fire – apagar un fuego / detener el fuego

Your honor – su señoría

Good gracious – caramba / válgame Dios *(mostrando gran sorpresa por algo)*

For now – por ahora

Made from – hecho de *(refiriéndonos al lugar en donde se hizo)*

Made of – hecho de *(refiriéndonos al material de que está hecho)*

Means of transportation – medios de transporte

Off you go – listo para irte / ya puedes irte

Right here – aquí mismo

Right there – allá mismo

That's where you're wrong – ahí es donde te equivocas / ahí es donde estás equivocado.

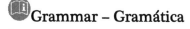Grammar – Gramática

Present perfect progressive – Presente perfecto continuo.

Este tiempo se usa más en inglés que en español. Usamos este tiempo cuando algo inició en el pasado, aún continúa pasando en el presente y puede que continúe en el futuro. Prestemos atención.

I've been waiting for you for five hours – he estado esperando por ti durante five horas *(comencé a esperar hacen five horas y aún sigo esperando)*

She *has been studying* since this morning – ella ha estado estudiando desde la mañana *(comenzó a estudiar en la mañana, aún está estudiando y puede que continúe estudiando)*.

I've been studying for three hours, but *I've only studied* five pages – he estado estudiando por tres horas, pero solo he estudiado cinco páginas.

Normalmente no usamos el presente perfecto continuo con estos verbos: *to belong, to hate, to know, to like, to love, to remember, to understand.*

Using "can't be" and "must be" – Usando "can't be" y "must be".

Usamos "can't be" cuando pensamos que algo está incorrecto y "must be" para indicar que algo más es lo correcto.

You *can't be* only twenty. You *must be* at least thirty. No puede ser que solo tengas veinte. Tú debes tener por lo menos treinta.

She *can't be* working. She *must be* resting – no puede ser que ella este trabajando. Ella debe estar descansando.

Por supuesto, no siempre los usamos juntos.

I don't know who she is, but she *must be* the teacher. – No sé quién es ella, pero ella debe ser la profesora.

She was sleeping just a minute ago. She *can't be*

working. – Ella estaba durmiendo solo hace un minuto. No puede ser que esté trabajando.

The word "As" – La palabra "As"

Ustedes saben que usamos la palabra "as" para comparación (*I am as smart as you* – *soy tan inteligente como tú*). Ahora vamos a ver otros usos de "as".

Podemos usar "as" para significar "*while – mientras*".

I sing *as* I work – canto mientras trabajo.

I remembered the dog *as* I walked out the door – recordé el perro mientras salía de la casa.

Podemos usar "as" para significar "*because – porque*".

As we had no option, we had to break the door – porque no teníamos otra opción, tuvimos que romper la puerta.

As you left the keys in the car, we had to break the window – porque dejaste las llave dentro del auto, tuvimos que romper la ventana.

También podemos usar "as" como preposición delante de sustantivos y pronombres. En este caso "as" funciona como comparativo "like, similar to".

I used to work *as* a teacher, and all the students learned *like crazy* – solía trabajar como profesor y todos los estudiantes aprendían como locos.

She used to work *as a cook*, and anyone who tries her food, *eats like a horse* – ella solía trabajar como cocinera, y todos los clientes comían como animales (caballos).

Verbs of Sense and Perception – Verbos de sentidos y percepción.

Eyes – Ojos

To look at – mirar / observar

I was *looking at* you – te estaba mirando.

To look like – parecerse.

It *looks like* an apple – se parece a una manzana.

To watch – mirar / observar

I am *watching* TV – estoy mirando TV

To see - ver

I *saw* something strange – vi algo extraño.

Ears – Oidos

To listen to – escuchar

I was *listening to* the radio – estaba escuchando la radio.

To hear – oír

I *heard* people speaking – oí personas hablando.

To sound (like)

The music *sounded* very loud – la música sonaba muy alta.

It *sounded like* a disco – sonaba como una disco.

Nose – Nariz

To smell (like)

It *smells* good – huele rico.

She *smells like* flowers – ella huele como a flores.

Mouth – Boca

To taste – probar / saborear

It *tastes* delicious – sabe delicioso.

It *tasted like* an orange – sabía a naranja / tenía un sabor a naranja.

Fingers / Hands – Dedos / Manos

To touch – *tocar o palpar*

I *touched* your skin – toque tu piel.

To feel - *sentir*

It *felt like* heaven – se sintió como el cielo.

It *felt* warm – la sentí caliente.

También podemos usar "*to seem (like)* – *parecerse*" y "*to appear to be* – *aparentar ser o estar*" para describir cosas.

The sun *seems* hot today – el sol parece caliente hoy.

The sun *appears to be* hot today – el sol parece estar caliente hoy.

It *seems like* she's getting better – parece como que ella se está recuperando.

She *appears to be* getting better – ella aparenta como que se está mejorando.

También podemos usar "*to look like*" y "*to sound like*" para decir lo que pensamos sobre algo, como ya hemos visto anteriormente.

That *sounds like* a good idea – eso suena como una buena idea.

That *looks like* a good plan – eso parece un buen plan.

The passive voice – La voz pasiva

Usamos la voz pasiva cuando no sabemos quién hizo algo o cuando queremos enfatizar algo que fue hecho en vez de quién lo hizo. Recuerden, siempre habrá una forma en la voz pasiva para decir exactamente lo mismo que lo que queremos expresar en la voz pasiva.

Active voice
Someone stole my dog – alguien se robó mi perro.

Passive voice
My dog *was stolen* – mi perro fue robado.
Si queremos indicar quien lo hizo en la voz pasiva, entonces usamos "by".
My dog *was stolen by someone* – mi perro fue robado por alguien.
The homework *was done by someone* – la tarea fue hecho por alguien.
Pueden usar la voz pasiva en todos los tiempos. Veamos algunos ejemplos.
My money *is kept* in the bank (present) – mi dinero está guardado en el banco.
My money *is being kept* in the bank (present progressive) – mi dinero está siendo guardado en el banco.
My money *was kept* in the bank (simple past) – mi dinero estaba guardado en el banco.
My money *will be kept* in the bank (future) – mi dinero será guardado en el banco.

The impersonal "you" – El "you" impersonal.
Cuando usamos "you" en una oración con sentido general, nos referimos a nadie en específico, más bien a todo el mundo.
You should speak English in class – se debe hablar inglés en clase.

Everybody should speak English in class – todos deben hablar inglés en clase.

English should be spoken by everyone in class – el inglés debe ser hablado por todos en clase.

You can't smoke here – no se puede fumar aquí

Nobody can smoke here – nadie puede fumar aquí.

This place *can't be used for smoking* – este lugar no puede ser usado para fumar.

Como pueden ver, todas estas frases significan lo mismo; estamos usando el "you" en sentido general.

Adjectives – Adjetivos
Several - varios
Steady – estable / firme
Bright – brillante / claro
Close (to) – cerca de / junto a
I am close to the restaurant – *estoy cerca del restaurante.*
I am close to you – *estoy junto a ti.*
Dark - oscuro
Horrible - horrible
Incredible - increíble
Latest – lo más reciente / último
Ordinary – común / ordinario
Steep - empinado

Regular verbs – Verbos regulares
To design – designed – designed - diseñar
To equip (for / with) – equipped – equipped – equipar (para / con)
To export – exported – exported - exportar

To import – imported – imported - importar
To invent – invented – invented – inventar / crear
To manufacture – manufactured – manufactured – fabricar / manufacturar
To park – parked – parked - parquear
To pedal – pedaled – pedaled - pedalear
To produce – produced – produced - producir
To protect (from) – protected – protected – proteger (de)
To raise – raised - raised – criar / levantar
To appear – appeared – appeared – aparecer / parecer
To chuckle – chuckled – chuckled – reírse entre los dientes
To seem – seemed – seemed - parecer
To sound – sounded – sounded - sonar
To touch – touched – touched – tocar / palpar
To wonder – wondered – wondered – preguntarse / asombrarse / maravillarse
To develop – developed – developed - desarrollar
To divorce – divorced – divorced - divorciarse
To dream – dreamed – dreamed - soñar
To launch – launched – launched – lanzar / inaugurar
To snore – snored – snored - roncar
To test – tested – tested - probar / examinar

Irregular verbs – Verbos irregulares
To wind up – wound up – wound up – dar cuerda
To go on – went on – gone on – continuar / avanzar / seguir

To light – lit – lit – encender / iluminar
To shake – shook – shaken – agitar / sacudir

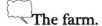The farm.

Farmer Joe has been trimming weeds in the grape vineyard for the past few days. He's hoping to finish today. He gulps down his breakfast and heads outside, his dog Lucky following behind him. An extension converts his tractor into a mechanical weed trimmer. But it's still really hard work. He throws some dry bread to his ducks and some of last year's hay to the goats. They gratefully reach out for a head scratch. Lucky growls, and Joe laughs.

This is Joe's favorite time to work. The sun over the horizon gives the grape leaves a yellowish hue. The cool, dewy air fills Joe's lungs, and the birds sound happy it's a new day. Lucky tries to shake the moisture off his feet, with no success. Joe checks the gas and scrapes dried weeds off the extension; then he powers up the tractor and heads out to the vineyards. Lucky runs before the tractor, avoiding the blades, then after the tractor, avoiding the wheels. As it draws near to lunchtime, Joe tries to get just a little bit more work done. There really isn't enough time in a farmer's schedule to pull the weeds, and even trimming them takes too long, but Joe hates using herbicides in his vineyards. And the freshly cut weeds smell heavenly.

When Joe goes inside, he finds his wife setting the table. "Chicken salad today, with carrot sticks and chips," she tells him.

"Wonderful," he answers, washing his hands in the kitchen sink to avoid walking around the house and dropping weed clippings everywhere. He and his wife enjoy conversation over lunch, while Lucky looks through the screen door longingly. Then Joe goes back out to work some more. Working especially hard, he manages to finish weeding by six o'clock. He sets the timer on the irrigation system and heads inside for dinner. Lucky is hanging around on the deck, hoping for a bit of dinner. It's venison roast in mushroom gravy, and it smells good! The dog is finally in luck. Since there's banana cream pie for dessert, there will be a little extra meat for the dog.

Exercises – Ejercicios

Exercise 4.1: Write the correct form of the phrase: *can't be, must be,* or *seems like.*

Example: They _seemed like_ they were sincere. They were very generous.

The cake _____ gone! I just made it this morning.

You _____ tired. You haven't slept well all weekend.

It _____ I've seen her before. She looks vaguely familiar.

They _____ here already. It's supposed

to take two hours to get here.

He _____ angry. He didn't say anything all evening.

You _____ so sad. He was a very sweet dog. I'm sorry he's gone!

It _____ made of plastic. It's too light to be metal.

She _____ my mother. I don't look anything like her.

It _____ they were impatient. Maybe they were planning to escape.

He _____ a nice guy. Invite him over so we can meet him.

Exercise 4.2: Complete the sentence. Write the verb in present perfect progressive.

My cousin _____ websites. He's very good at it! (design)

We_____ English teachers for ten years. (train)

That lime tree _____ much fruit lately. (not produce)

What's wrong with the dog? He_____

for thirty minutes. (shake)

My grandchildren _____ chickens! (raise)

I_____ if you would tell him about the burnt chicken. (wonder)

When will you take a break?

You_____ for six hours straight. (paint)

Strange lights _____ above the house at night. (appear)

You're still parking the car?

You_____ the car for ten minutes! (park)

Please don't throw that out. I_____ it for a project. (save)

Exercise 4.3: Write the verb in the passive voice and the tense given.

Coffee _____ in more than fifty countries. (grow-simple present)

Your purchase _____ on file for three months. (keep-*will* future)

Apple tart _____ with apples, flour, butter, and brown sugar. (make-simple present)

It looks like they're outside, but that movie

_____ in the studio. (film-simple past)

That brand _____ exclusively in the US, but not anymore. (produce—used to)

Yes, they _____ to the police. (report-present perfect)

Lesson 5
The state – El estado

Conversation

Jim: Nothing ever changes.

Harry:　　Nope.

Jim: We've been cheated out of our hard-earned money for centuries.

Harry:　　Centuries.

Jim: And do we ever get anything for all that money?

Harry:　　Never.

Jim: No, we don't. And if we ask them what they did with it, they just make up a bunch of lies.

Harry:　　A bunch of lies.

Jim: They say things will change, but they're all the same.

Harry:　　All the same.

Jim:　　They say they'll save us money, but prices keep getting higher.

Harry:　　Higher and higher.

Jim:　　They say there will be more jobs, and instead unemployment increases.

Harry:　　Always increasing.

Jim:　　They say they'll improve health care, but they just keep taking away our benefits.

Harry:　　Yeah.

Jim: First, they take away our dental care and eyeglasses. And now we have to order our prescriptions through the mail or pay for them out of pocket. And if there is no generic, it takes forever to prove we absolutely need it.

Harry: Forever.

Jim: But what can we do?

Harry: There's nothing we can do.

Jim: If I were president, I'd—

Harry: What would you do?

Jim: Well, I'd—

Harry: Oh, come on.

Jim: Huh?

Harry: You'd be the same.

Jim: Yeah, I guess you can't do it all by yourself.

Harry: Can't do anything.

New words – Nuevas palabras
Advice - consejo
Chain - cadena
Government - gobierno
Health - salud
Inflation – inflación
Position – posición
Real estate – bienes raíces
Tax – impuesto / gravamen
Wealth – riqueza
Weekdays – días de la semana
Wish - deseo
Army – ejército

Chore – tarea – asignación
Couple - pareja
Event - evento
King - rey
Lawn – césped
Lawnmower – podadora / corta césped
Machine – máquina
Occasion – ocasión
Prince - príncipe
Princess - princesa
Queen - reina
Uniform - uniforme
Advantage - ventaja
Agriculture - agricultura
Candidate - candidato
Crop – cosecha / cultivo
Defense - defensa
Development - desarrollo
Education – educación
Election – elección
Information – información
Investment – inversión
Percent – porcentaje
Otherwise – de lo contrario / por lo demás / de otra
manera
Reward – premio
Strike - huelga
Unemployment – desempleo
Vote – voto
Voter – votante

Words Definitions

Advantage: *a better chance or opportunity than someone else has.*

Education: *what you learn in school or at home. The teachings of your parents and teachers.*

Election: *a time when a country starts to select a new president. A time or process for selecting a candidate.*

Inflation: *when the cost of living goes higher.*

Left: *whatever still remains after everything or everybody is gone.*

Occasion: *a time for something or when something happens.*

Strike: *when people stop working because they want better conditions or are demanding something from the government or an institution.*

Successful: *when you have accomplished what you wanted to.*

Tax: *whatever money you have to pay to the government.*

Uniform: *special clothes people wear for school, work, or any institution.*

Wish: *something you want to happen.*

Phrases and Expressions - Frases y expresiones

To break the news – dar las noticias de último minuto

In order to – para

*I went to your house **in order to** see you* – fui a tu casa para verte. (Siempre le sigue un verbo)

Worth it – lo vale / vale la pena

By hand – a mano *(hecho a mano)*

To leave someone alone – dejar a alguien solo *(no molestar a alguien)*

To make someone + adjective – hacer ... a alguien. *(to make someone happy – hacer feliz a alguien). Siempre usaremos cualquier adjetivo para indicar lo que queremos decir.*

To stay after school – permanecer en la escuela castigado *(cuando ya todos se han ido y tú no puedes irte, porque estas castigado)*

To give away - regalar

To give trouble to – darle problemas a alguien

If I were you – si yo fuera tu

In a difficult position – en una difícil posición

What more...? - ¿Qué más?

Would rather – preferiría

Grammar – Gramática

Conditional type 2 – Condicional tipo 2.

Ya vimos y aprendimos el condicional tipo 1; ahora vamos a ver el tipo 2. Si algo pasó *(pero suponemos que no pasará)* o si algo fuera cierto *(pero suponemos que no es así)* entonces algo más pasaría.

If I had a lot of money, *I'd give* some of it away – si tuviera mucho dinero, regalaría parte de él.

I'd give some money away, *if I had* a lot of it – regalaría algo de dinero, si tuviera mucho.

En la forma condicional, usamos el pasado después de "if". Fíjense que la forma del verbo "to be" es "*were / weren't*".

If I were you, *I'd invest* in stock – si fuera tú,

invertiría en la bolsa de valores. *(Aunque estamos hablando de "I", debemos usar "were" en este modo)*

She'd probably **hate** me **if she weren't** my wife – probablemente ella me odiaría si no fuera mi esposa. *(Aunque estamos hablando de "she", debemos usar "weren't" en este tiempo)*

También usamos "were / weren't" después del verbo "wish".

I wish she were here – desearía que ella estuviera aquí.

I wish he were in better condition – desearía que el estuviera en mejor condición.

El condicional de "can" es "could".

If I took the plane, **I could** get there on time – si tomaba el avión, podría llegar a tiempo.

Some uses of "would" – Algunos usos de "would".

Ya hemos visto cómo usar "*would*" en el condicional; veamos algunos otros usos. Algunas veces usamos "*would*" en lugar de "*used to*".

When I was young, I **would (used to)** walk to school every day – cuando era jóven, solía caminar hasta la escuela cada día.

I'd always **forget** my books when I was a kid – siempre olvidaba mis libros cuando era chico.

I always **used to** forget my books when I was a kid – siempre solía olvidar mis libros cuando era chico.

Algunas veces usamos "would" para indicar atención o prediccion en el pasado.

I knew she would tell you about it – sabia que ella te lo diría.

Algunas veces hacemos énfasis en la palabra "would" para mostrar que esperamos que algo suceda y que no estamos contentos con eso o desaprobación por lo que consideramos una conducta típica.

You *would* do it, wouldn't you? – Lo harías, ¿o no?

The government *would* spend all our tax money on guns – el gobierno gastaría todo el dinero de nuestros impuestos en armas.

The verb "to wish" – El verbo "to wish".

Usamos "to wish" más el pasado para indicar como nos gustaría que sean las cosas.

We *wish (that) we were* pretty – desearíamos que fuéramos hermosas.

She *wishes she had* a car – ella desearía tener un carro.

Don't you wish that you didn't have to work? - ¿no desearías que no tuvieras que trabajar?

Usamos "to wish" más "would" para indicar como nos gustaría que las cosas cambien.

I wish he wouldn't smoke in the house – desearía que él no fume en la casa.

I wish it wouldn't rain so much – desearía que no lloviera tanto.

She wishes you would listen to her – ella desearía que tú la escucharas.

The passive voice – La voz pasiva

Ya aprendimos como usar la voz pasiva; vamos a ver la voz pasiva en pasado simple en contraste con el presente perfecto.

Recuerden que el pasado simple habla de un

tiempo finito o de una acción terminada. El presente perfecto habla de un tiempo indefinido o de una acción que puede aún estar pasando. Ambos tiempos pueden ser usados en la voz pasiva.

The president *was elected* last month – el presidente fue elegido el mes pasado. *(Tiempo definido)*

The president *has been elected* – el presidente ha sido elegido *(tiempo indefinido)*

A lot of teenagers *were arrested* during the strike – muchos jóvenes fueron arrestados durante la huelga.

A lot of teenagers *have been arrested* – muchos jóvenes han sido arrestados.

Fijense bien en la estructura y la diferencia entre ambos tiempos.

Nouns formed from verbs – Nombres formados de verbos.

Veamos cómo se forman algunos nombres o sustantivos usando los verbos como base.

To develop – desarrollar
Develop*ment* - desarrollo
To equip – equipar
Equip*ment* – equipo
To invest – invertir
Invest*ment* – inversión
To apply – solicitar
Applic*ation* - solicitud
To inform – informar
Inform*ation* – información

To invite – invitar
Invit*ation* – invitación
To elect – elegir
Elec*tion* – elección
To invent – inventor
Inven*tion* - invento
To suggest – sugerir
Sugges*tion* - sugerencia
Como pueden ver, conociendo un verbo podemos formar palabras usando ese verbo como base. Presten mucha atención al concepto y practíquenlo muy bien. No hay una regla directa para aprender este concepto; deberán prestar atención y aprender en el proceso.

Adverbs – Adverbios
Ever before – nunca antes / más que antes
We are studying more than ever before – estamos estudiando más que antes (más que nunca. Deben entender que no significa nada negative solo)
Anyway – de todas formas / de cualquier modo
Backward – hacia atrás
Forward – hacia adelante
Rather (than) – preferir
I'd rather go home – preferiría irme a casa (usamos would con rather)
I'd rather go home than stay here – preferiría irme a casa que permanecer aqui. (Usualmente usamos than despues de rather)
Therefore – por tanto / por lo tanto
Adjectives – Adjetivos

Alive - vivo
Dead - muerto
Foreign – extranjero
Necessary - necesario
Successful - exitoso
Worth – digno / de valor
Left – remanente / resto (lo que queda de algo)
Mad – loco / demente / furioso
Willing – dispuesto / complaciente

Regular verbs – Verbos regulares
To encourage – encouraged – encouraged – animar / alentar / estimular
To explain – explained – explained - explicar
To fire – fired – fired – disparar
To invest – invested – invested - invertir
To suppose – supposed – supposed - suponer
To wish (for / that) – wished – wished – desear (por / que)
To allow – allowed – allowed – permitir / autorizar / dejar
To bake – baked – baked - hornear
To dress up – dressed up – dressed up – vestirse / disfrazarse
To milk – milked – milked - ordeñar
To mow – mowed – mowed - podar
To agree (with) – agreed – agreed - acordar
To elect – elected – elected - elegir
To inform – informed – informed - informar
To offer – offered – offered - ofrecer
To organize – organized – organized - organizar

To plant – planted – planted – plantar / sembrar
To reelect – reelected – reelected - reelegir
To vote – voted – voted - votar

Irregular verbs – Verbos irregulares
To freeze – froze – frozen - congelar
To feed – fed – fed - alimentar
To let – let – let – dejar / permitir
To shoot – shot – shot – disparar / tirar / arrojar

Ancient times and nowadays.

Cinthia wished she could go back to the days of chivalry. She could imagine herself as a beautiful damsel in distress, waiting for her prince in shining armor to come and rescue her, just at the last possible moment. She was most captivated by these dreams when it was time to do her chores. She was Cinderella sweeping and mopping, cooking and washing. Never mind the fact that she had disposable cloths so she could sweep and mop at the same time, she bought frozen meals to save time on cooking, and she had a washing machine and dryer so she could do all the wash in a few hours.

As a little girl, Cinthia used to ride her dog around and pretend he was a pony. She would braid her hair with ribbons and practice royal etiquette with her dolls and stuffed animals. When she entered the room, all the bears stood up. She was addressed as "Your Highness." She walked with perfect posture and was careful not to talk too much. At meals, she always ate small amounts of food, she kept her mouth wiped clean with a napkin, and she never put her elbows on the table

As a princess, she wouldn't waste her time on menial tasks. She wouldn't even have to do her hair. Her meals would be cooked for her. Her house would be cleaned by servants. She would supervise household meals and finances. She might do some needlework or dance a little. She would never be bothered with dusting.

It wouldn't be near as much fun to be a modern princess. She'd have to do photo shoots and worry about always looking perfect. How do you look like a princess in a day when so many girls use makeup and designer clothes! She'd have to go around doing good works and avoid any possibility of scandal. But there would always be journalists who would make up rumors. Imagine your face on those cheap newspapers in the grocery aisle—or on TV! No, it would just be too much work. She sighed as she settled down with a latte to watch her favorite history program on TV. Life in medieval times must have been so much simpler.

Exercises – Ejercicios

Exercise 5.1: Write the correct form of the verb in the passive voice.

I _____ always _____ to follow my dreams (encourage—simple past).

The president _____ in a time of unemployment and inflation (reelect—simple past).

Nobody would eat the tomatoes that _____ in the garbage pile (plant—simple past).

He can't stay home. A birthday party _____ for him (organize—present perfect).

Unfortunately, your money _____ in an unstable company (invest—simple past).

Exercise 5.2: What is the meaning of *would* in each sentence: past intention, result of a wish, typical "bad" behavior, or used to.

_____ They said they would hire her if she made a small investment in the company.

_____ I'm not surprised you got stuck doing everything; she would "forget" to do her chores.

_____ I wish he wouldn't always talk about his work.

_____ That man! He would dump his garbage in front of my house.

_____ He would whistle when he had to go home in the dark.

_____ I wish she would study more.

_____ We would visit my maternal grandparents on Christmas Eve.

_____ When I went home, I thought I would have time to relax.

_____ They would have a garage sale every summer to get rid of the toys they didn't play with anymore.

_____ I wish you wouldn't make fun of me.

Exercise 5.3: Second conditional: write the verbs in the correct form.

If I _____ (have) a million dollars, I

_____ (buy) you a car.

If she _____ (be) here, she _____ (tell) you the truth.

If Mom _____ (try) the cake, she _____ (recognize) her secret recipe.

If they _____ (wear) coats, they _____

(not be) cold.

If the Smiths _____ (agree) to sell the farm,

their children _____ (cry).

Lesson 6
The mystery – El misterio

Conversation

Chuck: That was a great meal.

Frank: Thanks! I'm pretty good at pork chops.

Chuck: They were perfect—tasty and tender! So, how have you been?

Frank: Okay. Well, . . .

Chuck: What's the matter?

Frank: You're not going to believe me, but I think there's a ghost in the house.

Chuck: Seriously?

Frank: I can hear a baby crying in the house.

Chuck: All the time?

Frank: No, just at night. I think the previous owners had a baby and maybe it got sick or—

Chuck: Do you hear it all over the house?

Frank: No. Just in the dining room and bathroom. And when I turn the lights out, I see little lights flickering around the house.

Chuck: Hmmm. Let's see. Both of these rooms have windows facing that house over there. Do they have a baby?

Frank: I don't know—well, now, I think they do.

Chuck: So don't you think you might hear their baby crying?

Frank: Well, I thought it was closer. You think I'm just a superstitious old man, don't you?

Chuck: Superstitious? No. You're just hard of hearing, old man!

New words – Nuevas palabras
Bargain - ganga
Block – cuadra / bloque
Bottom – fondo / trasero
Brick – ladrillo / block
Furnace - horno
Garbage – basura / desperdicio
Garbage can – zafacón / bote de basura
Ghost - fantasma
The inside – el interior
The outside – el exterior
Owner - dueño
Plumbing - plomería
Roof – techo / tejado
Shopping center – centro comercial
Store - tienda
Top – cima / tope
Wiring - cableado
Argument – argumento / alegato
Coincidence – coincidencia
Cousin -primo
Crystal ball – bola de cristal
Fortune – fortuna / suerte
Fortune teller – adivino
Nonsense – disparates / majaderías
Prediction – predicción

Relative – pariente
Carpet - alfombra
Copy - copia
Elevator - elevador
Feather - pluma
File - archivo
File cabinet – archivero
Jam – mermelada / atasco (cuando un papel se atasca)
Jar – taro / frasco
Lock - candado
Watchman - vigilante
Photocopier - fotocopiadora
Safe – caja fuerte
Wastebasket – zafacón
Wire - cable

Word Definitions

Ahead of: something that is about to happen, something coming, something in front of.

Argument: when you have a fight using words only.

Block: in a square area, a block represents the space surrounded by four streets.

Finally: after waiting a long time for something and it arrives, after everything else, last. Used to introduce the last of a group or series"

Previous: the one before.

Silly: someone or something that is full of nonsense.

Superstitious: a person that believes all kinds of

tales and stories with no reason at all and is afraid of things because they might bring bad luck.

Unlucky: *someone who brings bad luck or someone that does not have good luck.*

Phrases and Expressions - Frases y expresiones

To ask someone over – invitar a alguien a tu casa

To clean up – asear / limpiar / enderezar / reformar

For example – por ejemplo

To give someone a bath – darle un baño a alguien

To go right – salir bien *(cuando algo sale bien)*

To go wrong – salir mal *(cuando algo sale mal)*

To make matters worse – empeorar las cosas

To come true – hacer o volverse realidad

To leave home – dejar tranquilo o solo a alguien, no molestar a alguien

To leave something to someone – dejarle algo a alguien.

Sometime – algún día *(en el futuro, alguna vez)*

To tell someone's fortune – leer la suerte a alguien

That's nothing new – eso no es nada nuevo *(no es sorpresa, eso siempre sucede)*

Can afford *(can't afford)* – poder costear *(no poder costear) / poder permitir (no poder permitir)*

For sale – en venta

To move in – mudarse *(cuando ingresamos o mudamos en una casa, apartamento, etc.)*

To move out – mudarse *(cuando egresamos, salimos de una casa, apartamento, etc.)*

Now and then – algunas veces *(no muy a menudo)*

A number of – un numero de *(varios)*

Such – tan *(you are such a fool – tú eres tan tonto.*
It is such a lovely evening – es una velada tan
hermosa)

Grammar – Gramática
To have + noun + past participle – To have +
sustantivo + pasado participio.
Cuando no podemos hacer algo nosotros mismos,
o no queremos, hacemos que alguien lo haga por
nosotros. Ahí es cuando usamos la combinación con
el verbo "to have – haber o tener". Veamos.
I always *have my nails done* at Tiffany's – siempre
me hacen las uñas en Tiffany.
I never *have my hair cut* at Thomson's – nunca me
corto el cabello en Thomsons.
Are you having your house redecorated? – ¿vas a
mandar a redecorar tu casa?
I am *having a tooth pulled* – me van a sacar una
muela.
Fíjense que siempre usamos el verbo "to have" más
el sustantivo y después siempre el verbo va en pasado
participio.

To need + ing – To need + ing
Algunas veces usamos "to need" más el presente
participio en vez de la voz pasiva.
My house is dirty. It *needs painting* (it needs to be
cleaned) – mi casa está sucia. Necesita pintura
(necesita ser pintada).
My car is broken. It *needs servicing.* (it needs to be

serviced) – mi carro está dañado. Necesita mecánica (necesita ser reparado)

Agreeing and disagreeing – Acuerdos y desacuerdos.
Vamos a aprender las variaciones cuando estamos de acuerdo con alguien, cuando no estamos de acuerdo y cuando no estamos seguros.

I think Kennedy will be reelected – creo que Kennedy será reelegido.
When you agree – cuando estás de acuerdo.
So do I – yo también
I do too – yo también
I am sure he will – estoy seguro que sí
I am absolutely positive he will – estoy completamente positivo que lo será
Oh, definitely – o, definitivamente.
Of course (he will) – por supuesto (él lo será)

When you disagree – cuando no estás de acuerdo.
I don't – no.
No, he won't – no lo será.
I don't think so – no lo creo.
Of course he won't – por supuesto que no lo será.

When you aren't sure – cuando no estás seguro.
Maybe (he will) – tal vez (lo será)
Perhaps (he will) tal vez (lo será)
He may – puede que sí.
Possibly – posiblemente

Probably – probablemente
I am not sure – no estoy seguro
I guess – supongo
I suppose so – supongo

I don't think he'll be reelected – no creo que será reelecto.
When you agree – cuando estás de acuerdo.
Neither do I – yo tampoco
I don't either – yo tampoco
I am sure he won't – estoy seguro que no
I am absolutely positive he won't – estoy completamente positivo que no lo será.
Oh, definitely not – o definitivamente no.
Of course he won't – por supuesto que no lo será.
When you disagree – cuando no estás de acuerdo.
I do – yo sí
Yes, he will – sí, él lo será.
Sure he will – seguro él lo será.
Of course he will – por supuesto que lo será.
When you aren't sure – cuando no estás seguro.
Maybe (not) – tal vez (no).
Maybe he won't – tal vez no lo será
Perhaps (not) – tal vez (no)
Perhaps he won't – tal vez no lo será
Possibly not – posiblemente no.
Probably not – probablemente no.
I guess not – supongo que no.

Conjunction "so that" – Conjunción "so that"
Usamos "so that" para indicar el por qué de algo.

Podemos usar el "so" solo; el "that" es opcional. Veamos.

Speak loud *so (that)* they hear you – habla alto para que te escuchen.

Speak softly *so (that)* they don't hear you – habla bajo para que no te escuchen.

I am making dinner *so (that)* you can eat – estoy haciendo la cena para que puedas comer.

La idea es la misma y podemos usarlo en cualquier tiempo.

Adverbs – Adverbios
Away (from) – lejos (de) (lejos de algún lugar)
Quite – muy (this is quite good – esto es muy bueno "very")
Abroad – fuera del país – en el extranjero
Absolutely – absolutamente
Possibly – posiblemente
Finally – finalmente

Adjectives – Adjetivos
Away (from) – lejos (de) (lejos de algún lugar)
Quite – muy (this is quite good – esto es muy bueno "very")
Abroad – fuera del país – en el extranjero
Absolutely – absolutamente
Possibly – posiblemente
Finally – finalmente

Regular verbs – Verbos regulares
To collect – collected – collected – cobrar /

recolectar

To disappear – disappeared – disappeared - desaparecer

To knock on – knocked on – knocked on - tocar

To manage – managed – managed – dirigir / manejar

To notice – noticed – noticed – notar / percibir

To own – owned – owned - poseer

To realize – realized – realized – darse cuenta / entender

To redecorate – redecorated – redecorated - redecorar

To service – serviced – serviced – dar servicio o mantenimiento a un aparato

To shop – shopped – shopped – comprar (en tiendas)

To predict – predicted – predicted - predecir

To empty – emptied – emptied - vaciar

Irregular verbs – Verbos irregulares
To build – built – built - construir

Constructions tools

Building a house is a complicated process. Once the land is purchased, the placement of the house and driveway can be planned. You will want to have the architect design the house so that water flows away from the foundation; the structure must be made to survive typical weather conditions for the region (for example, tornadoes, snow storms, or flooding), and windows placed to take advantage of sunlight. Make sure you decide first where you will need any special plumbing and wiring before you have the plans made. When the design is complete, you will need to get a building permit. You can request it yourself, or you can hire someone to supervise the project and get all necessary permits (septic, electric, plumbing, etc.).

Before building, you need to get insurance to protect the construction workers and the building. Then, the process of building can begin. First, the foundation is laid, with special attention to the natural flow of water across the land. The frame will probably be made with cement block and filled in with cement. Make sure the placement of the walls is square and level, and install the floor after having plumbing lines installed. Next, the walls will be framed and built according to the blueprint. The studs must be made level and then nailed in place.

You can purchase prefab roof trusses or have your builders put them together. If you are in a region that receives a lot of snowfall, make sure the roof can handle the increased weight of snow during a snowstorm. Protect the roof from moisture damage; then install siding, doors and windows. Finally, finish off the roof.

On the inside, install water and sewage pipes, the central cooling and heating system, electrical wiring and fixtures, and insulation. Then, install the ceilings. You can now add plumbing fixtures—toilets, sinks, and bathtubs, finish off the walls, and add flooring. After the building passes inspection, you can bring in your appliances and have the utilities turned on. And you're ready to move in! Enjoy filling in the spaces you visualized with your furniture, window treatments, and decorations!

Exercises – Ejercicios
Exercise 6.1: Match the actions to the cause.

_____ Jorie had a part-time job

_____ She left her dog with her sister

_____ She spent the afternoon at her sister's house

_____ She bought some peanuts

_____ She waited until her husband got out of work
A. so she could save money on a taxi.
B. so he wouldn't be too lonely.
C. so she could pay for her daughter's music lessons.
D. so she could get a ride home with him.
E. so she wouldn't be hungry.

Exercise 6.2: Write a sentence using the structure (a) *needs* + gerund and (b) *have* + past participle.
Example:
paint + nails ___My nails need painting.___ I'm going to have my nails painted.
hem + pants ___Mark's pants need hemming.___ He is going to have his pants hemmed.

trimming + hair _____;

she's going to _____

repair + shoes   _____;

I want to _____replace + tires

we want to _____

harvest + corn_____;

they plan to _____
dry clean + shirts

_____;
George is going to

_____

Exercise 6.3: Functions: complete the sentence according to the function in parentheses.

My aunt would never lie to me. (agree)

Of course _____.
Your teacher didn't complain about you. (disagree)

I am absolutely positive _____.
Were you here on time? (agree)

Oh, yes. _____ definitely _____.
The fair won't affect my business. (not sure) Well, I

guess _____.
Cats can't swim. (disagree)

Really? I think _____.
Koalas are pretty stupid. (agree)

Yeah, _____ probably _____.

Lesson 7
Telling the truth – Diciendo la verdad

Conversation

Mom: Where did you get those chips?

Mark: I found them.

Mom: That's dangerous! You can't eat food that you find lying around. It could be poisoned.

Mark: Well, I mean, I found $1, and I used it to buy the chips.

Mom: Oh, where did you find the dollar?

Mark: In front of the apartment building.

Mom: Was anybody standing outside?

Mark: Yes.

Mom: Did you ask them if they had lost some money?

Mark: No. I mean, they didn't look like very nice people.

Mom: Why didn't you cross the street to avoid walking by them?

Mark: Well, I was with my friend who lives in that apartment building.

Mom: Ah, and he didn't see the dollar bill?

Mark: No, I saw it after he went inside.

Mom: So you were alone with the bad people?

Mark: Just for a second.

Mom: But they didn't see you picking up the money?

Mark: No, they were distracted.

Mom: What were they doing?

Mark: I think they were selling drugs or something.

Mom: And you didn't report it to the police?

Mark: No.

Mom: We need to tell them that people sell drugs outside that building.

Mark: No, Mom. . . . I mean, it was probably just this one time.

Mom: Mark, are you sure you found that money?

Mark: Um, maybe not.

Mom: Where did you get it?

Mark: I took it from your purse. I'm sorry, Mom.

Mom: You have to be careful, Mark. If you start stealing and lying, it will become a habit. You'll become a slave to your bad habits, and who knows where you might end up? Stealing and lying affect your relationships. You'll attract the worst type of friends, and you might even end up in jail!

Mark: I'm sorry, Mom.

Mom: Well, why don't you wash the dishes so you can earn that dollar?

New words – Nuevas palabras
Choice – elección / opción / alternativa
Liar - mentiroso
Lie - mentira
Truth - verdad

Cause - causa
Cement - cemento
Group - grupo
Hammer – martillo
Hardware – ferretería
Nail - clavo
Lumberyard – maderería / almacén de madera
Opinion – opinión
Orphanage – orfanato
Pliers - alicates
Responsibility - responsabilidad
Saw – sierra / serrucho
Screw – tornillo / tuerca
Screwdriver - destornillador
Tool - herramienta

Word Definitions
Lie: when you say something you know that isn't true.
Lumberyard: the place where you buy wood
Tool: the things you need or use to repair or do something.

Phrases and Expressions – Frases y expresiones
After all – después de todo
How did it go? - ¿Cómo estuvo? / ¿Cómo te fue?
To make someone do something – hacer que alguien haga algo. *(Cuando hacemos que alguien haga algo que no quiere, por fuerza o insinuación)*
To have someone do something – hacer que alguien haga algo *(cuando hacemos que alguien*

haga algo voluntariamente o pidiéndolo adecuadamente o sugerir que alguien haga algo. Casi siempre sería cuando tienes autoridad "su madre o jefe" o mucha confianza (familia, mejor amigo)

To open up – abrir / abrirse

To tell on – delatar / contar

To tell the truth – decir la verdad

As far as I'm concerned – por lo que a mi concierne

Easier said than done – es más fácil decirlo que hacerlo

For a good cause – por una buena causa

For heaven's sake – por al amor de Dios

For someone's sake – por al amor de alguien *(let's do it for the children's sake – hagámoslo por amor a los niños)*

For nothing – por nada / de gratis

For very little – por muy poco

In my opinion – en mi opinión

To mind your own business – meterte en tus propios asuntos

To raise money – levantar fondos / recolectar dinero *(usualmente para una causa)*

The way I see it – como yo lo veo / de la forma que yo lo veo.

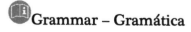**Grammar – Gramática**

The auxiliary verb "ought to" – El verbo auxiliar "ought to".

Este verbo auxiliar "ought to – deber" es una forma

intermedio entre "should" que es normal y "must" que es más fuerte y con más autoridad. Por lo general solo se usa en afirmativo. "Ought to" expresa ideas tales como deber, necesidad y obligación moral. Normalmente en su forma presente, siempre le seguirá un verbo. Veamos.

We ***ought to be*** punctual – debemos ser puntuales.

We ***ought to help*** orphan children – debemos ayudar a los niños huérfanos.

You ***ought to visit*** your parents once in a while – debes visitar a tus padres de vez en cuando.

Normalmente indica el tiempo presente con acción futura. Puede indicar pasado cuando es seguido por el pasado perfecto infinitivo.

You ***ought to have visited*** them – debiste haberlos visitado *(era tu responsabilidad, pero no lo hiciste).*

We **ought to have helped** the children – debimos haber ayudar a los niños *(era nuestra responsabilidad, pero no lo hicimos)*

Fíjense bien que "ought to have" está en presente y el siguiente verbo "esta en pasado participio".

Adverbs – Adverbios
Lousy – malísimo / horrible / terrible
Personally - personalmente / por lo que a mi concierne.

Adjectives – Adjetivos
Concerned – preocupado / interesado
Fair – justo *(cuando recibes lo que mereces)*
Honestly – honestamente / realmente

Regular verbs – Verbos regulares

To adopt – adopted – adopted - adoptar

To care – cared – cared – cuidar / atender / preocuparse / importar

To disagree – disagreed – disagreed – disentir / discrepar

To interrupt – interrupted – interrupted – interrumpir

To lie - lied – lied - mentir

To treat – treated – treated – tratar / atender / curar

To trust – trusted – trusted - confiar

Irregular verbs – Verbos irregulares

To beat up – beat up – beaten up – golpear / ganar una pelea *(cuando golpeas a alguien tan fuerte que le haces daño o lastimas. También tiene el sentido de ganar una pelea)*

To swear – swore – sworn – jurar / prometer

The orphanage

Zoe: Hi, Mackenzie, what's new?

Mackenzie: Actually, Dan and I have decided to adopt.

Zoe: Really? Locally?

Mackenzie: No. We thought maybe someone from Latin America or Asia.

Zoe: Easier said than done.

Mackenzie: How's that?

Zoe: Well, first of all, you have to meet the

requirements for your state. They'll check your house, and they have all kinds of checks to make sure you're able to provide a good home. Then you have to meet the requirements of the other country. For instance, China requires adopting parents to be at least thirty years old and to have a certain level of net wealth. Many countries prefer to give the children to someone local. Adoption can be stressful for children, especially when it means changing cultures.

Mackenzie: Wow. Well, the way I see it, we have foster homes and lots of people waiting to adopt here. But in other countries, so many children spend their whole lives in an institution. I've even heard that in some places, the children are kidnapped as soon as they leave the orphanage. If we can help those children to have a better life, I think we ought to do it.

Zoe: It might take a couple years.

Mackenzie: That's okay. It'll give us time to prepare—financially and emotionally. To tell the truth, we've already gone through the initial stages. They told us the orphan will probably need his own bedroom, so we're raising money to add on.

Zoe: Oh, really? How is that coming along?

Mackenzie: Well, I've been making baked goods and crafts to sell. Friends have been donating things, and we've had a few garage sales already. Then there are websites that allow your friends to help you financially. Of course, Dan works overtime when he gets the chance.

Zoe: That's nice. Have most of your friends

been supportive of your choice to adopt internationally?

Mackenzie: Yes. Well, there are always some people who disagree. Some people say it's not fair for the adopted child because you'll never love him as much as your own, but I think we will. We know a lot of families who have adopted, and the children seem very happy.

Zoe: I'm sure you'll be an amazing family to some child who really needs one!

Exercises – Ejercicios
Exercise 7.1: Write the verb with "ought to."

Example: You really _ought to eat_ more vegetables. They're so good for your health (eat).

You really _____ your husband. He's killing himself with this new project, and he needs your help (support).

You really _____ someone to teach your son guitar; he's pretty good (find)!

I can't believe you're not participating in the talent show. You have a great voice; you

_____ (sing)!

You know, we _____ our extra room to one of the families that lost their homes in the tornado (offer).

If anyone _____ homeless people, we should; we can make a community pantry where everyone in the area can contribute (help).

Exercise 7.2: Write the letter of the logical response.

But Mom, you didn't tell me you didn't want to me to take the TV apart.

Can you believe they repaired a paved road by pouring dirt over it?

You let your son join the soccer team? What grade did he get in his math class?

How do you get your kids to do their homework?

I went to my first job interview yesterday!

I make them do it. They don't get any privileges— TV, cell phone, going to friends' houses—until they're done.

Really? How did it go?

I don't mean to be rude, Mrs. Smith, but it's really none of your business.

To tell the truth, I'm not surprised. The township saves money in the strangest ways.

Oh, for heaven's sake, couldn't you figure that out on your own?

Conversational Level Three – Nivel de Conversación Tres

Tour across USA

Brenda: What are you doing, Luke?

Luke: I'm planning my trip.

Brenda: What trip?

Luke: I'm going to take a trip to California.

Brenda: Really? How are you going to get there?

Luke: On the bus, of course.

Brenda: You can't be planning to go by bus?

Luke: Why not?

Brenda: You'll go right by the Grand Canyon and miss it! Why don't we all go? There's room in the van for us and our luggage.

Luke: Because you'll turn it into a shopping trip. It'll take us two weeks just to get there, and we won't have any time left to spend in San José.

Brenda: Well, some of us prefer to enjoy the trip than just hurry to get there.

Luke: But that's what my trip is all about—my job interview in San José. I need to see where I can live, too.

Owen: The van needs servicing anyway. It's always reheating and it even shakes!

Cole: Well, if we all **pitch in**, we can get it repaired. We can take turns driving so that we have enough time to enjoy the most important places along the way.

Luke: Well, okay.

Brenda: That sounds good.

Cole: Let's see, there are five of us. I think we could cover the costs with $100 each. Then we'll need another $100 each for gas and tolls. That's if we don't stay in hotels on the way. Everyone pays for their own meals and whatever they want to buy, of course. And we might stay in a suite so we can share the cost of the hotel room in San José.

Owen: Only one suitcase per person, you hear? I'm not going to go all the way across the country with one suitcase under my feet and another one on my lap.

Luke: That's fine by me.

Brenda: Since you were planning to go on the bus anyway.

Luke: Yeah, well, it is my job interview.

Cole: Okay, okay

Luke: When can we leave? Tomorrow? They said I can come anytime I want.

Owen: Are you kidding? It's going to take a week to have the van repaired. And I have to get off work.

Luke: Well, I guess it can wait another week.

Cole: All right. We just have to ask Dad.

Owen: Oh, yeah. Dad.

[Brenda and Luke groan]

Visiting Disneyland

Martina was a hard worker. Her mom worked full

time, so Martina had to learn to take care of herself. One day at school she saw an advertisement online for a free trip to Disneyland. She clicked on the link, but a lot of little windows opened up, so she closed the browser. Martina asked her teacher about it. "I've been thinking about going to Disneyland," she said. "How can I do it?"

Her teacher just stared at her. Martina was not rich; her mother struggled to pay the rent. Their family could probably never go on vacation. But the teacher did not want to hurt her feelings. "You have to work and save up a lot of money—a lot of money. You'd have to buy a plane ticket and tickets to the park, plus you would need money for food and a hotel. You would need a visa, and lots of other things, too."

Martina was not discouraged: "I saw on the Internet that you can win a trip to Disneyland."

"Nothing in life is free, Martina. Be careful of scams. A lot of people make up lies in order to get your information. Be very careful."

"Thank you, Teacher." Martina sat down at her desk, but she did not stop thinking about her dream. She started making plans: she would sell tortillas at first. Then she could save up enough money to sell tamales. Maybe she could even set up a stand to sell food outside the convenience store near her house. Martina had trouble concentrating in class that day.

Martina's mom wasn't very excited about the idea, but she didn't want to discourage her little girl. Martina was surprised at how long it took her to save up a little bit of money. She saved for a few weeks before she was able to make tamales. She worked for several hours and still didn't sell all her tamales. She was so discouraged. She wished she had a storefront, so that she could make money faster. The convenience store manager felt bad for Martina and let her sell outside his business, but he knew she would never make enough to go to Disneyland. He told her she could leave her tamales inside the store, and he would sell them for her. Soon, she had tamales in stores all over town. She started to make more money. She opened a bank account to store her savings. It took two years, but Martina made it. She was able to take her mom to Disneyland! And when she came back, she went back to her tamale business and saved up money for college!

Republicans and Democrats

Matt: Hey, Dad, I went to register to vote, but they asked what party I wanted to vote for in the primaries.

Dad: Yes. That's the policy in our state.

Matt: But what party should I choose?

Dad: You have to decide that, Matt.

Matt: But Dad, I don't understand which party is better. Your family is kind of grass-roots conservative, but you're a democrat, and mom is from a more liberal, change-the-world background, and she's a republican.

Dad: Yes, that is kind of ironic. We usually think of the republican party as conserving traditional values and keeping the government from limiting individual rights, whereas the democratic party is more often associated with big government and help for minorities, trying to change society. But you shouldn't join a party just because your mom or I did. You need to make your own decision. And you don't have to vote for the party you join. Neither of them is perfect. In fact, we both vote for people from both parties.

Matt: What about the other parties?

Dad: Oh, I don't know. They never seem to have much of a chance to win, and so we don't usually vote for them. People say a vote for a third-party candidate is a vote wasted. But you ought to research all the candidates and decide who you agree with most. Then, whoever you choose, you can register for that party and vote for him or her in the primaries.

Matt: I don't think I really agree with any of them completely.

Dad: I understand. It's hard to know what politicians really believe anyway. A lot of people end up voting for the person they consider to be the lesser of two evils.

Matt: Who do you think will win?

Dad: I wish I knew. If I knew that, I'd be a very rich man. Let's do this. Go do some more research. Write down each party and the candidates for that party. Then write the pros and cons of each candidate, and come back and tell me who you agree with most. Then you can either register for that party and vote in the primaries, or wait and vote in the general election.

Matt: Okay, Dad.

College system in US

There are five main stages to school in the US. These are preschool/kindergarten, elementary school, junior high, high school, and college (university level). The requirements for each level are mainly determined by the state. Each state publishes requirements for certifying teachers and standards that the teachers have to cover in class and include in their portfolios. The state also determines requirements for people who want to educate their children at home. Often, home schoolers have to take a portfolio to an authorized evaluator so that they can continue home schooling the next school year.

States decide at what age schooling becomes compulsory. A few states require children to begin schooling at age five, many more at age six. Pennsylvania and Washington allow children to begin as late as age eight! In preschool, children can learn numbers, shapes, patterns, and alphabet sounds. In kindergarten, they study **phonics** so that they can learn to read. English spelling is no longer closely related to pronunciation ever since French was spoken in England for over three centuries. So now, English-speaking children must study rules of spelling, learning how to pronounce particular vowel and consonant combinations in "word families."

In elementary school, grades one to six, children

learn how to learn. They learn the basics of math, English (reading comprehension and writing), science, and history/geography/social studies.

In junior high, seventh to ninth grade, the standard is raised a bit higher. Students become more autonomous, with regular homework assignments and tests that require more memorization and independent study. Junior high is also called middle school.

The next step is high school, grades ten to twelve. If students want to go to college, they have to make sure they are in the college preparatory track in high school. Some high schools use terms such as the basic, advanced, and honors tracks to distinguish those students who are completing studies in order to immediately join the work force (basic), those who want to go to college (advanced), and those who want to test out of some college courses (honors) so that they can earn their college degree earlier.

Technically, there are several colleges in a university, but most people call university "college." In a liberal arts college, students take more general courses in the first two years, and courses specific to their major in the last two years. Underclassmen are called freshmen the first year, sophomores the second year. Upperclassmen are juniors their third year and seniors their final year. Universities have a special system for showing students' grade point averages based on the letter (A-B-C-D-F) and the number of credits earned. A good average will earn cum laude upon graduation. An excellent average earns magna cum laude, and a nearly perfect average earns suma cum laude.

University System in US

Today's **job market** requires a college-level education in order to maintain a **decent standard of living**. However, college is expensive! Community colleges offer significant discounts for local students, but what if you want to study humanities, and the local schools offer only science and law majors? There are huge books and entire websites dedicated to describing fellowships, loans, and scholarships available for students. Most of them are available to students in a particular field, **e.g.**, law, science education, foreign languages. Fellowships require the student to do something in exchange for the money; for instance, a science student might be asked to do research. Loans, of course, must be repaid. Scholarships are sometimes offered to anyone studying a particular major, to people within a particular minority group (e.g., women, Hispanics), to students with an outstanding GPA (Grade Point Average) in high school, or to the student who writes the best essay on a particular subject.

There are many opportunities for international students in the US, with scholarships offered exclusively for them nationwide and at many colleges. In fact, most colleges will probably have discounts (**i.e.**, small scholarships) for international students and minority groups. Once you arrive, you will probably have to maintain a particular GPA in order to keep the scholarship, but a good GPA can also help you to earn additional scholarships. Some organizations and colleges may offer a full scholarship (100% of **tuition** and possibly also housing/food) for students who they think may make the world a better place.

In any case, make sure you can prove that you can pay for your schooling before you enter the country. Talk with the school you plan to attend to get help securing your student visa. If you plan to get a work scholarship or to get a job on the side, discuss these plans with your admissions counselor. There are limitations on working under a student visa. Make sure that you can have your high school transcripts sent to the school and that they will be accepted. Some schools also require a certain level of English-speaking ability for admittance. Others will admit students with lower English ability but require them to take extra courses in English (at the normal cost of college tuition).

American music

The United States owes much of its musical heritage to the African-American slaves. Slaves had to work long hours in the fields, and they were not allowed to speak their native languages or complain about their situation. So when slave owners encouraged them to go to church, they were glad to have the opportunity to socialize and talk a little bit more freely. Inspired by hymns of the Great

Awakening, African-Americans made up songs to sing at church and in the fields. It's not hard to imagine why the slaves identified with the Jews: "When Israel was in Egypt's land, Let my people go; Oppressed so hard they could not stand, Let My people go."

Negro spirituals give encouragement to endure the difficulties of slave life, and they give hope of freedom. These messages were veiled in biblical allusions, so that slave owners would not prohibit them from singing these songs that gave them hope of one day being free.

Since slaves were not allowed to learn to read, they had to sing the songs from memory. Usually one person would sing a line, and the others would repeat it. Some of the spirituals, such as "Swing Low, Sweet Chariot" and "The Gospel Train," may have hidden meanings referring to the Underground Railroad, a route to Canada for escaping slaves. "Canaan" may refer to Canada, "home" might be freedom. These songs definitely encouraged slaves with the possibility of deliverance. Most of these songs are still popular. If you ever feel like quitting, you can sing the "Gospel Plow," which alludes to Luke 9:62 in the lyrics "keep your hand on the plow." Don't give up!

These songs gave back to the genre that inspired them; the genre of negro spirituals inspired gospel songs such as "Just a Closer Walk With Thee." Jazz, which is now popular all over the world, was also developed by, and usually interpreted by, African-Americans such as Louis Armstrong. This music uses

European instruments and harmony, but definitely has African rhythm and style.

Another distinctly American genre is bluegrass, which originated in the Appalachian region. This music became extremely popular when recordings were made in Bristol, Tennessee. And these recordings led to the development of another popular American genre—country music.

Level Three Tests – Examenes del Nivel Tres

Estos son los exámenes para pasar el nivel tres. Asegúrense de tomar su tiempo y completarlos correctamente. Una vez los hayan completado y estén completamente seguros que han terminado. Pueden presentarlos a un amigo de habla inglesa para que los revise y les diga si lo hicieron bien, o pueden enviarme un email con sus exámenes. Sin en algún punto, aun están dudosos, deberán repasarlo y asegurarse de dominarlo muy bien. El tercer nivel es esencial para todo el aprendizaje, sin dominarlo bien, no podremos aprender bien. Es imperativo dominar a la perfección cada uno de los conceptos presentados en este nivel. *Good luck once again!*

Test: Units 1-3

Test 1.1: Underline the correct form of the verb.

When she heard the news, her eyes **fill/filled/filling** with tears.

She was **hold/held/holding** the ruby when the detective arrived.

You can't play games with me! This **means/meant/meaning** war!

That poor girl looks like she is **runs away/ran away/running away** from home.

Why does she need a new coat? Has she **wears out/wore out/worn out/wearing out** the old one

508

already?

The slave **hides/hid/hidden/hiding** above the barn until they stopped looking for her.

You have to **tear/tore/torn/tearing** the pages out and put them in a **three-ring binder**.

There isn't any ice. The ice cubes haven't **freeze/froze/frozen/freezing** yet.

Oh, no! He **throws away/threw away/thrown away/throwing away** all of the bank records!

I really enjoy **teach/taught/teaching**!

Test 1.2: Underline the correct word or group of words.

My grandparents are visiting. They **may/maybe** stay for a month!

Mom likes chocolate. Dad likes strawberry. I like mint **herself/ourselves/myself**.

I **can/could/was able to** finish the report last night!

There used to **is/are/was/be** an Italian restaurant on this street.

My mom has trouble **get/got/gotten/getting** to sleep.

You can watch **wherever/whenever/whatever** you want. Just don't turn on the TV.

Whoever/wherever/whatever ate the ice cream, you had better buy some more!

We bought ice cream and cake, but the birthday girl didn't like **one/both/either** of them.

If it rains, you **are going to get/will get/got** wet.

Mom asked **if you want/do you want** to come to our house.

Test 1.3: Write the letter to complete the sentence.

_____ If you don't eat your vegetables

_____ He must be sick;

_____ I can't decide which purse to buy;

_____ If we don't go now,

_____ We can't be out of sugar;

A. we'll never make it to their house before dinner time.
B. I want all of them!
C. you'll probably get sick.
D. I just bought a two-pound bag yesterday!
E. he would never say no to pecan pie if he felt okay.

Test 2: Units 4-7
Test 2.1: Correct the error in each sentence. There is one grammatical error in each sentence.

What have you been do lately?

Look at that man dancing in the rain! He must is crazy.

If I had more money, I help you.

I wish I have a bigger house.

You really ought to bought more fruit.

Test 2.2: Underline the correct form.

You **can't be / must be** serious! I just saw her last

week, and she was fine! How can she be dying?

The store **can't be / must be** closed. Look there's only one light on, and I don't see anyone inside.

He **can't be / must be** the thief. I know him. He's a very nice guy, very honest too.

She **can't be / must be** hungry. It's been five hours since she had lunch.

They **can't be / must be** angry. He was so rude to them!

Test 2.3: Complete the sentence: Underline the correct form.

This is how to make fettuccine alfredo: First, the pasta **has been boiling / is boiled.** ...

The bread **has been taking / is taken** from the oven every morning at 7:00.

We **have been opening / is opened** the store early ever since Easter.

Clocks **have been turning back / will be turned back** next week.

The supervisor **has been asking / is asked** for a raise. What should we do?

Test 3.1: Underline the logical word/phrase.

If you're going to Niagara Falls, you have to take your passport. **Likewise / Otherwise**, they won't let you back into the United States.

When Amy thought she might get scarlet fever, she decided **to leave her dad alone / to leave her pictures to her dad.**

Are you watching soap operas? I **can't stand / can't wait** them!

I forgot my homework. And **to make matters worse / that's nothing new**, I didn't study for the test.

My aunt says it's bad **to tell someone's fortune / to tell the truth.**

Don't worry about losing the lottery. Maybe it's **the way I see it / for the best.** You won't have to worry about people asking you for money all the time.

Well, it's been nice seeing you. **Help yourself! / Take care!**

So you're Trixie? It's nice to finally meet you in person. **Keep in touch! / Welcome aboard!** You are going to love it here!

Good luck / Good gracious, I left the dog in the car!

I can't believe it. It looks like my dream of going to college is finally **coming true / getting to the point.**

This phone is **good gracious / good for nothing.** It won't even turn on anymore!

Please **have a seat / pay attention.** The doctor will see you in a few minutes.

That's a lot of money to pay for a balloon, but I guess it's **for a good cause / for nothing.**

If I were you / The way I see it, I would just calm down and wait to see what the doctor says.

Someone stole my wallet, but **it depends / thank goodness,** I ran into Uncle Joe, and he gave me a ride.

Now and then! / What do you say? Can we get a cat?

No, I'm not offended that you called me old. **After all / Day after day,** no one will ever believe that I'm older than you.

Son, it's very important not **to tell the truth / to tell on your classmates.** You won't have any friends!

Shut up! / Darn! That's not how you should talk to your grandpa!

Hurry up! It's time to go. **Come true / Come on,** let's go.

Test 3.2: Write the correct form for the first or second conditional.

If they had a dog, a burglar **won't / wouldn't** be able to break into their house.

If I raise enough money, I **will / would** go to Ireland.

If you were my dad, you **won't / wouldn't** talk to me that way.

If I had a car, I **will / could** get a better job.

If we leave now, we **will / would** have time to stop at a restaurant.

Test 3.3: Underline the correct form of the verb.

Metamorphosis was writing/written by Franz Kafka.

I've been waiting/waited for fifteen minutes.

Watergate salad is making/made with pistachio pudding, pineapple, nuts, and whipped topping.

Garbage used to be burning/burnt in people's back yards.

Mark has been studying / studied for a very difficult test.

Verb list – Lista de verbos
To adopt – adoptar
To agree (with) – acordar

To allow – permitir / autorizar / dejar
To appear – aparecer / parecer
To arrange – organizar / arreglar
To arrest – arrestar
To ask for – preguntar por / pedir
To bake – hornear
To be able - ser capaz
To beat up – golpear / ganar una pelea
To belong – pertenecer
To blow up - explotar
To break down - dañarse
To build – construir
To burn – quemar
To camp – acampar
To care – cuidar / atender / preocuparse / importar
To check – chequear / verificar
To cheer – animar / alentar
To chuckle – reírse entre los dientes
To collect – cobrar / recolectar
To cure – curar
To decide - decidir
To deserve – merecer
To design - diseñar
To develop - desarrollar
To disagree - disentir / discrepar
To disappear – desaparecer
To discuss – discutir
To divorce - divorciarse
To dream – soñar
To dress up – vestirse / disfrazarse
To drop – caer / dejar caer

To drown – ahogarse
To elect – elegir
To empty – vaciar
To encourage – animar / alentar / estimular
To equip (for / with) – equipar (para / con)
To explain – explicar
To export – exportar
To fall down – caerse
To feed – alimentar
To fill – llenar
To fire – disparar
To freeze – congelar
To go on – continuar / avanzar / seguir
To grow – crecer
To hide – esconder
To hijack – secuestrar
To hire – contratar / emplear
To import – importar
To inform – informar
To interrupt – interrumpir
To interview - entrevistar
To invent – inventar / crear
To invest – invertir
To knock on - tocar
To laugh – reír
To launch – lanzar / inaugurar
To let – dejar / permitir
To light – encender / iluminar
To manage – organizar / lograr / administrar
To manufacture – fabricar / manufacturar
To marry - casarse

To mean – significar / querer decir
To mess up – desordenar / estropear / arruinar / ensuciar
To milk – ordeñar
To move – mover
To mow – podar
To notice – notar / percibir
To offer – ofrecer
To organize – organizar
To own – poseer
To paint – - pintar
To park – parquear / estacionar
To pedal – pedalear
To plant – plantar / sembrar
To pray – orar
To predict – predecir
To produce – producir
To protect (from) – proteger (de)
To pull – halar
To push – empujar
To put away – guardar / retirar
To raise – criar / levantar
To realize – darse cuenta / entender
To redecorate – redecorar
To reduce – reducir
To reelect – reelegir
To return – regresar
To roast - asar
To run away - run away - huir
To sail – navegar
To save – salvar / guardar

Nivel Tres

To score - anotar
To seem - parecer
To serve – servir
To service – dar servicio o mantenimiento a un aparato
To settle down – establecerse / resolver / sentar cabeza
To shake – agitar / sacudir
To shoot – disparar / tirar / arrojar
To shop – comprar (en tiendas)
To smile – sonreír
To snore – roncar
To solve - resolver
To sound - sonar
To spend – gastar
To stop – detener
To straighten up – enderezar / ordenar
To suggest – sugerir
To suppose – suponer
To surf – surfear
To swear – jurar / prometer
To teach – enseñar
To tear – rasgar
To test – probar / examinar
To throw away – botar / arrojar / desechar
To touch – tocar / palpar
To train – entrenar
To treat – tratar / atender / curar
To trouble – molestar / preocupar
To trust – confiar
To try on – probarse (ropa)

517

To vote – votar

To wear out – gastar / desgastar

To welcome – dar la bienvenida

To wind up – dar cuerda

To wish (for / that) – desear (por / que)

To wonder – preguntarse / asombrarse / maravillarse

Grammar Summary

Lesson 1

Pronouns and adverbs – Pronombres y adverbios

Reflexive – Emphatic pronouns – Pronombres reflexivos y enfáticos.

Pronoun + of – Pronombre más of

Adjectives – Adjetivos

Regular verbs – Verbos regulares

Irregular verbs – Verbos irregulares

Lesson 2

Forms of "Can" and "To be able to" – Formas de "Can" y "To be able to".

Forms of "must" and "have to" – Formas de "must" y "have to".

The Adverb "Back" – El adverbio "back".

Indirect Commands – Órdenes indirectos.

Reported Speech – Discurso indirecto

Conditional (type 1) – Condicional (tipo 1).

Conjunctions – Conjunciones.

Adjectives – Adjetivos

Regular verbs – Verbos regulares

Irregular verbs – Verbos irregulares

Lesson 3

The auxiliary "May" and "Maybe" – El auxiliar "May" y "Maybe".

"There is / are" with auxiliary verbs – "There is / are" con verbos auxiliares.

Verbs plus "ing" form – Verbos más la forma "ing".

Reported Speech in Present and Past – Discurso indirecto en presente y pasado.

Reported questions "ask" – Preguntas discurso indirecto "ask".

Adverbs – Adverbios
Adjectives – Adjetivos
Regular verbos – Verbos regulares
Irregular verbs – Verbos irregulares

Lesson 4
Present perfect progressive – Presente perfecto continuo.

Using "can't be" and "must be" – Usando "can't be" y "must be".

The word "As" – La palabra "As"
Verbs of Sense and Perception – Verbos de sentidos y percepción.

The passive voice – La voz pasiva
The impersonal "you" – El "you" impersonal.

Adjectives – Adjetivos
Regular verbs – Verbos regulares
Irregular verbs – Verbos irregulares

Lesson 5
Conditional type 2 – Condicional tipo 2.
Some uses of "would" – Algunos usos de "would".
The verb "to wish" – El verbo "to wish".
The passive voice – La voz pasiva

Nouns formed from verbs – Nombres formados de verbos.

Adverbs – Adverbios
Adjectives – Adjetivos
Regular verbs – Verbos regulares
Irregular verbs – Verbos irregulares

Lesson 6

To have + noun + past participle – To have + sustantivo + pasado participio.

To need + ing – To need + ing

Agreeing and disagreeing – Acuerdos y desacuerdos.

Conjunction "so that" – Conjunción "so that"

Adverbs – Adverbios
Adjectives – Adjetivos
Regular verbs – Verbos regulares
Irregular verbs – Verbos irregulares

Lesson 7

The auxiliary verb "ought to" – El verbo auxiliar "ought to".

Adverbs – Adverbios
Adjectives – Adjetivos
Regular verbs – Verbos regulares
Irregular verbs – Verbos irregulares

Answers to exercises – Respuestas de los ejercicios

Como terminaron sus exámenes y se aseguraron de dominar cada concepto, pueden verificar las respuestas al final del libro. Me he tomado la libertad de ofrecerles las respuestas de todos los ejercicios de cada lección asi también como los del examen de nivel. Pero no hagan trampa, solo ustedes pierden si hacen trampa. *See you on the fourth volume.*

Lesson 1
Answers to Exercise 1.1:
myself
themselves
ourselves
itself
yourself
Answers to Exercise 1.2
whenever
Wherever
Whatever
whoever
whatever
Answers to Exercise 1.3:
b
d
a
e

c

Answers to Exercise 1.4:
by the way
Help yourself
Take care
You're kidding
come on

Lesson 2
Answers to Exercise 2.1:
can
cannot/can't
was able to
could
not been able to
can
could
not be able to

Answers to Exercise 2.2:
A/P
A
A
A/P
A
A
A
A
P
P

Answers to Exercise 2.3:
need
brought
walk back
gave
give
coming back
take
drove
want
ran back

Answers to Exercise 2.4:
The policeman says (that) you win a bicycle if you collect four of these (those) tickets.

The teacher says to bring pictures to class tomorrow.

Uncle Jerry says (that) you catch more flies with honey.

The veterinarian says (that) the best thing is to wash him (the dog).

The mechanic says (that) the car will be as good as new.

Answers to Exercise 2.5:
will get/gets
will take/can take
make
will kill
won't have

Lesson 3
Answers to Exercise 3.1:
Mark said he loved her.
They said this/that town was beautiful.
He asked where he/she was.
Her parents promised that they would not throw away her toys. / Her parents promised that they were not going to throw away her toys.
He told his daughter to go to sleep.
The player said he scored more points than any other player.
John said there might be mice down here/there.
The policeman said he found that hard to believe.
The principal asked if she was sure her husband would come.
Mac reported that Tom stopped to help a lady cross the street.

Answers to Exercise 3.2:
be
eating
drinking
travel
hiring
to rain/raining
watching/to watch
to pay/paying
to finish
to visit

Answers to Exercise 3.3:
sweetly
nice
neat
nervously
definitely

Lesson 4
Answers to Exercise 4.1:
can't be
must be
seems like
can't be
must be
must be
must be
can't be
seemed like
seems like

Answers to Exercise 4.2:
has been designing
've been training
hasn't been producing
's been shaking
have been raising
've been wondering
've been painting
have been appearing
've been parking
've been saving

Answers to Exercise 4.3:
is grown
will be kept
is made
was filmed
be produced
have been reported

Lesson 5
Answers to Exercise 5.1:
was ... encouraged
was reelected
were planted
has been organized
was invested

Answers to Exercise 5.2:
past intention
typical
wish
typical
used to
wish
used to
past intention
used to
wish

Answers to Exercise 5.3:
had; would buy

were; would tell
tried; would recognize
wore; wouldn't be
agreed; would cry

Lesson 6
Answers to Exercise 6.1:
c
b
a
e
d

Answers to Exercise 6.2:
Her hair needs trimming; she's going to have her hair trimmed.

My shoes need repairing; I want to have them [my shoes] repaired.

Our tires need replacing; we want to have them [our tires] replaced.

Their corn needs harvesting; they plan to have it harvested.

George's shirts need [dry] cleaning; he plans to have them dry cleaned.

Suggested answers to Exercise 6.3: Answers will vary.
Of course she wouldn't; Of course not
I am absolutely positive she did
I definitely was
not; I guess it might; I guess it could

they can; they might be able to
you're probably right; that's probably true

Lesson 7

Answers to Exercise 7.1:
ought to support
ought to find
ought to sing
ought to offer
ought to help

Answers to Exercise 7.2:
e
d
c
a
b

Answers to Level Three Tests – Respuesta de los Examenes del Nivel Tres

Answers to Test 1.1:
filled

holding

means

running away

worn out

hid

tear

frozen

threw away

teaching

Answers to Test 1.2:
may

myself

was able to

be

getting

whatever

Whoever

either

will get

if you want

Answers to Test 1.3:
c

e

b

a

d

Answers to Test 2.1:

have you been do → have you been doing

must is crazy → must be crazy

I help → I would help

I wish I have → I wish I had

ought to bought → ought to buy / ought to have bought

Answers to Test 2.2:

can't be

must be

can't be

must be

must be

Answers to Test 2.3:

is boiled

is taken

have been opening

will be turned back

has been asking

Answers to Test 3.1:

Otherwise

to leave her pictures to her dad

can't stand

to make matters worse

to tell someone's fortune

for the best

Take care!

Welcome aboard!
Good gracious
coming true
good for nothing
have a seat
for a good cause
If I were you
thank goodness
What do you say?
After all
to tell on your classmates
Shut up!
Come on
Answers to Test 3.2:
wouldn't
will
wouldn't
could
will
Answers to Test 3.3:
written
waiting
made
burnt
studying

Nevil Tres Conclusión

Muchas gracias por seleccionar el *Curso Completo de Inglés – Nivel Tres* por Yeral E. Ogando para su aprendizaje. Por fin, han llegado al final del tercer nivel, por lo tanto, ya pueden hablar inglés fluido y están listos para el nivel cuatro.

Les exhorto que continúen practicando y hablando inglés en todo momento, ya les he dicho que la Practica hace al Maestro. Visiten mi pagina de internet para más información.

God bless you and see you in volumen three.

Dr. Yeral E. Ogando
www.aprendeis.com

Nivel Tres BONO GRATIS

Estimado Estudiante,

Necesitas descargar el audio MP3 para usar este increíble método para aprender inglés. Visita este link:
http://aprendeis.com/ingles-audio-nivel3/
Usuario "ennivel3"
Contraseña "en32016"

Solo tienes que descargar el archivo comprimido, descomprimirlo y estas listo para iniciar tu experiencia al mundo del inglés.

Si quieres compartir tu experiencia, comentario o possible sugerencia, siempre podrás contactarme a info@aprendeis.com

Muchas gracias por estudiar el *Curso Completo de Inglés – Nivel Tres* y por escuchar mis instrucciones.

Caros afectos,
Dr. Yeral E. Ogando

Curso Completo de Inglés

Teach Yourself English

Habla Inglés desde la primera lección.
Nivel Cuatro avanzado.
Aprenda Inglés sin profesor hoy.

Dr. Yeral E. Ogando

Lesson 1

Crime doesn't pay – El crimen no paga

Conversation 1

Hank: You coming?

Morris: Yeah, yeah, I'm coming. Just a minute, okay?

Hank: Don't have all day.

Morris: I know. I don't think that guy will come after us though. Didn't you see how scared he was, begging for his life?

Hank: Maybe, but he seemed to be looking at something out of the corner of his eyes. I think he might have something up his sleeve.

Morris: That sheriff was sure a lousy shooter.

Hank: No, he wasn't.

Morris: Yes, he was.

Hank: No, he wasn't.

Morris: Yes, he was. Didn't get me.

Hank: He wasn't trying to shoot you, Stupid. He was trying to shoot the gun out of my hand.

Morris: Haha, good thing he didn't get it, right?

Hank: Sorry, Partner, he did.

Morris: We don't have a gun?

Hank: Nope.

Morris: Great! We're unarmed. We don't have anything to defend ourselves.

Hank: Don't worry. We're almost to the border anyway. They don't have anything against us in Montana. But get a move on!

Conversation 2

Morris: Hey, Partner, what's that up ahead?

Hank: Don't see nothin'.

Morris: Looks like someone coming this way.

Hank: Where?

Morris: See that cloud of dust?

Hank: Oh, heck, and there's no place to hide here.

Morris: Don't suppose they'll recognize us?

Hank: You kidding? They come all the way out here to get us but don't know who we are?

Morris: You're the one with all the answers. What do you say we do?

Hank: I say, let's run for it!

Morris: The riders are gaining on us.

Hank: Can't you move any faster?

Morris: This old horse doesn't move too fast.

Hank: Well, make him move. Dig your spurs into his side.

Morris: Last time I tried that, he dumped me. Hey, look! A cattle drive. Maybe we can get "lost" among the cattle.

Hank: We'd better get around them, or we'll have nowhere to go. Come on!

Morris: I can't go any faster.

Hank: Well, you're on your own. I'm out of here!

Sheriff: Put up your hands, you varmits. Heading for the border, huh?

Morris: Darn, we almost made it.

Sheriff: What's your hurry?

Morris: We wanted to—

Hank: My wife's awful sick, and she really needs some money for medicine.

Sheriff: Right. Come back to town, and we'll see if we have some medicine for her. Might have something for you, too!

New words – Nuevas palabras
The backyard – el patio / la parte trasera
Badge - insignia
Bar - bar
Bartender - bar ténder / cantinero
Beard - barba
Cage - jaula
Cattle - ganado
Cowboy - vaquero
Crime - crimen
Director - director
End - final
Hero - héroe
Heroine – heroína
Land - tierra
Lion - león
Mustache - bigote
Outlaw – forajido / bandido
Partner - compañero
Prison – prisión

Ranch – rancho
Saloon – salón / taberna
Sheriff – alguacil / sheriff
Stranger – forastero / desconocido / extranjero
The West – El Oeste
Accomplishment - logro
Activity - actividad
Announcement - anuncio
Attention – atención
Audience - audiencia
Auditorium - auditorio
Degree – título
Farewell – adiós / despedida
Grade - grado
Meaning - significado
Microphone - micrófono
Mind - mente
Play - obra
Rehearsal - ensayo
Retirement - retiro
Speech - discurso
Stage - escenario

Words Definitions -
Cattle: *when you raise cows for selling, usually for food.*

Crime doesn't pay: *this expression indicates that if you do something wrong or illegal, in the end, you will always get caught.*

Ranch: *a large farm where you raise cattle, sheep, goats, chickens, and so on.*

Take it easy: this expression is used when telling someone to stay relaxed or not to get excited about something.

Degree: the certification or title you get when you finish college or university.

Play: when an actor or actress tells a story on a stage, normally in a theater.

Grateful: when you are happy or thankful about something that someone gave or did for you.

Phrases and Expressions - Frases y expresiones

Around here / there – en esta (esa) área, por estos (esos) lados / Por aquí, por allá.

Crime doesn't pay – El crimen no paga.

In case – en caso de *(en caso de que algo pueda suceder, a veces se usa "just in case"-"solo por si las moscas", "por si acaso")*

In the end – al final

It's my turn – es mi turno

From the corner of his eyes – de reojo

Kind of – un poco de *(it is kind of hot today, isn't it? – está un poco caliente hoy, ¿no es así? I am kind of busy - estoy un poco ocupado)*

Lousy shot – mal tirador *(una persona que no dispara bien "bad shooter")*

These days – estos días / hoy en día

To beg for your life – rogar por tu vida

To flunk a test – quemar / tronar un examen

To give a speech – dar un discurso

To give up – rendirse / darse por vencido

To pass a test – pasar un examen

To take it easy – tómalo con calma / tranquilízate / relájate

To take part in – tomar parte en / participar en

To throw a party – armar una fiesta / organizar una fiesta.

Unarmed – desarmado

What's on your mind? - ¿Qué pasa por tu mente? / ¿Qué quieres decirme? / ¿Qué tienes pensado?)

Grammar – Gramática

Incomplete sentences – Oraciones incompletas

En conversación muchas veces tenemos oraciones incompletas cuando el significado es obvio o puede ser entendido sin completar la oración. Las palabras que omitimos en inglés usualmente son pronombres, verbos auxiliares y formas del verbo "to be".

Ready? – *¿listo?*

Como pueden ver, esta oración es solo una fracción de la frase completa. La oración completa tanto en inglés como en español sería"Are you ready?" - ¿estás listo?

See you later (I'll see you later) – nos vemos más tarde

Anybody home (is anybody home)? -¿hay alguien en casa?

Know me (do you know me)? - ¿me conoces?

Know her (do you know her)? - ¿la conoces?

El concepto es simple y sencillo; mientras más lo usen más lo aprenderán.

Present tense describing the past – Tiempo

presente describiendo el pasado.

Recuerden que a menudo usamos el presente simple o presente progresivo para hablar de las cosas que pronto sucederán.

When does Daddy arrive? - ¿Cuándo llega (llegará) papi?

He's coming soon – él viene (vendrá) pronto.

Del mismo modo cuando hacemos cuentos o chistes en inglés, muchas veces usamos el tiempo presente aún cuando estamos hablando del pasado. Veamos.

Finally the sheriff *comes* into the station, *goes* to his desk, and *asks* for the report. "He *wants* the report," *shouts* the assistant. *He's starting* to get angry, when the assistant *says*, "*Well, if you ain't got any work, I'll just have to go home.*"

Lean muy bien el corto párrafo y presten mucha atención. Verán que la estructura completa está en presente, cuando realmente están contando algo que sucedió en el pasado en forma de broma.

The auxiliary verb "Shall" – El verbo auxiliar "Shall".

Usamos "*shall*" cuando ofrecemos hacer algo, para sugerir que tú o alguien más haga algo o para pedir consejos o sugerencias. Normalmente se usa con "*I*" y "*We*".

Shall we go? - ¿nos vamos?

Shall I take your luggage? - ¿puedo tomar su equipaje?

Shall we talk now? - ¿hablamos ahora?

The pronoun "One" – El pronombre "One".

Usamos "One" como pronombre para indicar "*anybody, everybody, nobody*". Ésta es una forma muy formal; normalmente en vez de "one" se usa "*you*" o "*they*".

One never knows – uno nunca sabe.

One should never speak loudly in a hospital – uno nunca debe hablar alto en un hospital.

Nouns that end in "Er / Or" – Sustantivos que terminan en "Er / Or".

Hemos visto ya algunos de estos sustantivos en lecciones pasadas. Podemos agregar "*er*" *y* "*or*" a muchos verbos para formar el nombre de la persona, herramienta o maquinaria que hace tal cosa.

To swim – nadar

Para nombrar la persona que "nada", es decir, el "nadador" solo agregamos "er" al verbo quitando la partícula "to". Veamos.

A swimmer swims – un nadador nada

A teach*er* teaches – un profesor enseña

A sail*or* sails – un marino navega

A play*er* plays – un jugador juega

A writ*er* writes – un escritor escribe

A read*er* reads – un lector lee

A refrigerat*or* refrigerates – un refrigerador refrigera.

Como aprenderán, la terminación "er" es mucho

más común y puede ser usada en casi cualquier verbo. Veamos algunos otros ejemplos.

A driv*er* drives – un conductor conduce

A drink*er* drinks – un bebedor bebe

A runn*er* runs – un corredor corre

A danc*er* dances – un bailarín baila

A travel*er* travels – un viajante viaja

A fish*er* fishes – un pescador pesca

To have something + infinitive – Tener algo + infinitivo.

Podemos usar esta frase en todos los contextos y tiempos: "To have something – tener algo".

I have something to say – tengo algo que decir.

She has something to work for – ella tiene algo por lo que trabajar.

We have something to do – tenemos algo que hacer.

They had something to show you – ellos tenían algo para mostrarte.

He has something to dream for – él tiene algo por lo que soñar.

En español se puede traducir tanto como "tener algo para o tener algo que". También se puede usar *anything (casi siempre con el negativo), nothing,* o incluso *anyone* en lugar de *something*:

You have something to discuss – ustedes tienen algo que discutir o ustedes tienen algo para discutir.

Now that she has adopted her nephew, she has someone to live for – ahora que adoptó a su sobrino, tiene alguien para quien vivir.

Adjectives – Adjetivos
Brave – bravo / valiente
Common – común
Dull – aburrido *(what a dull story – historia tan aburrida)*
Dusty – lleno de polvo
Wild – salvaje / silvestre
Active - activo
Grateful - agradecido
Impossible - imposible
Possible - posible
Upset – enojado / furioso
Useful - útil
Useless – inútil / inservible

Exercises – Ejercicios

Exercise 1.1: Write the verb in the noun form.

My daughter is an excellent _____ (read).

Great! I need a _____ with this project (help).

What about that _____ (report). I thought she was helping you.

She was in an accident! Yeah, I know! It was really

a _____ (shock).

The car's _____ was unconscious

(drive).

Exercise 1.2: Complete the sentences. Add the omitted words.
All gone!

You hungry?

Coming!

Ready?

New here?

Exercise 1.3: Write the verb in parentheses in the correct form.
Example: I'm so hungry. Isn't there anything _to eat_ in this old place (eat)?
You're always bugging me. Don't you have

anything else _____ (do)?

Your honor, I have nothing _____ about the crime (say).
I'm so excited about the party. It gives me

something _____ to (look forward).
I don't want to go to your club. I don't have anyone

_____ to (talk).

Now that I know the potential of this new product,

it really gives me something _____ for (work).

Lesson 2
Crossing the border – Cruzando la frontera
Conversation 1

The border is a popular place. Even when three bridges are available within ten minutes of each other, they're always full of people waiting to cross. What makes them drive hours to wait in long lines? Why would they want to change their money at a depressing exchange rate? Why pay all that money for gas, tolls, and food on the trip? Shopping—that's why! Multiple department stores offer sales on toys, housewares, and clothing—clothing that is more durable, more comfortable, or more fashionable. For those looking for a bargain, there are discount stores, and electronics are nearly always cheaper.

But the trip is not without its risks. Roads to the border can be dangerous, not just because of the occasional flat tire but because of people who frequently cross the border with illegal goods. Border towns can be areas of conflict, too. And what do you do if you get a ticket for a burnt out headlight or if you are involved in a car accident? You might have to go to court and pay huge fines! But of the many people who cross the border every day, few people ever experience these problems, so the lines continue to grow and the bridges multiply. The shopping options, the smoothly paved streets, the hundreds of restaurants and fast-food eateries—all make a border crossing an expensive but thrilling experience.

Conversation 2

The boats lined up for the beginning of the race. At the signal, they were off. Each hurried along, the wind behind them. The contestants watched each other nervously. It would be a very close race. One boat was slightly bigger, but the other was more aerodynamically constructed. It was imposible to be sure which one would come out first. As one boat gained the lead, the owner's heart jumped, and his eyes shone with happiness. Then his mouth went dry as his boat slowed down on the next curve.

At last, they came up to the finish line. They were nose to nose when one boat started to sink! All was lost.

"Ha! Your boat sank!" the competitor gloated.

"So what? It's just a piece of paper. That sure was close! Let's make another one and try it again!"

The boys raced back to the bridge to fold better boats. "Best out of three?" asked the one who had lost the race.

"Okay!" said the other, and they both set their boats for another race.

New words – Nuevas palabras
Border – frontera / borde
East - este
Happiness - felicidad
Limit - limite

Nivel Cuatro

North - norte
Point – punto / punta
Sign - señal
South - sur
Speed limit – límite de velocidad
Traffic – tráfico
West - oeste
Accommodations - alojamiento
Ad – anuncio - aviso
Advertisement – promoción / anuncio
Carpeting - alfombras
Circle - círculo
Fireplace – chimenea
Fine - multa
Flat - apartamento
Highway - carretera
Roommate – compañero de habitación
Taste – gusto / sabor
Tracks – pistas / carrera de caballo
Transportation – transporte
View – vista / visión / perspectiva
Dark - oscuro
Light - claro

Word Definitions -
Flat: British term used for an apartment.
Point: the end of a pencil, pen or a knife.
Expressing a main or important idea.
Roommate: a person who shares a room with you and usually is not your relative.
So what?: when nobody cares about something and

it is not important at all.

Taste: *referring to the kind of things that you like. It also refers to the particular perception of different things in your mouth, such as sweet, sour, bitter, or salty.*

Traffic: *when speaking about cars, trucks, and so on that are on the road at the same time.*

View: *referring to what you can see from a place where you are.*

Phrases and Expressions - Frases y expresiones

Couldn't care less – me importa un bledo / me importa un comino *(usamos esta expresión para indicar que algo no nos importa en lo absoluto)*

From here on – de aquí en adelante / de ahora en adelante

Miles per hour – millas por hora

To serve someone right – tener lo que se merece *(se usa esta expresión para indicar que alguien recibe lo que se merece)*

So what? - ¿Y eso qué? / ¿y eso qué importa? *(usamos esta expresión para decir que a nadie le importa y que no es importante)*

To talk something over – discutir un problema

That's not the point – ese no es el punto

Yeah, sure –sí, seguro *(usamos esta expresión cuando queremos salir de alguien y no creemos lo que esa persona está diciendo)*

To leave it up to someone – dejar que alguien más decida.

🔵Grammar – Gramática
Adverbs – Adverbios
At last – por fin / finalmente
Se usa cuando hemos sido impacientes por motivo de una larga espera.
I have been waiting for hours. *At last* you are here. – he estado esperando por horas. Por fin estás aquí.

Pretty – algo / bastante
It was a *pretty good* conversation – fue bastante buena la conversación.
It is *pretty hot* here – está algo caliente aquí.
I am *pretty sure* she's lying – estoy algo seguro que ella está mintiendo.

Sure – realmente
It sure was a good conversation – realmente fue una buena conversación.

Way – mucho
The fight *was way too* slow – la pelea fue demasiada lenta.
It's *way over* 40 degrees – está mucho más de 40 grados.
Cuando se usa "way" como adverbio, por lo general se usa con "*too*", "*over*" y "*under*"

Forming nouns from adjectives – Formando sustantivos de adjetivos.
Formamos nuevos nombres o sustantivos agregando "*ness*" al adjetivo. Veamos.

Crazy – loco   *craziness* – locura
Dry – seco   *dryness* – sequedad
Como habrán notado, cuando un adjetivo con más de una sílaba termina en "y", cambia por "i"; pero si es un adjetivo de una sílaba no cambia como en "*dryness*".

Ill – enfermo   *illness* – enfermedad
Glad – alegre   *gladness* – alegría
Happy – feliz   *happiness* – felicidad
Sad – triste   *sadness* – tristeza
Sick – enfermo   *sickness* – enfermedad
Sleepy – soñoliente   *sleepiness* – somnolencia

Prefixes "Un / Im / In" – Prefijos "Un / Im / In".
Antes algunos adjetivos y pasado participios usados como adjetivos, "*un / im / in*" denotan el significado de negación, es decir "*not*".

Successful – exitoso
Unsuccessful (not successful) – fracasado / infructuoso / sin éxito
Happy – feliz
Unhappy – infeliz
Able – capaz
Unable – incapaz
Usual – usual
Unusual – inusual
Comfortable – cómodo
Uncomfortable – incómodo
Prepared – preparado / listo
Unprepared – no preparado / no listo
Possible – posible
Impossible – imposible

Perfect – perfecto
Imperfect – imperfecto
Moral – moral
Immoral – inmoral
Expensive – caro
Inexpensive – barato
Accurate – exacto
Inaccurate – inexacto
Eligible – elegible
Ineligible – inelegible
Organic – orgánico
Inorganic – inorgánico
Decent – decente
Indecent – indecente
Sane – sano
Insane – loco / insano / demente

Recuerden que al usarlo la oración casi siempre estará en positivo, porque el prefijo indica la negación.

This is possible – esto es posible.
This is not possible – esto no es posible
This is impossible – esto es imposible.

This is accurate – esto es correcto
This is not accurate – esto no es correcto
This is inaccurate – esto no es correcto

I am able to help you – puedo ayudarte
I am not able to help you – no puedo ayudarte
I am unable to help you – no puedo ayudarte.

The suffix "ful" – El sufijo "ful".

Cuando colocamos *"ful"* al final de algunos sustantivos, se convierten en adjetivos describiendo algo similar o la complexión del sustantivo. Recuerden que siempre será con una sola *"l"* al final.

Faith – fe
Faithful – fiel
Help – ayuda
Helpful – provechoso / servicial
Use – uso
Useful – útil
Peace – paz
Peaceful – pacífico
Power – poder
Powerful – poderoso
Beauty – belleza
Beautiful – hermoso / lindo / bello
Color – color
Colorful – colorido

No olviden que la letra "y" antes de "ful" se cambia por "i". Pero cuando le precede una consonante, entonces no cambia.

Playful – alegre / juguetón

Adjectives – Adjetivos
Plain – ordinario / simple
Public – público
Round – redondo
Wall to wall – de pared a pared

Cardinal points – Los puntos cardinales

Recuerden que los puntos cardinales se pueden unir unos con otros formando otros significados. Se escriben en minúscula a menos que formen parte de un nombre propio.

East - este
West - oeste
North - norte
South – sur
Southeast - sureste
Nothwest – noreste

I am heading east – me dirijo al este
I am in South Africa – estoy en Suráfrica.
They are in North America – ellas están en Norteamérica.

También se usa la palabra "bound" junto al punto cardinal, formando una sola palabra indicando que vamos o nos dirigimos en esa dirección.

An *eastbound* train – un tren dirigiéndose al este
A *westbound* trip – un viaje dirigiéndose al oeste.

Regular verbs – Verbos regulares

To hurry up – hurried up – hurried up - apresurarse

To owe – owed – owed – deber (cuando se tiene que pagar)

To slow down – slowed down – slowed down – ir despacio / retrasar

To spoil – spoiled – spoiled – echar a perder / dañar

To advertise – advertised – advertised – promocionar

To share – shared – shared - compartir
To surprise – surprised – surprised - sorprender

Irregular verbs – Verbos irregulares
To let go (of) – let go – let go – dejar ir / soltar
To take away – took away – taken away – llevarse / quitar *(quitarle algo a alguien y no devolvérselo)*

Exercises – Ejercicios
Exercise 2.1: Write the correct adverb: *way, sure,* or *pretty.*

He was going _____ too fast. He almost ran the red light.

The play was _____ good, but it could have been better.

You _____ don't see one of those every day!

I was surprised to see him there, but he

_____ didn't work for long!

You were _____ too loud. Everyone heard you.

The kids were _____ good. You know, kids will be kids!

We not only met the goal; we went _____ over it!

The lights were _____ bright. The singers were sweating.

Oh, no! It's _____ past our bedtime!

They _____ don't make toasters like they used to!

Exercise 2.2: Underline the correct form of the word.

The dictator liked to feel **power/powerful/powerness**.

This song always filled her with **happy/happiful/happiness**.

The **crazy/craziful/craziness** turkey flew into the car's windshield.

This purse is quite **use/useful/useness**. It's big and has a zipper.

We heard about her **ill/illfull/illness**, but we didn't know it was that bad.

My hands are always very **dry/dryful/dryness**.

Everyone hopes for **peace/peaceful/peaceness** and an end to war.

Now that her children were gone, she felt a strange sense of **empty/emptiful/emptiness**.

You should be **care/careful/careness**, or your cell phone might be stolen!

The **sad/sadful/sadness** music made her cry!

Lesson 3
Stepping on the gas - Acelerando

Conversation 1

Policeman: Ma'am?

Carol: Yeah?

Policeman: You need to move your car.

Carol: Why?

Policeman: You're parked in a fire lane.

Carol: Oops! How was I to know?

Policeman: The area is clearly marked right there with the diagonal lines.

Carol: Oh, haha. I can't tell the difference.

Policeman: Being able to recognize places where you can legally park is part of the driving regulations for the state. You studied them in the driving manual in order to obtain your license, right?

Carol: Of course. So where can I park?

Policeman: I don't know, ma'am, but you'll have to move.

Carol: But I'm okay as long as there isn't a fire, right?

Policeman: No, ma'am.

Carol: The thing is, I'm waiting for someone. He's expecting me to be here.

Policeman: That's too bad. If you don't want a ticket, you'll have to move now.

Carol: Okay. [She changes gears but discovers that the car is in reverse.]

Policeman: Stop! Put on the brakes!

Carol: [But she steps on the gas instead. She hits the car parked behind her—the policeman's patrol car.]

Policeman: What on earth are you doing?

Carol: Oops! I stepped on the gas instead of the brakes.

Conversation 2

Carol: Hi, Your Honor, this is what happened—

Judge: Please, keep your distance, young lady. You may stand over there.

Carol: Okay, so I was waiting for my father, who happens to be a policeman, and this guy—

Judge: We'll hear the patrol officer's report first.

Carol: Oh, right. Where is he?

Judge: He isn't here yet.

Carol: What happens if he doesn't come?

Judge: The charges would be dropped.

Carol: How long do we wait—

Policeman: You received my report, Your Honor?

Judge: Yes, would you like to read it aloud?

Policeman: *Yes.* On Tuesday, the 11th of October, the defendant, Carol Marie Larson parked in a fire lane. She was asked to move several times, and when she finally agreed to do so, she started to back up instead. I ordered her to stop the car, but she accelerated and hit the patrol car.

Judge: [turns to look at Carol] Why did you hit the patrol car, Miss Larson?

Carol: I forgot to take it out of reverse.

Judge: But the patrolman warned you to stop.

Carol: I meant to hit the brakes, but I stepped on the gas instead.

Judge: It sounds, Miss Larson, as though you might be a bit of a menace on the roads.

Carol: Haha. No, Your Honor, it was just an accident.

Judge: In other words, it won't happen again?

Carol: No, Sir.

Judge: You refused to move the car?

Carol: I didn't mean to be rude, but my dad was expecting me to wait for him outside, and it was the only place available on the street.

Judge: I will take that into consideration.

New words – Nuevas palabras

Background – antecedentes / historial / fondo

Environment - ambiente

Friendship - amistad

Looks – apariencia / aspecto

Marriage - matrimonio

Personality - personalidad

Relationship – relación

Sense of humor – sentido del humor

Temper - temperamento

Brakes - frenos
Court - corte
Leash – laso / cordón
Witness - testigo
Arrangement – arreglo / acuerdo / gestión
Catalog – catálogo
Commission – comisión
Complaint - queja
Delay - retraso
Discount - descuento
Dozen - docena
Line - línea
Merchandise – mercancía
Percentage – porcentaje
Quality - calidad
Quantity - cantidad
Representative - representante
Shipment – cargamento

Word Definitions -

Background: *knowing who your parents were, the things they did, what they looked like. Knowing where you come from and how you were educated and raised.*

Discount: *when prices for a product or merchandise are lower than their regular prices for a specific time.*

Down to earth: *when people have their feet on the ground, their ideas are practical and not crazy.*

Gentle: *when someone does not hurt others and is very kind toward people.*

Hard working: *when someone works a lot and likes to work.*

Practical: *when someone understands the important points and does the easiest and best thing.*

Reliable: *when you can trust in someone.*

Rude: *when someone says things to upset, hurts others, and interrupts conversations.*

Selfish: *When someone doesn't share with others and thinks only about himself.*

Temper: *when someone gets angry very easily and quickly gets in a bad mood.*

How was I to know?: *when we were not aware or did not know about something and we want to excuse ourselves for something we have said that was inappropriate.*

Witness: *someone who sees something and can tell others about it.*

Phrases and Expressions - Frases y expresiones

To change your mind – cambiar de opinión

To get along with – llevarse bien con alguien

To take something into consideration – considerar algo o tomar algo en consideración

As I was saying – como estaba diciendo

For ages – antiguo / viejo / por mucho tiempo

In ages – en siglos, en mucho tiempo

How was I to know? - ¿Cómo lo iba a saber?

In other words – en otras palabras

On earth – no puedo creerlo *(se usa después de una palabra interrogativa para indicar nuestra sorpresa o lo difícil que es creer lo que acaba de*

pasar o acaban de decir (why on eath did you do that?
- ¡no puedo creer lo que hiciste!)

To tell the court – decirle al juez o a la corte
(cuando se está frente a una corte)

You know me – ya me conoces *(sabes como soy)*

Difference between - deferencia entre does cosas
(the difference between you and me – la diferencia
entre nosotros dos)

In-law – *(se una al nombre familiar para referirse a*
los familiares políticos o de nuestra pareja) father in-
law

Happen (ed) to – sucede (esta expresión es usada
con el infinitivo del verbo para hablar sobre algo que
no estaba planeado o que pasó por casualidad, sea
bueno o malo) *I happen to be a teacher – sucede que*
soy profesor. She happened to be there when the thief
pulled the trigger – por casualidad ella estaba ahí
cuando el ladrón jaló el gatillo.

Grammar – Gramática
Conjunctions – Conjunciones

Tanto "as long as" y "provided that" se pueden usar
en sustitución de "if - si condicional" para expresar
una condición. "Provided that" es más formal.

As long as – mientras que / siempre que

You can stay **as long as** you keep quiet – te puedes
quedar siempre que te estés tranquilo.

We'll get along just fine **as long as** you mind your
own business – nos llevaremos muy bien, siempre
que no te metas en lo que no te incumbe.

You can go out tonight *as long as* you get back by midnight – puedes salir esta noche, siempre que estés de regreso para la media noche.

Provided that – mientras que / con tal que

You can go out tonight *provided that* you get back by midnight – puedes salir esta noche, siempre que estés de regreso para la media noche.

We're going camping next Sunday *provided that* there's time – iremos de campo el próximo domingo, siempre y cuando haya suficiente tiempo.

What if – ¿y si? ¿Qué tal si...?

What if you are not accepted? - ¿Qué tal si no eres aceptado?

What if I tell you the truth? - ¿Y si te digo la verdad?

Though – sin embargo

Se usa para contrastar una idea o pensamiento.

He is a great friend, *though* he is not very responsible – él es un gran amigo, aunque no es muy responsable.

Peter is an excellent student, *though* he flunked the exam – Peter es un excelente estudiando, aunque se quemó en el examen.

The suffix "ship" – El sufijo "ship"

Algunas veces agregamos "ship" a nombres y algunos adjetivos para describir la condición, carácter, posición, o estado de la palabra a la que se adhiere.

Champion*ship* - campeonato

Citizen*ship* - ciudadanía
Dictator*ship* - dictadura
Fellow*ship* - compañerismo
Friend*ship* - amistad
Hard*ship* – penurias / calamidades
Leader*ship* - liderazgo
Member*ship* - membrecía
Partner*ship* - sociedad
Relation*ship* – relación
Scholar*ship* - beca

The suffixes "y, ty, ity, nce, ncy" – Los sufijos "y, ty, ity, nce, ncy"

Cuando usamos estos sufijos, convertimos el adjetivo en nombre o sustantivo.

Difficult - difícil
difficulty - dificultad
Safe – seguro
Safety - seguridad
Active – active
Activity - actividad
Distant – distante
Distance - distancia
Intelligent – inteligente
Intelligence - inteligencia
Urgent – urgente
Urgency - urgencia
Special – especial
Specialty - especialidad
Stupid - estúpido
Stupidity - estupidez

Complex – complejo
Complexity - complejidad
Inferior – inferior
Inferiority - inferioridad
Humid – húmedo
Humidity - humedad
Necessary – necesario
Necessity - necesidad
Eternal – eterno
Eternity - eternidad
Credible – creíble
Credibility - credibilidad
Responsible – responsable
Responsibility - responsabilidad
Sensible – sensible
Sensibility - sensibilidad
Divine – divino
Divinity - divinidad
Secure – seguro
Security - seguridad
Curious – curioso
Curiosity - curiosidad
Generous – generoso
Generosity – generosidad

Future time in the past – Tiempo futuro en el pasado

Usamos "was / were going to + infinitive" para hablar de algo que se creía que pasaría pero ya no.

She ***was going to study*** English (but she didn't do it) - ella iba a estudiar inglés (pero no lo hizo)

I didn't know they *were going to move* (but they did) – no sabía que se mudarian (pero se mudarían)

I *was going to visit* you yesterday (but I didn't) – te iba a visitar ayer (pero no lo hice)

Relatives pronouns – Pronombres relativos

Which – el cual / la cual

Se usa cuando nos referimos a cosas, nunca sobre personas. También se puede usar "that", pero *which* es más formal.

It's the book *which* my father gave me – es el libro el cual mi padre me dio.

It's the book *that* my father gave me – es el libro que mi padre me dio.

Recuerden que podemos omitir ambos "which – that" de la oración y el sentido es el mismo.

It's the book my father gave me – es el libro que me dio mi padre.

This is the car *which* I told you about – este es el carro del que te hablé.

This is the car *that* I told you about – este es el carro del que te hablé.

This is the car I told you about – este es el carro del que te hablé.

Who – quien

Se usa cuando nos referimos a personas solamente. También se puede usar "that" en su lugar. "Who" es más formal que "that".

This is the woman *who* stole my heart – ésta es la mujer que robó mi corazón-

This is the woman *that* stole my heart – ésta es la mujer que robó mi corazón.

Adjectives –Adjetivos

Acceptable – aceptable

Down to earth – con los pies sobre le tierra / una persona práctica

Due – esperado (*the bus was due "to arrive" at 1:10 – el autobús se esperaba para la 1:15. The rent is due in two days – la renta se vence en dos días*)

Due to – por motivo de / por causa de (*I am tired due to late sleeping – estoy cansado por dormir tarde*)

Gentle – gentil / amable

Good natured – agradable / fácil de llevarse bien

Hard working – trabajador / una persona que trabaja duro

Interested in – interesado en

Nine to five – de nueve a cinco (trabajo de 9-5)

Perfect - perfecto

Poisonous - venenoso

Practical – práctico

Reasonable - razonable

Reliable - confiable

Retail – al por menor / al detalle

Rude – grosero / mal educado

Selfish - egoísta

Slippery - resbaladizo

Stupid – estúpido / tonto

Understanding - comprensible

Wholesale – al por mayor

Nivel Cuatro

Adverbs – Adverbios
A whole lot – mucho (forma coloquial)
Exactly – exactamente
Fairly – bastante / justamente / limpio

New regular verbs – Nuevos verbos regulares
To matter – mattered – mattered - importar
To imagine – imagined – imagined - imaginar
To ruin – ruined – ruined – arruinar
To skid – skidded – skidded – patinar / resbalar / deslizarse
To step on – stepped on – stepped on - acelerar
To cancel – canceled – canceled - cancelar
To delay – delayed – delayed - retrasar
To depend on – depended on – depended on – depender de
To increase – increased – increased - aumentar
To order – ordered – ordered – ordenar / mandar / pedir / encargar
To ship – shipped – shipped – enviar / embarcar *(enviar paquetes)*

New irregular verbs – Nuevos verbos irregulares
To bring up – brought up – brought up – criar / educar / traer a colación
To run into – ran into – run into – chocar con / encontrarse con *(golpear, usualmente con un vehículo)*
To run over – ran over – run over – atropellar *(usualmente con un vehículo)*

Exercises – Ejercicios

Exercise 3.1: Add *provided that* or *as long as* where appropriate.

Example: He loves me, I can face whatever comes my way!

I'll write the preface you give me the outline.

They won't face as many hardships this winter the pipes don't freeze.

They promise not to foreclose on the house you make all of your payments from now on.

You keep providing the materials, I'll be glad to make visuals for your class.

I'll give you free meals you give me a discount on the rent.

Exercise 3.2: Write the letter of the most logical answer.

_____ What if aliens take all of our chocolate?

_____ What if we run out of fossil fuels?

_____ What if the economy goes into a recession?

_____ What if you had to speak English in order to keep your job?

_____ What if you lost your voice on the day you agreed to speak to the high school students about your career?

A. We'll have to learn to economize and enjoy the simple things.

B. We will have to learn to use hydrogen energy.

C. I'd practice all day long.

D. I'd project a visual presentation and type anything else I wanted to say.

E. We will have to survive on cheesecake.

Exercise 3.3: Which sufffix goes with the following words? List the word in the correct column: distant, fellow, partner, prudent, responsible, safe

Ence   (i)ty   ship

_____   _____   _____

_____   _____   _____

Lesson 4
The weatherman - El meteorólogo
Conversation 1

Weatherman: It's going to be quite a day out there for pranksters.

News anchor: Is that so?

Weatherman: Yes, weather conditions will be particularly favorable to hiding and sneaking up on people today. It's going to be very foggy, so drive slowly, use your fog lights, and be cautious. The temperature will be dropping throughout the day as well, so dress warm. In fact, we're expecting an ice storm and a white out.

News Anchor: Really?

Weatherman: April Fools! No ice storm, just fog and cold temperatures. But I'm definitely going to buy myself some hot chocolate to combat this depressing weather!

News Anchor: In addition to playing tricks on unsuspecting people?

Weatherman: April 1st gives us something to look forward to on these bleak, cold days of spring.

News Anchor: Yes, make sure you tune in to your public radio station today to hear some of the more creative classical pieces. You will hear works that are poorly constructed, such as Mozart's "A

Musical Joke," and music that imitates animals, such as the "Duetto Buffo Di Due Gatti." Lots of fun. If you tune in and the music sounds boring, enjoy it! It's part of the joke.

Conversation 2

Manager: Hi! The employment agency sent us your résumé along with four others. You have a good GPA and excellent computer skills. What other qualifications do you have for this job?

Applicant: Well, I was assistant to the head of the Financial Aid department at school, so I had to learn a little of everything—accounting, communication skills, project management, and so on.

Manager: Wow. You sound almost overqualified to work as a receptionist. It's quite a step down from what you've been doing. How do you feel about that?

Applicant: Well, I need work right now, and I think I'll do a good job. You can contact my references. I'm responsible, honest—

Manager: But will you be happy here? Do you think your skills are wasted on a job as receptionist?

Applicant: Well, I probably won't stay here forever. I would like to eventually move on to other things. I enjoyed management.

Manager: How are you at taking orders?

Applicant: No problem at all, Sir. You see, I was the assistant; I took orders from the head of my department and other administrators. I had to help everyone in the department as well.

Manager: Do you know how to transfer calls and manage several phone lines?
Applicant: No, Sir. But I learn quickly.
Manager: Great! How soon could you start if you are hired?
Applicant: Anytime.
Manager: All right, we'll get back to you.
Applicant: Thank you!

New words – Nuevas palabras
Cloud - nube
Effect - efecto
Fog - neblina
Forecast – pronóstico
Moisture - humedad
Play-off – eliminatoria / partido de empate
Ski - ski
Stuff - cosas
Surgeon - cirujano
Weatherman – meteorólogo
Wind - viento
Alarm - alarma
Barn - granero
Cause - causa
Death - muerte
Destruction – destrucción
Device – aparato electrónico
Drop - gota
Film - película
Fire department – departamento de bomberos
House call – visita médica

Property - propiedad
Seafood - mariscos
Short circuit – corto circuito
Sidewalk - acera
System - sistema
Upset stomach – mal de estómago
Virus - virus
Accountant – contable / contador
Accounting - contabilidad
Employee - empleado
Employer - empleador
Employment - empleo
Employment agency – agencia de empleo
Engineering - ingeniería
Head – cabeza
Qualification – calificación (habilidades y destrezas)
Reference - referencia
Requirement - requisito
Résumé – currículo
Tow truck – grúa / camión de remolque
Zero - cero

Word Definitions -

Full time: when an employee works regular hours five days a week, around 8 hours a day. When you dedicate all your time to something.

Can't keep anything down: when it doesn't matter what you eat, you throw up.

Homeless: a person who does not have a home and sometimes lives in the streets or shelters.

House call: when the doctor pays you a visit to your house.

You have my deepest sympathy: when something really terrible happens, or when someone dies , we say this.

Stuff: when we don't know the name of some things or how to call them, we use this expression. We basically use it with anything.

Phrases and Expressions - Frases y expresiones

Is that so? – ¿realmente? / ¿estás seguro?

Quite a – bastante *(se usa para decir que algo es muy grande. Quite big – bastante grande. Quite heavy – bastante pesado)*

To drop / fall (temperature) – bajar la temperatura

To stand / be in line – pararse o estar en una fila

Can't keep anything down – todo lo vomito

To catch fire – coger fuego

To get out of – salir (se) de

Long weekend – fin de semana largo *(cuando no tienes que trabajar o viernes o lunes y el fin de semana es largo)*

Not any / no use – no importa lo que hagas *(usamos esta expresión cuando nada resolverá el problema del que hablamos o tenemos)*

Since when? - ¿desde cuándo? ¿Cuánto tiempo ha pasado desde…?

You have my deepest sympathy – mis más sinceras condolencias / cuánto lo siento.

To give someone a hand – darle una mano a alguien *(ayudar a alguien)*

To give up + ing – dejar o parar de hacer algo por siempre *(I gave up drinking – deje la bebida)*

If you don't mind my saying so – si no te importa que te dé mi opinión.

To keep + ing – hacer algo una y otra vez *(she kept coming every day – ella seguía viniendo todos los días)*

Might as well – también podrías / porque no *(you might as well try – también podrías tratar de hacerlo así)*

So far – hasta ahora

Won't accept / take no for an answer – no aceptaré / tomaré un no por respuesta.

Grammar – Gramática

The auxiliary verb "might" – El verbo auxiliar "might"

Usamos "might" de la misma forma que "may" para hablar de algo que pueda estar pasando o que pueda pasar. *No se usa para pedir permiso; en ese caso se usa (may-can).*

It *might* rain today – es posible que llueva hoy.

We *might* play cards tonight – es posible que juguemos cartas esta noche.

Peter *might* be at church already – es posible que Peter ya esté en la iglesia.

I *might not* call you tonight – es posible que no te llame esta noche.

Cuando usamos el "might" en el presente perfecto o presente progresivo, "might have" puede dar la idea de "may" o "could".

She *might have left* – puede que ella ya se haya ido.

She *might have been cleaning* when you called – puede que ella haya estado limpiando cuando llamaste.

The expression "had better" – La expresión "had better".

Usamos esta expresión igual que "should" o "ought to" para dar consejos. Cuando lo usamos seguido del pronombre personal, por lo general va en su forma de contracción.

You *'d better* come home quickly – será mejor que llegues a casa rápido.

She *'d better not* say anything – es mejor que ella no diga nada.

Peter *had better not* cancel the reservation – será mejor que Peter no cancele la reservación.

Muchas personas, cuando hablan en forma coloquial, a veces no usan el "had" y solo dicen la frase normal.

You *better* come – será mejor que vengas

She *better* not say anything – será mejor que ella no diga nada.

Question word "which one of" + noun / pronoun – La palabra de interrogación "which one of" + sustantivo / pronombre

Recuerden que cuando usamos "which", es porque tenemos elección y muchas veces va seguido de "of".

Which one of you drank my milk? – ¿Cuál de

ustedes se bebió mi leche?

Which one of the cars do you prefer? - ¿Cuál de los carros prefieres?

Which of the songs do you want to listen? - ¿Cuál de las canciones quieres escuchar?

The pronoun "those of "+ pronoun + "who" – El pronombre "those of" + pronoun + "who"

Cuando hablamos de unas pocas personas o cosas en un grupo, usamos *"those of"* más un pronombre en plural, haciendo la oración más clara.

Those of you who are going to the movies tonight had better get ready – los que (de ustedes) irán al cine esta noche, será mejor que se alisten.

Those of us who play golf have different strategies – los que (de nosotros) jugamos golf, usamos estrategias diferentes.

Supposed to – Supuesto a / tener que

Usamos "supposed to" para indicar algo que deberíamos "should" y describiendo algo que se espera o que es necesario. Recuerden, siempre vendrá un verbo después del "supposed to".

Teachers are *supposed to* educate students – los profesores tienen que educar los estudiantes.

Nurses are *supposed to* save lives – las enfermeras están deben salvar vidas.

Cuando usamos "supposed to" con el pasado, estamos indicando algo que debió haber pasado, pero no pasó o algo que no debió pasar pero pasó. Fíjense que la negación está en el verbo *"to be"*.

I *was supposed to* come at 5:00 – tenía que haber venido para las 5.

I *was not supposed to* be here – no tenía que haber estado aquí.

También puede explicar el por qué algo fue hecho.

Why are you here? – because I *was supposed to* be here - ¿Por qué estás aquí? Porque tenía que estar aquí.

Why didn't you go to school today? Because I *was not supposed to* go to school today. It's Saturday - ¿Por qué no fuiste a la escuela hoy? Porque no tenía que ir a la escuela hoy. Hoy es sábado.

No olviden que "*supposed*" también es el pasado participio del verbo "*suppose – suponer*" y algunas veces lo usamos en la voz pasiva para indicar creencia o pensamiento.

The robbery was *supposed to have happened* around noon – Se supone que el robo pasó como a mediodía.

Collective nouns – Nombres colectivos

Algunos nombres tales como "couple, team, police department" describen a más de una persona, pero están en singular y la forma verbal también está en singular.

The *team plays* tonight – el equipo juega esta noche.

The *police department works* very hard – el departamento de policías trabaja muy duro.

That *couple wants* to have a baby – esa pareja quiere tener un bebé.

Pero cuando usamos un pronombre en vez del

nombre colectivo, entonces usamos "they".

The *team wants* to practice tonight so *they are* getting ready now – el quipo quiere practicar esta noche, así que se están preparando ahora.

Presten mucha atención a la segunda parte de la oración con el pronombre personal y verán que están en plural usando "they".

The verb "to try + infinitive / gerund" – El verbo "to try + infinitivo / gerundio"

Cuando usamos el verbo "*to try*" con el infinitivo o el gerundio "*ing*" algunas veces tienen el mismo significado, pero en otras ocasiones tienen significado diferente.

Try to give the child some food – trata de dar al niño algo de comida.

Try giving the child some food – trata de dar al niño un poco de comida.

I *tried to hire* you when you came – traté de contratarte cuando viniste (pero no pude).

I *tried hiring* you when you came – traté de contratarte cuando viniste (pero no pasó)

Generalmente, expresamos las ideas con los siguientes significados.

Try + infinitive

Presente y futuro muestra un plan o una orden.

She always *tries to be* on time – ella siempre trata de estar a tiempo.

En el tiempo pasado incapacidad de hacer algo.

I *tried to stop* him, but it was too late – trate de detenerlo, pero era demasiado tarde.

Try + gerundio "ing"
Presente y futuro muestra esperanza o sugerencia. Perhaps you should *try getting up* earlier in the morning. – talvez deberías tratar de levantarte temprano en la mañana.

En el tiempo pasado muestra no tener buenos resultados.

I *was trying to* fix my computer – estaba tratando de reparar mi computadora.

The verb "to remember + infinitive / gerund" – El verbo "to remember + infinitive / gerund"
Cuando usamos "to remember" con el infinitivo es para indicar que no debemos olvidar algo.

Remember to drink your pills – recuerda tomar tus pastillas.

Remember to go to school – recuerda ir a la escuela.

Remember to study – recuerda estudiar.

Cuando usamos "to remember" con el gerundio es para indicar que estamos recordando algo del pasado.

I *remember taking* clases with you – recuerdo cuando tomaba clases contigo.

I *remember calling* you every night – recuerdo cuando te llamaba todas las noches.

Adjectives – Adjetivos
Central – centro / central
Depressed - deprimido
Depressing - depresivo
Eastern - oriental

Foggy - nebuloso
Northern - norteño
Southern - sureño
Western - occidental
Electrical - eléctrico
Exact - exacto
Homeless – sin hogar
Overworked – con exceso de trabajo
Pregnant - embarazada
Employed - empleado
Full time – tiempo completo
Overqualified – sobre calificado
Part time – tiempo compartido / medio tiempo
Qualified - calificado
Unemployed - desempleado
Unqualified – incompetente / no calificado

Adverbs – Adverbios
Generally - generalmente
Mostly – mayormente
Overnight – durante la noche
Partly - parcialmente

Regular verbs – Verbos regulares
To affect – affected – affected - afectar
To doubt – doubted – doubted - dudar
To operate – operated – operated - operar
To ski – skied – skied - esquiar
To cause – caused – caused - causar
To destroy – destroyed – destroyed - destruir
To injured – injured – injured – lesionar / herir
To kick – kicked – kicked - patear

To warn – warned – warned - advertir
To accept – accepted – accepted - aceptar
To recognize – recognized – recognized - reconocer
To require – required – required - requerir

Irregular verbs – Verbos irregulares
To beat – beaten – beaten - vencer
To blow – blew – blown - soplar
To rise – rose – risen – subir / aumentar / levantar
To throw up – threw up – thrown up - vomitar

Exercises – Ejercicios

**Exercise 4.1: Write the appropriate phrase: *might,*
had better, or *be supposed to.***
I have a lot of homework, Mom. We

_____ invent a new product and try to
sell it to our classmates.

You _____ wash those dishes right now,
or you won't use the computer for the rest of the day.

I _____ be late tomorrow. My cell phone
is broken.
We _____ finish this project tonight.
Tomorrow, we have to get ready for our trip.

They _____ cancel her account. She
didn't know how to use the confirmation code they
sent her.

I feel bad for Cindy. She _____ write a song for the next commercial.

It _____ rain tomorrow. There's a hurricane near the southern coast of the country.

Exercise 4.2: Match the sentences with the logical end.

_____ Which one of the rings

_____ Which one of these shoes

_____ Which one of the glasses

_____ Which one of these desserts

_____ Which one of the students

_____ Which one of the personality types

A. won the award?
B. is the one you prepared?
C. describes you best?
D. fits your ring finger best?
E. did you clean with the hydrogen peroxide mix?
F. did you drink out of?

Exercise 4.3: Write the verb after _remember_ as an infinitive or gerund.

Please remember _____ the trash (take out).

I remember _____ the marigolds in Grandpa's garden (pick).

Do you remember _____ breaded crab in Cancun (eat)?

Did she remember _____ the gas bill (pay)?

We don't remember _____ pizza (order).

Lesson 5
Visiting the bank – Visitando el banco
Conversation 1

Client: Hi, I'd like to make a deposit.

Teller: Okay, you'll need to fill out a deposit slip. They're over there on the counter.

Client: Thanks. . . . Okay, I'm ready now.

Teller: Did you forget something?

Client: Um, I don't think so.

Teller: It says here you have two checks to deposit.

Client: Yes.

Teller: Do you have the checks?

Client: Oh, yeah, haha.

Teller: So that's a deposit into your checking account. Would you like to make a payment on your loan today?

Client: Oh yeah, that's due this week, isn't it?

Teller: Yes. So is the credit card payment, but that will just accrue interest if you prefer to wait.

Client: And the loan?

Teller: The interest for a missed payment on the loan is a little higher.

Client: Ah, in that case, can we put one of the checks on the loan?

Teller: We can make a quick transfer from checking.

Client: Great! So I'm all set?

Teller: Yes! Have a great day!

Conversation 2

Judy: Oh, no! We're out of gas!

Gary: I didn't bring my cell phone either! We'll have to go get gas.

Judy: If we leave the car here, someone could hit it.

Gary: But if we leave the emergency flashers on, we'll run down the battery. We'll just have to pull over as far as we can off the road and go get some gas. Do you want to stay here? It's nice and cozy in the car right now.

Judy: No, I don't want to stay here alone.

Gary: Okay, let's go.

Judy: It's not so bad when you're moving. I'm almost hot!

Gary: As long as it doesn't snow. Just think, you won't have to go to the gym tomorrow. You're burning plenty of calories out here! [10 minutes later]

Judy: My toes are numb. I wish I had worn boots.

Gary: Come on. There has to be something soon.

Judy: My face is wet. If only it would stop snowing, we could see what's up ahead.

Gary: If you'd stayed in the car, you would still be warm.

Judy: If I'd stayed in the car, I'd be worried sick. Look, there's a barn. We could take shelter there.

Gary: If there's a barn, there's also a house. Come on, Hon, I think I see some lights ahead.

New words – Nuevas palabras
Account - cuenta
Checkbook – talonarios de cheque / libro de control
Checking account – cuenta de cheque
Client - cliente
Credit - crédito
Deposit - depósito
Deposit slip – comprobante de depósito
Funds - fondos
Guard - guardia
Interest - interés
Loan - préstamo
Mattress - colchón
Pickup truck - camioneta
Rule - regla
Safe deposit box – caja de seguridad / caja fuerte
Savings - ahorros
Savings account – cuenta de ahorros
Teller - cajero
Withdrawal - retiro
Withdrawal slip – comprobante de retiro
Advertising - publicidad
Budget - presupuesto
Can - lata
Commercial – comercial (especialmente comercial de TV)
Cottage – cabaña / casa de campo

Exam - examen
Lighter - encendedor
Publicity - publicidad
Raincoat – chamarra / impermeable
Shampoo - champú
Shelter - refugio
Side - lado
Situation - situación
Slogan - eslogan
Stew – guisado / estofado
Voice - voz
Beauty shop – salón de belleza
Cavity - cavidad / caries
Day off – día libre
Drill – taladro / barrena
Filling - empaste
Fingernail – uña de la mano
Injection – inyección
Nail - uña
Sergeant - sargento
Shot – inyección
Toe – dedo del pie
Toenail – uña del pie
While - mientras

Word Definitions –

Budget: *when you make a plan to know how much money you can spend on things.*

Cozy: *when the inside of a building, apartment, or house is small, comfortable, and warm.*

Drill: *a tool we use to make a hole. Dentists also*

use a drill to remove a cavity.

Funds: *money that you have at your disposal and can use for a particular purpose.*

Loan: *money that you borrow from a person or an institution and have to pay back.*

Numb: *when you can't feel a thing.*

Shelter: *anything that can protect you from the weather, disasters, or bombs. It could be a room underground, a house, and so on.*

Stew: *when you cook different types of meat with vegetables together in a pot.*

Phrases and Expressions – Frases y expresiones

All done – todo listo / terminado / completado

As well – también

By mistake – por error

Come on! – apresúrate / ven conmigo *(también se usa esta expresión cuando no creemos lo que nos están diciendo)*

It's time – es hora / es tiempo

Open wide – abre bien *(cuando un dentista o doctor te dice que abras la boca)*

To do business with – hacer negocios con

To go bankrupt – caer en quiebra / bancarrota

In that case – en ese caso

To make a deposit – hacer un depósito

To open a bank account – abrir una cuenta de banco

To take care of – encargarse de

To take out money – retirar dinero

To have your hair done – arreglarte el cabello

(cuando alguien te arregla el cabello)

To have your nails done – hacerse las uñas *(cuando alguien te hace las uñas)*

You won't feel a thing – no sentirás nada

What's that? - ¿Qué es eso?

When / while someone has the chance – cuando / mientras alguien tiene la oportunidad

Grammar – Gramática

Giving advice – Dando consejos

Usamos el verbo "to suggest – sugerir" para consejos u órdenes indirectas. Se puede usar tanto el infinitivo como el gerundio.

Why don't you eat an apple? ¿Por qué no te comes una manzana?

She *suggested eating* an apple – ella sugirió que comiera un manzana.

She *suggested that I eat* an apple – ella sugirió que comiera una manzana.

I wouldn't eat an apple if I were you – no comería una manzana si fuera tú.

She *suggested not eating* an apple – ella sugirió que no comiera una manzana.

She *suggested that I not* eat an apple – ella sugirió que no comiera una manzana.

She *suggested that he eat* an apple – ella sugirió que él comiera una manzana.

Presten mucha atención a la estructura. Como pueden ver, pueden usar tanto el verbo como el infinitivo o el gerundio. Recuerden, el uso del "that" fue opcional. Fíjense de la construcción en negativo.

Nivel Cuatro

También es muy importante que cuando usamos una tercera persona singular (he / she) después del verbo "to suggest", el verbo siguiente no lleva "*s*".

Past conditions – Pasado condicional

Usamos el pasado y condicional perfecto para hablar de algo que no pasó, pero que pudo haber pasado o que deseamos que haya pasado.

If I'd known you were coming, **I'd had dressed up** properly – si hubiese sabido que vendrías, me hubiese vestido apropiadamente.

If I'd studied English, *I would have gotten* that job – si hubiese estudiado inglés, hubiera conseguido ese empleo.

Recuerden que la "if clause" puede estar tanto en la primera o segunda parte de la oración.

I'd have dressed up properly, if *I'd known* you were coming – me hubiese vestido apropiadamente, si hubiese sabido que vendrías.

The expression "if only" – La expresión "if only".

Usamos esta expresión en el presente, pasado y pasado perfecto. En el presente indica cosas que deseamos que sucedan. En el pasado indica cosas que hubiésemos deseado que sucedieran o algo que lamentamos no haber hecho.

If only they avoid riots, everything will be OK – si solamente previnieran las huelgas, todo estaría bien.

If only we had more time, we could go to the beach – si solo tuviéramos más tiempo, podríamos ir a la playa.

If only we hadn't eaten that much, we could have been swimming all this time – si solo no hubiésemos comido tanto, podríamos haber estado nadando todo este tiempo.

Cuando usamos "if only" con el verbo "to be" en el pasado simple, siempre usaremos "were", nunca "was".

If only she weren't so sweet – si solamente ella no fuera tan cariñosa.

The verb "to wish" plus past perfect – El verbo "to wish" más el pasado perfecto.

Podemos usar "to wish – desear" con el tiempo pasado para hablar de cosas que lamentamos.

I *wish you'd waited* – desearía que hubieras esperado.

I *wish you were* here – desearía que estuvieras aquí.

I *wish you'd be gone* – desearía que te fueras.

The verb "to do" and its uses – El verbo "to do" y sus usos.

Usamos "to do" para hacer y responder a preguntas.

Do you like to eat? - ¿te gusta comer?

Yes, *I do.*

No, *I don't.*

A menudo usamos "to do" para hablar de una actividad, usualmente se sobreentiende de lo que estamos hablando.

Did you clean your bedroom yet? - ¿ya limpiaste tu

habitación?

No, *I haven't done* that – no, aún no lo he hecho.

Aren't you cleaning your bedroom? - ¿no estás limpiando tu habitación?

Why *should I do* that? - ¿por qué debería hacerlo?

Algunas veces usamos "to do" con mandatos para hacer una sugerencia o invitación dándole un tono más formal.

Do come in – por favor entre

Do have a seat – por favor siéntese

Do have some more – por favor sírvase más

Algunas veces usamos el presente o pasado simple del verbo "to do" con otro verbo para enfatizar o disentir lo que alguien haya dicho.

I hope you like your meal – espero que te guste tu comida.

Oh, I *do like it* – sí me gusta.

You should have told him – debiste haberle dicho

I *did tell* him – sí le dije

Did you tell her about the problem? – ¿le hablaste del problema?

I *did tell her* about it – si le hable del problema.

Do you like your present? – ¿te gusta tu regalo?

I *do like* my present, thanks so much – síme gusta mi regalo, muchas gracias.

Adverbs – Adverbios

Right away – de inmediato / inmediatamente

Almost - casi

Twice – dos veces

Hardly – a penas

Adjectives – Adjetivos
Bankrupt – bancarrota
Each - cada
Named – llamado / con el nombre de
Overdrawn – sobregirado
Cozy - acogedor
Worthwhile - valioso
Awake - despierto
Numb – anestesiado / entumecido
Separate - separado

Regular verbs – Verbos regulares
To advise – advised – advised – aconsejar
To credit – credited – credited – acreditar
To deposit – deposited – deposited – depositar
To remind – reminded – reminded – recordar
To wire – wired – wired – enviar dinero de un banco a otro / cablear
To avoid – avoided – avoided – evitar
To dry – dried – dried – secar
To pour – poured – poured – verter / echar / server *(algo liquido)*
To regret – regreted – regreted – lamentar
To bother – bothered – bothered – molestar / fastidiar
To choke – choked – choked – ahogarse / sofocar
To criticize – criticized – criticized – criticar
To join – joined – joined – unirse
To remind of – reminded of – reminded of – recordarse de

To separate from – separated from – separated from – separarse de

Irregular verbs – Verbos irregulares
To withdraw – withdrew – withdrawn – retirar

Exercises – Ejercicios

Exercise 5.1: Match the problem with the advice.

_____ I just had my wisdom teeth removed, and I'm hungry.

_____ We don't know where to go on vacation.

_____ I'm so cold.

_____ I need to learn more English.

_____ I never have enough money.

A. Why don't you put a sweater on?
B. I suggest you go to Pigeon Forge, Tennessee.
C. If I were you, I would buy some diet supplement drinks.
D. My teacher recommends watching videos in English, with no captions.
E. Mom suggested I put half of my money in the bank and put the rest in labeled envelopes for paying bills, buying food, and so on.

Exercise 5.2: Write the verb in the correct form: *had* + past participle or *would/could have* + past participle.

We _____ (buy) your sofa if we had known you were selling it.

If you _____ (buy) that coat, you would have something to match your boots.

I would have put the milk away if I _____ (see) it.

If they had accepted my offer, they _____ (install) the new system my now.

Mrs. Smith _____ (buy) some chocolate bars if she had known you were selling them.

Exercise 5.3: Identify the use of *do* in the sentences: negative, question, activity, polite invitation, or emphasis.

_____ Does Susy have her calculator?

_____ I don't like strawberries.

_____ Please do come with us.

_____ Norman does aerobic exercise every day.

_____ I did finish my homework, but the dog ate it.

Exercise 5.4: Complete the sentence with the correct form of the verb.

Example: If only we _had gone_ (go) to camp with the others, we would have had a great summer!

If only we _____ (wait) to buy the oven, it would have been on sale!

If only they _____ (tell) us about the bird-watcher's bed and breakfast, we would have stayed there!

I wish you _____ (finish) school before getting married.

I wish I _____ (ask) her to come to my party.

BJ wishes he _____ (forgive) his friend.

Lesson 6
The date – La cita

Conversation 1

Jack: Hi. The name's Richardson.

Hostess: Did you see our sign?

Jack: What sign?

Hostess: It says no sleeveless, no flip-flops. This is a formal restaurant. We ask that our clients dress formally.

Nancy: These aren't flip-flops. They're dressy sandals.

Jack: As I was saying, I have a reservation for two under the name Richardson.

Hostess: Richardson, let's see. . . . I'm sorry. We don't have a reservation under the name Richardson.

Jack: Try Jack.

Hostess: I'm sorry, Sir. Maybe you made the reservation for another day?

Jack: No, I just made the reservation yesterday. I talked to Jose.

Hostess: I'll talk to the manager and see if we can find a table for you. . . . There is a booth on the balcony.

Jack: It's a little cold for that, but okay. [One hour later, the man's bill is returned by the manager with the credit card.]

Manager: I'm sorry. We're not accepting credit

cards right now.

Jack: You've got to be kidding! It says outside that you accept all four major cards.

Manager: Yes, but the system's down right now, so we're only accepting cash.

Jack: But you didn't tell me that when we got here.

Manager: It went down only five minutes ago.

Jack: So what am I supposed to do? I didn't bring any cash because I planned to pay with credit.

Manager: I suppose we'll have to bill you. We don't need any help with the dishes right now. Haha.

Jack: Listen, I have never had such a terrible experience in my life. We will never be coming here again.

Manager: I'm sorry you feel that way. Can I see your driver's license, please?

Conversation 2

Leila: Are you still there, Marge?

Marge: Yep.

Leila: Did I tell you about the puppy yet?

Marge: No, you have a puppy?

Leila: Yes, well, the kids brought it home. I told them I didn't want a puppy, but they promised to take care of it. And they said it was free.

Marge: Free for them, but what is it going to cost   you? So are they taking caring of it?

Leila: They feed the puppy five or six times a day and play with it all the time, but they haven't cleaned up any of its messes yet.

Marge: Oh, no. Has it ruined anything?

Leila: Only my clothes, the sofa, some collectible figurines, slippers, and toys.

Marge: Wow! It's been busy! If I were you, I'd get rid of that thing right away. If you don't, you'll be cleaning up after it all day long, and your house will be a disaster.

Leila: Yeah. You know I love animals, but this has just gone too far.

Marge: Listen, I have to go, but I'll be online later on tonight if you want to talk, okay?

Leila: Okay, bye!

Marge: Bye!

New words – Nuevas palabras
Cancellation – cancelación
Case – caja / estuche
Cash - efectivo
Charge - cargo
Cigar - cigarro
Delivery - entrega
Extra – extra / adicional
Falls - cascada
Inch - pulgada
List - lista
Lunchtime – hora del almuerzo
Ocean - océano
Rate – tarifa / tasa (de moneda)
Reservation – reservación
Sunglasses – lentes de sol
Threat - amenaza

Trick - truco
Violin – violín
Waiting list – lista de espera
Warning - advertencia
Waterfall - cascada
Ant - hormiga
Basket – canasto / cesta
Bull - toro
Fly - mosca
Jack – gato (para levantar carros) / enchufe
Moment - momento
Mosquito - mosquito / zancudo
Page – página
Picnic – picnic
Puppy - cachorro
Rag – trapo / harapo
Spot - lugar / sitio / espacio / mancha

Word Definitions -

Booked up: *when a hotel or place is full and they cannot accept any more reservations.*

For crying out loud: when everything we are doing or happening in our lives is going wrong, we use this expression.

Rag: a piece of an old cloth.

Threat: a very strong warning, especially when someone tells you that he or she will do something bad to you.

To run for your life: when you are running very fast from a very bad and dangerous situation.

Trick: when something is funny to watch and hard to do.

Warning: *when you tell someone about danger.*

Phrases and Expressions - Frases y expresiones
By this time tomorrow – para esta hora mañana
From now – desde ahora
From now on – desde ahora en adelante
To give someone a warning – darle una advertencia o amonestación a alguien
I ('ll) bet – apuesto
To make a reservation – hacer una reservación
To make a stop – hacer una parada
To make a delivery – hacer una entrega
To make sure - asegurarse
To play dirty – jugar sucio / hacer trampa
To play a trick on someone – hacerle una jugarreta o broma a alguien
To be freezing – estar congelándose
For crying out loud – por el amor de Dios
To get through – comunicarse *(cuando haces una llamada y puedes o no comunicarte)*
To let in – dejar entrar
To let out – dejar salir
To run after – correr detrás de / tratar de atrapar *(cuando se corre detrás de alguien tratando de atraparlo)*
To run for your life – correr por tu vida
You see? - ¿lo ves? *(usamos esta expresión para decir, "viste, te lo dije")*
You can't miss + noun / pronoun – no puedes dejar de ver algo o a alguien / no te lo puedes perder

Grammar – Gramática

The future progressive – El futuro progresivo

Este tiempo se forma con "will be" más el gerundio. Lo usamos para hablar de algo que estará pasando en el futuro o para sugerir que algo ya ha sido preparado para el futuro

I *will be meeting* with the school president tomorrow – me estaré reuniendo con el presidente escolar mañana.

She *will be coming* home next week – ella vendrá a casa la semana entrante.

Will you *be traveling* for a long time? - ¿estarás viajando por mucho tiempo?

They *will be having* a good time on their vacation – ellas estarán pasando un tiempo maravilloso en sus vacaciones.

Using "The" with noncount nouns and the plural – Usando "The" con nombres que no se cuentan y con plural.

No usamos "the" con la mayoría de las palabras en plural o que no se cuentan, a menos que estemos hablando sobre algo definitivo.

I love *parties* – me encantan las fiestas *(como estamos hablando en plural general, no usamos "the")*

I love *the parties* you organize – me encantan las fiestas que tú organizas. *(Como estamos hablando de unas fiestas en específico, usamos "the")*

Water doesn't have any color – el agua no tiene ningún color. *(Como el agua no se puede contar)*

The water at the beach was blue – el agua de la playa estaba azul. *(Como estamos hablando de una agua en específico)*

Cuando nos referimos a nombres propios, es decir, de personas, lugares, y cosas como canciones, libros, películas, obras, barcos y más, no usamos "the" y *recordemos que los nombres propios se escriben con mayúscula.*
Con excepción de los nombres propios de:
Algunos países (the United States, the Soviet Union, etc).

Ríos, océanos y mares (the Amazon, the Atlantic, the Mediterranean, etc)

Sierras montañosas (the Alps, the Andes), pero no con nombres de montañas.

Use of "should have / shouldn't have" – El uso de "should have / shouldn't have"
Lo usamos para criticar, para hablar del por qué las cosas salieron mal, y sobre cosas que deseamos que fueran diferentes.
You *should have* told her. She deserved to know – debiste habérselo dicho. Ella merecía saberlo.
You *shouldn't have* spanked her. She did't deserve it. – no debiste darle nalgadas. Ella no se lo merecía.

I *should have* studied English; if I had, then I wouldn't be asking you to interpret for me – debí haber estudiado inglés, si lo hubiese hecho, entonces no estaría pidiéndote que interpretes para mí.

Making commands stronger – Haciendo los mandatos más fuertes

Cuando damos una orden, normalmente usamos el nombre de la persona o un pronombre para que no haya confusión.

Don't you do that again – no hagas eso de nuevo *(nunca lo vuelvas a hacer)*

Don't you say that again – no digas eso de nuevo *(nunca más vuelvas a decirlo)*

Tiffany, clean up this mess and *do* the dishes – Tiffany, limpia este desorden y friega los platos.

Listen, everyone! – escuchen todos.

Cuando usamos "you" al inicio de la orden, lo hace más fuerte.

You pay attention to me ¡Tu préstame atención.

Algunas veces usamos una cláusula condicional al inicio o después del mandato para volverlo una amenaza. Tiene el mismo significado que si estuviéramos enojado.

If you do that again, you'll be in trouble – si haces eso de nuevo, estarás en problemas.

If you say that again, you'll get me into trouble – si dices eso de nuevo, me meterás en problemas.

I'll spank you, *if you do* that – te azotaré, si haces eso.

Regular verbs – Verbos regulares

To attack – attacked – attacked - atacar

To charge – charged – charged – cobrar / cargar a una cuenta o tarjeta

To confirm – confirmed – confirmed - To climb – climbed – climbed – escalar / trepar / subirse

confirmar

To crash – crashed – crashed – chocar / estrellarse

To cough – coughed – coughed - toser

To deliver – delivered – delivered - entregar

To envy – envied – envied - envidiar

To reserve – reserved – reserved - reservar

To sunbathe – sunbathed – sunbathed – tomar el sol

To pack – packed – packed - empacar

To spank – spanked – spanked – azotar (dando nalgadas)

To step in – stepped in – stepped in – poner un pie dentro de algo / entrar

To step on – stepped on – stepped on - pisar

Irregular verbs – Verbos irregulares

To bite – bit – bitten - morder

Exercises – Ejercicios

Exercise 6.1: Add three missing definite articles ("the") to the text.

Mom loves scarves. She wears them to church and parties. Scarf she likes most is a turquoise one with a paisley design. Right now, it's popular to wear scarves in many different ways in United States, but she was only person who wore them all the time a couple decades ago.

Exercise 6.2: Write sentences with *should have* and the verb provided.

I forgot to pay the electric bill, and they turned the

electricity off._____ (send) the check the same day it arrived.

I didn't want to wake up the baby, so I didn't give

him a bath._____ (bathe) him yesterday afternoon.

My friend's mom gave all her money to a

confidence trickster. Your friend _____ (report) the man to the police.

It's been raining for two weeks, and all the clothes

are dirty._____ (go) to the laundromat.

My sister loves desserts and sweet drinks, and now

she has diabetes._____ (go) on a diet years ago.

Exercise 6.3: Choose the command appropriate to the context and relationship.

A father finds his little girl playing with sharp sewing scissors.

Don't you ever play with those scissors again.

If you don't put those scissors down, I'm going to call the police.

It might be a good idea to play with something else.

One could get hurt playing with scissors.

The IT man is deleting files that are no longer needed.

If I were you, I wouldn't delete my performance reports.

Shall we leave my performance reports?

Please don't delete my performance reports.

You'd better leave my performance reports.

A man wants his wife to make him chocolate cake.

Why don't you make some chocolate cake?

What if you make chocolate cake?

Listen, you make some chocolate cake, okay?

You're supposed to make me chocolate cake.

A student refuses to sit down and do his worksheet.

I was going to suggest you sit down.

What if you sit down and do your work now?

Listen, sit down and do your work now.

Remember to do your worksheet before the end of class, okay?

Exercise 6.4: Write the verb in future progressive.

I won't be able to answer the phone then. I

_____ (work out).

We _____ (have) dinner around 6, so we'll want dessert before 7 p.m.

We'll never catch them that way. The criminals

_____ (cross) the border by that time.

They _____ (open) their gifts around 9, so we'd better get there before then.

Nivel Cuatro

She _____ (recover) from minor surgery, so please make sure she doesn't do any heavy lifting.

Lesson 7
The musical – El musical

Conversation 1

Jason: I'm so nervous.

Mom: Just relax. Don't think about it.

Jason: I can't help it, Mom.

Mom: You'll do fine. Just think of it as an exciting adventure.

Jason: I think I'm going to be sick.

Mom: Sick of practicing?

Jason: No. I'm going to throw up.

Mom: No, you won't. Look, if you keep talking about being nervous, you are going to get sick, and I'm going to lose my temper. So just stop thinking about it. Relax. Practice if you want. Or you can do your homework.

Jason: It's almost time to go!

Mom: Are you ready?

Jason: Noooo!

Mom: Let's go. Are you going to wear sneakers with your dress pants?

Jason: I told you, I can't even think straight.

Mom: Just change your shoes.

Jason: [At the recital] Mom, look! They put me last on the program!

Mom: That's a good thing. It means you're the

best!

Jason: It means I have to be nervous the whole time! Ow! You stepped on my foot!

Mom: Oh, I did? I'm sorry. Just shut up and listen.

Teacher: [20 minutes later] Last on our program is Jason Fuller playing Scarlatti's Sonata No. 5 in C major.

Mom: [Afterwards] What did I tell you? You were great!

Jason: I still feel sick.

Mom: Too bad. We could have gone for pizza.

Jason: Actually, I think I am feeling a little better.

Conversation 2

Harry: [coughing] Hey, babysitter.

Leanna: The name's Leanna.

Harry: [coughing] Just for your information, I don't need a babysitter.

Leanna: Uh-huh. I'm here so you can take care of me, right?

Cinthia: Shhhhh, I'm trying to hear the TV.

Leanna: You shouldn't watch soap operas.

Cinthia: I can't help it. Look at him. Isn't he gorgeous? I fell in love the moment I saw him.

Leanna: When was that?

Cinthia: Five minutes ago.

Leanna: Turn it off.

Cinthia: Hey!

Leanna: Where's the cough medicine?

Harry: What are you doing?

Leanna: Putting sugar in your cough medicine. You know, a teaspoon of sugar is supposed to help you take the medicine.

Harry: I think it already has sugar in it.

Leanna: Do me a favor.

Harry: What?

Leanna: Get lost.

Harry: I'm going to tell my mom.

Leanna: Go ahead. Do you think people are just lined up out there begging to watch you two?

Cinthia: What's for dinner?

Leanna: It's eight o'clock. Haven't you eaten yet?

Harry: No.

Leanna: Have some cereal.

Harry: You're supposed to take care of us.

Leanna: Do you want to go to bed now?

Harry: No, I'm going to go get some cereal.

New words – Nuevas palabras
Balance - balance
Bolt - tornillo
Drum – tambor (de música)
Firewood - leña
Gallon – galón
Gram - gramo
Half - mitad
Instrument - instrumento
Liter - litro
Musician - músico

Nut - tuerca
Ounce - onza
Part - parte
Pint - pinta
Pound - libra
Producer – productor
Quart - cuarto
Roast – asado / tostado
Tablespoon - cucharada
Teaspoon – cucharadita / cucharilla
Adventure - aventura
Babysitter - niñera
Ending - final
Lobby - vestíbulo
Maid – criada / camarera
Mayor - alcalde
Musical - musical
Novel - novela
Parking lot - parqueo
Sex - sexo
Someplace – algún lugar
Even though – sin embargo

Word Definitions -
Favor: something nice you do for someone else without expecting anything in return.

Ingredients: several things you need to prepare or make something else.

Why's that?: when we wonder why things happen and ask for an explanation.

Adventure: when something exciting happens to

you.

To fall in love: *when you start being interested in someone.*

Get lost: *when you tell someone to disappear, go away (not a nice word).*

How dare you: *when someone does something that makes us angry or something that we cannot believe they would do.*

I beg your pardon?: *when we want the person to repeat what they said, because we didn't understand it or because we can't believe what they said.*

Obscene: *when pictures, books, plays, and so on have too many references to sex or immorality.*

Phrases and Expressions - Frases y expresiones

Can't help + ing – no puedo evitarlo / no puedo dejar de *(siempre se usa el verbo que le sigue en gerundio. I can't help laughing – no puedo dejar de reir. I can't help crying – no puedo dejar de llorar.)*

To do someone a favor – hacerle un favor a alguien

Don't mention it – de nada *(cuando hacemos un favor, y decimos, "ni lo menciones")*

To keep someone or something from + ing – evitar que alguien haga algo o que algo suceda *(I try to keep from crying – trato de no llorar. You kept me from leaving – evitaste que me fuera o no me dejaste ir)*

Why's that? - ¿Y eso por qué? ¿Por qué haces eso? ¿Por qué pasa eso?

To fall in love - enamorarse

Get lost – piérdete / lárgate

How dare you – como te atreves...

I beg your pardon? – perdón? No entendí. ¿Qué dijiste?

To live happily ever after – vivir felices para siempre

To lose your temper – perder la compostura

To take place – suceder o pasar *(indicando cuando y en qué lugar acontece o aconteció un evento)*

Grammar – Gramática

The gerund after prepositions – El gerundio después de preposiciones

Siempre usamos la "ing" del verbo después de preposiciones (excepto cuando viene antes del infinitivo o mejor conocido como partícula).

Books are *for reading*, not *for writing* in – los libros son para leerlos, no para escribir en ellos.

Before adding the ingredientes, make sure you crack the eggs – antes de agregar los ingredientes, asegúrate de romper los huevos.

I can't get *used to living* like this – no puedo acostumbrarme a vivir así.

I look *forward to hearing* from you – espero escuchar de ti.

Adjectives – Adjetivos

Amusing – divertido / gracioso

Entertaining - entretenido

Fond of – aficionado *(cuando algo nos gusta muchísimo)*

Obscene - obsceno

Sold out – vendido *(cuando se vendió todo y no queda más)*

Regular verbs – Verbos regulares

To add – added – added - agregar

To boil – boiled – boiled - hervir

To loosen – loosened – loosened - aflojar

To lower – lowered – lowered - bajar

To mash – mashed – mashed – amasar / triturar

To mix in – mixed in – mixed in - mezclar

To peel – peeled – peeled - pelar

To raise – raised – raised – levantar / elevar

To record – recorded – recorded - grabar

To rush – rushed – rushed - apresurarse

To select – selected – selected - seleccionar

To stir – stirred – stirred – agitar / revolver / atizar

To tighten – tightened – tightened - apretar

To shorten – shortened – shortened - acortar

To flatten – flattened – flattened - aplanar / alisar / achatar

To lengthen – lengthened – lengthened – alargar / prolongar

To sadden – saddened – saddened - entristecer

To threaten (with) – threatened – threatened – amenazar (con)

Irregular verbs – Verbos irregulares

To spread – spread – spread – untar / esparcir / propagar

To deal with – dealt with – dealt with – lidiar con

Exercises – Ejercicios

Exercise 7.1: Write the correct form of the word.

1. We can't help . _____ (laugh) at him, but he thinks we're making fun of him.

2. You have to keep him from _____(jump) off the roof.

3. You'll just have to get used to _____(take) cold showers, because the water heater s topped

4. _____ (work).

5. We're looking forward to . _____ (hear) you play at your recital tomorrow.

6. I'm very fond of . _____ (sew),

7. but I don't like . _____ (read) about sewing.

8. How dare you _____ (eat) my dessert?

9. Can you do me a favor? Can you help me with .

_____ (mix) the dough?

10. He's used to _____ (sleep) after lunch

Lesson 8
Murder in the suburbs – Asesinato en los suburbios

Conversation 1

Gail: Did you see the murder mystery last night?

Brenda: Yeah. It was okay.

Gail: Okay? It was so exciting. I could have watched it three times.

Brenda: It may have been exciting, but it wasn't realistic. How many criminals leave that many clues? And do you think little pieces of our clothing could be found wherever we've gone?

Gail: Yeah, I see your point.

Brenda: Probably most murders will never be detected.

Gail: What do you mean?

Brenda: Well, for instance, your neighbor suddenly moved out. You never saw her move out, but the family said she moved out. Do you know she moved out?

Gail: I guess not. Do you think she was killed?

Brenda: Probably not. If we suspect everyone of murder, we'll never be able to sleep at night! But a smart murderer doesn't want everyone to be suspicious of her. She'll choose a time when no one would suspect anything was wrong. And by the time anyone investigates, all the evidence will have been destroyed.

Gail: Wow. I don't think I'll be sleeping well from now on. I think I need some comfort food.

Brenda: Don't worry. You don't have a fortune to inherit or a dubious past. And the whole neighborhood looks forward to receiving your edible gifts!

Conversation 2

You must have been told about the importance of birth control in school, at the doctor's office, and on television programs. Teen pregnancies have been increasing, and children are being raised in difficult family situations. If young people do not use birth control—it is argued—there are multiple negative results: an unwanted birth, the possible interruption of the parents' education, a premature end to the parents' childhood, and a child raised in an environment of resentment.

However, birth control does not come without risks. First of all, most birth control methods do not protect the parents from sexually transmitted diseases (which may represent a higher threat at a younger age), nor do they protect them from the emotional and relational effects of a promiscuous lifestyle. Some methods of birth control may be related to emotional instability, circulation problems, and an increased risk of getting cancer. Furthermore, most methods of birth control still permit a five percent chance of pregnancy.

Very few doctors tell their patients about birth control methods that track the woman's cycle. And even fewer recommend the most natural prevention method of all. Sadly, peer pressure drives many young people to become sexually active early and does not give them a complete picture of the risks and benefits of the various options. And we call this being informed?

New words – Nuevas palabras
Enemy - enemigo
Fact – hecho
Governor – gobernador
Headline - encabezado / titular
Murder – homicidio / asesinato
Murderer – homicida / asesino
State - estado
Yacht - yate
Achievement - logro
Birth control – control natal
Cancer - cáncer
Cure - cura
Expert - experto
Grandchild - nieto
Growth - crecimiento
Hunger – hambruna
Institute - instituto
Life expectancy – esperanza de vida (cuantos años promedio vive una persona)

Method - método
Natural resource – recurso natural
Reality - realidad
Robot - robot
Science - ciencia
Secret - secreto
Feeling - sentimiento
Pit – pozo / hoyo / fosa
Tranquilizer – tranquilizante

Phrases and Expressions - Frases y expresiones

Can tell by – from – poder notar algo por *(you can tell they are intelligent by the way they speak – puedes notar que ellas son inteligentes por la forma en que hablan. You can tell she is kind from the way she treats people – puedes notar que ella es bondadosa por la forma en que ella trata a las personas)*

A great deal – una gran cantidad

Here goes – aquí vamos *(cuando vas a hacer algo ahora)*

How come? - ¿Cómo así? ¿Por qué? *(how **come you aren't** ready? - ¿cómo puede ser que no estás lista? Fíjense la estructura)*

In spite of – a pesar de

Pull yourself together - compórtate / modérate / cálmate / detente

To go bad – salir mal / dañarse

To lose your head – perder la cabeza *(cuando hacemos algo sin pensar, un tontería o algo que normalmente no haríamos)*

To run for – correr por *(postulándose para un cargo o una position. I am running for president – estoy postulándome para presidente)*

To a certain extent – hasta cierto punto

To call the whole thing off – cancelar todo el asunto

The computer is up / down – la computadora está funcionando / no está funcionando

To get dressed - vestirse

To give a hand to – aplaudir *(dar una mano en aplauso)*

To go through with - continuar con algo *(continuar algo que estaba planeado aunque no quieras hacerlo)*

To have the time – tener el tiempo

To lose your mind – perder la cabeza / volverse loco

The pit of your stomach – la boca del estomago

To shake like a leaf – temblar como una hoja *(cuando estás tan nervioso o tienes tanto frío que estás temblando)*

Who knows? – ¿Quién sabe? *(yo no sé; lo sabes tú)*

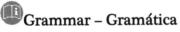Grammar – Gramática

Using "must have / can't have / couldn't have" – Usando "must have / can't have / couldn't have"

Usamos "must have" más el pasado participio para expresar lo que pensamos que probablemente pasó.

She **must have had** plastic surgery – ella debió haberse hecho una cirugía *(porque se ven tan bien que no es natural)*

It *must have rained* yesterday – debió haber llovido ayer *(porque hay mucha agua)*

They *must have won* the match – ellos debieron haber ganado el partido *(porque hay un trofeo aquí)*

It *must have been* love – debió haber sido amor *(porque nadie haría tales cosas si no estuviera loco de amor)*

Usamos "can't have " y "couldn't have" más el pasado participio para decir lo que pensamos que probablemente no sucedió.

They *can't have eaten* all that candy – ellos no pueden haberse comido todos esos dulces *(porque estarían enfermos)*

She *couldn't have done* all that by herself – ella no pudo haber hecho todo eso ella sola *(porque es demasiado para una sola persona)*

I *couldn't have said* that – no pude haber dicho eso *(sería imposible que yo dijera algo así)*

The passive voice – La voz pasiva

Usando *"may / might / could (n't) / must have"* más *be* + el pasado participio en la voz pasiva.

I can't find my wallet – no puedo encontrar mi cartera.

It *may have been stolen* – puede que se la hayan robado.

It **might have been stolen** – puede que se la hayan robado.

It *could have been stolen* – puede que la hayan robado.

It *couldn't have been stolen* – no puede ser que se

la hayan robado.

It *must have been stolen* – seguramente se la han robado.

The future perfect – El futuro perfecto

Usamos el futuro perfecto para hablar de algo que pasará antes de cierto tiempo en el futuro.

By the year 2025, people *will have cloned* humans – para el 2025, las personas habrán clonado humanos.

By the time she gets there, *I'll have left* already – para cuando ella llegue, yo ya me habré ido.

By Monday, *I'll have fixed* your car – para el lunes, habré reparado tu auto.

También podemos usar el futuro perfecto en la voz pasiva.

By then I hope that the boys *will have been finished* – para entonces, espero que los chicos hayan terminado.

Using "may have" in the future – Usando "may have" en el futuro.

Cuando usamos "may have" para hablar sobre algo en el futuro, es porque no estamos seguros si habrá pasado o no.

They *may have realized* by tomorrow morning – puede que ellas se hayan dado cuenta para mañana en la mañana.

We *may have finished* by Monday – puede que hayamos terminado para el lunes.

She *may have gotten* there by tonight – puede que ella esté allá esta noche.

Using "two-word" verbs – Usando los verbos de dos palabras.

Algunos verbos son formados al agregarles una preposición o un adverbio al verbo. A estos llamamos verbos de dos palabras o frases verbales; usualmente su significado cambia y difiere del significado de la palabra por si sola. Ya hemos visto algunos en nuestro aprendizaje.

Algunos de ellos pueden usar un pronombre directo que usualmente se coloca o en medio de las dos palabras del verbo o después de ambas.

To try on

Let's *try* these pants *on* – probémonos estos pantalones.

Let's *try on* these pants – probémonos estos pantalones.

To give away

Don't *give* the puppy *away* – no regales el cachorro.

Don't *give away* the puppy – no regales el cachorro.

To turn off

Why don't you *turn* that thing *off*? - ¿Por qué no apagas esa cosa?

Why don't you *turn off* that thing? - ¿Por qué no apagas esa cosa?

To talk over

Can we *talk over* this problem? - ¿podemos discutir

este problema?

No, we cannot *talk* it *over* – no, no podemos discutirlo.

No, we cannot *talk* this problem *over* – no, no podemos discutir este problema.

Recuerden,
Cuando es pronombre tiene que venir entre las dos palabras del verbo.

The prefix "ex" – El prefijo "Ex"

El prefijo "ex" es usando al igual que en español para indicar un estado anterior o pasado.

Ex-wife – exesposa
Ex-president – expresidente
Ex-marine – exmarino

Adverbs – Adverbios

Apparently - aparentemente
Next door - al lado
Necessarily – necesariamente

Adjectives – Adjetivos

Afraid of – tener miedo de (I am afraid of you – te tengo miedo)
Jealous – celoso
Ripe – maduro
Amazing – increíble
Certain – cierto
International – internacional
Optimistic – optimista
Pessimistic – pesimista
Scientific – científico

Alike – igual
Calm – calmado
Out of order – fuera de servicio / fuera de orden

Regular verbs – Verbos regulares
To attach – attached – attached – adjuntar / adherir
To applaud – applauded – applauded - aplaudir
To call off – called off – called off - cancelar
To consider – considered – considered - considerar
To continue – continued – continued - continuar
To calm down – calmed down – calmed down - calmarse
To carry on – carried on – carried on – continuar / proseguir
To discover – discovered – discovered - descubrir
To double – doubled – doubled - duplicar
To exist – existed – existed - existir
To ignore – ignored – ignored - ignorar
To introduce – introduced – introduced – introducir / presentar a alguien
To lock – locked – locked – cerrar con llave / encerrar
To murder – murdered – murdered – asesinar / cometer homicidio
To strangle – strangled – strangled - estrangular
To stare – stared – stared – mirar fijamente / quedarse mirando a alguien
To suspect – suspected – suspected - sospechar
To trick – tricked – tricked – engañar / jugarle una broma a alguien
To triple – tripled – tripled - triplicar
To unlock – unlocked – unlocked – abrir un

cerradura o candado / dejar libre

To use up – used up – used up – usar todo de algo / acabar

To work out – worked out – worked out – salir bien *(cuando algo da buen resultado)* / hacer ejercicios

Irregular verbs – Verbos irregulares

To break down – broke down – broken down – dañarse / romperse

To put off – put off – put off – posponer / postergar

To show up – showed up – shown up – llegar / aparecerse

To take after – took after – taken after – ser como alguien / seguir los pasos de alguien *(I take after my father – soy como mi padre)*

To take over – took over – taken over – discutir algo

Exercises – Ejercicios

Exercise 8.1: Write the best modal phrase: *may have, must have, can have, can't have, could have,* or *couldn't have.*

1. Jo: What do you think Mom

_____done with my pet turtle?

2. Ty: She 2. _____ given it away.

3. Jo: No. She. _____ done anything like that. She knows I love my little Speedy.

4. Ty: Yeah. Well, she. _____ put

it somewhere out of the way so she wouldn't have to smell it.

Exercise 8.2: Write the verb in parentheses in future perfect.

A: "I'll see you at the party around midnight."

B: "I _____ (go) home by then."
My aunt is going to come live with me when

I'm forty. I _____ (make) a lot of money by then.

By the time you finish that piece of pizza, I

_____ (eat) the rest of the pizza.

Be careful! Your neighbors probably

_____ (frustrate—passive) by your pranks.

Hopefully by the time he turns ten he

_____ (adopt—passive).

Exercise 8.3: Underline the best two-word phrasal verb for the context.

I **put / gave / took** the Christmas tree away because we never put it up anymore.

Please **turn on / try on / switch on** these pants before I give them away. They might still fit you.

Nobody's watching the TV. Could you please **take /**

turn / put it off?

We haven't decided yet, but we'll **hand / look / talk** it over tonight.

Conversational Level Four – Nivel de Conversación Cuatro

The filming

Monday

Josh, this place is so awesome. We went on a safari today in the Masai Mara. It's this huge park where animals just roam free. We got to see lions on the hunt! The chased down a gnu and ate it alive. Mom was kind of freaked out, but Brandon and I were just eating it up. Seriously, you gotta see this. It's amazing. I mean, it's just raw nature.

This man said the park is getting smaller. He said there's more people and hunting and less water and land. Too bad!

Tuesday

I seriously wanna open up a restaurant here. I mean, you got gnus, zebras, buffalo, and wildebeest here. You can offer some seriously crazy dishes. Wildebeest is pretty popular. Dad says its illegal poaching. But you gotta eat, you know? Dad's busy working on the storyline for the film, so I'm bored.

Wednesday

This park is huge, no matter what they say about it shrinking.

Dad's team has a drone for shooting—I mean, filming, you know—the elephants. I guess they can kill you pretty easy, and Dad's no crocodile hunger, so the drone does the hard work. He said they used to have to hang out of helicopters with the camera. I can just see him dropping the camera. Haha! It'd be okay, maybe, as long as he didn't fall out! This is kind of dangerous work, I guess.

So Dad asked a guide about getting local food, and we had ugali and vegetables. It's kind of a big blob of boiled corn flour. It's okay. It's not bushmeat. ☹ You use your right hand to eat it. That's the best part. No silverware and napkins in the Serengeti!

Thursday

You'll never believe this. A lot of hunting goes on at night, so Dad's group put out infrared cameras to pick up on some of the action. And some of the cameras disappeared. Well, they got a couple of them back, and you can see that hyenas took them. It looks like they tried to eat the cameras. Really! They picked the things up in their mouths and took them off. Man, that's crazy. Truth is stranger than fiction, you know? That's what Grandma says.

Friday

I have to go home tomorrow. I wanna learn some

Swahili before I go, but I'm always with Dad's team, and their interpreter is usually too busy to talk to me. Oh, well. I don't wanna go home!

The indecent neighbor

Dear Jake,

I really like my new house. I sure didn't expect to like it so much. You know we old folks don't like change, but it's pretty comfortable. It's clean, there are lots of places for my knick-knacks, and I love to just sit in the breakfast room and enjoy the view and the breeze. I'm having the roof repaired because some of the loose shingles make a racket up there, but other than that, it's perfect.

My neighbors are very nice. Many of them are retired, like me. There are also lots of children, but they aren't too wild, and they make the neighborhood more cheerful. The only neighbor I don't like is the man across the street. He's just downright indecent. He mows the lawn in his underwear! Suzie, my new friend down the street, says they're spandex. I can't bear to look out the window when he's outside. It's just gross.

And he has ever so many girlfriends. I don't see what they see in him. He's not handsome, rich, or funny. When I was a girl, we all liked the handsome boys, or the ones who could make you feel really special. Girls must be desperate these days.

Doctor put me on a diet. She says no more sugar, salt, or oil, and she wants me to eat about two cups of food per day tops. What's the joy of life without food? I'd rather go happy than suffer a dull life forever.

So anyway, the indecent neighbor invited some of us over for a cookout for Labor Day. I asked Suzy, "Do you think he'll wear clothes?" She thinks he will. I still don't know if I'll go. He kind of gives me the creeps.

I wish you were here to enjoy my breakfast room with me. Do you think you might come for Thanksgiving? I suggest you bring that nice girlfriend of yours, too. You know this house has plenty of room for all of us. Then I could show her my salt- and pepper-shaker collection. I gave some of them away to my dearest friends by my old house before the move, but I still have my favorites. I'm sure she would enjoy relaxing in the beautiful out-of-doors here, if only she could get away from her cell phone for a little bit.

Now, don't you forget about your old granny, you hear? You come and see me soon!

Hugs and kisses,
Grandma Silvie

Men and women expressing themselves differently.

Research in the last forty years shows that women

and men usually express themselves differently. In writing, women are supposed to use more dashes. But most research focuses on speech. Look at the following four language "functions" as probably expressed by men and women. Can you tell the difference between the two? Label the women's language "W" and the men's "M."

Suggestion:

_____ Don't you think it's a little cold in here? Maybe we should turn up the heat.

_____ It's cold. I'm going to turn up the heat.

Complaint:

_____ We need to go out more. What do you say we go see a movie tonight?

_____ I just feel like we never go out anymore. It's kind of depressing. Wouldn't it be nice to go out once a week or so?

Apology:

_____ Oh. Sorry.

_____ Oh, I'm so sorry. I didn't see your purse there. Here, let me help you pick up your things.

Prediction:

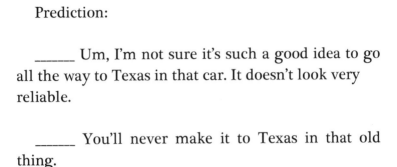

_____ Um, I'm not sure it's such a good idea to go all the way to Texas in that car. It doesn't look very reliable.

_____ You'll never make it to Texas in that old thing.

The answers are Suggestion 1 W 2 M, Complaint 1 M 2 W, Apology 1 M 2 W, Prediction 1 W 2 M. Now, not all men and women speak with such a marked difference in directness. Some researchers think the difference may not be naturally a difference between men's and women's speech but more a difference in power and powerlessness. In fact, there is some debate about how women bosses should speak. Apparently, some men are disturbed when these women speak with authority. But if she's the boss, she's supposed to give orders, right? And she'll probably have more to say than the people who work for her.

So here are some characteristics of the indirect language often associated with either women or with people who are not in a position of power:

Using why-questions or other roundabout ways to make a suggestion:
Why don't we go to the store today instead of tomorrow?

Your hair's getting kind of long, isn't it?

Limiting or qualifying what you say:
It seems like this wall is kind of crooked.
I think the pipes are leaking.

Use more correct and proper language:
One of the people who comes here disagrees with my writing grammar and etiquette books.

I like to say "goodness" or even "good gravy" rather than anything stronger.

So, put your new knowledge into practice: can you determine whether a man or woman wrote this article?

The dream man

Who do you think is the typical dream man—Brad Pitt or Gilbert Blythe? A muscle man or the guy next door? Popular wisdom says girls marry a guy who resembles their dad. According to a survey conducted by iVillage, property of NBC, girls want a muscular guy who is six feet tall, has brown eyes and dark hair, and doesn't have much body hair. Another British study showed guys may be even more demanding than women in their concept of a girl's perfect man. For a long-term relationship, girls chose a typical guy with a little extra weight while guys thought they would want the man with perfect hair and muscle tone.

Physical appearance probably becomes less important than personality factors as we get older. Older women hint that the number of requirements for a good partner decreases with age. One woman jokes on her blog about only requiring someone with good hygiene.

The 1950s song "Mr. Sandman" specifies that the dream man be cute and have soft lips and wavy hair. Other than that, he just had to really want a girl. Makes sense. Girls don't want to be tied to a guy who could "take or leave" her. Modern girls still want a sense of security. Besides having a college degree and making good money, he should love his mom and want his own family.

In fact, even younger girls are willing to sacrifice perfect looks provided a guy has a great personality. According to the iVillage study, the ideal man must balance contrasting with and complementing his girl. He should know how to do manly things but also enjoy shopping. He should be both funny and sensitive. Girls don't ask much, right?

We are generally attracted to someone who is similar to us and who we spend a lot of time with. In a December 2, 2014 article in *Psychology Today,* Noam Shpancer describes research findings by Shackelford, Schmitt, and Buss: women value "status, emotional stability, and intelligence" more than men. Intelligence and social skills are also deciding factors.

However, there's really no one definition of the dream man that will work for everyone. In the words of author Francoise Sagan, "There is no such thing as an ideal man. The ideal man is the man you love at the moment."

The dream woman

What is the ideal woman like? Is she slender or curvy? In control or carefree? The definition depends on who you ask. A popular men's magazine says guys want a girl with a big chest, no hips, long legs, and small feet. Sounds like a popular doll, right? A dating website that sells first dates tried to define the perfect woman based mainly on her physical appearance, education, and vices (such as a smoker), and the physical definition varied greatly from one person to the next. Some like blond hair, some brown, and some red. Some like blue eyes, others brown. So while physical appearance sure is important to men, there are many different definitions of physical beauty.

What about her personality: does that matter? The modern ideal woman must be educated and able to make money (quite a reversal of traditional expectations), but she shouldn't express her opinions too loudly. She should smile and laugh at a guy's jokes. But apparently, it doesn't matter what she's actually thinking or feeling, what her interests are, or what kind of character she has. But then again, it depends on who you ask. A Christian author surveyed groups of men across the country who agreed that a woman should take care of her appearance, show him respect, and be sincere. Many of them admitted that they are attracted to women who are not very discreet but said that they would advise their little sister to dress in a way that makes people value her personality over her body.

One mother told her son to look for a woman who would dress nicely, work hard, help others, and speak kindly (the "virtuous woman"). Modern psychology recommends looking for a woman you like a lot, but not someone perfect.

A girl who wants to attract a man as fast as possible might stop eating, stop talking, start smiling and laughing more in order to match up to the images of fake women posted all around highways and grocery stores. But these tactics will not help her to find true love. If you want to develop a long-term relationship, find a girl who takes care of herself, is a good friend, and enjoys life. And watch out for the color red.

To be a Christian or not to be

Around the year 60 AD, King Agrippa told the apostle Paul, "You almost persuade me to be a Christian." In the United States, seventy-five percent of adults consider themselves Christians, but what does it mean to be a Christian? Let me tell you the story of two people, and you can tell me who was a Christian.

One man was a political leader who made Christianity legal in his kingdom. He stopped sacrifices to pagan gods and had religious buildings constructed. When his subjects were divided over religious differences, he called a council to end the disagreement. He passed some humane laws, but he also had some of his family members executed.

Another man who lived hundreds of years later believed that the Bible, rather than the traditions of the established church, should determine what Christians would believe and do. He worked in hiding to translate the Bible into the language of the people. He was betrayed by a friend to the government, strangled, and burned at the stake.

Today, there are many different people who say they are Christians. Some believe in the authority of the Bible, and some do not. Some believe that Christ was God; some do not. A look at the history of early Christians shows many people dying for being a Christian. In some countries, people are still arrested and even killed for being Christians. But there are others who become rich by asking for money in exchange for prayers or blessings.

Christ said his followers would have problems and would be persecuted. Christianity isn't something you can use for financial or political advantage. The true Christian helps the widow and orphan, controls his words, stops sinning, Christ is not someone just to be admired or quoted but someone to follow and obey.

Christians are people who have exchanged their sin for Christ's righteousness. They are ambassadors for Christ, people who beg others to repent of their sin and to be reconciled to God.

Young girls sang as they were attacked by lions. They could have saved their lives provided that they deny their faith. But they did not. If you knew you might be killed for becoming a Christian, would you be publically baptized? Would you be proud to identify yourself with Christ?

Level Four Tests – Examenes del Nivel Cuatro

Estos son los exámenes para concluir este nivel y curso. Asegúrense de tomar su tiempo y completarlos correctamente. Una vez los hayan completado y estén completamente seguros que han terminado. Pueden presentarlos a un amigo de habla inglesa para que los revise y les diga si lo hicieron bien, o pueden enviarme un email con sus exámenes. Sin en algún punto, aun están dudosos, deberán repasarlo y asegurarse de dominarlo muy bien. Ustedes ya están listos para cualquier situación. Les felicito por haber llegado al final de este increíble método de aprendizaje. Es imperativo dominar a la perfección cada uno de los conceptos presentados en este nivel. *Congratulations, You've made it!*

Test 1-2

Test 1.1: Add the correct prefix or suffix: er/or, in/im/un, full/less/ness.

That soccer (1) play___ was (2) ___sane! He just kept arguing with the referree till he was kicked out of the game.

Yeah, it's (3) use___ to argue with a referee in these games, even if it was a bad call. It's (4) ___possible to convince them they're wrong.

Well, I guess it would be embarrassing to admit you're wrong in front of everyone. But it's (5)

_____moral to lie about it!
Everyone lies nowadays. It's a widespread (6)

sick_____.

Test 1.2: Add the missing phrases to complete the conversation.

at last   have them altered   pretty well   shall
we   something to do

Lucy: These pants fit _____.
Nora: Really? Mine are too long. I'm going

to _____.
Lucy: Why not give them to me? It'll give

me _____.
Nora: Okay. I'm just so happy to find some

jeans in my size. _____, a pair that isn't too tight
or too loose!
Lucy: Pretty exciting! Well, I'm done.

_____ go now?

Test 1.3: Read the text and answer the questions.

When you take a standardized test, you should start studying far ahead of time. Study a test-preparation book for short periods of time and practice a lot. You can find websites with exercises for many different tests. Make sure you get plenty of sleep the night before the test. No late-night studying! Eat your breakfast, so you have plenty of energy. And remember to take regular pencils and a traditional pink eraser.

1. You should study _____.
❑ the night before the test
❑ only two or three times
❑ for one or two hours at a time
❑ for three or more hours at a time

2. On the day of the test, it's important to _____.
❑ eat breakfast
❑ take a pencil
❑ have lots of energy
❑ all of the above

3. According to the test, how can you prepare for the test?
❑ Study a dictionary.
❑ Practice online.
❑ Stay up late reading.
❑ Watch videos.

Test over units 3-5

Test 2.1: Complete the sentence with the appropriate form of the verb.

If only we _____ (keep) our dog, he

would _____ (protect) us from burglars.

I wish I _____ (like) fish. It looks like that's all we'll be eating this week.

You'd better _____ (go) soon, or it'll be too dark to see the road.

Remember _____ (call) me when you get home. I worry about you when you travel!

If only there _____ (not be) so many speed

bumps, we would _____ (be) there already.

If you _____ (tell) me you had a test today,

I would _____ (remind) you to study.
     Your spelling is terrible, Dear. But take heart!

Santa Clause might _____ (visit) you tonight and write your essay!

We were _____ (watch—future of past) a movie, but the electricity went out!

You're supposed _____ (go) to school tonight and talk to my teachers.
     They'll give us free shipping, provided that we

_____ (spend) $100.

Test 2.2: Correct the verb errors.

I wish you can go to college.

The team were exhausted after the game.

If only he was here, he would fix everything.

Danielle has a great trainer in the competitions who always help her.

Which one of the ducks have a broken leg?

Test 2.3: Correct the prefix/suffix errors. There is one error in each sentence.

He had an inferiority complex in spite of his incredible leaderance skills.

Her generosity led to her popularship.

Being a factory employee is a necessity for memberance in this organization.

In her urgenceship, she forgot her prize from the championship.

She won a scholarity due to her incredible intelligence.

Test 6-8

Test 3.1: Write the verb in the correct form for future continuous or future perfect.

By the time we finish eating, the streets will

have been _____ (plow).

At 10:00 p.m., Grandma will be _____ (prepare) for bed.

Hopefully in May she'll be _____ (graduate) from college.

Let's see. By that time, I should have

_____ (finish) writing my thesis.
When you retire, Mayberry will be

_____ (celebrate) its 300th anniversary.

After this class, we'll be _____ (enjoy) a cup a hot chocolate and some donuts in honor of our principal's birthday.
When will she arrive? She'll be _____ (come) around that corner any minute now.

Just keep eating, and you'll have _____ (eat) all your vegetables before you know it.

If you help me out, we'll have _____ (finish) cleaning the house by noon.

This Saturday, I think he'll be _____ (discuss) the importance of talking to your children.

Test 3.2: Write the correct form of the action word.

She can't help _____ (fall) in love with you!
Out of revenge, they kept Mark from

_____ (see) the girl of his dreams.

I just can't get used to _____ (eat) meat every day.
We really look forward to _____ (spend) Christmas with you!

My son is very fond of _____ (train) animals.

You have to consider the appropriateness of

_____ (insult) your neighbor.

Test 1-8

Test 4.1: Write the correct form of the action word.

I need to have my hair _____ for my sister's wedding (do).

As long as you _____ attention, you shouldn't have any problems on this job (pay).

I remember _____ Christmas cookies with Grandma (make). It was so fun!

My boy sure _____ pizza (like)! He asks to eat it every day!

Shall we _____ (go)? It's getting kind of late.

I don't have anything _____ to the party (take)! Can we stop and buy a present?

You're supposed _____ anyone who offers to help you (thank).

You should _____ (study) English

before _____ (travel) around the world.

What if it _____ really cold (get)? Do you

think the baby might _____ (get) sick?

If we had _____ snacks, we wouldn't have to pay these high restaurant prices (bring).

If only she had _____ to me, she wouldn't be in so much trouble now (listen).

Please do _____ your dog with you (bring). We love pets!

I wish you _____ more patient with children (be).

In twenty years, we won't be _____ things with cash (buy).

They should have _____ the toll road (take). It's faster, and it's easier on your car.

Don't you ever _____ on the table again, young lady! (stand).

He talked for twenty minutes on the importance of

_____ your teeth (brush).

You couldn't have _____ the whole cake (eat).

You'd _____ sick right now (be)!

By the time you get here, we'll have _____ all of

our Thanksgiving supper (finish)!

Please try _____ here by 8 in the evening (be).

Test 4.2: Complete the conversation with the best adverb.

almost   alwaysgenerally   hardlymostly
next door   pretty   right away   sure

1. Once upon a time, there was a beautiful girl

   who was _____ smart too.

2. She was. _____ perfect, in fact,

3. because she was. _____ kind, and she

4. _____ did her work

5. . _____. Almost, I say, because she loved animals more than people.

6. She could _____ stand going to a party.

7. She _____ was destined to remain single! But as it turns out,

8. the boy who lived _____ liked animals more than she did.

9. And they were _____ happy for the rest of their lives because, as Longfellow says, "into each life a little rain must fall."

Verb list – Lista de verbos
To accept – accepted – accepted - aceptar
To add – added – added - agregar
To advertise – advertised – advertised – promocionar
To advise – advised – advised - aconsejar
To affect – affected – affected - afectar
To applaud – applauded – applauded - aplaudir
To attach – attached – attached – adjuntar / adherir
To attack – attacked – attacked - atacar
To avoid – avoided – avoided - evitar
To beat – beaten – beaten - vencer
To bite – bit – bitten - morder
To blow – blew – blown - soplar
To boil – boiled – boiled - hervir
To bother – bothered – bothered – molestar / fastidiar
To break down – broke down – broken down – dañarse / romperse
To bring up – brought up – brought up – criar / educar / traer a colación
To call off – called off – called off - cancelar
To calm down – calmed down – calmed down - calmarse
To cancel – canceled – canceled - cancelar
To carry on – carried on – carried on – continuar / proseguir

To cause – caused – caused - causar

To charge – charged – charged – cobrar / cargar a una cuenta o tarjeta

To choke – choked – choked – ahogarse / sofocar

To climb – climbed – climbed – escalar / trepar / subirse

To confirm – confirmed – confirmed - confirmar

To consider – considered – considered - considerar

To continue – continued – continued - continuar

To cough – coughed – coughed - toser

To crash – crashed – crashed – chocar / estrellarse

To credit – credited – credited - acreditar

To criticize – criticized – criticized - criticar

To deal with – dealt with – dealt with – lidiar con

To delay – delayed – delayed - retrasar

To deliver – delivered – delivered - entregar

To depend on – depended on – depended on – depender de

To deposit – deposited – deposited - depositar

To destroy – destroyed – destroyed - destruir

To discover – discovered – discovered - descubrir

To double – doubled – doubled - duplicar

To doubt – doubted – doubted - dudar

To dry – dried – dried - secar

To envy – envied – envied - envidiar

To exist – existed – existed - existir

To flatten – flattened – flattened - aplanar / alisar / achatar

To hurry up – hurried up – hurried up - apresurarse

To ignore – ignored – ignored - ignorar

To imagine – imagined – imagined - imaginar
To increase – increased – increased - aumentar
To injured – injured – injured – lesionar / herir
To introduce – introduced – introduced – introducir / presentar a alguien
To join – joined – joined - unirse
To kick – kicked – kicked - patear
To lengthen – lengthened – lengthened – alargar / prolongar
To let go (of) – let go – let go – dejar ir / soltar
To lock – locked – locked – cerrar con llave / encerrar
To loosen – loosened – loosened - aflojar
To lower – lowered – lowered - bajar
To mash – mashed – mashed – amasar / triturar
To matter – mattered – mattered - importar
To mix in – mixed in – mixed in - mezclar
To murder – murdered – murdered – asesinar / cometer homicidio
To operate – operated – operated - operar
To order – ordered – ordered – ordenar / mandar / pedir / encargar
To owe – owed – owed – deber (cuando se tiene que pagar)
To pack – packed – packed - empacar
To peel – peeled – peeled - pelar
To pour – poured – poured – verter / echar / server (algo liquido)
To put off – put off – put off – posponer / postergar
To raise – raised – raised – levantar / elevar
To recognize – recognized – recognized - reconocer

To record – recorded – recorded - grabar

To regret – regreted – regreted - lamentar

To remind – reminded – reminded - recordar

To remind of – reminded of – reminded of – recordarse de

To require – required – required - requerir

To reserve – reserved – reserved - reservar

To rise – rose – risen – subir / aumentar / levantar

To ruin – ruined – ruined – arruinar

To run into – ran into – run into – chocar con / encontrarse con (golpear, usualmente con un vehículo)

To run over – ran over – run over – atropellar (usualmente con un vehículo)

To rush – rushed – rushed - apresurarse

To sadden – saddened – saddened - entristecer

To select – selected – selected - seleccionar

To separate from – separated from – separated from – separarse de

To share – shared – shared - compartir

To ship – shipped – shipped – enviar / embarcar (enviar paquetes)

To shorten – shortened – shortened - acortar

To show up – showed up – shown up – llegar / aparecerse

To ski – skied – skied - esquiar

To skid – skidded – skidded – patinar / resbalar / deslizarse

To slow down – slowed down – slowed down – ir despacio / retrasar

To spank – spanked – spanked – azotar (dando

nalgadas)

To spoil – spoiled – spoiled – echar a perder / dañar

To spread – spread – spread – untar / esparcir / propagar

To stare – stared – stared – mirar fijamente / quedarse mirando a alguien

To step in – stepped in – stepped in – poner un pie dentro de algo / entrar

To step on – stepped on – stepped on - acelerar / pisar

To stir – stirred – stirred – agitar / revolver / atizar

To strangle – strangled – strangled - estrangular

To sunbathe – sunbathed – sunbathed – tomar el sol

To surprise – surprised – surprised - sorprender

To suspect – suspected – suspected - sospechar

To take after – took after – taken after – ser como alguien / seguir los pasos de alguien (I take after my father – soy como mi padre)

To take away – took away – taken away – llevarse / quitar (quitarle algo a alguien y no devolvérselo)

To take over – took over – taken over – discutir algo

To threaten (with) – threatened – threatened – amenazar (con)

To throw up – threw up – thrown up - vomitar

To tighten – tightened – tightened - apretar

To trick – tricked – tricked – engañar / jugarle una broma a alguien

To triple – tripled – tripled - triplicar

To unlock – unlocked – unlocked – abrir un

Nivel Cuatro

cerradura o candado / dejar libre

To use up – used up – used up – usar todo de algo / acabar

To warn – warned – warned - advertir

To wire – wired – wired – enviar dinero de un banco a otro / cablear

To withdraw – withdrew – withdrawn - retirar

To work out – worked out – worked out – salir bien (cuando algo da buen resultado) / hacer ejercicios

Grammar Summary

Future time in the past – Tiempo futuro en el pasado

Relatives pronouns – Pronombres relativos

Adjectives –Adjetivos

Adverbs – Adverbios

Lesson 4

The auxiliary verb "might" – El verbo auxiliar "might"

The expression "had better" – La expresión "had better".

Question word "which one of" + noun / pronoun – La palabra de interrogación "which one of" + sustantivo / pronombre

The pronoun "those of "+ pronoun + "who" – El pronombre "those of" + pronoun + "who"

Supposed to – Supuesto a / tener que

Collective nouns – Nombres colectivos

The verb "to try + infinitive / gerund" – El verbo "to try + infinitivo / gerundio"

Try + infinitive

Try + gerundio "ing"

The verb "to remember + infinitive / gerund" – El verbo "to remember + infinitive / gerund"

Adjectives – Adjetivos

Adverbs – Adverbios

Lesson 5

Giving advice – Dando consejos

Past conditions – Pasado condicional

The expression "if only" – La expresión "if only".

The verb "to wish" plus past perfect – El verbo "to

wish" más el pasado perfecto.

The verb "to do" and its uses – El verbo "to do" y sus usos.

Adverbs – Adverbios

Adjectives – Adjetivos

Lesson 6

The future progressive – El futuro progresivo

Using "The" with noncount nouns and the plural – Usando "The" con nombres que no se cuentan y con plural.

Use of "should have / shouldn't have" – El uso de "should have / shouldn't have"

Making commands stronger – Haciendo los mandatos más fuertes

Lesson 7

The gerund after prepositions – El gerundio después de preposiciones

Adjectives – Adjetivos

Lesson 8

Using "must have / can't have / couldn't have" – Usando "must have / can't have / couldn't have"

The passive voice – La voz pasiva

The future perfect – El futuro perfecto

Using "may have" in the future – Usando "may have" en el futuro.

Using "two-word" verbs – Usando los verbos de dos palabras.

The prefix "ex" – El prefijo "Ex"

Adverbs – Adverbios

Adjectives – Adjetivos

Answers to exercises – Respuestas de los ejercicios

Como terminaron sus exámenes y se aseguraron de dominar cada concepto, pueden verificar las respuestas al final del libro. Me he tomado la libertad de ofrecerles las respuestas de todos los ejercicios de cada lección asi también como los del examen de nivel. Pero no hagan trampa, solo ustedes pierden si hacen trampa. *You have reached to the end of this incredible course.*

Lesson 1

Answers to Exercise 1.1:
reader
helper
reporter
shocker
driver

Answers to Exercise 1.2:
It's all gone. / They're all gone.
Are you hungry?
I'm coming. / We're coming.
Are you ready?
Are you new here?

Answers to Exercise 1.3:
to do

to say
to look forward
to talk
to work

Answers to Exercise 2.1:
way
pretty
sure
sure
way (*Sure* is possible as well.)
pretty
way
pretty/sure
way (*Sure* is possible as well.)
sure

Answers to Exercise 2.2:
powerful
happiness
crazy
useful
illness
dry
peace
emptiness
careful
sad

Answers to Exercise 3.1:
I'll write the preface as long as /provided that you give me the outline.

They won't face as many hardships this winter provided that/as long as the pipes don't freeze.

They promise not to foreclose on the house provided that/as long as you make all of your payments from now on.

As long as/provided that you keep providing the materials, I'll be glad to make visuals for your class.

I'll give you free meals as long as/provided that you give me a discount on the rent.

Answers to Exercise 3.2:
e
b
a
c
d

Answers to Exercise 3.3:

Nce	(i)ty	ship
Distance	responsibility	fellowship
Prudence	safety	partnership

Answers to Exercise 4.1:
are supposed to
had better
might
had better
might
is supposed to
might

Answers to Exercise 4.2:

d

e

f

b

a

c

Answers to Exercise 4.3:

to take out

picking

eating

to pay

ordering

Answers to Exercise 5.1:

c

b

a

d

e

Answers to Exercise 5.2:

would have bought

had bought

had seen

could have installed/ would have installed

would have bought

Answers to Exercise 5.3:

question

negative
polite invitation
activity
emphasis

Answers to Exercise 5.4:
had waited
had told
had finished
had asked
had forgiven

Answers to Exercise 6.1:
Mom loves scarves. She wears them to church and parties. The scarf she likes most is a turquoise one with a paisley design. Right now, it's popular to wear scarves in many different ways in the United States, but she was the only person who wore them all the time a couple decades ago.

Answers to Exercise 6.2:
You should have sent
You should have bathed
should have reported
You should have gone
She should have gone

Answers to Exercise 6.3:
a
c
a

c

Answers to Exercise 6.4:
'll be working out
'll be having
will be crossing
'll be opening
'll be recovering

Answers to Exercise 7.1
laughing
jumping
taking
working
hearing
sewing
reading
eat
mixing
sleeping

Answers to Exercise 8.1: (Answers will vary. Suggested answers are as follows.)
could have
may have
couldn't have
must have

Answers to Exercise 8.2:
will have gone
will have made

will have eaten
will have been/gotten frustrated
will have been adopted

Answers to Exercise 8.3:
gave
try on
turn
talk

Answers to Level Four Tests – Respuesta de los Examenes del Nivel Cuatro

Answers to Test 1.1:
er
in
less
im
im
ness

Answers to Test 1.2:
pretty well
have them altered
something to do
At last
Shall we

Answers to Test 1.3:
for one or two hours at a time
all of the above
Practice online.

Answers to Test 2.1:
had kept; have protected/protect
liked
go
to call
weren't; be

had told; have reminded
visit; write
going to watch
to go
spend

Answers to Test 2.2:
can → could
were → was
was → were
help → helps
have → has

Answers to Test 2.3:
leaderance → leadership
popularship → popularity
memberance → membership
urgenceship → urgency
scholarity → scholarship

Answers to Test 3.1
plowed
preparing
graduating
finished
celebrating
enjoying
coming
eaten
finished
discussing

Answers to Test 3.2:
falling
seeing
eating
spending
training
insulting

Answers to Test 4.1:
done
pay
making
likes
go
to take
to thank
study; traveling
gets; get
brought
listened
bring
were
buying
taken
stand
brushing
eaten; be
finished
to be
Answers to Test 4.2:
pretty

almost
generally
always
right away
hardly
sure
next door
mostly

Nivel Cautro Conclusión

Muchas gracias por seleccionar el *Curso Completo de Inglés – Nivel Cuatro* por Yeral E. Ogando para su aprendizaje. Por fin, han llegado al final de este increíble curso, por lo tanto, ya pueden hablar inglés fluido y están listos para cualquier situación o conversación en inglés.

Les exhorto que continúen practicando y hablando inglés en todo momento, ya les he dicho que la Practica hace al Maestro. Visiten mi pagina de internet para más información.

God bless you and see you next time.

Dr. Yeral E. Ogando
www.aprendeis.com

Nivel Cautro BONO GRATIS

Estimado Estudiante,

Necesitas descargar el audio MP3 para usar este increíble método para aprender inglés. Visita este link:

http://aprendeis.com/ingles-audio-nivel4/
Usuario "4ennivel4"
Contraseña "4en42016"

Solo tienes que descargar el archivo comprimido, descomprimirlo y estas listo para iniciar tu experiencia al mundo del inglés.

Si quieres compartir tu experiencia, comentario o possible sugerencia, siempre podrás contactarme a info@aprendeis.com

Muchas gracias por estudiar el *Curso Completo de Inglés – Nivel Cuatro* y por escuchar mis instrucciones.

Caros afectos,
Dr. Yeral E. Ogando

Otros libros escritos por Yeral E. Ogando

Conciencia: El Héroe Dentro de Ti

Curso Completo de Inglés – Nivel Uno
Curso Completo de Inglés – Nivel Dos
Curso Completo de Inglés – Nivel Tres
Curso Completo de Inglés – Nivel Cuatro

Yeral E. Ogando Proviene de un origen muy humilde y continúa siendo un humilde siervo de nuestro Señor Todopoderoso; entendiendo que no somos más que recipientes y el Señor nos llama y nos envía también a hacer Su trabajo, no nuestro trabajo. Lucas 17:10 "Así también vosotros, cuando hayáis hecho todo lo que os ha sido ordenado, decid: Siervos inútiles somos, pues lo que debíamos hacer, hicimos".

El Señor Ogando nació en el Caribe, República Dominicana. Es el padre amado de dos bellas chicas Yeiris y Tiffany.

Jesús le trajo a Sus pies en la edad de 16-17 años. Desde entonces, ha servido como Co-pastor, Pastor, profesor de la Biblia en las escuelas, consejero de jóvenes, plantador y fundador de iglesias. Actualmente está sirviendo como Secretario para la Iglesia Reformada Dominicana así como de enlace para Haití y EE.UU.

Fluido en varias lenguas el Señor Ogando es el Creador y dueño de un Ministerio de Traducción On-line que opera desde el 2007; con traductores cristianos Nativos en más de 25 países.

(www.christian-translation.com),

Lo más apasionante acerca de su Ministerio de Traducción es que miles de personas están recibiendo la Palabra de Dios en su lengua nativa diariamente y cientos de ministerios logran llegar al mundo a través del trabajo de Christian-translation.com junto con su red de traducción de 17 sitios web relacionados con traducciones cristianas, a diferentes lenguas.